SOCIAL CHANGE AND ECONOMIC LIFE INITIATIVE

Series Editor: Duncan Gallie

EMPLOYER STRATEGY AND THE LABOUR MARKET

THE SOCIAL CHANGE AND ECONOMIC LIFE INITIATIVE

This volume is part of a series arising from the Social Change and Economic Life Initiative—a major interdisciplinary programme of research funded by the Economic and Social Research Council. The programme focused on the impact of the dramatic economic restructuring of the 1980s on employers' labour force strategies, workers' experiences of employment and unemployment, and the changing dynamics of household relations.

ALSO PUBLISHED IN THIS SERIES

EMPLOYER STRATEGY AND THE LABOUR MARKET

Edited by

JILL RUBERY

and

FRANK WILKINSON

OXFORD UNIVERSITY PRESS
1994

Oxford University Press, Walton Street, Oxford OX2 6DP

Oxford New York Toronto
Delhi Bombay Calcutta Madras Karachi
Kuala Lumpur Singapore Hong Kong Tokyo
Nairobi Dar es Salaam Cape Town
Melbourne Auckland Madrid
and associated companies in
Berlin Ibadan

Oxford is a trade mark of Oxford University Press

Published in the United States
by Oxford University Press Inc., New York

© the several contributors 1994

British Library Cataloguing in Publication Data
Data available

Library of Congress Cataloging in Publication Data
Employer strategy and the labour market | edited by Jill Rubery and
Frank Wilkinson.
(Social change and economic life initiative)
Includes bibliographical references and index.
1. Labor market—Great Britain. 2. Industrial relations—Great Britain.
I. Rubery, Jill. II. Wilkinson, Frank. III. Series.
HD5765.A6E46 1994 331.12'0941—dc20 93–49446
ISBN 0–19–827894–2
ISBN 0–19–827927–2 (pbk.)

1 3 5 7 9 10 8 6 4 2

Set by Hope Services (Abingdon) Ltd.
Printed in Great Britain
on acid-free paper by
Bookcraft (Bath) Ltd.
Midsomer Norton, Avon

FOREWORD

This volume is part of a series of publications arising from the Social Change and Economic Life Initiative—a programme of research funded by the Economic and Social Research Council. The major objectives of the programme were to study the nature and determinants of employer labour force policies, worker experiences of employment and the labour market, the changing dynamics of household relations, and the impact of changes in the employment structure on social integration and social stratification in the community.

The research programme focused on six local labour markets: Aberdeen, Coventry, Kirkcaldy, Northampton, Rochdale, and Swindon. These were selected to provide contrasting patterns of recent and past economic change. Three of the localities—Coventry, Kirkcaldy, and Rochdale—had relatively high levels of unemployment in the early and mid-1980s, whereas the other three experienced relatively low levels of unemployment.

The data collected by the Initiative give an exceptionally rich picture of the lives of people and of the operation of the labour market in the different localities. Three representative surveys were carried out between 1986 and 1987, providing fully comparable data across the localities. The first—the Work Attitudes/Histories Survey—was a random survey of the non-institutional population aged between 20 and 60, involving interviews with about 1,000 people in each locality. It provides information on work histories, current experiences of employment or unemployment, and attitudes to work. This was taken as the point of departure for the other two surveys, focusing respectively on the household circumstances of respondents and on the policies of their employers. In the Household and Community Survey approximately a third of the original respondents were reinterviewed to develop a picture of their household strategies, their organization of domestic work, their leisure activities, their friendship networks, and their attitudes towards welfare provision. Where people had partners, interviews were carried out both with the original respondents and with their partners. The Employers' Survey was based on telephone interviews with senior management in the establishments for which respondents in the original Work Attitudes/Histories Survey worked. A further non-random follow-up survey was carried out involving 180 of the establishments that had taken part in the initial survey. The details of the research design and sampling for the different phases of the programme are provided in an Appendix at the end of this volume.

In addition, related studies were carried out in individual localities, focusing in greater depth on issues that had been covered in the common surveys. These included studies of the historical context of employment practices, current processes of technical change, managerial employee relations policies, industrial relations, gender segregation, the relationship between employer and employee perceptions of employment conditions, and household strategies with respect to labour market decisions and the organization of work within the household.

The team that implemented the programme consisted of thirty-five researchers drawn from fourteen different institutions. It brought together sociologists, economists, geographers, social historians, and social psychologists. The major common research instruments were collectively constructed through a series of working groups responsible for particular aspects of the study. The programme involved, then, a co-operative interdisciplinary, research effort for which there are few precedents in British social science.

DUNCAN GALLIE
National Co-ordinator and Series Editor

PREFACE

This book is the product of the collective endeavour which was essential to ensure the success of the complex Social Change and Economic Life Initiative.

It would be impossible to name all the people who contributed to this research activity, but we must single out the following for special mention: the members of the Employer Survey working party; Michael White from PSI who conducted the telephone survey of employers; the researchers in the various teams who conducted the case-study interviews and/or analysed the survey data; the co-ordinating team who constructed the employer survey questionnaire and in particular Carolyn Vogler who co-ordinated the coding of the questionnaires; the participants in the working party on the Work Attitudes/Histories Survey which included a wide range of questions on employer policy and practice; Public Attitude Surveys for conducting that survey; and last, but not least, the employers and individuals who agreed to participate in the various and lengthy interviews on which the chapters in this volume draw.

From a more personal point of view, this book should also be seen as the outcome of collective and collaborative research with our immediate colleagues at Cambridge, through which many of our own ideas and insights into the relationship between employer strategy and the labour market were formulated. During the period of the SCELI research we were particularly indebted to Brendan Burchell, who took responsibility for all the technical aspects of data analysis and also contributed to all areas of the research from the statistical to the theoretical, thereby becoming the mainstay of the project. We are also indebted to contributions from Jane Elliott, Colin Fraser, Sara Horrell, Ray Jobling, and Catherine Marsh. The research on which our own contributions to this book are based started a long time before SCELI and emerged from the work of the

Labour Studies group at the Department of Applied Economics at Cambridge. Our two former colleagues Roger Tarling and Christine Craig played a large part in the development of the ideas presented here. Both Christine Craig and Catherine Marsh died during the preparation of this book and we should like to dedicate it to them.

J.R. and F.W.

CONTENTS

EMPLOYER POLICIES, EMPLOYMENT CHANGES, AND INDIVIDUAL PERCEPTIONS

LIST OF FIGURES

LIST OF TABLES

CONTRIBUTORS

BRENDAN BURCHELL is a Lecturer in research methods in the Faculty of Social and Political Sciences and a Fellow of Magdalene College, Cambridge.

JANE ELLIOTT is a Fellow of Newnham College, Cambridge.

DUNCAN GALLIE is an Official Fellow of Nuffield College, Oxford.

ANNE GASTEEN is a Lecturer in Economics at Glasgow Caledonian University.

BOB MORRIS is Professor of Economic and Social History at the University of Edinburgh.

ROGER PENN is Reader in Economic Sociology at the University of Lancaster.

MICHAEL ROSE is Visiting Fellow (formerly Reader) in Economic Sociology in the Centre for European Industrial Studies, University of Bath and a *Chercheur Associé* at the University of Paris-Nanterre.

JILL RUBERY is a Senior Lecturer at the Manchester School of Management, UMIST.

JOHN SEWELL is Professor and Dean of the Faculty of Economic and Social Sciences, University of Aberdeen.

JIM SMYTH is a Lecturer in the Department of History, University of Stirling.

MICHAEL WHITE is a Senior Fellow and Head of Employment Studies at the Policy Studies Institute, London.

FRANK WILKINSON is a Senior Research Officer in the Department of Applied Economics, University of Cambridge and a Fellow of Girton College, Cambridge.

Introduction

JILL RUBERY AND FRANK WILKINSON

Labour-market change in the 1980s and into the 1990s has been closely linked to the actions and policies of employers. Employment restructuring is seen to be the outcome of changes in industrial organization, including the closure or rationalization of capacity, the growth of small and decline of large employers, and the privatization of public services. Equal attention has been focused on the apparently widespread introduction by employers of new policies and practices, induced on the one hand by growing product-market uncertainty and, on the other, by the changed political climate and increased relative power of management in the workplace. High unemployment, coupled with evident rapid change in industrial organization, has switched attention away from the supply-side capabilities and preferences of labour to a concern with management policy and practice. This greater interest in the role of firms in the labour market coincides with a change of theoretical focus in a range of associated disciplines towards the role of organizations and management in structuring employment relationships. This change of focus was fully reflected in the design and implementation of the Social Change and Economic Life Initiative; the study of employer policy and practice was a central objective informing both the design of the overall project and the internal design of survey instruments. This volume brings together the main theoretical and empirical work on employer policy arising out of the initiative. Here we outline the theoretical debates and policy background which informed the research design, before describing the contributions of its findings to the development of the analysis of the interactions between employer strategy and labour-market structure.

EMPLOYING ORGANIZATIONS AND THE ORGANIZATION OF LABOUR: THE BACKGROUND TO THE RESEARCH

(i) *The theoretical debates*

From the vantage point of the 1990s, what is surprising about the renewal of interest in the role of firms in structuring employment which occurred in the early 1970s, is that it took so long for the analysis of labour organization to be clearly integrated into a modern approach to the analysis of the firm. Within industrial economics and sociology, and in organization theory, the concept of the firm as a 'black box' responding automatically to market signals had long given way to a more complex analysis of the determinants of competition and the range of strategies that firms could pursue without jeopardizing their survival. Concepts such as managerial versus competitive theories of the firm (Marris 1964), bureaucratic versus organic forms of organization (Burns and Stalker 1961), high-technology versus low-technology forms of labour organization (Blauner 1964), had all entered standard textbooks before there were wide-scale, serious, and systematic attempts to centre the analysis of the labour market at the level of the firm. There had been some progress in that direction in the 1950s with Kerr's (1954) analysis of balkanized labour markets, Lester's (1952) development of the range theory of wage differentials, and indeed Dunlop's (1957) analysis of wage clusters and wage contours. Becker's (1964) analysis of firm-specific skills in the 1960s provided a basis within neo-classical theory for introducing the role of employer policy, but firm-specific skills were treated as a special case to the more common situation of investment in general skills. Indeed, the concerns with employer policy in the 1950s gave way within labour economics to the empirically more tractable issues of the individual relationships between human capital formation and the individual's earnings function, while organization theory and industrial economics continued to develop the analysis of the emergence of the corporation, the visible hand of market forces, without exploring the consequences for labour organization of the existence of corporations with market power and the ability not to act as short-run profit-maximizers or wage-takers.

Thus the changes that took place in the 1970s emerged not so much from the discovery of new sets of concepts and ideas, but from a late realization of the need to integrate labour back into organization theory and industrial economics, and of the increasing empirical implausibility of maintaining the key features of a neo-classical perfectly competitive labour market. Within the UK and the USA a series of studies revealed the difficulties of explaining the characteristics of the labour market within a standard labour-market framework. In the UK, studies of local labour markets persistently revealed differences in pay levels between comparable workers in comparable firms (Robinson 1970; Mackay *et al.* 1971), suggesting that there was little tendency towards equalization of wage levels through the operation of competitive markets. In the USA the failure of programmes to extend training for the urban poor suggested that lack of human capital was at least not a sufficient explanation for labour-market disadvantage, and that inequality of access to employment structures may also be important (Thurow 1975; Doeringer and Piore 1971).

The outcome of these observations was the development of segmentation theory and of an analysis in which divergences in firms' employment policies provided the central basis for division in the labour market; this division was held to be independent of labour quality and to lead to cumulative divergence over time in the relative fortunes of those who secured employment in primary-sector firms compared to those who remained in the secondary sector. Thus the industrial structure not only reflected but also contributed to and created labour-market inequalities. Firms' employment policies were linked to divergences in their product-market positions and technological requirements; labour organization could thus be reintegrated into the analysis of industrial organization and product-market competition.

These provide the main analytical strengths of the original dual labour market approach to segmentation. Its weaknesses are by now well known. The theory lacked an adequate historical analysis of the emergence of employer policy, and in particular overlooked the role of worker organization in the establishment of differences in employer policy (Rubery 1978; Kahn 1975; Friedman 1978). The notion of dualism at best provided a static description of labour-market structures, but at worst it failed to capture the complexity and differentiation within firms' employment policies (Wilkinson 1981). The theory overstressed the technological determinism of employment policy and understressed the influence of managerial imperatives to control and motivate labour (Edwards 1979). It over-simplified the relationship between product-market structure and employment policy, emphasizing mass production as a necessary condition for high-wage stable employment just at a time when markets were fragmenting and firms required more flexible employment organization within their core labour forces (Atkinson 1985*a*; Piore and Sabel 1984). And finally the role of social disadvantage, and in particular racism and sexism, in the structuring of labour markets was underestimated (Barron and Norris 1976; C. Craig *et al.* 1982, 1985*a*). 'Secondary' employment conditions were found to be more associated with the employment of disadvantaged workers than with requirements for low technical skills.

This list of criticisms of the dual labour market model can be drawn up, with hindsight, due to the multi-layered analyses of employers' labour-market policies that developed alongside the simple dual labour market theory in the 1970s. For simplicity, these developments can be divided into the flexibility debate, the post-Fordist debate, the de-skilling debate, the gender debate, and the new industrial relations debate.

The *flexibility debate* which emerged in the 1970s can be seen to be a response to the increasingly uncertain economic conditions for the world order that prevailed after the first and second oil shocks. These revealed the dualist notions of the progressive development of stable oligopolistic markets, juxtaposed to unstable competitive markets in residual sectors, as untenable descriptions of the tendencies of world capitalism. Large firms, far from enjoying protection from competition, were active in the creation of new and more destabilizing forms of competition based around restructuring, relocation, and international integration of production. The questions then became, not why a residual secondary employment sector had persisted in the midst of affluence, but what would be the new boundaries between primary and secondary employment; to what extent would the secondary sector absorb the labour displaced from the primary sector (not, how could the primary sector be expanded to absorb the secondary labour); and to what extent would the new forces for competition lead to changes in the terms and conditions of employment, and in particular in the form of the labour contract.

The influential model of the flexible firm by Atkinson (1985*a*) led to the association of flexibility with a core–periphery strategy which operated within firms and between core and peripheral firms. Segmentation was thus as likely to be found within firms as between firms, and increasingly associated with new forms of the employment contract; atypical contracts for those in the periphery and more permanent employment relationships involving functional flexibility and internal labour market systems for those in the core. The increasing interest in 'functional flexibility', or multi-skilled workers with firm-specific training, has called into question the relevance of current occupational classifications for labour-market analysis and centred attention on employer policy in the development of training systems and formation of the skilled labour force (Marsden 1986; Streeck 1989). The search for flexibility was also associated with moves at a more macro level to change the nature of the employment relationship, in fact to deregulate labour markets so that they resembled the labour markets of neoclassical theory. The relationship between the flexibility debate and the new industrial relations debate will be discussed below.

The apparent undermining of mass production as the engine of growth in the 1970s gave rise to a much more general debate on the changing nature of industrial and labour organization than that associated with the flexible firm model. The notion of *post-Fordism* emerged to describe the search by capital to accommodate its productive system to the new economic order. While the Fordist model had been based on detailed division of labour and the application of technology to deskill the labour force, the move to more uncertain and more variable product markets required the development of more flexible systems of production which in turn would require more flexible and higher levels of labour skills. Within the post-Fordist debate, the system of labour organization has been linked to the system of industrial production at both a macro and a micro level; Fordism at the macro level required labour to benefit in the increasing productivity, to ensure an expanding demand for products (Boyer 1979; Aglietta 1979). This relationship was argued to be assured through the development of wage-determination systems which provided for steadily rising real wages in line with productivity. The search for accommodation to post-Fordist conditions not only called into question the evolution of the system of work organization required by firms, but also led to a fragmentation of wage-determination systems, reflecting the more fragmented and unstable system of industrial production. One further feature of post-Fordism is the increasing role for small firms, no longer considered the residual and peripheral elements of industrial organization. Increasing complexity in the analysis of product markets and forms of competition have also led to increased complexity in the analysis of inter-firm relations. These are seen not to be adequately described by market or exchange relations, as they may vary on a spectrum from subordination and dependency to high levels of trust and co-operation (Brusco 1982; Piore and Sabel 1984). These new forms of inter-firm relations are expected to thrive particularly in industrial districts—that is, geographical areas with concentrations of complementary firms, facilitating co-operative relations. Under this analysis inter-firm relations take on significance in explaining labour organization as well as the relations of individual firms to the market.

The *de-skilling debate*, indissolubly linked to the publication of Braverman's book in 1974, initially developed along very similar lines to that of the segmentation debate. The analysis suggested that the dominant imperative of capital was towards the application of technology and systems of work organization designed to reduce the scope for discretion and exercise of judgement by labour, concentrating the function of conception within management. Thus the dominant economic form would increasingly become the large, technologically sophisticated firm, utilizing Taylorist techniques of labour organization. Employer needs to exercise control over the labour process became the determining influence on the employment system. Inconsistencies with the segmentation approach were apparent; in Braverman the large, technically advanced firms had reached a higher stage of de-skilling, while in segmentation theories it was large firms that had most need of workers with firm-specific skills. For segmentation theorists it also was the large firms that provided good employment conditions, while Braverman's approach implied (although he was inconsistent on this point), that at least in the absence of unions, pay should have been lower in these types of plants which had been most subject to the Babbage principle of replacing high-paid by low-paid labour.

These problems were to some extent resolved, as in segmentation theory, by the admittance of a role for labour organization and worker resistance into the theory (Rubery 1978). Labour is not passive in response to de-skilling strategies, but may resist changes to jobs or may bargain for material compensation in return for acquiescence in the new systems of working. Moreover, firms' objectives are not necessarily satisfied through the technical de-skilling of work; labour still retains its own free will, which can be used against the interests of the firm even when exercising low levels of technical skill. Firms' concerns are broader than the development of technical constraints over labour; they also have to seek ways to legitimize the managerial hierarchy in the eyes of labour and to 'manufacture consent' (Burawoy 1979a).

Thus, over time the labour process debate has become less tied to the a priori notion of de-skilling and more associated with the analysis of multi-dimensional management strategies and equally complex responses by labour. Even within an analysis which accepts a tendency to de-skilling there remains the possibility of multiple outcomes in terms of work organization and employment conditions. However, the labour-process debate has also been influenced by the post-Fordist analysis which suggests that the assumption of a linear tendency towards de-skilling is erroneously predicated on the notion of a continued expansion of mass production. Firms' objectives are not to reduce uncertainty within a known production system, but to increase their capacity to respond to new market and technological conditions. Changes in markets and technologies may displace but also create new skills, and competitive success may be related more to gaining the active co-operation of the labour force than to reducing the scope for labour to intervene in the production process.

If worker organization and resistance is recognized to lead to different forms of work organization and systems of reward than those predicted by considerations of technical skill alone, then it also follows that, where disadvantaged workers are employed, firms may find it relatively easy to de-skill, or to pay lower wages and provide more insecure employment than might be merited by a simple consideration of technical skills. The wide-ranging research into the relationship between *gender* and employment structure over the past two decades does indeed suggest that firms relate pay and employment conditions as much to the differences in external labour-market opportunities of men and women as they do to the contribution of the work they perform to the productivity of the firm (Craig *et al.* 1985*a*; Phillips and Taylor 1980; Armstrong 1982). Gender is also related to firms' search for flexibility and their use of non-standard employment contracts, with female labour being more frequently available for part-time and temporary work than male, and men providing flexibility more through overtime, shiftworking, and self-employment (Horrell and Rubery 1991). Gender dimensions to labour organization have been placed increasingly centre stage in labour analyses, but gender differences are recognized as arising not out of natural or biological differences but out of social processes and the specific implementation of employment policies by employers. The gender debate has also served to remind scholars that in this demand-centred employer-policy analysis the structure of the labour supply still 'matters' and its structure and characteristics are in part conditioned and reproduced by firms' policies (see Scott forthcoming).

By the end of the 1970s, the concerns about how to improve and extend the labour-market regulation system to modify the effects of dualism and segmentation had given way to a debate over the merits of regulation *per se*, and over the advantages and disadvantages of a deregulatory strategy for industrial relations. Among the problems facing capital in adjusting to the new competitive conditions were argued to be the rigidities in labour organization that came from systems of employment protection. Firms were said to require new systems of work organization, employment contracts, and working-time arrangements that would provide the flexibility necessary to adjust to the recessionary conditions of the 1980s. This debate over the *new industrial relations* was initially concerned with moves by government and by employers, at least within Britain and America, to establish more authoritarian, or 'macho-management' styles of labour organization. However 'macho-management' increasingly seemed inappropriate for a new competitive order in which quality, design, and service appeared to be more important determinants of competitive success than simple price levels. Firms had to motivate their work-force to produce quality products on time, and this required commitment and 'loyalty' as much as high effort levels and direct control.

The continued success of Japan and the increasing infiltration of Japanese management techniques into production systems also raised interest in forms of the employment relationship which to some extent could be said to lie at the other end of the spectrum from the direct control, hire-and-fire policies of an 'ideal-type' American industrial relations system. The clear impossibility, in the context of the Japanese success, of maintaining that there is one best system of industrial relations for the new economic order, created difficulties with policy-makers keen to extend the pressure towards deregulation and flexibility. An ingenious resolution of these difficulties was presented by an OECD group of experts, which argued that Japanese and American systems were both relatively successful systems of industrial relations, the one providing internal and the other external flexibility (OECD 1986a). The fact that they stood at opposite ends of the spectrum was argued to be their strength; the problem cases were those, primarily European systems, that were hybrids of the two models and thus provided neither internal or external flexibility. Despite this attempt to rehabilitate the pure deregulationist argument, the subsequent debate over 'appropriate' industrial relations regimes has been as much concerned with new ways of increasing 'commitment' as with extending direct managerial control.

The human resource management literature (Storey 1989; Guest 1987) is predicated on firms having interests in establishing and developing long-term relationships with employees, so that the emphasis in the debate has shifted from rigidities related to individualized protection to distortions to the employer–employee relationship introduced by collective bargaining and employment regulation, which inhibits the development of appropriate individualized contracts and relationships. The attack on the 'old industrial relations' is thus still present but takes the form of providing alternative means of integrating employees on a long-term basis into the firm. Employer policy and employer style have also been given greater attention in the industrial relations literature of the 1980s (Purcell 1987). While industrial relations has traditionally been the study of union organization and policy, in the 1980s the focus switched to management policy and management style. Empirical research has attempted to establish different management strategies and to relate them systematically to industrial and organizational characteristics, but the most significant finding has been the absence of evidence of widespread strategic planning on the part of firms, with respect to their staff policies, and the absence of simple relationships between structural variables and the form of management style. Thus, in a recent survey, only 35 per cent of firms claimed to have any form of personnel strategy and only 11 per cent had an explicit policy of developing a core–periphery framework within their labour force (Hakim 1990). Most firms still fall into the 'opportunistic' category when researchers attempt to categorize staff policy, suggesting first that this is not always considered sufficiently central to competitive success for firms to have developed a coherent policy, and secondly that the obstacles to the adjustment of policies to fit current 'requirements' can be severe. These include the actual costs of making the transition, the problems of developing a coherent policy across different layers of management, and the costs of disrupting customs and customary expectations within a production system.

This integration of research on organizational policy-making into the analysis of how employment systems develop has revealed how naïve were, for example, early theories of segmentation which predicted a simple relationship between the structural characteristics of firms and their staff policies. Employment systems within firms and indeed within societies are subject to a process of evolution or gradual change, punctuated at times by dramatic reconstruction. Within this dynamic context, an emphasis on cross-sectional relationships, between structural variables and management employment policy, necessarily underestimates the weight of past and current policies on employment systems.

(ii) *The policy context*

The launch of the Social Change and Economic Life Initiative in 1985 came some fifteen years after the rekindling of interest, by social scientists, in the role of employer policy in the structuring of employment and employment opportunities. The burgeoning debate on the nature of labour-market structuring and its links with business organization tracked the growing crisis in capitalism, with the ending of the post-war 'Golden Age' and the acceleration of change in industrial and labour-market organization which contributed to and were precipitated by these developments. In Britain the crisis and the political response took an extreme form. The growing economic and increasingly social problems associated with long-term economic decline, exacerbated by the inflationary consequences of the two oil crises, encouraged a switch to policies which identified inflation as a monetary phenomenon and the relative inefficiency of the British economy as largely attributable to imperfections of the market mechanism, especially in the labour market. The resulting macroeconomic policy and the progressive deregulation of the labour market triggered a major recession, accelerated the industrial reconstruction away from manufacturing, and dramatically restructured the labour market. The launch of Social Change and Economic Life Initiative coincided with the recovery stage from the early 1980s recession. In the five or so years preceding the research, deep recession, tight monetary policies, and high exchange rates had meant that, for much of British industry, survival itself required major policy changes. At the same time, the deregulation of the labour market and the weakening of labour organizations by unemployment and legislation changes provided wide scope for managerial innovation in employment and labour organization strategies. This, and the improvement of the economic climate as the research got under way, provided a unique opportunity for observing what might have been expected to be a period of dramatic transformation of employment relationships.

(iii) *The survey instruments*

Employer policy was identified as a central issue for investigation by the Initiative. A specific employer-survey element was incorporated, including intensive case-studies of firms. Furthermore, the surveys of individuals and employers were linked by the inclusion within the individual work-history and work-attitudes survey of a wide range of questions concerning respondents' perceptions of employment structures and employment systems, and taking change of employer, along with change of occupation, working-time, and supervisory responsibility, as marking an 'event' in a respondent's work history. The link was made more direct by using the employers of the respondents to the survey of individuals to generate a sampling frame for the telephone survey of firms. The individual teams also conducted specific studies of firms and of the relationships between firms in specific industries, industrial districts, and labour markets. One of these linked firms and their work-force directly, by administering matched questionnaires to managers and employees within given organizations.

However, fundamental and arguably irresolvable problems remain as to how to design research methods for studying change in labour organization which give the appropriate equal weight to employer policy. In practice, the history of employing organizations cannot be easily studied by interrogating the current management, because of the central role of managerial and ownership reorganization in bringing about change—particularly in such a period as the early 1980s. Moreover, the use of the histories of existing firms to reconstitute the structure of labour demand in earlier periods is flawed because of the omission of the influence of firms which have since disappeared. Interpretation of employer policy through individuals' life histories is at best a poor substitute for direct knowledge of firms' policies, as it is not possible to determine whether changes in an individual's work history come about because of movement within stable structures or because of changes in employer policy or in the composition of firms. For these various reasons it is more difficult to build into the analysis of the structure of labour demand the kind of retrospective element evident in, for example, the analysis of individual work histories. Consequently, the current context and change over the recent past forms the main focus of the research. Nevertheless, two of the papers have been able to extend the relatively short time horizon with historically based analyses of changes in employer policies using more qualitative research techniques and historical materials collected outside the core SCELI surveys.

Within these methodological constraints, the Social Change and Economic Life Initiative can be seen to have made a novel and significant contribution towards integrating employer policy more directly into social-survey research. This book demonstrates the fruitfulness of this approach by bringing together work on the relationship between employer policy and the labour market which draws upon the whole battery of survey and other research methods deployed in the SCELI. The richness and diversity of the data sets and related studies provide a unique opportunity to explore from perspectives of segmentation, de-skilling, flexibility, new competition forms, and innovative industrial-relations hypotheses, the increasingly complex debate on the role of employer policy.

THE STRUCTURE OF THE BOOK

(i) *Markets, employers, and employment policies*

The first section of the book includes four chapters which in different ways seek to provide a general overview of the relationship between employer policy and employment systems.

The first paper, by Rubery, criticizes the ideal-type models of segmentation theory which assume that firms can be divided or dichotomized into primary or secondary, or into those using internal and bureaucratic models of employment and those operating under competitive conditions. In the second part of the paper these criticisms are illustrated drawing on case-studies from the Northampton employer survey.

Rubery's critique consists of four elements. First, empirical evidence suggests that most firms benefit from continuous, stable employment relationships with 'committed' workers; it is thus more plausible to look at the different constraints that firms face in developing policies to match their needs than to seek to divide the industrial structure into those where labour continuity and commitment matters and those where employment is casual and unskilled. Second, as a consequence of segmentation on the supply side of the labour market, resulting both from the selective employment policies of firms and from social disadvantage, firms do not necessarily have to provide objectively high pay and good promotion prospects to secure a stable and committed labour force. What matters is how pay and promotion compare to the employee's own external opportunity wage and prospects. For many workers this may in fact be social security, or even if other jobs can be obtained, a reduced wage level, because of age or other barriers to re-employment. This segmentation on the supply side allows for a wider range of employment policies that are compatible with the objective of 'internalizing' the labour force than is assumed in the internal-labour-market literature. In particular, it suggests that there should be a distinction made between internal labour markets in which most employees have promotion prospects and those where most higher level vacancies are filled by internal recruits. The latter was found in the Northampton area study to be relatively frequent but to provide promotion prospects for only a minority of existing employees.

The third and fourth criticisms relate to the way in which internal and external labour markets are conceptualized. The switch to an employer-based or organizational-level analysis of employment policy has led to an overemphasis on change within organizations as the motor of change in employment systems. Changes in the external environment, in the supply of labour or the provision of industry-wide training, may be more important than change in firm-specific requirements. The flexible-firm model purported to show that the move to increase numerical flexibility was primarily related to changes in firms' technological and market constraints, but evidence suggests that these strategies might equally well be interpreted as opportunistic responses to high levels of unemployment. Changes within firms have to be related to both internal and external conditions, mediated of course through the impact of organizational structures.

While the organization-based approach has neglected the influence of the external labour market on the internal, it has also left the external labour market as a black box equivalent to the black box of the firm in neo-classical economics. The role of firms' employment policies in structuring the external labour market has been largely unexplored and internal labour markets are still often seen as deviations from a competitive norm. In practice, the external labour market takes its form through the influence of a whole range of institutions, including the family, the state, the educational and training system (Maurice *et al.* 1986), and employing organizations. The importance of internal factors to employment systems can be seen to be sufficiently strong that even those workers with relatively transferable skills can face very different employment conditions in different firms. Thus mobility between firms involves moving from one slot in one firm's internal labour market to another slot in a different internal-labour-market system. Only when employers collude together to establish common pay and grading systems (or strong occupational associations fix pay levels) does a going rate of labour necessarily prevail. Institutions, organization, and administrative rules are equally important in structuring opportunities in the external environment as in the internal.

Chapter 2, by Gallie and White, utilizes the opportunities offered by the Initiative to provide rigorous and systematic empirical tests of the standard hypotheses of segmentation theory and the flexibility debate. The data sets used apply to all six areas and include the employer telephone survey and the work-attitudes and work-history surveys. The first part of the paper analyses responses generated by the telephone survey, asking: is it possible to divide the sample of employers into primary and secondary employers on the basis of combinations or profiles of their work-force policies, and is there any relationship between structural characteristics, such as size of firm or industry, and employment policy, as predicted by segmentation theory? Although information was collected in the telephone survey on the use of five different types of work-force policy (share of part-timers, rate of recruitment, rate of internal promotion, use of individual assessment systems, and proportion of marginal workers), firms could not be divided into segments with systematic combinations of these different work-force policies. There were associations, both negative and positive, between pairs of these policies, but these did not provide a basis for systematic classification of firms' employment policies. Similarly, the results on structural variables such as industry and size were inconclusive.

The second part of Chapter 2 explores the extent to which there is a relationship between employment contract status and primary and secondary employment conditions, drawing on data from the work-attitudes/work-history survey. These questions are influenced by the fusion between the segmentation and the flexibility debates; over time secondary employment conditions have been increasingly associated with atypical and marginal employment. However, analysis of the SCELI data again suggests that these hypotheses have over-simplified the relationships: instead of atypical employment being subject to 'mutually reinforcing disadvantage', different types of atypical employment were found to have different types of advantage and disadvantage. Contract and temporary work was most subject to job insecurity, but scored highly in terms of skills and career progression, while part-time workers were, for the most part, in stable jobs, but had poor pay, skills, or employment prospects. Subjective measures of job quality complicate the picture further, with part-timers having higher levels of both pay and job satisfaction than other workers.

This empirical rejection of the simplistic models of segmentation and flexibility theory leads Gallie and White to make suggestions for more fruitful approaches. The first is to explore the reasons for the adoption of specific types of employment policy, instead of searching for a profile of different elements of employment policy. This approach may be particularly important to understand the concentration of marginal employment, and indeed part-time employment, in a relatively small share of establishments; instead of looking for general explanations of these employment forms we need to focus more specifically on why certain firms choose to make extensive use of a particular employment contract. The second suggestion is to recognize the constraints that firms face in adjusting to their employment systems and to see their current practices as representing 'an accretion of choices made over a considerable period'. Under this approach it may be more fruitful to concentrate attention on the factors leading to change in employment policy, even of an incremental nature, rather than attempting to explain the structure of employment practices by reference to structural or conjunctural variables.

The third chapter in Part I, by Wilkinson and White, in fact takes up this proposal for research by exploring the relationship between changes in the product-market environment of firms over the previous five years and analysing the relationship between product-market pressure and changes to employment policies and practices. This study is based on the responses to the employer telephone survey in the six areas. Included in the survey were a range of questions relating to firms' practices with respect to the use of marginal workers and the extent to which they had made changes in work-force practices. Some of these practices could be considered as policies to improve qualitative flexibility of labour (shiftworking, training to provide cover, use of incentive schemes, personal appraisal, and work study), while others were more directly related to quantitative flexibility (shedding of surplus labour, employment of labour on a part-time or contract basis). Statistical analysis of the data confirmed associations between these groups of employment practices. Firms were also asked about changes in the competitive environment over the previous five years. Reflecting the influence of the 'post-Fordist' debate, the questions asked not only about changes in the level of demand for products and intensity of price competition but also about pressures to reduce batch size, improve design and quality, meet delivery dates, provide increased credit to customers, and deal with foreign as well as British competitors. Firms subject to increased competitive pressure along these different dimensions were found also to be those that had made most changes to the effort they put into design, quality, work scheduling, and use of technology. Moreover, statistical analysis revealed a relationship between moves to increase qualitative flexibility of the labour force and improvements to the non-price elements of the firm's competitive strategies, while those firms which had made increased use of quantitative flexibility were more likely to have been subject to price-based competition. Explanations of the current system of employment by reference to these product-market variables were less successful than the attempt to explain recent changes in labour policy, thereby supporting the conclusions of Gallie and White in Chapter 2 on the potential advantages of studying changes in employment practices rather than levels. Nor, with the exception of part-time working, was the use of structural characteristics particularly helpful as a means of explaining differences in overall employment policies, again showing the weakness of standard segmentation models.

The Wilkinson and White paper is novel in two ways. First, the paper successfully demonstrates the need to develop a more complex analysis of the relationships between firms and their product markets than has been present in segmentation theory, and shows the strength of this approach in shedding light on the determinants of *change* in employers' employment policies. The second novel feature is the application of a similar analysis of 'product-market pressure' and its relationship to employment policy change to the public sector, using concepts such as 'pressure on costs' as equivalent to price pressure, and pressure to improve quality of service as equivalent to quality pressures in the private sector.

Chapter 4, by Rose, addresses another of the key debates on employer policy: employer policy and the new industrial relations. The paper uses material drawn primarily from the SCELI data set of intensive employer interviews carried out in the six areas combined. Questions in the SCELI survey about the time horizon over which firms planned their business operations were used to divide the sample into 'strategists', 'planners', and 'improvisers'. The paper then documents the extent to which there is evidence, for the sample of firms as a whole, and for these three subsets, of employers introducing policies to introduce staff flexibility, to change work operations, or change the system of employee representation. The overall findings confirm the common view of British firms as 'improvisers and empiricists'. Even where evidence of strategic behaviour was found, it applied only to a small minority of firms and stopped short of the more extreme theories of companies developing strategic management for social control, found in much of the literature. Marketing factors dominated over labour issues and only 3 per cent claimed to have positive personnel policies. Nevertheless, the division between strategists and improvisers provided a useful distinction for the analysis of employer practice, indicating that divisions do exist between forms of management style and policy. While the strategists were found, as predicted, to be more involved in flexible contracts and in functional flexibility, they were also found, against predictions, to have the highest levels of unionization and to be the most committed to union regulations. These firms were also the most likely to have introduced quality circles and the like, but these did not represent a challenge to unionization. Little support was thus found for either the 'macho-management' hypothesis or the hypothesis that 'deunionization' is associated with the adoption of more human-resource-centred management strategies.

The first section of the book thus provides an empirical and theoretical critique of the conventional models of employer policy and the labour force while presenting some specific suggestions for the development of a more general approach to the analysis of employer policy, not tied to simplistic stereotypes or dualist divisions, and in which the historical specificities of the firm, the industry, and society can be allowed to play a part.

(ii) *Localities, industrial organizations, and labour-market policies*

In Part II the interplay between geographical and historical specificity and theoretical models of industrial and labour organization is explored further through three chapters which study industrial and employment systems within particular localities according to particular historical conditions. The first two chapters have an explicitly historical focus. Chapter 5, by Penn, analyses the evolution of Rochdale as an industrial district. Identified as an ideal-type industrial district by Marshall in 1923, it is particularly appropriate to use Rochdale to explore the increasingly influential model of the industrial district which has emerged in the Third Italy but which is also argued to have developed in certain parts of the UK (Pyke 1988). The paper traces the development of the industrial structure of Rochdale through various phases of interrelated and interconnected growth of specific industries, including textiles, paper, and engineering. These overlapping and interconnected industries provide a plausible example of an interconnected industrial district where complex subcontracting relationships between firms could be expected to have emerged, based on various subordinate or co-operative relationships. However, analysis of firms' relations with other firms reveals that, instead of this structure fostering internal linkages, most firms' ties to local industry and markets are in fact weakening and their involvement in external and international relations are strengthening. Thus the textile industry in Rochdale increasingly sources its machinery abroad and the engineering firms specialize in products with an international rather than a local dimension. There is little evidence of widespread subcontracting, particularly of key production processes. Relationships between large firms and their subcontractors can be categorized as subordinate and not co-operative, and small firms have failed to develop any effective form of inter-firm co-operation; their existence thus remains precarious and isolated from any form of support structure. Interestingly, the only area where firms in Rochdale appear to have retained their historical co-operative relationships is explicitly in the area of labour relations. Firms still exchange information on wages and co-operate on training, resisting attempts to force Rochdale to give up its independence under the new system of Training and Enterprise Councils.

Assumptions of a general trend towards co-operative inter-firm relations and complex systems of subcontracting are revealed by this chapter to be misplaced, even in an area with long-established industrial cultures and traditions. It also shows that industrial districts are by no means new, although their form and operation may change over time. The second chapter in this section, that by Morris and Smyth, also shows that employer policy has a long pedigree as the major structuring influence on a local labour market. The paper uses oral history and documentary materials to trace the employment policies of two firms in the area of Kirkcaldy. Far from adopting the casual employment practices of neo-classical textbooks these firms both adopted a policy of paternalism to maintain, control, and reproduce their labour forces. The strong relationship between the institution of the family in structuring labour supply and firms' employment policies is brought out clearly in the paper. Not only do the firms have specific employment preferences between male and female, young and old labour, but they also use the domestic commitments of individuals to support and maintain the family as a means of creating a tied labour force, although in this case instead of the conventional male breadwinner it is the young women who inherit the obligation to work in the mills so that the family retains access to housing. Finally, the ideology of the family is reinforced through the 'theatre of paternalism', the linkage of events and privileges within the firm to events connected with the owners' family. The historical evidence revealed that these firms were not obliged to provide the whole range of good employment conditions to secure a stable labour force; instead, the guarantee of employment and the dependency of the families on housing allowed firms to keep direct wage levels at a low level. Moreover, the restricted opportunities which the firms' employees faced were not so much a result of the free play of market forces but the consequence of employers' strategies to create a closed 'industrial district', restricting mobility to other firms through control of housing and no-poaching agreements between neighbourhood firms.

The chapter looks at how the development of other institutions have changed the scope and form of employer policy. Using SCELI data on housing tenure and fringe benefits the authors show how in the modern period the state has taken over the role of the employer in the provision of housing, freeing up the choices of employees to move between firms but also shifting the burden of responsibility for social reproduction from employers to the state. Employers are now content to limit their non-cash payments to sponsorship within the community, and to providing benefits to higher level employees through provision of cars, pensions, and health benefits. Changes in the institutional conditions for the reproduction of labour have thus had a major impact in modifying and redefining the scope for employer policy in the generation and maintenance of its labour supply.

Chapter 7 in this section does not have a long historical perspective but has similarities to the other two in several respects. It is concerned with an industrial district, namely the oil industry in Aberdeen; it deals with a very particular period in Aberdeen's history, the oil boom of the late 1970s and early 1980s, and as a consequence of the oil slump in the middle of the research period, is also able to look at the switch from boom to slump, thus tracing two important periods of Aberdeen's history within a very short time-scale. The specific focus of the paper by Gasteen and Sewell is on the use of flexible employment forms and core–periphery strategies in the Aberdeen oil and oil-related industries. The overall effect of the study is to reveal the inadequacy of the flexible-firm model as a description of the factors that lead to and the problems caused by the use of atypical or flexible employment forms. The oil boom led to the development of a complex system of subcontracting and flexible employment systems which were only in part related to the volatility or unpredictability of product-market conditions. Of equal importance was the division of the oil-production process into a number of distinct stages, requiring different skills through the product cycle, and the associated high levels of specialization which led to the growth of subcontracting to increase functional flexibility. Labour-supply factors also proved important in the development of these networks. Agency or subcontract work tended to be higher paid than regular employment and thus was a favoured option during the boom; self-employment also became very much part of the culture and expectations of the oil industry and the Aberdeen labour market. Moreover, by adopting flexible employment contracts the industry was able to extend its effective labour market, attracting in labour from outside Aberdeen for intensive work periods, who would then return to their families for extended breaks. Thus the particularities of the oil industry, the general boom, and the specific labour-supply requirements, all helped to foster the development of flexible working. This culture of flexibility also had an influence on how the industry adapted to the recession which had hit the industry shortly before the field-work. Initially, the existence of flexible employment forms provided an immediate means of labour-force reduction; peripheral workers were dispensed with and the core protected. Later the core was also reduced and more staff transferred to peripheral status. The flexible employment forms then became a means to reduce overheads and labour costs, instead of a way to expand labour supply under shortage conditions. Without the culture of flexibility it might have been more difficult for the oil companies to pass on the costs of adjustment so easily to the labour force.

In addition to providing a wealth of detail and information on the complexities of the subcontracting and flexible-employment system Chapter 7 also highlights some of the control aspects of the use of flexible employment that have often been overlooked in the description of the benefits of flexibility. For example, firms found that the use of contract labour paid at higher wages than permanent staff was only viable when they were employed on different tasks than permanent staff. Otherwise the permanent staff resented their lack of commitment to the firm and their higher pay. Problems of loyalty and commitment by subcontractors was less of a problem when specialist subcontractors were used, since these were more concerned about maintaining their reputation for quality to secure the next contract. Finally, firms had to choose between a range of different ways of introducing flexibility into their employment contracts; some preferred to use open-ended contracts, but with the understanding that all jobs were in principle temporary, so as to avoid the potential for conflict among a work-force composed of both permanent and temporary staff. Others preferred to gain the loyalty of permanent staff by separating them out from the temporary staff. The possibility of combining temporary employment status with a permanent contract suggests that in Britain, where employment protection laws are weak, researchers have placed too much emphasis on the explicit use of temporary contracts and not enough on actual employer policy with regard to provision of continuous employment opportunities.

(iii) *Employer policies, employment changes, and individual perceptions*

The final section of the book is concerned with the impact of employer policy on individuals in the labour market. Chapter 8, by White and Gallie, addresses this issue by reference to the impact of employer policy on occupational attainment, net pay, and satisfaction with pay and job security. The data used for this investigation come from the work-attitudes/work-history survey for all six areas. As the employers of the respondents were used as the sample frame for the telephone survey, it proved possible to link these data sets to provide information on employment policies for some 2,000 or more respondents. The types of employer policies investigated include their use of internal development policies (internal promotion), their employment of part-time and marginal workers, and their recognition of trade unions.

The data sets also allowed the effects of structural variables such as industry, size of establishment, and extent of technological change to be analysed. Three dependent variables—occupational attainment, pay, and satisfaction—were used to measure differences in labour-market outcomes for individuals. Analyses were able to investigate the impact of employer policy on these outcomes, controlling for a wide range of other variables including the respondents' gender, their qualifications and work experience, their social class of origin, their status as part-time or marginal workers or as permanent full-time workers, their trade-union membership, and their occupational position in their previous job. The objective was to identify the effects of employer policies, net of the effect of human capital and work experience (although these are not necessarily themselves independent of employer policy). The results found the expected strong effect of human capital and gender on occupational attainment and net pay, but employer employment policies were found to have independent and significant effects over and above the gender, human capital, and social class effects. Employees in firms with internal development policies were likely to have both higher occupational attainment and higher net pay levels. Occupational attainment of employees in firms with high levels of part-time working were similar to those in firms with low levels of part-time working, but net pay was significantly lower. Interestingly, those actually employed on a part-time basis had considerably lower occupational attainment than their full-time equivalents but in fact received higher net pay, after adjusting for differences in human capital, although this difference was largely accounted for by the tax system.

Amongst the other variables examined for their impact on pay and occupational attainment, temporary workers were found to have the lowest occupational attainment but fixed-contract workers the worst rates of pay; union recognition was found to have no effect on pay levels, but respondents who were actually union members, and not just employed in firms which recognized unions, did in fact receive higher pay. These effects were independent of the mark-up associated with internal development policies. Structural variables such as industry, size, and technology had less clear-cut effects on pay than firms' employment policy variables.

Turning to the effect of employer policy on satisfaction variables, the most noticeable impact of general employer policy on satisfaction was recent experience of work-force reductions, which was associated with a lower satisfaction with job security for all groups of workers, including those on permanent contracts. Employer policy, such as internal development policy, appeared to have little effect on pay satisfaction. Here the most noticeable result was the higher satisfaction score for part-time workers, possibly associated with their higher net pay relative to human capital.

The overall conclusion to this statistical investigation of the impact of employer policy on labour-market outcomes is that there does appear to be an impact on employee life chances in terms of pay and occupational attainment, if not on work satisfaction. Atypical employment policies also seem to have some spin-off effects on workers employed within the establishment, for example reducing pay levels in firms with high ratios of part-time working. The impact of atypical employment status on individuals was, however, mixed. Occupational attainment of part-time and temporary staff was low, but net pay relative to human-capital and pay satisfaction scores was above those for full-timers. These results are, of course, predicated upon the possibility of estimating pay and job attainment 'net of human capital', that is that there is a common human-capital element in all pay structures, and it is important not to lose sight of the absolutely low pay levels of part-timers, and indeed of female full-timers. Comparisons of female part-timers with male full-timers would certainly not suggest that part-timers were relatively well-paid, even 'net of human capital'. Nevertheless, these findings do indicate again that there has been perhaps too much attention focused on specific employment contracts, particularly marginal employment contracts; the findings on the impact of work-force reductions on satisfaction with job security certainly indicate that insecurity can extend easily into labour-force segments with so-called permanent jobs.

The final two chapters in Part III take up a somewhat different theme: the exploration of how individuals themselves interpret and view the labour market, firms' employment policies, and their own employment prospects. Chapter 9, by Burchell, Elliott, and Rubery, looks at these issues using the work-attitudes/work-history survey for Northampton. It explores how individuals came to be in their current jobs, how they perceive employers' policies with respect to recruitment and promotion for people in their types of jobs, and what they consider their prospects in the labour market to be. The chapter explores the extent to which individuals' interpretation of the functioning of the labour market fits with existing models of how labour markets work, and discusses the extent to which current theories have underestimated the importance of individuals' interpretation of the labour market in predicting responses to employer policy. A continuing theme throughout the paper is the difference in responses by gender.

In many respects, the findings do provide confirmation for existing models of segmented labour markets. Women, for example, are less likely to have promotion prospects in their current job and more likely to consider that they could obtain a similar job in the external labour market. However, some results are less obvious: even though women consider that they could get an equivalent job in the external labour market they are no less likely than men to consider that their best chances of a better job would be to stay with their own employer. In contrast, although men are more likely to have promotion prospects in their current job which should encourage them to stay with their current employer, they are just as likely as women to consider that their best chances lie in changing employers, presumably because they are more likely than women to have promotion prospects outside as well as inside. These findings indicate that the interpretation of the impact of internal labour markets must be related to individuals' own external labour-market opportunities, in terms of pay and promotion possibilities.

Perceptions of the labour market are difficult to interpret because of the confounding of personal factors, such as age, life-cycle, and material situation, with perceptions of structural factors. For example, the most frequent factor causing people to view their chances of getting a better job was age, but once those mentioning age were omitted from the sample the next most frequent factor mentioned was a structural constraint, namely lack of jobs to apply for. With the exception of age, respondents were not particularly likely to identify direct forms of personal discrimination as the main constraint on obtaining a better job. Almost all women chose to see barriers to getting a better job to be related to having domestic commitments and not simply to being a woman. The complexities of these results, and the clearly personal ways in which labour-market processes are interpreted by individuals—that is, relative to their own expectations and labour-market opportunities—suggests that it is necessary for employers, if they aim to use explicit personnel policies to achieve given objectives, to pay more attention to the way these policies are likely to be interpreted by existing and potential employees. Individuals' perceptions of their current position and future prospects are clearly related to their own past experience and their domestic and family circumstances (Burchell and Rubery 1990).

More evidence that we need to take perceptions seriously is provided in the final chapter, which reports on a special study carried out by the Cambridge team of twenty firms, where directly matched questionnaires were administered to managers and employees. One particular focus of these questionnaires was the firms' employment policies. The survey explored five areas of firms' employment policies that are relevant to internal labour market theory: pay levels relative to similar firms, frequency of promotion opportunities, external opportunities of employees, career orientations of employees, and keenness of employees to undertake training. Managers and employees were asked directly matched questions relating to their perceptions of these practices, whether they considered themselves to have a career, were likely to find a job outside, and their own personal keenness to undertake training. Burchell and Rubery explore two questions. Was there any evidence that employers actually pursued policies with respect to pay and promotion? How correlated were employer and employee perceptions of firms' policies or of employees own opportunities and attitudes?

Evidence in favour of the view that firms pursue policies was provided by the range of responses to questions relating to level of pay and frequency of promotion. Firms without explicit policies could have been expected to score around the mid-point of the scale on the 'about average' points. Employees also spread their responses, showing again that they held more definite views about their firms' employment policies than that they were 'about average'. What emerges clearly from the data, however, is a lack of congruence between employer and employee perceptions of firms' employment policies. Employers in general were considerably more optimistic about the level of pay and opportunities for promotion they provided than were their employees; in the latter case, the disagreement was often of the order of three points on a five point scale. Nor were employers any more 'canny' about their employees' attitudes and opportunities; only with the question of career orientations was there found to be any real degree of correlation between manager and employee perceptions. What these results demonstrate is that while it is clearly 'neater' and less time-consuming for researchers to collect information on employment policies from employers, they must not make the assumption that these descriptions of employment policy necessarily fit actual practice (a long-established caveat to manager-based research), nor that, even if they do approximate to actual practices, will employees necessarily perceive that their firms, for example, offer better pay or promotion prospects than in the external labour market. These themes are also taken up by Morris and Smyth in Chapter 6, where employees of the paternalistic employers were found to regard their employers' policies as harsh and restrictive, though accompanied by some degree of security. This provides a counterbalance to simplistic views that paternalism induces loyalty and consensus. If the purpose of employment policies is to influence behaviour, then it is not only researchers but also managers who need to pay serious attention to the way employees perceive their policies.

CONCLUSIONS

Perhaps the most notable feature of the chapters which constitute this volume is how little empirical support they give to theoretical predictions of how managers will reorganize labour when faced by intensified product-market pressure and when given new opportunities to tighten control by government-inspired labour-market deregulation and by high unemployment. There is little general evidence that employers have systematically pursued such objectives as greater labour-force flexibility, de-skilling, human resource management, or have adopted the 'new industrial relations'. The poor performance of such hypotheses can possibly be explained by reference to the quality of British management, or by the length of time it takes to introduce new management systems, so that it is too soon to make a final judgement. But before any such conclusions can be drawn it would seem necessary to consider more carefully the nature of the labour process, and locate the hypothesis of labour management more directly in its product- and labour-market contexts than is usual in most theoretical work on these questions. This analysis suggests that explanations can be found in the range of objectives of employer policy, many of which are not necessary mutually compatible.

Firstly, it is important to differentiate between the *technical* and *social* relations of production. In production, the different types of labour and machines which constitute the process of production are mutually dependent in a technical sense: one cannot operate without the others. Consequently, the essence of their joint activity is co-operation and the more effective this is the more efficient production will be. Within this context, the social relations of production have two functions: co-ordination and control. The co-ordinating function of the social relations provides the way by which effective co-operation in production is achieved. Production co-ordination requires direction, essentially a managerial role, but also a network of less formal interpersonal relationships—the social framework for individuals to work together. The control function of the social relations of production involves the exercise of power and the imposition of sanctions necessary to secure compliance in co-operation, and again these may operate at the formal managerial and informal intra-group level.

Apart from their function of securing co-operation, the social relations of production have a more coercive role in distribution. For, whilst the means of production and labour necessarily work together in production, they nevertheless compete over shares in the proceeds of their joint activity. This does not raise problems in the simplest forms of orthodox economics because relative prices (and hence distributional shares) are given to the firm by the market. Moreover, under the assumptions of orthodox economics, each of the co-operators will secure the compliance of the others in production because they can choose alternatives from amongst a large number of perfect substitutes. The problems arise when would-be co-operators bargain on unequal terms. Asymmetry in bargaining power results from, amongst other things, inequalities in economic resources, limitations on the numbers of alternative trading partners, and differential access to information. These inequalities are unlikely to be all on one side. For example, capital's economic superiority and control of the means of production is countered to varying degrees by trade-union organization, skill scarcity, and the privileged access labour has to information about production processes acquired by work experience and in the process of learning-by-doing. Moreover, the exercise of bargaining power is ultimately limited by the risk that one or the other of the partners will withdraw co-operation, so that the loss in production will swamp any gain from an increased share.

Employers can thus be seen to have a range of objectives which are not necessarily mutually compatible. The need to exercise control for distributional reasons and to ensure compliance with the co-operative requirements of production may inhibit the co-ordinating role by creating resistance. The need to manufacture and maintain consent may be an important constraint on the exercise of power by managers, requiring a governance structure in which the different interests are represented and procedures by which differences can be resolved and changes implemented. Job design, terms and conditions of employment, promotion systems, the form of the labour contract, the choice between internal and external provision of labour services, and other aspects of the labour organization, can be expected to reflect the compromises between the distributional and production objectives of employers and the need to maintain an institutional framework necessary to sustain that compromise.

From within this understanding, two explanations can be suggested of why there has been no widespread extension of the use of non-standard job forms or other such radical changes. First, the requirements of production are for permanence in employment relationships, not only because production is continuous and because of the need to build up and retain specific skills, but also to create the necessary conditions for effective co-operation. Secondly, in making changes, attention needs to be paid to the effects on the social relations of production and how this might influence productive performance. For these reasons, employers might be reluctant to introduce radical new departures from past practices and will experiment rather carefully with such innovations. Even in the Aberdeen oil industry, where the technical discontinuities in the exploration, development, and production chain created a culture of self-employment, short-term contracts, and subcontracting, the increased casualization of the work-force following the collapse of oil prices was not unproblematic. Increased use of non-standard employment contracts posed problems of quality control, reliability, and the risk of disaffection by permanently employed key workers. It is also notable that the one oil firm in the Aberdeen sample which was exclusively engaged in the continuous process of oil production extended its internal labour market by incorporating staff previously employed on short-term contracts.

The demands of the technical and social relations of production are not the only constraints on the ability of employers to pursue particular employment policies: this is also importantly conditioned by the product- and labour-market structures and the institutional environment within which they operate. In a seller's market producers find it easier to impose their production requirements on consumers and this should be reflected in the variety and quality of goods they supply. They will also be well placed to pass on to their customers the price and non-price costs of their labour organization policy. In a buyer's market, on the other hand, the need to pay closer attention to consumer needs will place constraints on employers' labour organization strategies by increasing the requirement to pay closer attention to product design, variety, quality, and reliability, as well as price. In these circumstances, the ability to escape from uncertainty and price pressure, by adopting employment strategies based on wage and employment flexibility, is constrained by the requirement to pay closer attention to non-price aspects of competition. Such product-market demands necessitate higher skill, more functional flexibility, and higher levels of work-force (or subcontractor) trust and co-operation, none of which are likely to be fostered by greater wage and employment uncertainty or by conflictual industrial-relations strategies.

The fact that the effects of labour organization strategies are likely to be imprinted on the quality of products and services limits the scope of policies producing inferior terms and conditions of employment in highly competitive markets where product quality matters. From this perspective it is perhaps not surprising to find standards of services are generally low by international standards in hotels, catering, and distribution in Britain, sectors which are relatively closed to international competition and which are typified by poor terms and conditions of employment. Moreover, the public sector, where consumers have little power to impose service standards, is where casualization and the worsening of terms and conditions of employment have often been taken furthest.

Segmented labour markets with comparable labour available at different terms and conditions provide the opportunity for employers to tailor their labour-market strategies to their own needs without necessarily sacrificing the benefits of an established and committed work-force. This is strongly suggested by the evidence that part-time workers on low rates of pay are generally permanent workers, that they see their current employment as offering the best job prospects, despite the ease of getting a comparable job in the external labour market, and that they have high levels of job satisfaction. Thus employers have the best of several worlds: the domestic circumstances of married women, for example, provides the basis for a flexible, committed but cheap labour force: primary workers at secondary prices. Age and job shortages also trap individuals in the internal labour market by lowering their value in the external labour market so that their pay need not reflect their primary status.[1] In these circumstances, it is not surprising that non-standard job forms have not become more common; employers can achieve their objectives without them.

Finally, institutions also exert permissive and constraining influence on employer strategies. Chapter 6 demonstrates how the discriminatory letting of company houses within a paternalistic employment framework, coupled with employer collusion restricting labour mobility, secured long-term commitment from, and the orderly social reproduction of, a low-paid and reliable workforce. However, the strategy was undermined by state-provided social welfare, local-authority housing, and full employment. Penn's study of Rochdale also demonstrates how local labour-market institutions were modified by changing industrial organization, the increasing internationalization of firms, product markets, and supply networks which weaken local inter-firm linkages. However, the withdrawal of firms from locally based interest groups was not complete: continued common interests in local labour markets are reflected in collaboration in training and wage-fixing.

Trade-union organization, employer associations, and collective bargaining serve both to limit the range of options open to management and to provide a procedural framework for securing change. Training systems, recognized qualifications, and standardized pay levels narrow the range of alternative strategies open to employers and structure the job opportunities and promotion paths of individuals, both inside the firm and in the external labour market. The role of unions in governance structures within firms are indicated in Chapter 4 by the association between active labour organization strategies, higher levels of unionization, and employer commitment to union regulation. It is not unreasonable to suppose that strong union representation constrains employers from adopting policies counter to the interests of the incumbent work-force. But this success puts the unions in a position where, in the interest of their members and their members' jobs, they are obliged to negotiate over the introduction of new forms of work organization and to use established procedures for this purpose.

Perhaps the most important institutional forces structuring the labour market are the employment strategies of employers themselves. These create the rules, norms, and structures which shape wage, job, and promotion opportunities in both the internal and external labour market and through which individuals progress, enhancing or diminishing their labour-market credentials. They also create for each individual employer the labour-market environments, internal and external to the firm, which act as important constraints on the range of employment strategies that an individual employer can devise and deploy.

NOTE TO INTRODUCTION

1. It should be noted that this line of reasoning turns the conventional insider/outsider models on their head: in both cases restricted external-labour-market chances provide opportunities for rent extraction by employers.

I
Markets, Employers, and Employment Policies

1

Internal and External Labour Markets: Towards an Integrated Analysis[1]

JILL RUBERY

Internal labour markets have provided a major focus of labour-market analysis in the 1970s and 1980s. This interest has come from a number of sources; from institutional economists associated with the labour market segmentation debate (Doeringer and Piore 1971; Wilkinson 1981; Osterman 1984); from the neo-institutionalists within the neo-classical tradition and some Marxist economists concerned with information and transactions costs (Williamson 1975; Bowles 1985; Lindbeck and Snower 1985); from sociologists and economists analysing the organization of the labour process (Friedman 1978; Burawoy 1979b); from economists concerned to relate forms of labour-market organization to macro-economic conditions (Boyer 1979; Gordon et al. 1982); and from policy-makers and practitioners concerned with explaining the existence of different employment forms and the apparent success of the Japanese form of internal labour market (OECD 1986b).

The term 'internal labour market' can be given a wide or a narrow definition. The most exclusive definition links internal labour markets to a specific form of labour-market organization: to the development of internal job ladders with limited ports of entry, offering recruits the prospect of job security, internal promotion prospects, and higher lifetime earnings than they could command on the external labour market. This definition is associated with Doeringer and Piore's internal labour market model and with Williamson's model of hierarchies. A weaker definition would include employment systems which tend to protect insiders from external labour market conditions and to provide better terms and conditions of employment than they could find in the external labour market. This definition is associated with 'insider–outsider' models of the labour market. At an empirical level, the existence or otherwise of internal labour markets is usually measured according to the level of pay, the extent and frequency of job promotions, the degree of job security, and the sensitivity of pay settlements to internal or external factors (Blanchflower and Oswald 1988).

Within this literature it is often argued that firms can be arrayed along a spectrum according to the degree of internalization of their employment systems, or more frequently dichotomized into those operating an internal system and those using employment systems driven by external market conditions. This type of dichotomization is evident in the dual labour market literature, in the core–periphery approach to flexibility (Atkinson 1985*a*), and even in the neo-institutional approaches, with firms using high pay to reduce shirking necessarily contrasted with those basing pay on external opportunity wages[2] and in the distinction between 'markets and hierarchies'. The notion of a competitive and unstructured labour market thus tends to be retained alongside the notion of structured internal-labour-market systems. The extent of internalization over time is argued to be related to changes in firms' technological or market requirements, in terms of firm-specific skills or more recently in needs for commitment and loyalty.

The move from the market-oriented approach which dominated the debate in the 1960s, through the emphasis on human-capital theories, to a firm- or organization-centred approach in the 1970s and 1980s, represents a considerable advance in labour-market theory.[3] To pursue a market approach based on the analysis of spot contracts, in the face of clear evidence of the importance of continuous employment contracts and divergent employment practices between firms, was clearly inappropriate (Mackay *et al.* 1971; Maurice *et al.* 1986 appendix). However, the development of an organizational level approach to the structuring of labour markets in itself does not necessarily provide an adequate framework for analysis. There may be problems with the way organizations and organizational practices are theorized, and the relationship between organizations and their external environment may be neglected. In recent literature there are three main areas where problems can be identified.

The first is a tendency to assume both compatibility and coherence between firms' employment systems and their employment needs or requirements (see in particular Doeringer and Piore's (1971) analysis of the relationship between demand for firm-specific skills and the use of primary employment policies, and Piore and Sabel's (1984) assumption that a move to flexible specialization on the production side will necessarily bring about a move to high trust relations on the employment side). This problem arises out of the general tendency for economists to engage in equilibrium and functionalist theorizing. Attention is paid to how firms move towards compatibility between their policies in the employment sphere, their production needs, and their financial constraints, and not to the potential for continual tension and incompatibility between these different aspects of economic organization. Analyses of firms' employment practices, with reference to pay, job stability, or promotion systems, do not necessarily give a clear indication of firms' relative needs for stable, committed labour according to production criteria. Differences in employment policies between firms may not simply reflect differences in, for example, skill requirements, but may be as much determined by differences in financial constraints or in levels of union organization (Rubery 1978).

The second danger of an employer-centred approach is that of neglecting the influence of external conditions on internal policies. External conditions provide the constraints and the opportunities which determine firms' room for manœuvre. A prime example of this danger was found in the 1980s debate over flexibility, where employers' moves towards a core–periphery strategy were interpreted within the framework of changing internal needs of firms for greater functional and numerical flexibility (Atkinson 1985*a*). Subsequent developments and analysis of labour-market change have suggested that such moves are more appropriately interpreted as firms' responses to changing labour-market conditions, which were likely to be reversed once the labour market tightened.

While the second problem with the employer-centred approach is a tendency to overstress the autonomy of employer action, the third danger is that of neglecting the cumulative and aggregative effect of employer policy on the organization of labour markets. The analysis of the role of institutions in structuring labour markets has tended to be limited to the specific operation of internal labour markets. The impact of these systems on the operation of the labour market at a more aggregate level has not often been systematically investigated. Some recent contributions to the literature have tended to remedy these defects. For example, Osterman (1988) has linked the development of long-term unemployment to the internal labour market policies of firms, and Marsden (1986) and Osterman (1987) have both investigated the role of firms' training and employment policies in breaking down the operation of occupation-based labour markets. These contributions remain, however, very much the exception, and the complex subject of the iterations between firm-based policies and the organization of the labour market remains a relatively unexplored terrain.

The thrust of these criticisms of the state of internal-labour-market research is to suggest that there need to be developments along three dimensions: a more sophisticated approach to the determinants of employer policy which allows for conflict and tensions in the formulation of employer employment policy; a greater integration between the analysis of external and internal influences on employer policy at the micro level; and the development of a more integrated analysis to the organization of labour markets at both a micro and a macro level. This study aims to make some contribution to these three objectives, by developing an analysis of labour-market organization which addresses macro and micro level phenomena through the same theoretical approach but without falling prey to the problem of generalizing from the micro to the macro from the unsound base of the so-called representative firm (Tarling 1981). The argument instead will be developed on the basis of heterogeneous firms operating in different segments of product and labour markets.

To illustrate the theoretical arguments we will draw upon case-studies of a wide variety of firms, in terms of size, product market, ownership, trade-union organization, and labour supply, carried out in the Northampton labour market as part of the Social Change and Economic Life Initiative (SCELI) between 1986 and 1988. The case-studies involved extensive interviews with personnel managers (and in some cases general management) covering the whole range of topics on employment policy: recruitment, pay, promotion, gender segregation, non-standard employment, working-time, technological, product and organizational change, trade-union structure, collective bargaining, and management style. This extensive empirical material will be used selectively here to provide illustrations and examples of different employer policies under various external conditions and opportunities—not to test the hypotheses developed here. The advantage of this case-study material is that it spans the whole range of employing organizations, from public to private, large to small, independent to multinationals, and thus provides a good basis for developing an analysis of the role of employer policy in structuring labour markets that is relevant to the labour market as a whole. However, the limitations of an area-based study also become apparent when moving beyond the micro or firm-specific level to the aggregate level. One relevant level of aggregation is at the local labour-market level, but so too is the industry, occupational, or company level (in the case of large corporations). Thus we will also make reference to how our case-study establishments' employment policies relate to their position in industrial, occupational, or company labour markets.

The study is organized in two parts. The first part is a theoretical analysis of how internal and external labour markets develop and operate. This gives rise to four key hypotheses. Illustrative case-study material relating to these hypotheses is presented in the second section.

INTERNAL LABOUR MARKETS AND EXTERNAL LABOUR MARKETS: AN ANALYTICAL FRAMEWORK

An appropriate framework for the analysis of labour-market structuring first requires a consideration of the incentives to 'internalize' labour; second, an exploration of constraints on employer employment policy; third, an analysis of the interrelationships between employer policy and the external environment, including the external labour market.

Incentives for firms to 'internalize' their labour

The growth of a range of different explanations of internal labour markets has drawn attention to the fact that, in contrast to early single-factor theories, the incentives for and pressures on firms to 'internalize' their labour forces are multi-dimensional. These incentives can be divided into three categories: those associated with labour as a factor of production; those associated with the system of competition; those associated with the system of production. Consideration of each of these issues in turn reveals a very wide range of reasons why, *ceteris paribus*, most firms are likely to prefer to continue to employ their existing work-force, to internalize their labour.

(i) *Labour as a factor of production*

The incentive to secure a return on investment in training used to be considered the main or prime factor in internalizing employment and providing workers with firm-specific skills with protection against economic downturns (Oi 1962; Doeringer and Piore 1971; Kerr 1954; Lester 1952; Becker 1964). This incentive was initially assumed to be limited to firm-specific skills but later writers have argued that firms are not in fact able to pass on the full cost of general training to employees (Marsden 1986; Osterman 1984, 1987; Sengenberger 1981), thereby creating the conditions for a more general hypothesis that, all things being equal, firms which invest in training will try to encourage continuity of employment in order to reap a return on investments.

The imperative to internalize has more recently been linked to managerial needs to control and direct the motivations, intelligence, and free will of labour. Neo-institutionalists such as Williamson (1975) have identified a management concern not simply to retain skilled labour within the firm but to ensure that skills and knowledge are used in the interests of the firm. It is not just the continuity of contract that is desired but the productive use of skills, or at a minimum an insurance that labour will not use its idiosyncratic knowledge against the interests of the firm or continually to force a renegotiation of the contract in the interests of the workers. Career structures and high lifetime earnings opportunities are seen to be ways of guarding against capricious behaviour on the part of workers with idiosyncratic knowledge.

Issues of motivation and morale have also been extended to workers without necessarily high levels of skill, but who are also hired on the basis that they will provide a given minimum level of labour effort. These problems have concerned both neo-classical and Marxist economists. Firms face costs in attempting to ensure that this wage-effort bargain is observed, both monitoring effort and in hiring and firing. Monitoring is argued to be most effective and cheapest if the control system is internalized, if the workers themselves can be relied upon to provide the effort with only a system of random checks. This self-monitoring system is expected to work if employees feel that they would suffer significant damages if caught 'shirking' on a random check; that is, if the job offers higher pay, security, or promotion than could be obtained on the external market (Bowles 1985; Lindbeck and Snower 1985). This notion that the job must be better than outside jobs of course rests on the assumption that workers find it easy to move between jobs in the secondary or competitive markets even if they have a 'dismissal' on their employment record.

A more positive reason for management's interest in stable employment systems has been found in the notion that labour brings certain unique properties into the firm which can add to the value of the resource to the firm. It is the differences in the characteristics of labour from other factors of production, namely the free will of labour and its associated ability to use intelligence and interpretation to resolve unspecified and unknown problems, which constitutes the advantages of labour to the firm (Storey 1989; Guest 1987; Pankhurst 1990). This contrasts with the shirking models, where these very same attributes constitute the problem of labour for firms. Williamson's model of course fits somewhere in between these two approaches, as on the one hand he stresses the practical significance of idiosyncratic knowledge, but argues that it is workers' tendencies to act 'opportunistically' that provide the incentive for the establishment of internal labour markets.

The human-resource-management debate has been implicitly concerned with controlling as well as motivating labour but the emphasis has been placed on 'unleashing' labour's potential productive capacity, once the employees' commitment and loyalty to the company's aims and objectives has been secured through appropriate management techniques. For some, this identification of the potential for labour to use its ability to problem solve, and to enhance the quality of production, is linked explicitly to the development of new forms of competition (Piore and Sabel 1984). For others this attribute of labour has always been present (Pankhurst 1990) and it was management's attraction to the apparent certainties of Taylorism and not the actual differences in competitive environment that was the main cause of the change in attitude to the role of labour. This approach is clearly linked to current interest in the apparent success of Japanese employment systems.

Whether or not commitment and loyalty can be secured through a change in terms and conditions and management style is clearly a matter for debate. Problems emerge at two levels at least: whether changes in management style do change attitudes and behaviour, and whether changes in management policy are in fact perceived by employees (see Chapters 8 and 9). The relative effectiveness of human resource management in raising productivity or reducing turnover may have some influence in the future on current management policies, but the significance of the human resources debate is possibly the way in which it has made clear that the inherent labour issue for management is not how to secure control over a known labour process and predictable levels of labour effort, but how to mobilize the capacities of labour to deal with the uncertainties of the labour process while retaining managerial control.

Finally, in this analysis of the role of labour as a factor of production, comes the characteristic of labour as the only factor of production responsible for its own reproduction. This gives rise both to opportunities for employers to 'exploit' labour, in the sense of not rewarding labour according to its relative skill and effort; and to the incentive for workers to combine together to improve the terms and conditions under which they are employed. The notion of an internal labour market has been developed on the assumption that, in the absence of a specific system of providing preferential treatment to internal employees in terms of pay and promotion, employers will face an inherently unstable and unreliable labour supply. The problem with this approach is that it overestimates both the power of individual labour in the external labour market and the willingness of workers to move between jobs. If jobs are scarce and workers have a tendency, all other things being equal, to keep the job they have, then employers may be able to combine their needs for stability with a low-paid and informal employment system. The problem of 'shirking' is here resolved by the absence of any alternative job opportunities.

Neo-institutionalists have a tendency to define all existing employment systems as representing employers' best interests. This *ex post* rationalization has been argued by Osterman (1984) to be incompatible with the evidence that firms have spent considerable efforts resisting what are now seen to be eminently rational and economically efficient systems of labour organization. In fact, labour and labour organizations have played a very significant role in the creation of structured and stable labour markets in the face of employer opposition (see Rubery 1978). It cannot therefore be assumed that firms always find it essential when operating with fragmented and disorganized labour to create a formal internal labour market to guarantee stability and commitment, nor that firms which provide good terms and conditions of employment do so to match their specific production and market needs. Employment policies and practices may need to be regarded as having emerged out of a range of influences, including production and market requirements, labour-market pressures and conditions, and the interplay of management policy and labour organization and bargaining strategies. Those firms without unions but with formal internal-labour-market systems may have developed these as much to pre-empt potential union organization as to meet current production requirements. Fine tuning of employment policy to either production needs or labour-market pressures cannot therefore be necessarily anticipated.

The above discussion suggests a whole range of motives, related to the characteristics of labour as a factor of production, as to why firms may wish to create internal-labour-market systems: to capture returns to training, to ensure a hard-working, motivated labour force, to unleash productive capacity to improve the effective performance of the organization, and to meet the demands of organized labour or reduce the likelihood of the development of collective organization of the work-force. This expanded list of factors, in comparison with the concentration in earlier literature on firm-specific skills, suggests that the incentives to internalize labour are general rather than confined to particular types of firms. However, one of the merits of the segmentation literature has been the identification of variety in systems of production and competition, in contrast to the 'black-box' approach to industrial organization and the assumption that competitive strategies can be adequately explained by cost or price minimization. The relationships between incentives to internalize labour and the characteristics of firms' production and competitive systems therefore need to be explored.

(ii) *Competitive conditions*

The dual-labour-market literature stressed the need for stable market conditions, associated with mass production systems as a necessary condition for establishing internal-labour-market systems (Berger and Piore 1980). Mass-production systems were also argued to have the greatest need for firm-specific skills. Later work has stressed that, under the new competitive conditions associated with the 'post-Fordist' market system, labour takes on an enhanced role in the firm's competitive strategy, as firms require key workers with firm-specific skills to aid the development of more competitive products and systems, and demand greater commitment from all employees to ensure higher quality standards (Best 1990; Hirst and Zeitlin 1989). This analysis can be extended from manufacturing to services, with firms using the personal and the intellectual skills of labour to establish their position in service product markets. While these latter arguments can be increasingly applied to large firms, the recognition of the role of labour in establishing firms' specific competitive advantage or niche position also reveals the inadequacy of the dual labour market formulation. Stable mass-production firms may have had the financial capacity to establish internal labour-market systems, but this did not mean that these firms were the most reliant on the firm-specific skills of their labour force.

The advancement of a more complex approach to the competitive process, where firms do not only compete on price, has opened up the range of types of firms that can compete effectively within apparently similar product-market areas (Rubery *et al.* 1987). This heterogeneity of firms can also be expected to be associated with heterogeneous employment systems. However, in contrast to the dual labour market literature, there is not likely to be an easy divide between those firms that have to and those that do not have to internalize their labour for competitive reasons. In fact, the multiple functions of internal labour markets, as outlined above, and the multiple competitive strategies which are now recognized to be a feature of most product markets create the possibility that, *ceteris paribus*, most firms would find advantages in an internalized employment system (except of course to the extent that they can shift costs of training by recruiting from the external labour market). However, the renewed emphasis on competitive strategies suggests that the types of labour that employers strive to 'internalize' may be found in areas which are central to the overall effectiveness of the organization and not simply related to technical skills.

(iii) *Production conditions*

The advantages to firms of long-term employment are likely to be greater the more that training is firm-based and firm-specific, the wider the variety of tasks to be learnt, the more knowledge of tasks and systems is cumulative, the more importance is attached to factors such as quality, reliability, and innovation in production over cost minimization, the greater the impact of personal relations within the firm or outside on competitive success, and the greater the costs of monitoring work effort and performance. The variety of factors under consideration again points to heterogeneous firms with heterogeneous systems sharing a common need to create long-term employment relationships based on trust and commitment. Firms will vary in the weight they attach to the use of internalizing policies to increase effort levels or to expand skills, and these differences in emphasis will have an effect on the specific form of internal labour market which is created, but the range of production conditions which favour continuity and trust suggests that the differences are more ones of degree than of divergence.

The establishment of a common need for a stable and committed labour force does not necessarily imply that all firms are able to pursue this objective or do so through the standard policies of high pay and promotion opportunities. There may be wider differences in firms' employment policies than in their employment needs (C. Craig *et al.* 1985*a, b*; Rubery 1987). The explanation of this greater divergence between policies and needs requires first of all an analysis of the constraints that operate on firms in developing policies to match their needs and secondly a consideration of how firms may develop different policies to meet similar needs, through the utilization of inequalities and segmentation in the external labour market.

Constraints on firms' employment policies

The problems firms face in developing employment policies to match their production and market requirements can be divided into two categories: financial and organizational. These constraints are in addition to those arising from the need to match the expectations and aspirations of collective and individual labour, as discussed above.

(i) *Financial conditions*

Employment policies of firms will be influenced by the extent to which they are concerned to generate short-term or long-term profits. While 'short-termism' may be used as a critical assessment of much of British management, it also has its roots in objective financial conditions. If a condition of remaining in business is maximizing short-term profits, then considerations such as the loss of skills through high labour turnover are likely to be given relatively low weight in firms' policies. Similarly, investment in training for the future is likely to be an area where cost-cutting strikes. Financial constraints affect both the ability to pay high wages and the ability to provide job security. Firms that have long relied on a paternalistic internal labour market system have found the credibility of their labour-market policy undermined when the severity of the recession or major changes in ownership or technical change leads to widespread redundancy (Lawson 1981). This credibility is difficult to restore even when prospects improve. Management's ability to develop a coherent employment policy thus depends on the short- and long-term financial position of firms. The prevalence of opportunistic policies (Purcell and Sisson 1983) and the absence of evidence of widespread strategic planning of work-force requirements (Hakim 1990 and Chapter 4 in this volume) may result from the incompatibility of firms' needs and firms' ability to finance, as well as from problems of developing effective and coherent management policies within organizations.

(ii) *Organizational factors*

Opportunities for and constraints on the development of internal-labour-market systems arise from both the structural characteristics of organizations and the policies and strategies pursued within organizations. At a basic level, the size of organization will determine the opportunities to provide career prospects. Small firms thus face great difficulty in internalizing labour through the offer of promotion opportunities, whatever their needs in terms of firm-specific skills. Effective size of organization is not, however, independent of managerial strategy. Those that use a decentralized system of managerial control will create different opportunities for career advancement than those that use a centralized policy. Under the former system it is likely that opportunities for advancement at the local level will be greater for any individual, as the effective pool of potential applicants is limited to the specific plant, but the length of the job ladder is likely to be limited to that establishment or product group[4] except for a small group of key workers who may be integrated into a centralized management labour market. Decisions to centralize or decentralize organizations are not likely to be driven primarily by labour considerations (Marchington and Parker 1990), so that the system of internal organization may in practice often act as an effective constraint on the firm's personnel policy.

Features of management style and policy are clearly also likely to have an effect on the extent to which the firm develops long-term employment relationships. Those that have a primarily opportunistic approach to policy will be more inconsistent in their employment policies, thus potentially reducing employee commitment to the firm and reducing the likelihood that employees will perceive themselves to be in a stable employment position with long-term prospects. The high costs of moving from one employment system to another is in part likely to explain the prevalence of an opportunistic approach, and the development of partial and inconsistent policies to retain labour may not prove effective. Firms which plan and include in their planning workforce requirements are perhaps the most likely to have an internal development policy. However, unforeseen circumstances can overtake even the most careful planners. Unanticipated expansion or contraction can have a major effect on the relative use of internal promotion to external recruitment. Expansion can lead to firms having to look outside even when committed to internal development policies. Equally, contraction may lead firms that have a policy of stable employment but not internal promotion to fill most vacancies with existing employees to facilitate redeployment. These observations suggest that firms' actual practice in promoting internally or recruiting externally cannot be taken as indicative of their preferred managerial policy in a 'steady state'. It may be in fact more appropriate to consider internal labour markets as 'adaptive organizational responses to a continually changing environment' (Bills 1987: 216). Managers may desire to implement certain employment policies but 'their ability to institute the desired changes may be growing or diminishing. Underlying imperatives are inevitably filtered through constrained managerial decision-making.'

Thus the search for classification of firms may at one level be considered too static and deterministic. Nevertheless, it is likely that more bureaucratically organized firms, and those in particular with highly developed systems of rules and procedures governing the employment relationship, can be expected to maintain an internal labour market system once it has been incorporated into the rule book, thereby limiting opportunism on the firm's part. However, rules may also act to restrict upward mobility of employees, by reserving jobs, for example, to craft-trained workers. Firms with no formal policy with respect to promotion may from time to time offer considerable chances for advancement to individuals, but as the promotion system is *ad hoc* and individualized it is unlikely to provide an incentive to stability for the majority of the work-force. In contrast, firms which have a codified promotion policy may benefit from greater stability, even if in actual practice the promotion opportunities for a low-grade employee are limited.

These examples suggest that there is no easy way of categorizing firms as having or not having an internal development or promotion policy. They also suggest that the existing system of employment within the organization necessarily constrains the organization in its policies and practices. The costs of changing employment systems are high and it is only when, for example, a promotion system has been in place for some time that it is likely to be recognized by the work-force as providing significant opportunities. Rapid adjustment of employment policies to current needs is both costly and potentially counter-productive; but at the same time firms have to respond pragmatically to situations that have not been anticipated, such as expansions or contractions in its employment demand. So far, however, organizations have been considered as responding to changes within the organization, to changing employment requirements associated with changing production, for example. Organizations also have to respond to conditions in their external environment, including the labour market.

Organizations, employment policies, and the external labour market

The labour market can influence both the extent to which firms need to internalize their employment systems and the type of employment system that will achieve their objectives. The first labour-market influence on internal labour markets comes from the training system. If institutions exist at the industry, national, or local level to provide a pool of generally skilled labour then firms may prefer to employ ready-trained workers over trainees. This strategy avoids the cost of training, particularly when there is a likelihood of poaching. Firms may still opt for the firm-specific training route if the general system of training is inappropriate, if the general system of training confers significant bargaining power on employees, or if a substantial element of firm-specific training is needed in addition (Marsden 1986; Osterman 1984). In the last case the likelihood of poaching is diminished if the employees do not have a general skill. In addition the ability to draw on a pool of labour is dependent on both geography and labour-market conditions. Firms may have to switch to the development of internal training systems in response to the closure of firms in the local area which had previously provided a potential supply of ready-trained labour. Labour-market factors are thus important in determining the extent to which firms provide internal training, a decision which is clearly not determined solely by technology but also by managerial policy and by labour-market institutions.

The scope for making choices between internal and external recruitment will also be influenced by other firms' employment policies. Labour mobility between firms is usually only really suppressed if firms collude together to agree not to poach. Where internal labour market systems prevail, workers may in fact be able to gain more in financial terms by moving between firms with different average levels of pay than would be the case in the occupational labour markets of economics textbooks, where pay for the same quality of labour is equalized between firms. The main constraint on mobility will be the extent to which skills are truly firm-specific or have transferable elements. If skills are transferable and firms have agreed to abide by a common pay system for a particular occupation—that is, there is a strong wage contour (Dunlop 1957)—the opportunities for advancement through change of employer are more limited.

The conditions in the labour market will also influence the extent to which firms internalize labour, in terms of both job security and pay levels. It has already been argued that workers with firm-specific skills may be able to move to another firm and earn higher pay, even if this meant some loss of their skill and occupational status. Equally, firms may be able to lay off workers with firm-specific skills and still be in a position to rehire them and recoup their investments. The extent to which firms have to internalize the costs of recession or variations in demand, or are able to pass these costs on to workers or the state, depends on conditions in the external labour market. If there is a low probability of laid-off workers being lost to the firm or the industry because of weak alternative employment opportunities, then even employees with high levels of firm-specific skills do not have to be offered employment security. The existence of advantaged and disadvantaged groups in the labour market, a phenomenon which can be labelled 'non-competing groups', or 'segmentation on the supply side', provides firms with different constraints and opportunities in determining their employment systems. If firms employ workers with few alternative employment opportunities, either because of the general state of the labour market or because they belong to a disadvantaged labour-force group, then the risk of un- or underemployment during a recession may be passed on to the work-force instead of being borne by the employer (Oi 1962).

The opportunity for firms to adjust their employment policies to match the specific opportunities of the labour-force group employed extends to all areas of employment, including pay as well as employment security. For each labour-force group that a firm employs and wishes to encourage to be stable and committed, the minimum requirement is that the firm should offer more stable and/or better conditions of employment than could be obtained in the external labour market.[5] The differences in 'opportunity wages' between groups provide the possibility for even low-paying firms to 'internalise' their labour forces. These firms may also be able to avoid the costs of promotion ladders. Such employees may be willing to expand and develop their skills without these being rewarded in the form of higher status jobs and higher pay.

The existence of disadvantaged groups in the labour market is in part the consequence of broader social forces leading to discrimination within the labour market and elsewhere in the social system. However, disadvantage is also created through the policies of employers. Employer policies on recruitment, retention, and training all imply selection and selectivity. To the extent that employers' policies and preferences are similar and reinforcing, they necessarily contribute to the creation of disadvantaged labour-market groups: those that are disenfranchised from primary segments on grounds of age, by the lack of transferable skills consequent on firms' specific training policies, on grounds of unstable work experience consequent upon economic instability of firms, and so on (Osterman 1988; Daniel 1990). Individual employers are able to take advantage of this effect of the cumulative actions of employers within the labour market, and to use these disadvantaged groups to provide the stability and commitment required in organizations which lack the financial and institutional conditions to establish a primary (high wage and good promotion prospects) internal labour market system.

This analysis suggests that segmentation in the labour market may be a way for firms to avoid the problems of divergences between production requirements in terms of a skilled and committed labour force and their financial and organizational conditions. It also suggests that the existence or otherwise of internal labour market systems cannot be 'read off' from an analysis of comparative pay levels, extent of job security, or indeed length of promotion ladders. What matters is not the actual level of employment benefits but how they relate to an individual's external opportunities in the labour market. The association of an internal labour market system with high pay, promotion prospects, and job security as a means of obtaining labour commitment is predicated on a view of the labour market where full employment is the norm, where pay reflects relative potential productivity, and where most workers expect career progression or promotion over their lifetime. Under a segmentation analysis, labour-market behaviour may be radically different: workers may regard any job as something to be prized, thereby leading to both stability and commitment; pay differentials may reflect social disadvantage and past work histories more than actual potential or contribution to the firm; promotion may only be expected by the advantaged, so that expanded job content does not always give rise to expectations of job-regrading and promotion (Rubery 1987). With respect to pay, firms only need to ensure that they pay above the external opportunity wage, or reservation wage if the alternative to work is likely to be unemployment. With respect to job security, firms only have to provide protection against cyclical variability if laid-off workers are likely to be lost to the firm or the industry. An intermediate position might be possible if workers bear the cost of downturns through work-sharing, through cuts in overtime, bonuses, or through short-time working.

With respect to promotions, firms only have to offer promotion opportunities to all workers if they could expect promotion and career progression outside. Otherwise, even if it is essential to fill higher level jobs with internal recruits, promotion need only be offered when vacancies arise. This type of internal labour market could be considered a *firm-oriented ILM* while ones where most employees are promoted could be considered an *employee-oriented ILM*. At the other extremes firms may just expect workers to take on more responsible work with no increase in status, and possibly even no increase in pay. For workers for whom pay promotion in the external market is more usual than job-based promotion, firms may use various incentive payments schemes or individualized pay as a means of reward instead of formalizing the change in job content through a job promotion ladder. The type of 'internal labour market' system in use may thus be linked directly to workers' opportunities in the external labour market; as this does not operate to equalize pay and promotion according to ability, firms have greater discretion over how to organize employment to achieve their objectives.

This discretion will be reduced the more firms are forced to adhere to given standards or rules in their employment system. Industry standards in training or in collective bargaining will restrict the scope for firms within the same industry to use different employment systems. Terms and conditions for occupations may be controlled by occupational and professional associations and occupational training systems. At the level of the firm, collective bargaining or the use of specific management systems, such as job evaluation, may force greater attention to be paid to job content and skills than to external labour market opportunities. Research has revealed that there are considerable differences within firms in the types of employment policies used for given job clusters (Baron *et al.* 1986) and that these differences are not explicable by differences in firm-specific human capital but 'are shaped in no small measure by political and institutional forces inside and outside organisations, for example, by gender differentiation, the presence of professional groups, unions and the institutional environment' (Baron *et al.* 1986: 270). Under these conditions, institutional mechanisms which integrate pay and employment practices between job clusters in the same organization will also serve to reduce the discretion of management to tailor internal systems to match external conditions. Production and social relations within the firm will impose constraints on management's abilities to differentiate conditions for similar groups of labour, but considerable discretion undoubtedly exists for firms to develop employment policies which differentiate by, for example, gender, working-time, or occupational status.

SUMMARY

This analysis of the factors associated with the development of internal labour market systems established first of all the likelihood that the incentives to internalize labour are much more widespread and general than has often been posited. Instead of internal labour markets operating as a special case it might be more appropriate to consider internalizing to be a general phenomenon, or at least objective, all other things being equal. This tendency emerges from a consideration of the particular characteristics of labour as a factor of production and from the development of a more complex analysis of the processes of competition and production than is allowed for in models which subsume production and competitive conditions within the umbrella proposition of price and cost minimization. However, all things are not equal and firms are constrained by their financial position and by organizational characteristics from pursuing an employment policy that is tailored to current production needs. Adjustment to current production needs and labour-market conditions is often precluded because of the cost of adjustment in terms of management time, impact on motivation and expectations, training costs, etc. Fine tuning of employment systems to firms' needs cannot therefore be expected. However, firms may still be able to adopt longer-term policies and strategies that enable them to overcome the obstacles to effective internalization that arise out of financial and organizational constraints. These strategies involve tailoring employment conditions not to average conditions in the labour market but to the specific labour-market opportunities of the work-force employed. Thus internalization can be achieved in financially constrained firms by targeting the employment of disadvantaged labour. As a general proposition, firms' internal employment policies are likely to be influenced by, although not determined by, conditions in the external labour market, including the level of unemployment, the structuring of labour supply into advantaged and disadvantaged groups, and indeed the supplies of skilled and trained labour.

This analysis of how the internal organization of employment is related to the opportunities on the external labour market has also indicated the ways in which the external labour market is structured by the policies and practices of firms. This two-way interaction suggests that the way forward may be towards developing an integrated analysis of the operation of internal and external labour markets, in which institutional factors are recognized to have as much influence on the external as the internal markets.

This discussion generates four key hypotheses which can be explored using examples and illustrations from the case-study material.

1. *Firms have a general need for a stable committed work-force.* However, not all firms are able to develop employment policies appropriate to their needs because of organizational and financial constraints.

2. *Segmentation in the labour supply increases employers' options.* Firms can secure stable and committed workers even at

low wages if they recruit from disadvantaged segments of the labour force.

3. *Internal and external factors influence firms' employment policies.* A firm's employment policies are shaped by the interaction of internal and external influences, mediated through the firm's current organizational system.

4. *Organizational and institutional processes structure external as well as internal labour markets.* The characterization of external markets as governed by market forces and internal markets by organizational and institutional rules and practices needs to be replaced by a more integrated analysis of the internal and the external, in which the role of organization in shaping the external labour market is explicitly recognized.

Illustrations are included to demonstrate how these hypotheses which have been derived from theoretical arguments have empirical relevance. These theoretical arguments in practice have been grounded on extensive empirical research by the Cambridge Labour Studies Group over a long period (see C. Craig *et al.* 1982, 1985) but have been further developed through the case-studies carried out as part of the SCELI employer survey in Northampton.

SOME EMPIRICAL EXAMPLES

Hypothesis 1: Firms have a general need for a stable committed work-force.

Small firms were the ones which seemed least able to develop employment policies to match their requirements. Two small engineering firms needed to employ skilled craft labour who were thus potentially mobile. The work also involved considerable firm-specific skills and training. However, because of the small size of the units, the management felt unable to provide the type of career progression necessary to maintain these key staff and, even though they used cash and other incentives such as company cars, they were unable effectively to 'internalize' these employees.

One small scaffolding company had been forced because of the recession to discontinue its internal management-training scheme.

It was fully aware that this policy was likely to cause problems in the future; firm-specific skills were so important that its only source of management recruits were ex-scaffolders whom the management believed lacked the appropriate education and other skills for managerial jobs.

Hypothesis 2: Segmentation in the labour supply increases employers' options.

The survey revealed a very wide spectrum of employment policies which were nevertheless all built around the notion of needing a stable and committed labour force and a desire to fill jobs with internal recruits. The organizations which conformed most closely to the standard model of a high-paying, secure employment system, offering at least some chance of advancement to most employees, were the two financial institutions. Nationalized industries also provided security and promotion through the ranks, but even though all jobs were filled internally, the actual share of the work-force who could expect to be promoted was relatively small and the pay levels for higher grade workers and managers were relatively low compared to average managerial salaries. Firm-oriented internal labour markets—when most vacancies are filled internally but the chances of advancement are slight—were found to be more common than the traditional model where most employees have some prospect of promotion. Often firms felt it was unnecessary to create higher grade openings to keep the staff as few expected to obtain promotion on the external labour market. Moreover, as the proportion of promotions to employees was so low, there was little problem in finding suitable candidates with the requisite firm-specific skills.

Some firms explicitly used internal training systems to reduce the average wage bill; for example, one large shoe company adopted a policy of internal training to ensure that their workers would not have the expectations of high wages for low effort that recruits from other shoe companies might bring with them. This firm provided greater opportunities to move up the job ladder to management than did other shoe companies, a factor which may have reduced the flow of labour to higher paying firms. One engineering company offered extensive internal mobility opportunities to unskilled engineering recruits, including the opportunity to take a degree, but the top salary for a graduate engineer in the company was below the median salary level for all male non-manual workers, thereby indicating that apparent length of the job promotion ladder was in this case longer than the length of the pay promotion ladder.[6]

More extreme examples were found of firms developing employment policies to provide a stable and committed labour force without offering the terms and conditions usually associated with such systems. For example, several firms targeted 'disadvantaged' groups who were available at pay levels which did not reflect their abilities. One computer firm hired unemployed youngsters who had been trained on a computer course. This course allowed for aptitude to be assessed. They were then taken on at low wages and the firm relied for stability on the youngsters' 'loyalty' to the firm that had given them a chance. A doctor's practice required intelligent and medically aware staff for reception and other duties and explicitly relied on recruiting married and non-mobile women, often with a medical or nursing background, from the local community. Considerable store was placed on stability but this was guaranteed more by the lack of alternative opportunities than by explicit employment practices.

Finally, at the far extreme of the spectrum was a packaging firm which provided neither high pay nor job security but nevertheless needed to have available a large and experienced supply of labour to meet orders at short notice. The strategy the firm adopted was to use labour primarily from an ethnic community group. It operated a casual employment system but expected to be able to rehire the same staff when orders increased. Moreover, those workers who proved themselves most able were promoted to a small core of around 60 employees (out of a total of 200 employees at maximum). These core workers became the supervisors in the busy season and the main production staff in the slack period. Without the possibility of rehiring the same workers the company did not feel it would be able to adopt this highly flexible employment policy and still have an efficient system of production. This firm provides a clear example of a core–periphery strategy but in this case both the core and the periphery were clearly located in the secondary sector.

Other examples were found of firms taking advantage of the recession to pass some of the costs of producing and maintaining skilled labour back on to the work-force. In one case, for example, a hotel had stopped providing training for chefs and expected them to come to the firm ready-trained, a policy change that had been facilitated by high unemployment. Other firms had moved from direct employment of young people to use of the Youth Training Scheme (YTS), with the government and families thus bearing the costs of this labour. The packaging company was the only firm to have based most of its employment and competitive strategy on the availability of a flexible reserve outside of the firm which still retained some level of firm-specific skills.

Hypothesis 3: Internal and external factors influence firms' employment policies.

The previous examples of different types of employment systems have illustrated some of the interrelationships between the internal and the external. Perhaps the best way to illustrate this interplay further, and to stress that such an approach should not lead to a deterministic explanation of employment choices in which the historical development of specific organizations and practices plays no role, is to analyse the process of change in employment systems.

Examples from the survey show that trends in the degree of internalization of the labour force cannot be solely attributed to changes in internal conditions. For example, several firms in the survey had been forced to move towards internal training because of the closure of other similar firms in the locality. Geographical isolation meant that 'poaching' of generally skilled labour was no longer an option. Sometimes the direction of change was in the opposite direction; several firms had moved towards more external recruitment of employees in the marketing area because of an expansion in general training or professionalism which the firm could take advantage of. In some instances there were changes within the organization and outside which combined together to change employment practices. One engineering firm which had traditionally recruited skilled craft workers had found difficulty in recruiting, due to the heavy redundancies the firm had made in the early 1980s which had destroyed its reputation as a good employer. The high level of unemployment and the establishment of the YTS scheme then provided the basis for a change of policy towards recruiting YTS trainees and developing firm-specific training systems.

Change in labour-market conditions was affecting several firms at the time of the survey. The drying up of ample labour supplies was forcing firms to provide better employment conditions in order to ensure stability and take up of vacancies. Several retail companies were moving away from YTS back to stable direct employment, for example. While many of the changes observed could be related to external factors, other developments also illustrated the significance of organization and competitive strategy in determining employment practice. Some firms had changed their policies towards particular occupational groups because of their increasing importance to the firm's business prospects. Receptionists in the hotel were being integrated into the management structure, because of the recognition of the importance of selling bedroom space to the overall profitability of the concern, and one knitting-wool manufacturer was integrating knitwear designers into the core labour force as design of new patterns was used increasingly as the means of marketing wool. These changes in status of employees within the employment system were in fact independent of any technical changes in job content, in training, or in labour-market conditions. These examples also provide further confirmation of the importance of competitive strategy over technical skills in determining employers' priorities in employment policies.

Organizational factors and tradition nevertheless intervene to limit the impact of any new competitive strategy, or indeed any change in external conditions, on employment policy. One construction firm stressed the increasing reliance of the company on the site foremen who acted as effective managers of the outside operations, but because of traditional employment practices it was the clerks in the office who received significant perks, such as free health care and pensions and life insurance, while the site foremen received sizeable earnings but no pension and minimal life cover.

Changes in organizational structure and ownership were in some cases a direct source of change in employment systems. A public house included in the survey probably had the most casual employment system amongst all the survey firms. However, as it was now owned by a large multinational there was the possibility for a motivated worker to move through this casual employment system, not only into pub management but into the management structure of the multinational. Opportunities for promotion were thus closely linked to organizational structure. Changes in public-sector organizational structure were also likely to have significant effects on promotion opportunities. The health service reorganization had increased the potential scope for promotion at the local level, as new layers of management had been added, but professional health workers were now in competition with potential external or non-specialized recruits for higher level jobs.

Finally, the rate of change in employment in the organization proved to be a very important determinant of the use of internal promotion. For some firms, internal promotion had declined as a proportion of total recruitment into higher grades, not because of any change in policy but because the pace of expansion had outstripped the availability of suitable internal recruits. For others, external recruitment had declined because the firm was declining and vacancies were reserved for internal employees to minimize potential redundancies. Some firms reported a deliberate change of policy towards external recruitment as a means of bringing new expertise into the organization at a time of change in systems or products.[7] Once these changes had been made the intention was to return to a policy of internal training and promotion, using these new recruits, into senior jobs as the source of necessary expertise. Some such examples were found in the public sector, including one hospital, where new blood at the top was considered necessary to raise the internal standards of training and skill development.

Measurement of changes in the share of internal promotion compared to external recruitment thus provides a very blurred picture of actual changes in long-term employment policy or the importance of firm-specific skills. Understanding of the dynamics of change has to be developed at the case-study level, but these case-study analyses have to be integrated into an analysis of the dynamics of change in the organization, on the one hand, and the dynamics of change in the labour market on the other.

Hypothesis 4: Organizational and institutional processes structure external as well as internal labour markets.

Case-study material of firms is clearly not the most direct way to investigate this proposition in full. The role of 'organization' in structuring the external labour market extends beyond the impact of employing organizations to include, amongst others, the family, the state and education systems. and trade unions (see for example Maurice *et al.* 1986 and 1984, where institutions at the national level are in fact seen to determine organization at the firm level, a result which would not be apparent if research was carried out only within a given nation state).

The influence of the family was evident indirectly in the case-studies, through the low wage rates at which specific groups, mainly women and young people, were available to the case-study firms; the ability of the packaging firm to lay off the ethnic community workers and thus pass the cost of economic downturn on to the extended family network; and the decline in potential recruits to YTS at the time of the survey, which may in part be related to the reluctance of the family in Britain to fund young people in training or education past the school-leaving age (as well as perhaps to the poor quality of the training provided).

However, the direct evidence that we have relating to this proposition from the case-study material applies mainly to the pattern and determinants of mobility between firms for workers in the labour market. Potential mobility by workers is seen by commentators such as Hicks (1963) to provide the main brake on firm-specific employment policies. What is apparent from our empirical work, here and elsewhere, is that the mobility options for groups are heavily circumscribed. Age, work experience, location, and other factors all restrict workers' mobility, in addition to the more overt discriminatory obstacles such as race and gender. Firms are not therefore forced by potential mobility to offer similar employment packages, since they may select from effectively non-competing groups, or they may create immobile pockets of labour through the development of firm-specific skills.

The development of firm-specific skills and payment structures does not necessarily isolate the firm from labour-market pressures. The variety of pay levels for similar types of labour that is now recognized to be a general phenomenon in local labour markets means that it is not necessary for workers to have fully transferable skills for it to be worthwhile for them to change employers. In fact, the implications of firm-specific labour markets is that a major source of differences in earnings is the nature of the employing organization. The only constraint on mobility comes from the presumed limited ports of entry and firm-specific skills. If, however, the internal labour markets are not entirely closed and employees' skills are not entirely firm-specific then they may move between firms for pecuniary advantage, even if in the process they have to abandon some of their firm-specific skill.

Moreover, employees with fairly general skills are also likely to be integrated into firm-specific payment structures, based around different average pay levels. As a consequence even those who are readily transferable can move between firms for monetary advantage. For example, many firms in the survey complained that they were unable to attract good clerical or secretarial staff because their rates of pay were low, but they felt unable to remedy this problem as the clerical rates were tied in to all other rates through job evaluation or other grading systems. Where the situation became critical, as in one building society, such that some improvement in pay was necessary, the solution applied was to change the grading structure, not the pay rates, to deflect comparisons from other groups. From this analysis we can see that, even for those with general skills, labour-market pressures (or wage contours in the language of Dunlop) are unlikely to be sufficiently strong to ensure comparable pay for similar workers. Those in low-paying firms are likely to be potential recruits for high-paying firms once vacancies arise.

This does not mean that the low-paying firm is unable to survive in the long term without raising rates, as those who are not immediately successful in moving may over time become increasingly trapped within the firm, through age discrimination, and through the damaging influence of length of experience with a poor employer on ability to move into jobs with a good employer. Low-paying firms may thus be under pressure from mobility but may still be able to retain some of their work-force without conforming to a 'market rate'.

In many ways, movement in the external labour market can be characterized as moving from one internal labour market to another, with the entry rate of pay and the grading and job status determined as much by internal as by external criteria. The only examples that we found in our survey where there was a generally recognized rate for particular occupations, and little opportunity for pay promotion through changing employers without a compensating job promotion, related to situations where employers acted together, in these cases through national collective bargaining to establish common rates of pay and pay structures. The main examples were in the public sector, where the use of national grading structures effectively rendered all employee moves as more akin to moves within the same employing organization or within an internal labour market than moves within the external labour market. Some public-sector employers pointed to the damaging effects this type of system had on their ability to recruit, as they were not able to offer any extra inducements for those making horizontal moves.

Thus, if the labour market in fact functioned as in simple neoclassical theory, with all jobs for the same types of worker paid at equivalent rates, there might be even less labour-market mobility than with the current firm-specific systems. These act in principle to restrict opportunities to move because of skill loss but in practice may act to increase them because of the opportunities for pay promotion. The only private-sector example of a regulated external labour market was the theatre, where rates of pay were again determined by national agreement and pay differentials depended strictly on size of theatre and job grade. Thus mobility in the theatre industry was also formalized, with pay promotion only possible by moving to larger theatres or to higher job grades.

These examples suggest that it is only through institutional organization, either by employer collaboration or the development of occupational associations, that similar terms and conditions for similar workers can necessarily be expected to prevail. External labour markets can be said to be as much subject to organization and institutional arrangements as internal structures, whether the institutions concerned are inter-employer or inter-employee, or the set of independent internal labour market systems.

CONCLUSIONS

Four reasons have been suggested in this analysis, at theoretical
and empirical levels, why a more integrated approach to the
analysis of labour markets is needed than that which juxtaposes
the internal to the external, the bureaucratic to the spot market,
the core to the periphery or the primary to the secondary. In the
first place it has been argued that the divisions that can be drawn
between firms in terms of their employment practice do not necessarily coincide with divisions in firms' labour-force requirements. Firms that need firm-specific skills are not necessarily in a
position to offer good employment conditions, and those that
make relatively little use of the skills of their work-forces may be
required through collective organization of the workers to provide primary-type employment conditions. A more general need
for stable and continuous employment relationships was identified than has been recognized in much of the internal labour
market literature, where firm-specific skills may still be regarded
as deviations from the norm of general skills.

Secondly, firms may be able to secure stability and commitment through a number of strategies, which may involve recruiting people whose opportunities in the external labour market are
highly constrained. Thus measurement of levels of pay or promotion opportunities do not provide an accurate guide to the
impact of these conditions on the behaviour of the work-force as
this will depend on the actual external opportunities of the
employees, which at the extreme may be unemployment, with or
without access to benefits. The third reason is that to develop an
analytical framework that is capable of explaining the dynamics
of change in the employment system it is essential to understand
the processes of change at the organizational level. This is in contrast to the market approach of the neo-classical economist, yet
at the same time it is necessary to understand the influences of
external conditions on internal employment practice. Case-study
and management analysis has veered too far towards seeing the
organization as isolated from its external environment. Business
strategy has been seen as a subject increasingly divorced from the
general analysis of economies and society.

Fourthly and fundamentally, the external environment is itself shaped by organization, including employing organizations. The dichotomization between internal and external reflects the persistence of an assumption that the external market needs to be analysed using abstract concepts of the market, of supply and demand, while the internal has to include organizational, institutional, and even political processes. The operations of the external labour market are thus not subjected to critical scrutiny, with all change being ascribed to mysterious workings of market forces over which institutions have little influence or at worst a damaging repressive impact. An institutional approach to the organization of employment cannot stop at the establishment or the company door. It needs to extend this analysis to the iterative relations between organizations and the operation of the labour market, in the hope that a direct analysis of the institutional relationships through which markets are created and structured will at last serve to reduce the pervasive power of the myth of the invisible hand.

NOTES TO CHAPTER 1

1. The author is grateful to the other members of the Cambridge SCELI team who participated in the survey of employers referred to in the paper, to members of the SCELI working party on employer strategy who commented on the paper, and also to the participants at the Labour Process conference at UMIST and the audiences at the Sheffield Employment Services conference on 'Employment and Unemployment in its Context' (Mar. 1992), and at the Dept. of Employment Labour Studies seminar (Jan. 1993), all of whom provided useful comments on a variant of this chapter.
2. In some versions it is assumed that all firms pay high wages, with the effect that unemployment rises above the equilibrium rate and workers are encouraged not to shirk because of the threat of unemployment. However, implicit in the efficiency wage models is the notion that firms do have some discretion over the wages they pay, but it is unlikely that all firms would be able to exercise the same degree of discretion.
3. Progress in economic theory is not always or usually linear. Much of what was presented as new in the 1970s and 1980s could be found in earlier institutional approaches to labour markets (Kerr 1943; Lester 1952).

4. The range of functions carried out at the local level will be greater under decentralization, so that the promotion ladder might not be as foreshortened as it at first appears. However there is a danger that this increased responsibility devolved to the local level will not necessarily be reflected in the salary and status structure.

5. One example of how firms consciously pursue this strategy is evident in the reluctance of firms to employ 'overqualified' labour for low-grade jobs. This may be in part because they are not the most able workers for this type of work but, in addition, firms may expect these workers to be less committed and stable employees than people selected from more disadvantaged groups. For similar reasons, firms may be reluctant to employ men who are temporarily unemployed in 'female-type' jobs because of an expectation that they will wish to move on to other work and thus may not take their contract seriously.

6. There has perhaps not been sufficient attention paid to the role of internal labour markets in cutting wage costs and not simply turnover costs. It is not simply that firms wish to save training costs (and ensure a supply of skilled labour to meet production requirements). They also do not want to pay the wages necessary in a tight labour market to retain their labour (Sengenberger 1981; Pfeffer and Cohen 1984).

7. This introduction of new expertise has similarities to the analysis of Wholey (1985) who distinguishes between external recruitment to fill vacancies and external recruitment as a strategic opportunity designed to build up the competitive strength of the firm (in this case a law firm) by buying in expertise that could not be obtained in-house.

2

Employer Policies, Employee Contracts, and Labour-Market Structure

DUNCAN GALLIE AND MICHAEL WHITE

The neo-classical vision of the labour market depicts individual outcomes primarily as the result of individuals receiving returns to their innate ability or to their investment in human capital by way of education and training. Within such theories, the employer is little more than a black box and employer policies merely reflect the impersonal laws of the market.[1] During the last two decades, however, there has been a growing concern to develop an alternative account of labour-market processes that gives a central place to employer policies in actively determining labour-market structures and outcomes. The most developed versions of such employer-centred theories are those loosely classified under the labels of 'dualist' or 'segmentation' theory. These not only assert a major causal role for employers, but elaborate a theory of the particular ways in which the labour market has become differentiated, and the implications of this for employee experiences. In this chapter, we will be concerned to examine empirically the particular conceptualization of the labour-market processes developed by segmentation theorists, focusing both on the nature of the policy mixes adopted by employers and on the employment experiences of those presumed to be in different labour-market segments.

Within segmentation theories, employers are depicted as deliberately structuring the terms of employment with a view to attracting and retaining particular types of labour. Typically, they select between two major strategic options: those of providing 'primary' or 'secondary' sector conditions of employment. In the former, they offer employees relatively well-paid and long-term jobs, with significant opportunities for upward career progression. In the latter, they offer poorly paid and insecure employment. Employers are sometimes seen as adhering exclusively to one or other type of strategic option. For instance, Edwards (1979) suggested that large employers would tend to offer 'primary' conditions of employment, while small employers would offer 'secondary' conditions. However, it has also been argued that a single employer may well utilize a combination of the strategic options, offering different employment conditions to different sections of its work-force (C. Craig *et al.* 1982). This version of the thesis has gained considerable currency in discussions of the growth of the 'flexible' firm (Atkinson and Meager, 1986).

At the institutional level such strategies are crystallized in the mechanisms governing recruitment and in the types of contracts that employees are offered. Employers offering primary-sector conditions are more likely to emphasize recruitment to posts through the internal labour market, since this is seen as a condition of providing the type of career structures that would secure employee commitment. Employers offering secondary-sector conditions, on the other hand, would rely primarily on the external labour market. At the same time, the recruitment of different types of labour involves a differentiation of types of contract. Employees recruited into the primary sector would be offered 'standard' employment contracts, which would provide them with full-time posts of indefinite duration, and institutionalized employment protection. Those recruited into the secondary sector, however, would be offered 'non-standard' employment contracts. These could be various in type, including temporary workers on short-term contracts and part-time workers whose hours of work made them ineligible for the most favourable types of employment protection. Whatever the specific mechanisms, the essential point was that the contractual conditions of this type of employee were such that the employee could be easily disposed of.

The factors that are seen to underlie the choice by employers of primary employment conditions vary between versions of segmentation theory. They include the implications of advanced technology for the need to retain firm-specific skills (Doeringer and Piore 1971), the desire by employers to exercise more effective control over work performance (Edwards 1979; D. M.

Gordon *et al.* 1982), and the influence of workplace unions in constraining employer choices (Rubery 1978; Berger and Piore 1980). However, a common feature of the different explanations is that they tend to be rooted in what are seen to be the evolving characteristics of private manufacturing industry. In most versions of the theory, the construction of a primary sector in which labour benefited from much more secure employment had as a necessary consequence the generation of a 'secondary' sector of employment. For Berger and Piore (1980), this resulted from the need to retain sufficient flexibility to cope with product-market fluctuations. For Edwards (1979), the maintenance of quite different categories of labour was seen as an important source of division between employees, and thus a major factor in maintaining employer strength in the longer term.

The implications of these strategies for employees was that they were confronted not by the relatively open and uniform labour market of neo-classical theory but by a highly differentiated structure of positions. Moreover, it was a type of differentiation that involved very generalized patterns of advantage and disadvantage. Those with non-standard contracts were exposed to the cumulative disadvantages of low pay, uninteresting work, tight supervision, poor career opportunities, and a high level of job insecurity. At the same time, it was a relatively closed labour-market structure that had powerful mechanisms for locking particular types of employee into specific sectors. The internal labour market was quite deliberately intended to undercut the easy transfer of employees between establishments and this, in turn, limited the opportunities for upward mobility for those in the secondary sector. Moreover, the constraints imposed by the institutional rules governing recruitment were reinforced by the very different emphasis placed on training and skill development in the two sectors. The disadvantaged 'secondary' or 'flexible' sector is seen as containing a substantial, and growing, proportion of all jobs. Indeed, Catherine Hakim (1987) has argued that it now represents fully one-third of the overall work-force.

In our empirical examination of labour-market processes we shall focus, in particular, on two issues: whether it is possible to distinguish types of employers with quite distinct policies with respect to the recruitment, retention, and use of labour; whether it is correct that employees become differentiated into separate labour-market 'segments' or 'sectors', in which those with 'standard' employment contracts benefit from generalized advantage and those with 'non-standard' employment contracts from generalized disadvantage.

THE ANALYSIS OF POLICIES AND STRATEGIES

The Social Change and Economic Life Initiative provided an important opportunity to assess the nature of employer policies. By comparison with previous research on labour-market differentiation, the Initiative's survey of employers offered unusually extensive data on local labour markets. The survey was carried out in six British localities, chosen to reflect contrasting labour-market conditions. Three of the localities (Coventry, Kirkcaldy, and Rochdale) had experienced relatively high rates of unemployment, while the other three (Aberdeen, Northampton, and Swindon) had known more prosperous employment conditions for the better part of the 1980s. The total of 1,300 employers, from the six localities, covered all sizes of establishment, private and public sectors as well as manufacturing and services. The range of topics covered in the survey was designed in the light of theories of labour-market differentiation, thereby permitting the development of analysis procedures to test notions of labour-market segmentation, and of strategic behaviour by employers, in a reasonably direct and concrete manner.

The perspective with which we approached this analysis was rather different from that of most exponents of labour-market segmentation theory. This is reflected in our preference for the broader notion of differentiation, rather than segmentation. We would suggest that both the proactiveness and the interconnectedness of employers' policies are constrained by limits upon calculative capacity. The notion of calculation, which was at the centre of Weber's exposition of bureaucratic rationality, suggests that the available means of calculation set bounds to rational action. There is a partial anticipation here of the organization theory of March and Simon, in which the notion of bounded rationality was greatly developed. According to March and Simon (1958) organizations respond to external pressures in a piecemeal manner, and by the application of decision rules which themselves have evolved in a piecemeal fashion and may be far from optimal.[2]

We therefore see little reason to expect employers in general to develop highly concerted sets of policies which would tend to place them in distinct segments of the labour market. But neither would we suppose that the only alternative is a neo-classical view, in which employers are no more than vectors transforming human inputs into economic outputs. Rather, there is scope for a wide diversity of policy mixes, some of which may indeed reflect concerted efforts on the part of particular groups of employers to differentiate themselves, while others reflect the accumulation of historical development and piecemeal response to one circumstance or another.

Conceptualization and validation of policy variables

The conceptualization of variables for the analysis of employer policies can be represented as a set of nested boxes, as shown in Figure 2.1. The innermost box contains the variables which have been given a central place in debates about the differentiating effect of policies. These can be divided into two compartments. One compartment of the inner box contains variables thought to be indicative of 'internal labour markets' and 'primary employers'. It is through the provision of training (specifically, training for promotion), the assessment of individual performance, and the filling of jobs through internal promotion, that employers can enhance specific human capital and reduce the transaction costs of employing labour.

The other compartment contains, first of all, the two variables thought to be most indicative of 'secondary' labour markets or employers. Through the employment of large proportions of part-time workers, along with high rates of recruitment, such employers are deemed to reduce worker bargaining power, both in relation to wages and in relation to the organization of work, and hence to facilitate a regime of low wages, de-skilling, low investment in human capital, and lack of security. Also in this compartment are located variables indicating the employment of casual, temporary, or contractors' workers, homeworkers, or agency staff, which we refer to generically as marginal workers. Such employment may suggest either that the employer is

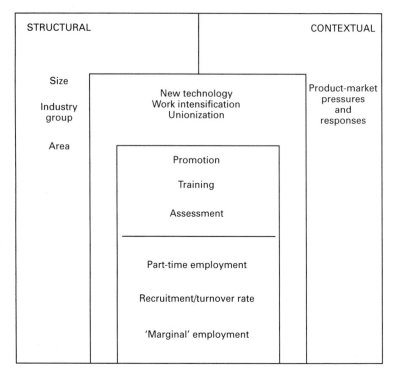

Fig. 2.1 Variables for assessing labour-market differentiation

'secondary', or that it is 'primary' with a 'periphery' of secondary jobs. In either case, the effect on the workers so employed is said to be similar to that of part-time employment, especially with respect to wages and security.

The next box outward contains further policy variables, less directly involved in the representation of labour-market differentiation, but having a number of possibly influential relationships upon differentiation. Here we place variables concerning the establishment's involvement in technological change; its adoption of various measures to increase work rationalization, intensification, or flexibility (such as the use of job interchange, of work measurement, of incentive schemes); its position regarding trade-union recognition, and its use of 'alternatives' to unionized relations, such as works councils or staff councils, or channels of group or individual communication and involvement. Outside these two layers of policy variables come structural and contextual variables. Structural variables are represented by area (the six localities, with contrasting labour-market conditions, which form the basis of the research design), by size, and by industry group. Contextual variables are represented by a set of indicators of product-market, financial, and competitive conditions and pressure experienced by the organization.

Policy should even within a 'bounded rationality' view of organizational behaviour, exhibit some adaptiveness to the external situation. We would therefore expect policy to be related to structural variables, representing the long-term location of the organization in the economy, and to contextual variables which reflect circumstances in the short or medium term. This is not to regard policy as determined by structural and contextual influences; on the contrary, organizations could be expected to vary greatly in their responsiveness, and to exercise choice even within a given level of response.

Of the three main structural variables, area or locality was given by the design of the overall Initiative. Size (number of employees) captures the stage of development of the organization, in relation to such fundamental organizational concepts as bureaucratization and internal complexity, and is believed from previous research to be generally related to many of the policy variables which we have enumerated.

Creating a suitable classification of organizations to represent stable divisions of the product market was more problematical. We wanted an a priori classification which would reflect salient differences in market relations, and at the same time have a plausible bearing on work-force differentiation. Much of the literature of labour-market segmentation has assumed that segments would be organized according to simple differences in product-market characteristics (sometimes cross-classified with a distinction between white-collar and blue-collar workers, as in D. M. Gordon *et al.* 1982). In addition, much of the literature has been preoccupied with the manufacturing sector, failing to take seriously distinctions between manufacturing and services, or distinctions within services (for instance between market and public services). The most obvious simple classification is first of all between production (manufacturing and construction) and services, and then between marketed and public services. We further decided to subdivide both marketed and public services into those which involve a high content of professional knowledge on one hand, and those where the service content is of a relatively routine kind. The resulting classification has five divisions: manufacturing and construction; knowledge-based marketed services (banking, business services, etc.); other ('routine') marketed services (retail, hotels and catering, transport, etc.); knowledge-based public services (education, health, and social services); other ('routine') public services (police, fire brigade, cleansing, recreation, etc.).

The industry classification was cross-validated with measures of work-force composition. The survey originally gathered twenty-eight independent work-force measures (seven job-group levels, by total and part-time employment, by gender) and these were summarized in twelve measures, following data-reduction procedures using partial correlation analysis and principal-components factor analysis. It was found, in a subsequent multiple discriminant analysis, that these twelve work-force composition measures correctly classified 60 per cent of establishments to their industry classification group (to be compared with a 20 per cent random chance of correct classification). The fivefold classification clearly provides a structural indicator with strong relationship to work-force composition, and so one which we can expect to be linked with differentiating policies.

Structural variables

The explanations given in the literature for the emergence of new managerial strategies usually imply that they develop primarily in the private sector and are closely related to the size of the employing unit. To begin with, the relations of the structural variables with the work-force policy variables were examined at the simplest level, using one-way analysis of variance and tests of association. The findings are summarized in Table 2.1, in the form of contingency coefficients. A number of points immediately emerge from these results. First, the frequency with which policies were used by employers did indeed vary by industry group, size of establishment, and also—though to a much lesser extent—by area. Several relationships, in the case of area, were either non-significant or lacking any discernible pattern. In the case of

TABLE 2.1. *Relations between work-force policies and structural variables*

	Area (6)	Size (7)	Industry group (5)
Part-time employment (6)	0.18	0.29	0.55
Recruitment rate (6)	0.24	0.24	0.31
Marginal employment (4)	0.18	0.39	0.23
Internal promotion (2)	n.s.	0.13	0.10
Individual assessment (2)	n.s.	0.28	0.12
Work intensification (6)	0.16	0.38	0.23
New technology (3)	0.12	0.38	0.35
Unionization (2)	0.14	0.28	0.45

Note: The number of categories in each variable is stated in brackets beside the variable name. The contingency coefficients tabulated are all significant at least at the 5% level. n.s. = not significant at 5% level.
Source: The Employer Baseline Survey

both size and industry group, however, the variations were always statistically significant and clearly patterned.

It was notable that two policies expected to be closely linked (part-time employment and recruitment rate, prime indicators of 'secondary employers') emerged as having stronger connections with industry group than with size. Another particularly strong connection of industry group was with trade-union recognition. Promotion, technological change, and work rationalization or intensification formed a somewhat contrasting group, having stronger connections with size than with type of industry. The measure of marginal employment conformed to the pattern of the promotion, technology, and rationalization variables, rather than of the 'secondary employment' variables, having a particularly strong relationship with size of establishment.

The measures of employers' policies do seem, then, to relate to structural factors. But closer inspection of the differences by size and by industry group shows that the patterns are not simple, and do not conform to some of the ideas about labour-market segments which have been proposed. This can be most forcefully illustrated by looking at the distributions of policies by industry group. For selected policies, we find that the difference in proportions run as follows:

For part-time employment, the knowledge-based public services (education, health, social services) came first, followed by
routine marketed services, with the remaining groups far behind,
especially production industries.

For recruitment rate, first place was taken by routine marketed
services, with knowledge-based public services in last place and
the remaining groups in between.

On union recognition, the public sector as a whole was easily
first, with the production industries next and the marketed services of all types much lower.

On work rationalization/intensification, both market production services and public routine services scored high, while knowledge-based public services scored low and the remaining groups
were intermediate.

In short, there was no pair of our key policy measures where the
ranking was identical across industry groups; each industry group
exhibited a unique profile of policy tendencies. With size, it was
true, the differences were more orderly, making it reasonable to
think of a progressive size effect for some of the policies. The use
of marginal workers, for example, was increasingly likely to be
part of employers' policies as their establishments grew larger,
and this also was clearly true of the use of promotion to fill jobs,
the adoption of new technology, and the recognition of trade
unions. There were, nevertheless, substantial complications. In
the case of part-time employment, for example, larger establishments tended to have less than 10 per cent if they had any at all,
while smaller establishments were much more likely than these to
have 25 per cent or more. But small and large employers were
about as likely to have no part-timers at all. Again, in the case of
recruitment rates, a linear pattern was hard to discern. Turning
to employment of marginal workers, while probabilities of
employing none decreased with size, and of employing a moderate proportion (up to 20 per cent) increased with size, the
employers with particularly high proportions (20 per cent or
more) were quite evenly spread across the size groups.

The diversity of policy profiles across industry groups, and the
absence of clear trends on size of establishment for several of the
policy measures, create obvious difficulties for anyone minded to
partition the market in terms of the standard structural variables.
Such diversity and non-linearity suggest that the influences of

industry group and size, if indeed they are to be seen as influences, do not operate across-the-board but perhaps in conjunction with other conditions. Nor do the results do anything to encourage the view that local labour-market conditions influence the growth or decline of one form of labour-market relation or another. Differences on the policy variables between the six areas of study, although sometimes significant at a simple level of analysis, were always of small magnitude and far less prominent than in the case of the other two main structural variables. The areas which had experienced relatively depressed conditions (Coventry, Kirkcaldy, and Rochdale) did not have consistently different policies from the more buoyant areas of Aberdeen, Northampton, and Swindon. When account is taken of the fact that areas differed both in terms of their size structure and of their industry-group structure, it becomes apparent that locality has no more than a limited role in the analysis of work-force policies. Such a role emerges in certain special cases which are discussed at a later point.

The final difficulty for theorists who have characterized secondary labour markets in terms of a combination of part-time and temporary or casual employment conditions is the rather obvious difference between part-time employment and what we have called marginal employment. Part-time work is specially prevalent in smaller establishments, in schools, hospitals, and social work, and in retailing, hotels, and catering. Temporary, casual, and other types of marginal employment policy are specially prevalent in larger establishments, in routine public services even more than in schools, hospitals, and social work, and in production industries. It is not at all obvious, if they are different forms of the same employment relation, why they should be so differently distributed.

Relationships between work-force policies

A question of considerable importance for theories of the labour market is the degree to which work-force policies can be seen as interconnected. Most versions of labour-market segmentation theory assume that a classification of employers corresponds to a division of work-force policies into contrasting sets. A dichotomization of organizations, as in dual-labour-market theory, indicates that there should be just two policy sets, one

corresponding to each type of organization. More elaborate classifications of employers would, naturally, point to additional policy sets, but the principle of one-to-one correspondence between
divisions of the labour-market and policy sets or clusters remains
the same. Finally, if employers' policies fall into definite clusters,
that would strengthen the presumption that their behaviour
towards their workers is strategic rather than piecemeal and *ad
hoc*.

Log-linear modelling was applied, both to establish the relations between the variables within a systematic framework, and
to assess the choice between different notions of the labour market. Five variables were chosen to represent the work-force policies of central importance, which were earlier described and
summarized in Figure 2.1. The 'primary labour market' policies
were reflected in promotion and use of individual performance
assessment. The 'secondary labour market' policies were represented by part-time employment, recruitment rate, and use of
marginal workers. Part-time working and the use of marginal
workers could also be connected with the notion of peripheral
workers in core–periphery theories.

A minimal requirement for most versions of dual and segmented labour-market theory is that the primary policies should
be positively related to one another, that the secondary policies
should be positively related to one another, and that the primary
policies should be negatively related to the secondary policies.
This would at least indicate a tendency towards grouping of policies in line with the supposed tendencies in the labour market.
Such a result, however, would not be sufficient to establish a
classification or partitioning of employers into distinct groups.
For that one needs to demonstrate a stronger configuration in
the data. Employers must be concentrated either in combinations
of high 'primary' policies and low 'secondary' policies, or low
'primary' policies and high 'secondary' policies, and must be
emptied from the remaining combinations. Such a configuration
would reveal itself in a high-order interaction effect, and can be
directly tested through log-linear modelling.

We first fitted a model consisting of the ten relations between
the five variables, taken in pairs,[3] but without any higher order
interactions (that is, relations involving more than two variables).
The goodness of fit for this model was highly satisfactory (likeli-

hood ratio chi-square 25.5 on 27 degrees of freedom; p = 0.55). Fitting a model of the five four-way interactions would use up 25 degrees of freedom, and therefore could not significantly improve the fit of the model. Since, however, one or more of the five four-way interactions might still be important, we fitted the model with all the four-way effects. None of the higher order effects was, in fact, significant. In short, there was no support for the notion that employers could generally be classified into two or even a few groups corresponding to higher-order combinations, or profiles, of work-force policies. Instead, we found that the simpler model consisting of the pair-wise relations between the five employer policy variables gave a good account of the data. Table 2.2 reports the parameter estimates for this model, while Table 2.3 summarizes the relationships less formally.[4]

The relationships summarized in Table 2.3 can be compared with the predictions from segmentation theory. The relationships according with the expectations of segmentation theory were the positive ones between part-time employment and recruitment and between use of promotion and performance assessment, and the negative ones between part-time working and promotion, and part-time working and performance assessment. Contrary to expectations was the positive relationship between recruitment rate and promotion, a relation which may reflect the fact that both promotion and recruitment can be depressed in static organizations. The relation between recruitment rate and use of performance assessment, although in the expected negative direction, fell well short of significance.

Most unexpected, however, were the relations of use of marginal workers with the other four work-force policies. The relationships with the remaining variables were positive in all cases, although with marked non-linearity. In other words, high levels of marginal employment accompanied both the use of part-time working and high recruitment rates, but also use of promotion and of performance assessment. Indeed, of all the significant associations identified in the model, much the strongest was that between use of marginal workers and use of promotion.

However, closer examination revealed a marked non-linearity in the relationship between marginal employment and promotion. It can be seen in Table 2.4 that those employers with a moderate proportion of marginal workers (1–19 per cent) were far more

TABLE 2.2. *A model of employer work-force practices*

Parameter	Estimate	Standard error
1	2.605	0.1620
PT (2)	−1.008	0.1778
REC (2)	0.6921	0.1587
PR (2)	0.6584	0.1606
IND (2)	0.6938	0.1610
MAR (2)	0.8843	0.1656
MAR (3)	−1.249	0.2478
PT (2).REC (2)	0.4765*	0.2357
PT (2).PR (2)	0.5121*	0.1297
REC (2).PR (2)	−0.6779*	0.1318
PT (2).IND (2)	0.4147*	0.1335
REC (2).IND (2)	−0.2023	0.1339
PR (2).IND (2)	0.4854*	0.1348
PT (2).MAR (2)	−0.4112*	0.1399
PT (2).MAR (3)	0.4820*	0.1861
REC (2).MAR (2)	−0.2363	0.1391
REC (2). MAR (3)	0.6113*	0.2030
PR (2).MAR (2)	−1.291*	0.1392
PR (2).MAR (3)	−0.6043*	0.1880
IND (2).MAR (2).	−0.4454*	0.1452
IND (2).MAR (3)	−0.581*	0.1921

Scaled deviance = 25.518 on 27 degrees of freedom.
Notes: The interpretation of the relationships being modelled is provided in Table 2.3. The labels in the table have the following meanings: PT = part-time employment (2 = high); REC = recruitment rate (2 = high); PR = promotion (2 = high); IND = individual assessment (2 = none); MAR = marginal employment (2 = moderate, 3 = high). Parameter values not shown are set to zero and * indicates the parameter estimate for association significantly different from zero.

likely to offer internal promotion than those with no marginal workers, but that as the use of marginal workers moved to more extreme levels, the proportion using internal promotion fell back somewhat, although it remained higher than in the case where there were no marginal workers. This pattern is repeated in relationships of marginal employment policy to a number of other policies, making it reasonable to infer that there are qualitative differences between levels of marginal employment. Moderate levels of marginal employment appear to accompany and support

TABLE 2.3. *Relationships among employers' policies established by log-linear modelling*

Combination	Relationship
Part-time employment Rate of recruitment	Positive: high part-time employment is associated with high rate of recruitment.
Part-time employment Marginal employment	Non-linear: high levels of marginal employment are linked to high part-time employment, but medium marginal employment to low part-time employment.
Part-time employment Promotion	Negative: high part-time employment is associated with no promotion.
Part-time employment Use of performance assessment	Negative: high part-time employment is associated with no assessment.
Rate of recruitment Marginal employment	Non-linear: high marginal employment is linked with high recruitment, but medium marginal employment is not.
Rate of recruitment Promotion	Positive: high recruitment associated with promotion.
Rate of recruitment Use of assessment	Not significantly related.
Marginal employment Promotion	Non-linear: high marginal employment linked to use of promotion (relative to no marginal employment) but medium marginal employment linked to promotion still more strongly.
Marginal employment Use of assessment	Positive: medium marginal employment is linked to use of assessment, high marginal employment still more so.
Promotion Use of assessment	Positive: use of promotion is associated with use of assessment.

what have been regarded as the policies of 'primary' employers, but where very high levels of marginal employment occurred, the association tended to weaken though remaining positive. The relationships with part-time employment and recruitment rates involved a somewhat different form of non-linearity. *Moderate* levels of marginal employment were related to somewhat *reduced* use of part-time working and lower recruitment rates, but high

TABLE 2.4. *Marginal employment and internal promotion*

Marginal employment as % of total	Internal promotion in past year (%)		TOTALS
	Any	None	
None	31	69	628
1–19	62	38	421
20–49	50	50	107
50+	39	61	54

Source: The Employer Baseline Survey.

levels of marginal employment were linked with high rates of part-time working and high recruitment rates.

The analysis, then, fails to produce evidence of any clear classification of employers. There are, to be sure, polarizing tendencies apparent within work-force policies, and the clearest opposition appears to be that between internal training and promotion on the one hand, and part-time working on the other. There are points at which the analysis appears to be in agreement with one or another version of segmentation theory, but in each instance other points fail to fit the theory. Most decisively, an associative model of the type fitted reveals the capacity of many employers to combine policies which are often portrayed as incompatible, and this is confirmed by inspection of the two-way tables. Even among employers with very high proportions of part-time workers and very high recruitment rates, substantial proportions make use of internal promotion and individual assessment of performance.[5]

Special cases

The limitations of a purely statistical approach to the issue to employers' work-force policies is that it may obscure, through processes of aggregation and averaging, extreme or special cases of considerable importance. We have already hinted at such special cases in the preceding discussion; even if 'primary' and 'secondary' employers do not characterize the labour market as a whole, there is still the possibility of them being considered as special cases. These, and other, special cases could exert a long-term influence upon the development of labour markets even if, in the shorter run, they are highly atypical.

By analogy with the statistical notion of outliers, we suggest that it may often be of particular interest to examine employers who are located at extreme points of the distribution of work-force policies. An important illustration concerns the employment of marginal workers: it has already been suggested that those employers with very high proportions of such workers may have differed qualitatively from those with more moderate proportions. About 5 per cent of the employers' sample employed one half or more of its work-force on a 'marginal' basis. With the aid of travel-to-work area tabulations from the 1984 Census of Employment, supplied by the Department of Employment Statistics Branch, we reweighted the sample both to a population establishment basis and to a population employment basis. The weighted analysis estimated that, across the six localities, the employers with these very high proportions of marginal workers represented about 3 per cent of establishments, and employed about 50 per cent of the individuals who were working under these contractual terms. This supports the point that special cases may be of considerable significance.

Further cross-tabulations were then conducted in an attempt to pinpoint the location of these employers more precisely, but this endeavour was only partially successful. Such extreme policies were about equally often found in small as in large establishments, in marketed and public routine services, and in marketed production industries. Even with this extreme group, then, it was difficult to make a simple identification either with (say) a small-firm-and-service 'secondary' sector, or with the 'peripheral' needs of large 'primary' employers. Case-study research by the Aberdeen research team (Sewel 1993) identified a group of oil-related production and service firms which made extensive use of marginal employment to absorb market volatility, and these cases, which constituted a particularly clear example of 'core–periphery' strategy, were also statistically detectable in our tabulations. But it is clear that Aberdeen was not typical of other areas, and there was no evidence that these special strategies within Aberdeen had systematically affected the whole labour market: Aberdeen employers were not more likely than those elsewhere to employ marginal workers. The assumption must be, on balance, that the extreme development of the marginal employment strategy arises from a variety of circumstances, which will only be understood through further detailed case-study investigation.

A more clear-cut result emerged from a similar analysis of extremely high levels of part-time working. On a weighted basis, some 7 per cent of establishments employed 75 per cent or more of their employees on a part-time basis. Not only were more than four-fifths of these in establishments with less than 50 employees, but the same proportion were in marketed routine services (retailing, hotels, and catering). There was, therefore, a most marked concentration of these special cases according to size and industry, and one which corresponds to some notions of the 'secondary' labour market. Moreover, many of these employers made relatively little use of the other policies which have been included in our review. In particular, only 7 per cent had introduced both computers and other equipment using microprocessors, although the corresponding proportion for the entire survey was 24 per cent; and only 24 per cent had introduced one or both of these forms of advanced technology, while in the whole sample the proportion was 60 per cent.

There would be, perhaps, some justification in asserting that these employers were focusing upon part-time working as their chief work-force strategy. But it is necessary to stress how small the proportion of employers was, to whom this rather clear and extreme picture applied. As one enlarges the view to include the more numerous employers with less extreme policies, the picture becomes progressively blurred. Our illustrations, therefore, while suggesting justifiable applications of some of the existing notions of segmented labour markets, confirm how narrow those applications are.

CONTRACTUAL TYPES AND CONCEPTUALIZATION OF LABOUR-MARKET STRATIFICATION

Segmented-labour-market and core–periphery flexibility models of the labour market usually postulate the division between a primary sector that has generalized advantages, in terms of employment stability, pay, skill, training, and career opportunities, and a secondary sector in which employees suffer generalized disadvantage along these dimensions. The 'secondary' or 'peripheral' sector, as it is generally conceived, comprises two principal categories of employees: temporary workers, who may either be hired on an individual basis by an employer or contracted through an agency, and part-time workers. In this section we are concerned with: (1) The adequacy of a model postulating an essentially homogeneous and generally disadvantaged secondary sector, and (2) the implications of such systematic labour-market disadvantages for employee experiences. In examining these issues, we were able to draw upon a second component of the data collected under the Social Change and Economic Life Initiative. In each of the six localities, a random sample of 1,000 people was interviewed, drawn from the non-institutional population aged 20 to 60. This provided extensive information both about people's current employment situation and about their past employment histories.

The first step was to operationalize a set of labour-market categories that corresponded to those that have been the focus of discussion in theories of the secondary sector. This was done by cross-classifying an indicator of contract length with that of full-time or part-time status. For contract length, people were asked whether their job was considered by their employer to be a temporary job (lasting less than twelve months), a fixed-term job (lasting between one and three years), or a permanent job, with no fixed period of time for ending. In practice, these categories covered nearly all employees, with only 1 per cent unable to classify themselves in one or other of them. Overall, we retained five distinct contract types: full-time temporary workers, full-time fixed-term workers, part-time temporary workers (including all those with contracts of less than three years), permanent part-time workers, and permanent full-time workers. Table 2.5 gives the relative importance of these categories in the employed workforce. By far the largest was that of the permanent full-time employees (74 per cent). This was followed by the part-timers, but it is notable that the great majority of these were in permanent jobs: 17 per cent of employees were permanent part-timers and only 3 per cent were temporary part-timers. Finally, 6 per cent of employees were in full-time short-term jobs, roughly

Duncan Gallie and Michael White

TABLE 2.5. *Percentage of employees by contract type*

	Men	Women	All
Temporary (< 12 mths)	4	2	3
Fixed-term contract (1–3 yrs)	4	3	3
Temporary PT	1	6	3
Permanent PT	—	39	17
Permanent FT	91	51	74
Total	2,146	1,650	3,845

Source: Table 2.5 to 2.15 are based on data from the work-attitudes/histories survey

evenly divided between those in temporary jobs lasting less than a year and those with fixed-term contracts for between one and three years.

Labour-market experience

To what extent do the categories that constitute the 'periphery' suffer from generalized disadvantage in terms of work and labour-market situation? The two defining characteristics of the secondary sector are low pay and job insecurity. A first point to note is that those on non-standard employment contracts were less well paid in terms of hourly gross earnings than permanent full-timers (Table 2.6). The lowest paid of all were temporary part-timers, followed by permanent part-timers. However, even the full-time temporary workers earned only 86 per cent of the

TABLE 2.6. *Hourly earnings by contract type*

	Average hourly gross earnings (£)			N
	All	Men	Women	
Temp.	3.81	3.91	3.54	106
Contract	3.54	3.72	3.12	108
Temp. PT	2.61	*	2.60	75
Perm. PT	3.21	*	3.17	560
Perm. FT	4.45	4.90	3.40	2,334

* N = less than 10

earnings of the permanent full-timers and among fixed-term contract workers the figure fell to 80 per cent. The differential between the earnings of permanent full-timers on the one hand and temporary and fixed-term workers on the other is even sharper for men. For women, on the other hand, while the earnings of permanent full-timers are higher than those of part-timers and fixed-term contract workers, they are lower than those of temporary workers. The cell numbers for women temporary workers (28) are low and it is probably not worth reading too much into this deviation from the general pattern. It should be noted that the differentials between the different contract groups tend to be much smaller for women than is the case for men. The earnings advantage of permanent full-timers in relation to most groups with non-standard contracts is also evident across age groups. The main exceptions are in the cases of very young part-time temps and full-time temporary workers in the 35–44 age bracket who secure unusually high earnings for those with this type of contract.

Theoretically, the most central characteristic of secondary labour is that it lacks job security; it is labour that can be easily disposed of to adjust to product-market fluctuations. The contract types outlined above reflect the level of formal security or insecurity inherent in a job. But it could be argued that they may underestimate in an important way the real extent of job security. A person might be formally employed on an indefinite basis, but know that their job was in practice insecure. It has been suggested that this is particularly likely to be the case for women part-time workers, because of the weaker legal provisions covering the redundancy of part-timers. Part-timers working more than 16 hours a week have to be employed with the firm for more than two years to have the same level of formal protection as full-timers, and the delay is five years for those working between 8 and 16 hours a week. Table 2.7 suggests that the contract types relate closely to perceived security for temporary workers and permanent full-time workers. The most interesting feature of the data, however, is the relative security of the part-timers and of the fixed-term contract workers. There is no evidence at all that the 'permanent' part-timers perceive themselves to be in insecure jobs. Indeed, exactly the same proportion considered their jobs secure as among permanent full-timers. The

TABLE 2.7. *Contract type by perceived security of job*

	Temp.	Contract	Temp. PT	Perm. PT	Perm. FT	All
Very secure (%)	11	23	16	51	54	50
Fairly secure (%)	25	41	33	40	37	37
Fairly insecure (%)	22	19	33	5	7	8
Very insecure (%)	42	17	18	3	2	5
N	118	125	104	643	2,773	3,762
% security has decreased over last 5 years	83	48	73	18	23	25

insecure, as one would expect, were the very small proportion of part-timers on short-term contracts. Among the full-time contract workers, the notable point is that, while the proportion of those that feel very secure is only about half that among those with permanent posts, none the less, a majority overall (64 per cent) regard their positions as either very or fairly secure. This holds true for both men and women on such contracts. This suggests that the formal time-limits of these jobs may not reflect accurately the possibilities of a continuing relationship with the organization. This might be the case because such contracts could be renewed or it might be that these jobs represent a transitional status to a more secure position within the organization. Overall then, while care must certainly be taken in making assumptions about the relationship between contractual statuses and perceived security, the error would not appear to be in the direction implied by segmentation theory. Permanent part-timers were not particularly insecure, while a proportion of short-term contract workers had a much higher sense of security than might have been expected. Certainly it is clear that the different categories of employee that tend to be placed together in an undifferentiated 'secondary' sector or 'periphery' are in fact very heterogeneous in terms of the central defining characteristic of secondary-sector employment—job security. Indeed, in these terms, permanent part-time employees cannot be meaningfully classified as 'secondary-sector' workers.

Turning to past labour-market experience, the expectations from the segmentation literature are that such employees will have been locked into insecure labour-market positions over time or that they will have entered them through downward mobility from a more privileged sector of the labour market. A picture of past occupational mobility can be obtained from comparing the ranking of a person's current occupation on the Hope–Goldthorpe scale of occupational desirability with that of the person's previous occupation. This confirms that temporary workers, temporary part-timers, and permanent part-timers were significantly less likely to have been upwardly mobile than permanent full-timers, although it would be misleading to regard upward mobility as particularly widespread even among the latter. Whereas 35 per cent of permanent full-timers had improved their occupational level in moving into their current job, the proportion among temporary workers fell to 27 per cent and among permanent part-timers to 25 per cent. Further, a substantial proportion of people in these categories had been downwardly mobile. This was the case for 32 per cent of temporary workers and of temporary part-timers and for 36 per cent of permanent part-timers, compared with only 21 per cent of permanent full-timers. It is notable that the pattern for temporary and part-time workers is inversed for full-timers. For the former, downward mobility was a more common experience than upward mobility, whereas for the latter upward mobility was more common.

It is once more the fixed-term contract workers that fail to fit the pattern for 'secondary'-sector employment. Of these, a relatively high proportion emerge as having been upwardly mobile and, indeed, upward mobility is more common than downward. The contract workers are as likely to have been upwardly mobile as the permanent full-timers.

The past labour-market experience of those in the 'secondary' sector should also be characterized by greater job insecurity. The nature of the transition into people's current occupation suggests this was the case for some of the non-standard contract groups. The great majority of permanent full-timers (86 per cent) had moved into their present job directly from their previous job (Table 2.8). The proportion of such direct movers, however, was 69 per cent among fixed-term contract workers, 52 per cent among temporary workers, 48 per cent among permanent part-timers, and 35 per cent among temporary part-timers. In the case of temporary and fixed-term contract workers, this was clearly due to the fact that more people had taken up their current job after a spell of unemployment: 37 per cent of temporary and 27 per cent of fixed-term contract workers, compared with only 10 per cent of permanent full-timers, had been unemployed immediately before their present job. Such prior experience of unemployment was particularly high for men on such contracts. Women on fixed-term contracts were almost as likely to have moved straight from a secure job as permanent full-timers. For part-timers, the major cause of the low level of direct job moves was that people had been non-employed prior to their current job. Over half of temporary part-timers and 48 per cent of permanent part-timers had previously been non-active. The proportion of permanent part-timers coming from unemployment (5 per cent) was notably lower than among permanent full-timers.

Finally, the theory of the 'secondary' sector would lead us to expect a major difference between those in standard and non-standard forms of employment in terms of their perception of their future job opportunities, with the former seeing far greater chances for upward career mobility. The data in Table 2.9, however, suggest again major variations between the non-standard contract groups in their views about future opportunities. The part-timers were certainly those that saw future opportunities as most closed, with only 35 per cent of the temporary and 37 per cent of the permanent part-timers thinking they had a chance of getting a better job over the next two years. But the full-time temporary and contract workers are, if anything, even more optimistic about the future than permanent full-timers. Overall, more than half (56 per cent) of fixed-term contract workers thought they had a reasonable chance of getting a better job. This was even more the case for women (65 per cent) than for men (52 per cent). The major difference between the permanent full-timers and the temporary and fixed-term contract workers lay in the extent to which they saw their opportunities as lying primarily within the internal or external labour market. Much as segmentation theory would predict, the permanent full-timers looked mainly to the internal labour market (62 per cent), whereas this was the case for only 32 per cent of temporary and 44 per cent of fixed-term contract workers.

TABLE 2.8. *Type of transition into current job*

	Temp.	Contract	Temp. PT	Perm. PT	Perm. FT	All
From secure job (%)	41	54	25	39	75	65
From insecure job (%)	11	15	10	9	11	10
From unemployment (%)	37	27	15	5	10	11
From non-activity (%)	11	5	51	48	5	14
N	116	116	102	618	2,673	3,626

TABLE 2.9. *Perceived labour-market opportunities*

	Temp.	Contract	Temp. PT	Perm. PT	Perm. FT	All
Promotion opportunities have increased over last 5 years	27	40	13	14	31	28
Chances of getting better job over the next 2 yrs very or quite good	48	56	35	37	45	44
Best opportunities with current employer	32	44	48	51	62	58

Work situation

It is notable that the 'secondary sector' groups are very heterogeneous in terms of the skill level of their work. The concept of skill is controversial and it is important to consider a variety of indicators that reflect different dimensions of skill (Gallie 1991). In Table 2.10, the contract groups are examined in terms of the level of qualifications required of new employees, the amount of training undertaken for the job, the on-the-job experience needed before it could be done well, the supervisory responsibility, and the individual's own assessment as to whether or not the job was skilled. In practice, these provide a very similar picture of the skill levels of the different contract groups. The lowest level of skill was to be found in the two groups of part-timers, followed by the temporary workers.

Again the fixed-term contract workers stand out sharply from the other categories of 'precarious' labour. They were much more likely to be in jobs where 'O' level or higher qualifications were required and a majority had received training for their work. Indeed, 'O' levels were as likely to be required for fixed-term contract workers as for permanent full-timers. In terms of training, on-the-job experience, and supervisory responsibility, the fixed-term contract workers are only slightly below the levels of skill to be found among the permanent full-timers, while they are the group most likely to consider their own work to be skilled. In fact, it is only among men that contract workers come lower on these skill criteria than permanent full-timers. Women contract workers are indistinguishable from full-timers in terms of experience and responsibility and they are actually more likely to have received training and to be in jobs requiring 'O' levels.

The 'secondary sector' groups are also sharply differentiated by recent experiences of change in skill. The part-timers were not only the lowest skilled on all criteria, but they were far and away the least likely to have experienced an increase in either skill or responsibility over the previous five years (Table 2.11). Indeed, the temporary part-timers were the only group in which more people had experienced a decrease in their skill over this period than an increase. In contrast, a majority of fixed-term contract workers had experienced an increase in their skills (54 per cent), a proportion that was twice that among part-timers. The experience of

TABLE 2.10. *Skill characteristics by contract type* (%)

	'O' Level currently required	No training	Learnt to do job < 1 month	Responsible for work of others	Consider job skilled
Temporary	45	70	31	16	59
Contract	65	46	24	40	85
Temp. PT	26	71	58	12	38
Perm. PT	23	78	58	10	39
Perm. FT	60	45	18	43	78
All employees	52	52	27	36	69

TABLE 2.11. *Changes in skill and responsibility over previous five years by contract type*

	Temp.	Contract	Temp. PT	Perm. PT	Perm. FT	All
Skill						
decrease	23	10	29	10	7	8
no change	35	36	49	63	36	40
increase	43	54	22	26	57	52
N	83	77	59	463	2,501	3,182
Responsibility						
decrease	25	14	28	10	5	7
no change	27	33	44	56	29	33
increase	48	54	28	35	66	60
N	84	79	59	462	2,498	3,182

Note: Only asked of those that had been in work five years previously.

improving their skills was particularly common among women on fixed-term contracts (71 per cent). Taking the overall pattern, the skill experiences of fixed-term contract workers were very similar to those of permanent full-time employees.

In some versions of segmentation theory, the distinction between sectors is also a distinction in forms of control over work. Indeed, this is a central pivot of Edwards's (1979) theory of labour-market differentiation. The growth of the primary sector is a response to the growing difficulties of winning sufficient employee commitment through traditional forms of direct supervisory control. This is resolved through introducing forms of 'bureaucratic' control for the upper, more skilled part of the core work-force, while controlling its lower section through the mechanical pacing of work ('technical' control). Secondary-sector workers, however, remain subject to direct ('simple') supervisory control—a situation necessitated by their low levels of skill and short experience in the organization. In general, control over work performance in the primary sector is held to be looser and more indirect, while that in the secondary sector is relatively tight.

There is some evidence that permanent full-timers are, indeed, allowed greater discretion in their work than those employed on non-standard contracts. For instance, more than half (54 per cent) of the permanent full-timers said that they had a great deal of choice over the way they did their job, whereas the proportion was lower for each of the other contract types, with temporary workers feeling that they had the least discretion (Table 2.12). This is confirmed, although in a weaker way, by responses to a question about the factors that determine how hard people work. The permanent full-timers were marginally more likely to stress the importance of their own discretion. However, it is only with certain of the non-standard contract groups that this can be held to reflect tighter forms of supervision. Certainly, the temporary and fixed-term contract workers were the most likely to say that their supervisor determined their work pace, but it is notable that supervisory pressure was least marked of all in the case of the permanent part-timers. In contrast, the permanent part-timers were more likely than any other group to see their work effort as determined by clients or customers, although the picture of part-timers given by Table 2.13 is of a category with particularly few

TABLE 2.12. *Amount of choice over way job is done*

	Temp.	Contract	Temp. PT	Perm. PT	Perm. FT	All
Great deal	37	44	41	47	54	52
Some	32	34	32	28	29	30
Hardly any	12	9	12	11	8	9
No choice	20	14	16	13	8	10
N	119	124	105	629	2,765	3,742

TABLE 2.13. *Factors determining how hard employee works (%)*

	Temp.	Contract	Temp. PT	Perm. PT	Perm. FT	All
Own discretion	51	60	58	60	63	62
Supervisor	32	43	29	19	28	17
Machine/assembly line	6	4	4	4	8	7
Customer/clients	24	37	30	42	37	37
Fellow workers	39	42	29	23	29	29
Pay incentives	13	20	7	7	18	16
Reports/appraisals	19	21	9	7	17	16

pressures for greater work effort. While in general, then, those with non-standard contracts had less discretion at work, this only reflected tighter supervision in the case of the full-time temporary and contract workers.

Overall, in terms of work and labour-market situation, it is clear that the set of non-standard contract groups that tend to be lumped together into an undifferentiated 'secondary' sector have in fact quite different patterns of past and current experience, and possess to very different degrees the defining characteristics of secondary workers. Given the centrality of job security to theories of the 'secondary' sector, it is the temporary and contract workers that conform most clearly to criteria of secondary employees. They are more insecure both in terms of their past and their present work. However, in other respects, the contract workers—those with fixed-term jobs of between 12 months and 3 years duration—fit the model poorly. A significant proportion of them rank highly in terms of the various skill criteria. Moreover, far from seeing themselves as having particularly limited career opportunities, they are the group with the highest proportion thinking there are future opportunities for upward mobility. In terms of pay, skill, and mobility characteristics, it is the part-timers that conform most closely to the image of secondary-sector work. They receive the lowest hourly pay, they were particularly likely to have experienced downward mobility in relation to earlier jobs, and they had the least optimistic view about future opportunities. However, part-time workers fail to fit the model on the critical issue of security, where they are virtually indistinguishable from permanent full-timers.

The fundamental difficulty, then, for theories of the 'secondary' sector is that the assumption that different types of labour-market disadvantage are mutually reinforcing would appear to be unfounded. Rather, groups appear to suffer from very different sources of disadvantage and these are likely to lead to different experiences of employment and the labour market. The concept of the 'secondary' sector, as it is used in segmentation theory, fails to define empirically adequate common criteria for allocation to sectors and it veils rather than illuminates the crucial differences between contract groups.

Contract types and job satisfaction

What was the effect of the different contract types on satisfaction with work and employment conditions? Taking first overall job satisfaction, it is notable that, on a 0–10 scale measure, both the most and the least satisfied groups were non-standard contract groups. For instance, if the top third of scores are taken as indicating satisfaction, it is the full-time temporary workers that come out quite clearly as the least satisfied (54 per cent) (Table 2.14). However, at the other end of the spectrum, it is not the permanent full-timers that have the highest level of satisfaction but the permanent part-timers (85 per cent). The fixed-term contract, temporary part-time, and permanent full-time workers form an intermediate group that are much closer to each other than to either the temporary workers or the permanent part-timers. If an alternative indicator of overall satisfaction is taken, based on whether or not people would wish to change jobs if there were plenty of jobs available, exactly the same pattern emerges (Table 2.15). The temporary workers were far and away the most likely to want to change jobs (68 per cent), while the permanent part-timers were the least likely (38 per cent).

Turning to specific aspects of the employment situation, people were asked how satisfied they were with their prospects, their pay, their relations with supervisors, their job security, the ability of management, the actual work, their ability to use their own initiative, and their hours of work. Once more the general pattern re-emerges, with temporary workers being the least satisfied on the greatest number of issues (5 out of 8), and the second most dissatisfied group on the three remaining issues. In contrast, permanent part-timers were the most satisfied group on seven out of eight issues. The issues on which temporary staff were least satisfied were job security, promotion, the ability of management, and pay. However, their attitudes also appear to reflect resentment of the tighter supervision and relatively low skilled work that were noted earlier. The highest level of satisfaction of permanent part-time workers, and indeed the point on which they stood out most clearly from other groups, was in their satisfaction with their hours of work. However, they also appeared to appreciate the high level of security, the relatively loose supervision, and the scope for discretion in the job. The area in which it

TABLE 2.14. *Job satisfaction by contract type*

| | % Satisfied | | | | | |
	Temp.	Contract	Temp. PT	Perm. PT	Perm. FT	All
Promotion	17	34	14	29	37	34
Pay	41	38	48	58	49	50
Supervision	63	61	74	80	71	72
Security	15	33	24	80	74	70
Ability of management	38	46	57	64	49	51
Ability to use own initiative	59	76	76	84	84	83
Actual work	54	72	69	78	77	76
Hours	56	58	69	85	67	70
Overall satisfaction with job	54	73	71	85	76	77

TABLE 2.15. *Respondents who would wish to change job if there were plenty of jobs available*

	Temp.	Contract	Temp. PT	Perm. PT	Perm. FT	All
All	68	43	46	38	41	42
Men	76	51	78	82	43	45
Women	48	28	41	37	38	38

is difficult to see the satisfaction of part-timers as reflecting objective rewards of the job is that of pay. While the pay satisfaction of part-timers was not particularly high (58 per cent), it was higher than that of any other group, despite objectively low hourly rates. This suggests a substantial difference in levels of expectation, possibly in part deriving from a trade-off between pay and other job rewards or from differences in perceived need. It may also reflect a greater concern with *net* hourly pay, which is more favourable to part-timers, than with gross pay (see Chapter 8). The sole issue on which part-timers appeared to have rather low levels of satisfaction related to their promotion opportunities. As was seen earlier, this reflected the fact that such opportunities were very poor.

While temporary workers give a generalized picture of very low levels of satisfaction and permanent part-time workers of high levels, the picture for fixed-term contract workers and temporary part-timers is one of rather more mixed attitudes to their employment situation. For instance, temporary part-timers were the least satisfied of all with the promotion opportunities available to them (only 14 per cent could be classified as satisfied in this respect). Further, as with full-time temporary workers, they have a very low level of satisfaction with the security of their job. On the other hand, they were nearly as satisfied as permanent full-timers with their pay, and they showed even higher levels of satisfaction than permanent full-timers with supervision and their hours of work. The fixed-term contract workers, like the temporary workers, were less satisfied than permanent full-timers on every issue, but the difference was generally far less sharp. In particular, fixed-term contract workers were considerably more satisfied than any of the other non-standard contract groups with their promotion opportunities and, indeed, they were very close to the permanent full-timers. This fits well with the earlier evidence that they were particularly likely to believe that there would be opportunities for getting a better job over the next couple of years. On the other hand, fixed-term contract workers had particularly low levels of satisfaction with their pay (where they were the least satisfied of all) and with their job security.

The significance of particular types of contract differed to some degree between men and women. The very high satisfaction rankings of the part-timers reflect primarily the attitudes of women part-timers. Although the sample numbers for male part-timers are small, implying that conclusions about them should be treated as very tentative, they would appear to be more dissatisfied than full-timers with their pay and much more likely to want to change their job. There was also a difference between men and women on fixed-term contract. It was noted earlier that women were more likely than men on such contracts to have high levels of skill, to have experienced recent increases in skill, and to believe that they had reasonable opportunities for future promotion. This difference is reflected very clearly in the measures of satisfaction. Male contract workers were intermediate between the temporary and the full-time workers in their satisfaction with all aspects of their job situation. In contrast, female fixed-term contract workers were *more* satisfied than female full-timers about their ability to use their initiative, the nature of the work itself, and their future promotion opportunities. It was only with respect to pay, supervision, and security that they were less satisfied. There was also a difference on the overall job satisfaction measure. Men on fixed-term contracts were less satisfied overall with their jobs than the full-timers; in contrast, women on fixed-term contracts had a higher level of overall satisfaction than full-timers. Exactly the same pattern emerges if the desire to change jobs is taken as a measure of satisfaction (Table 2.15). The lack of homogeneity of the 'secondary' sector, then, emerges even more clearly when one takes account of gender.

In short, while non-standard employment status tends to be associated with relative disadvantage in at least certain aspects of the work or labour-market situation, there is no simple reflection of this in the levels of satisfaction with employment. The temporary workers come closest to a case in which fairly generalized disadvantage led to exceptionally low levels of satisfaction. While fixed-term contract and temporary part-time workers saw significant disadvantages in certain aspects of their work situation, these were balanced by issues on which they had relatively high levels of satisfaction. Permanent part-timers stood out as a group which, despite its non-standard contract status, would appear to have a relatively high level of satisfaction with most aspects of the employment situation than even the 'core' work-force of permanent full-timers. It is only by excluding the permanent part-timers that it would be possible to sustain the argument that secondary-sector work is associated with conditions of employment that are likely to generate lower levels of satisfaction with work. Even then, sharp differences between the permanent full-timers and the 'secondary' work-force only emerge with respect to temporary workers.

CONCLUSIONS AND IMPLICATIONS

Theories of labour-market segmentation have provided the main alternative view of the labour market from that of neo-classical economics, during the past two decades. The present study provides a particularly rich opportunity for the assessment of such theories, because of the availability of both individual and establishment data. A practical difficulty in carrying out this task is the existence of a number of different variants of segmentation theory. Rather than reviewing these one by one, we have focused on a number of broad propositions or assumptions which appear to underlie the more influential versions. In particular, we have been concerned to examine the assumption that the labour market can be meaningfully divided into a primary and a secondary sector.

First, we considered the view that 'primary' and 'secondary' employers, distinguished in terms of relatively advantageous and disadvantageous policies, also tend to be distinguished in terms of structural characteristics, notably industry and size. For example, it has often been assumed that 'primary' policies are to be found within larger employers, especially those in manufacturing. The evidence that has been examined suggests that there is no clear patterning of the relationships of employers' policies in terms of industry group or size of establishment. The ordering of industry and/or size groups in terms of their positions on policy dimensions was inconsistent; so no derivation of two or more segments of the labour market could be achieved.

Second, we sought a rigorous test for the notion that employers might be categorized by combinations, or profiles, of their work-force policies. If this were so, then such combinations would prove necessary for a multivariate model of the relationships between the work-force policies. This would appear in the form of significant high-order interaction effects. But, in fact, a model consisting of the simple associations between a set of five policies provided a good fit, and higher order interactions were non-significant. A weaker notion of 'policy combinations' might be defined in terms of the patterns of simple associations. For example, there might be two groups of policies, within each of which the associations were positive, but across which the associations were negative or zero. In fact, however, no grouping of the policy variables fitted such a picture.

Third, we examined the view that 'secondary' jobs can be defined in terms of non-standard employment contracts. It has been commonly assumed that such contracts (part-timers, temporaries, fixed-term engagements) provide essentially similar (and highly disadvantageous) employment conditions. These non-standard contracts are then equated with 'secondary' employment, and the provision of such contracts is equated with 'secondary' policies on the part of the employer. The evidence of the present survey was inconsistent with the notion that there exists a group of 'secondary' workers definable in terms of non-standard contracts.

Within the group of non-standard contractual types, differences in the objective situation, and in individual perceptions and satisfactions, were extremely large. There was no basis for considering them as a single group. Furthermore, those on non-standard contracts did not fare consistently worse than those on standard contracts. For instance, the differences in favour of full-time over part-time work were in many respects very small. Similarly, workers on 1–3-year fixed-term contracts reported a mixture of advantages and disadvantages, rather than uniformly disadvantaged circumstances. Fixed-term contract workers enjoyed some advantage in terms of the occupational level of their employment and promotion opportunities, although pay was relatively low and there was low satisfaction with job security. Women on fixed-term contracts fitted particularly poorly the usual criteria for 'secondary' sector labour. The most adverse experience was undoubtedly that of individuals on employment contracts of less than one year, and the notion of 'secondary' employment could reasonably be applied to this group. However, it constituted only 3 per cent of the sample.

In short, neither the analysis of employer policies nor of the implications of contract statuses for employee experiences offer support for the central proposition of segmentation theory that there is a meaningful division between a primary and a secondary sector of the labour market. It should be stressed that this assessment is based on a cross-sectional survey of six local labour markets. It does not exclude the possibility that segmentation processes, of the kinds discussed, have operated historically or in other settings. It is also possible that particular employers, or small groups of employers, use work-force policies in the ways visualized by segmentation theory, even though this does not apply to employers in general. Nor, of course, does this analysis exclude other forms of differentiation of life chances through labour markets, such as gender segregation of occupations or divisions between non-manual and manual workers.

One of the general implications of the research has been that the focus of explanation should shift towards the differential use of particular policies. For example, we need to understand why some employers have large proportions of part-time workers, while others have few or none. Detailed analysis of such questions has tended to be ignored because of the assumption that part-time employment policy is part of a more general 'secondary' employment profile. In view of the findings of this chapter, it is necessary, on the contrary, to find a form of explanation which permits part-time employment to be mixed rather freely with other policies, such as internal training and promotion policies. The issues raised concern both the influences upon the adoption of particular policies at particular times, and the evolution of combinations of policies to produce the observed mix at a given time.

The choice of work-force policies might be accommodated within a general framework of organizational change under bounded calculative rationality. The resulting picture is a familiar one (e.g. Weber 1947; March and Simon 1958). The progress of organizations towards an optimal mix of choices may be hindered by numerous factors. Calculative capacity will be limited, and may take the form of slow and cautious trial-and-error learning. Knowledge of, and search for, new policy options may be limited, so that the available new options may diffuse quite slowly, in the manner of other kinds of innovations. Organizations may have limited resources to manage change, and are generally biased towards the status quo; policies are not continuously reviewed, and changes for the most part take place as a result of pressures. In addition, the objectives, and hence the choices, of organizations may not be wholly economic in character: coalitions have to be maintained and authority legitimated, in order to ensure survival, and these considerations may also bias choices. Such a model accommodates the wide variation in policy mixes observed in this study, and explains why there is not a convergence on just a few near-optimal sets of work-force policies. At any one time the observed distribution of policies represents an accretion of choices made over a considerable period.

A general model of this kind does not, in itself, take one very far. It does, however, suggest that research could usefully focus upon the margin of change and upon the pressures which are likely to be operating at that margin. Two of an organization's boundaries with its environment which are likely to be experiencing frequent pressures are those with the product market and those with the labour market. Sets of variables relating to change around these boundaries, and the associated changes in workforce policies, afford a promising focus for developing empirically grounded accounts of policy development. Investigations using the present data, and relating to these areas of change, are reported elsewhere (Chapter 3; Elias and White 1991). Substantially more research of this kind will be needed to develop satisfactory models of policy development.

There is also scope to identify and examine 'special cases' which, though untypical, may exert leverage upon the labour market and provide examples which, in the longer run, other employers may begin to follow. There may even be 'labour-market niches' which, in a small way, represent similar processes of division within the labour market to those talked of in segmentation theory. The interpretation of such 'special cases' or 'niches' will be improved by setting them within the context of an analysis of the labour market as a whole. This relationship between the general picture and the extreme or outlying cases of employer policy will form the subject of a separate paper (White, forthcoming).

Finally, it is necessary to explore empirically the extent to which specific policies influence employee experiences. We have been sceptical about the particular way in which segmentation theorists have conceptualized employer policies and their implications for the structure of the wider labour market. However, this is by no means incompatible with the view that differences in employers' policies do affect outcomes for individuals in important ways, and hence that the life chances of individuals, with equal endowments, may diverge as they encounter differing employment conditions. Indeed, as we will show in Chapter 8, this assumption can be strongly supported. What is needed, however, is a better account of how this comes about. An improved account will explain and illuminate both the differences in policies adopted by employers and the differences in outcomes experienced by individuals.

NOTES TO CHAPTER 2

1. There have been numerous variations or elaborations on the neo-classical, human capital model in recent years, and some of these may superficially appear to attribute some active role to the employer. However, even in the case of efficiency wage theory (Lindebeck and Snower 1985), it seems rather that it is the optimal behaviour for employers as a whole which is modified than that employers separately exercise divergent or distinctive policy choices. Employer behaviour continues to be fully determined by the costs of and returns to labour, but the costs are more broadly conceived.
2. For a review of more recent institutionalist theories of the firm, see Jacquemin 1987.
3. For a multi-way table of k dimensions (or variables), there are $k(k-1)/2$ pairs of simple associations or marginal two-way tables. In the present case, with five variables, there are $5(5-1)/2 = 10$ simple associations. Our analysis, therefore, fits a model consisting of the complete set of such associations.
4. Table 2.2 may need some explanation for those unfamiliar with this form of analysis. It should first be noted that since four of the five

variables are dichotomous, while one has three categories, the full five-way table has $2^4 \times 3 = 48$ cells. The model of the table, consisting of the 10 relations between pairs of variables, requires 21 parameters. These consist of: the constant term; one main effect parameter for each of four dichotomous variables, and two main effect parameters for the single three-valued variable (these main effect terms, however, are not separately interpretable in a model with higher-order terms); one parameter for each of the six 2×2 marginal tables; and two parameters for each of the four 2×3 marginal tables. The degrees of freedom are $(48-21)$, as stated in the text.

It will be observed that Table 2.2 looks like the results of a regression analysis, and this is helpful for an understanding of the model. Log-linear modelling is one case of the general linear model, which includes regression analysis, and all applications of the general linear model have a common form. In the present case, the observations which the model seeks to fit are the counts in the cells of the five-way table (or rather, the natural logarithms of those counts), while the explanatory factors are the first-level interactions between the variables, often also referred to as associations. The parameters are estimated weights (like regression coefficients), which, if applied in combination to the appropriate cells, will reproduce the overall table as closely as is possible under the assumed model. All combinations of values of the pairwise variables which are not shown in Table 2.2 are (as with the reference values of dummy variables in a regression analysis) implicitly set to zero. It is also possible to exponeniate the parameter estimates and interpret them as odds-ratios, and in much log-linear modelling this is the main focus of interest. In the present case, however, we are interested in the form of the model, and the significance of the parameters, rather than the magnitude of the odds-ratios. (For further explanation of log-linear modelling, see Everitt 1977 or Gilbert 1981.)

5. It might be claimed that the observed relationships would be consistent with a 'core–periphery' version of segmentation theory (Atkinson and Meager 1986), since positive associations between 'primary' and 'secondary' policies could occur as a result of their application to different groups of employees within each organization. A full discussion is not possible here, as we do not aim to address the many specific versions of segmentation theory. However, advocates of a 'core–periphery' approach should at least note the following points. First, if 'core–periphery' theory is intended to distinguish between groups of employers in terms of their profiles of labour policies, then it is not supported by the present results. The lack of explanatory force in the higher-order interactions of the model tells against all segmentation theories making these types of strong claim, whatever

3

Product-Market Pressures and Employers' Responses

FRANK WILKINSON AND MICHAEL WHITE

INTRODUCTION

In the crisis which culminated in the recession of the early 1980s, increasing attention was given to the responsiveness of employers to product-market pressures and particularly their need to be more flexible. In this debate the early focus was mainly on the use of labour. Flexibility was regarded as synonymous with the close adjustment by the firm of the labour it employs, the way labour is utilized and the wages paid to changing levels of output, and the prices of products. A wide range of strategies for this purpose were identified. These were neatly categorized by Atkinson (1985*b*) as financial, numerical, functional, and distancing. Labour-force flexibility is achieved 'financially' by adjusting wage levels; numerically, by adjusting the labour force and/or hours worked; 'functionally', by reorganizing work and by multi-skilling workers to enable them to undertake a variable range of tasks; and 'distancing', by subcontracting or otherwise 'putting-out' processes, the production of components, finished products, and the provision of services previously supplied internally. By any, some, or all of these routes the firm can adjust its unit labour costs to increase profitability or to track revenue more closely.

This approach takes technology and products largely as given and concentrates attention on cost adjustments. Justification for this can be found in the fact that the immediate responses of firms to product-market changes may be restricted to reducing employment and other ways of cutting labour costs which may be more directly under their control than other items in the budget. But even within this short-term perspective, the nature of product-market competition may be such that labour costs are not the only or even the most important consideration. Product-market pressure based on non-price attributes of goods—quality, design, batch size, timing of delivery, credit terms—cannot be simply countered by cost cutting. Difficulties in meeting these standards may result from systems of work organization and methods of wage payments; under these conditions tighter controls might make matters worse. Quality is a notable victim of piece-work and especially speed-up (Haraszti 1977). Scientific management, it is argued, has made the firm incapable of responding to demand for greater variety by rigidly separating conception from execution, by finely dividing labour, and by the imposition of hierarchical management to 're-coordinate' production (Piore and Sabel 1984). Fordist systems have also been identified as counter-productive, in terms of quality and even labour costs, by reason of the attitudes they engender in workers, the employees' ability to resist control, and the adversarial relations they promote (Fox 1974; Hyman 1988; Konzelmann Smith 1991). A condition for flexibility may be, therefore, the exercise of more discretion over the labour process by the work-force (Fox 1974), responsible autonomy (Friedman 1978), team-work (Brown and Reich 1989) and a necessary prelude to this may be a radical restructuring of management (Konzelmann Smith 1991).[1] There is also growing awareness of the contribution to be made by workers if their knowledge of products, the work process, and the benefits of their 'learning by doing' can be tapped by management. This is accompanied by the increasing recognition that hierarchy is perhaps not the only or even the best means of overcoming this 'information impactedness' dimension of transaction costs (Williamson 1986). More recent recommendations are that worker/management co-operation and the development of corporate culture are more effective managerial strategies in this respect than traditional approaches to industrial relations (Kochen *et al.* 1986).

Moreover, it is increasingly recognized that marketing, production, work-organization, and labour-market policies of employers are interrelated and are importantly influenced by economic and technical change, and by the shifting balance of power within the firm and between firms and their customers and suppliers. One problem with the academic debate on this subject is its polarization: what might be described as its inflexible specialization. In some accounts, power relationships are played down. Strong emphasis is placed on the potential of the interaction between general purpose technologies, a multi-skilled and flexible workforce, and co-operative relations within and between firms, to create high rates of product and process innovation and product markets responsive to consumer needs (Best 1990; Sabel 1989). The opposing view emphasizes the control elements in new technology and the potential of more co-operative forms of work organization, new forms of industrial relations, and training programmes to incorporate workers and emasculate their independent organizations as part of a general trend towards a new 'neo-Fordist' social framework for accumulation (Hyman 1988; Mehaut 1988; Meegan 1988).

Ultimately, whatever view is taken of the dynamics of the social relations of capitalist systems, long-term competitive viability crucially depends on securing new markets; developing new competitive strategies; the designing of new, and the redesigning of existing, products; an increase in the responsiveness to product change; the adoption of new technologies; and the reorganization of production (Skinner 1986). Such developments have implications for the quantity and quality of labour required by the firm and the terms of employment, wage payments, and systems of work organization. But these can be expected to be both a response to and a determining factor in technical, market, and organizational change. Adaptation by the firm should therefore be regarded as an interactive process, involving changes in product-market conditions, technology, managerial, and labour organization (Rubery *et al.* 1987). How these relate become the important questions to ask, rather than whether employers have adopted in isolation this or that labour organizational strategy with this or that degree of success.

The addressing of these wider issues requires some view of the dominant forces inducing change and a range of quantitative and qualitative data by which to assess the impact. For the first of these purposes, we assumed that the main pressure for change was coming from the product market, on the expectation that this could elicit a range of possible product, production, technical, and/or labour organizational responses.[2] The data are from the SCELI 'baseline' survey of firms, a telephone inquiry which achieved a good response from large samples but which allowed only relatively simple, straightforward questions to be asked. A range of questions were included, designed to investigate the nature of the product-market pressures to which organizations were subjected, followed up by others enquiring about the product, process, and new-technology response to these pressures. Tapping this information required different types of questions for the public and private sector; some questions did not have equal relevance to all sectors and were therefore excluded from some parts of the survey; and the analysis was confined to establishments with twenty or more employees.[3] However, the survey was designed to identify the dominant tendencies in product-market developments, the ways organizations were responding to these changes, and the extent to which these applied generally. The baseline survey also provided the opportunity to compare the product-market changes with the work-organization and labour-market strategies.

This paper is concerned primarily with a statistical analysis of the interaction between product-market pressures and the responses of employers. It reveals a significant relationship between the qualitative (i.e. non-price) changes in the competitive environment and qualitative aspects of product and process development and the organization of labour.

Product-market pressures

The changes in the product-market environment over the five years up to 1986, roughly covering the period from the depth of the post-1979 recession to the strong recovery phase of the cyclical upswing, were explored in the baseline survey by a series of questions about changes in the level of demand; in the intensity of competition and the direction from which the increased competition had come; and the changing nature of the demands made of the sellers of products and services by buyers. The extent of the increase in product-market pressure and the form this took are summarized in Table 3.1.[4] Demand had increased for 62 per cent of private-sector organizations, and for half of these the improvement was substantial, whilst demand had declined for 23 per cent of the respondents. But clearly the

TABLE 3.1. *Product-market pressures in the private sector*

Areas in which increases reported	% of establishments	Total no. of respondents
Level of demand	62 (60)	646
Competition from:		
home	49 (52)	647
abroad	31 (38)	647
Greater buyer selectivity in:		
quality	84 (86)	641
price	84 (84)	636
delivery dates	80 (78)	623
design	66 (68)	617
Buyer delivery requirements		
shorter delivery periods	66 (69)	411
smaller orders	47 (46)	412
Buyer credit requirements		
longer to settle account	51 (46)	547
more credit	50 (50)	517

growth in demand had been taking place in a buyer's market and one in which foreign and domestic competition was intensifying, so that the securing of orders was not unconditional. More than 80 per cent of the organizations found their customers to be more selective in terms of price, quality, and delivery dates; and two-thirds found buyers paying more attention to design. The suppliers had also come under increasing pressure over the delivery of goods and services and the amount of explicit and implicit credit required. A significant increase in the number of small orders and of those with a shorter delivery date had been experienced by 47 and 66 per cent of the organizations respectively, half registered a notable increase in the amount of credit required by their customers and a similar proportion had found their customers were taking longer to settle accounts. In addition to pressure from their buyers, more than one-third of the organizations surveyed had been affected by increasing foreign and around a half by increasing British competition.

Questions were designed to explore the economic context in which the public-sector establishments operated and Table 3.2

reveals considerable increased pressure.[5] 'Product-market' pressure on the public sector had increased in both quantitative and qualitative terms. Over the previous five years, 66 per cent of the public-sector establishments surveyed had experienced an increase in demand for their services whilst 15 per cent suffered a decline. Meanwhile, the standards required of the services provided had risen for 82 per cent of the establishments; 65 per cent experienced changes in what the public wanted and 28 per cent had come under increased competition from the private sector. There is no direct equivalent in the public sector to the financial pressure private firms come under from prices and the customers' demands for favourable credit terms. Public-sector services, for the greater part, are funded directly by the central or local state. However, financial pressures analogous to those in the private sector are felt when the state adjusts its funding arrangements and 89 per cent of the public-sector establishments surveyed reported changes in financial practices of government.

TABLE 3.2. *External pressure on the public-sector service*

Pressures reported	% of establishments	Total no. of respondents
Changes in financial policies of the government	89 (93)	273
Requirements for higher standards of services	82 (78)	271
Increase in the level of demand	66 (85)	277
Changes in what the public wants	65 (73)	276
Increases in competition from the private sector	28 (43)	277

CHANGES IN PRODUCTS, PROCESSES, AND EMPLOYMENT PRACTICES

In response to product-market pressures the organizations surveyed adopted a variety of measures. Table 3.3 shows that changes in competition led to a significant increase in the attention paid to the scheduling of work, in design and development

TABLE 3.3. *Responses to changes in competition in the private sector*

Areas in which increases were reported	% of establishments	Total no. of respondents
Attention paid to scheduling work	74 (76)	643
Effort put into design and development	72 (73)	639
Use of new technology	64 (69)	646
Range of products and services supplied	54 (59)	646

input, and in the use of new technology by 74, 72, and 64 per cent of the respondents respectively, and 54 per cent of the employers widened the range of their products or services. Similar questions were not addressed to public-sector employers but, as Table 3.4 shows, 67 per cent of the public-sector establishments were offering a wider range of services and almost all were struggling with increased cost pressure on services. A large majority of employers, therefore, experienced increased market pressure, or the equivalent in the public sector, from multiple directions and responded by qualitative changes in their product, process, and delivery systems.

In both the public and private sector a significant proportion of the firms in the survey had taken action in the two years previous to the interview to modify work organization, pay systems, training, and employment policies. The incidence of these changes are recorded in Table 3.5. Apart from the reduction in the number of workers surplus to requirement, which was reported by 30 per cent of the employers, 'numerical' flexibility

TABLE 3.4. *Responses in the public sector*

Response reported	% of establishments	Total no. of respondents
Pressures of services against costs	96 (99)	268
Wider range of services required	67 (63)	217

TABLE 3.5. *Labour-market, pay, and labour organization policies: public and private sectors*

Qualitative policies	% of establishments	Numerical policies	% of establishments
Training employees to cover jobs other than their own	45 (47)	Reduction of numbers employed surplus to requirement	30 (33)
Use of individual performance assessment	35 (39)	Replacement of some employees with contract or agency staff or casual or temporary workers	11 (17)
Use of work measurement or method study	21 (21)	Replacement of some full-time with part-timers	13 (15)
Shiftworking	17 (24)		
Use of group or collective pay incentives	16 (17)		

through the substitution of part-time workers for full-time was undertaken by 13 per cent of the employers and the use of various forms of non-permanent employment contracts were extended or adopted by 11 per cent. By contrast, measures to make more effective use of the existing labour force were more widespread. Training for the interchangeability of workers between jobs had been undertaken by 45 per cent of the sample and 35 per cent had made increased use of individual performance assessment. The increased use of work measurement and method study was less common, affecting only 21 per cent of the establishments, 16 per cent had made greater use of various forms of group incentives, and 17 per cent had increased shiftworking.

PRODUCT-MARKET PRESSURES AND RESPONSES

The results of the baseline survey paint a picture of increasing pressure in the product market due to more demanding buyers and a higher level of competition from other domestic and foreign sellers. It also shows considerable changes being made in products and processes and, although to a lesser extent, in the way labour is employed and organized. The question then arises as to how, if at all, these changes are related. For the purposes of this analysis the data were grouped into product-market 'pressures', which include the level of demand, price, and non-price factors; product-market 'responses', which include the range of products, design and development effort, use of new technology, and attention to the scheduling of work; and labour policy 'responses', which were divided into 'qualitative' flexibility (shift-working, training to provide cover, group incentive schemes, personal appraisal, and work study) and 'numerical' flexibility (shedding surplus workers and the employment of part-time workers and those on non-standard contracts). When possible the public sector is included in the analysis but, as the signals produced by the public and private 'markets' are not identical, the same variables could not be generated for the two sectors. However, as the public sector is generally cash limited, 'pressure on costs' seemed likely to have similar consequences to 'price pressure' on private firms and it was therefore felt that these two variables were comparable. In the same way, the 'quality of service' question asked of public employers seemed close enough to the comparable question used in the private-sector questionnaire (including for private-sector services) to merit its inclusion in the analysis. Identical labour-policy questions were addressed to public- and private-sector employers.

Influences of product-market pressures on product-market responses

The first stage in the analysis was to explore the influence of product-market 'pressures' on product-market 'responses'. The distinctness of pressures from responses was first established by a principle component factor analysis. The four questions conceptualized as responses[6] together emerged as a very clear leading factor from this analysis. The items conceptualized as pressures were more heterogeneous, although there was sufficiently strong inter-correlation between the three non-price pressures (quality, delivery, and design) for these to be reasonably treated as a group. Consequently, the independent variables used in the regression analysis were changes in demand, price pressure, and the composite non-price 'product-market pressures', and the dependent variable was the composite 'product-market response'. The equation also included eleven dummy variables to control for area, industry group, and size.

The regression analysis (details of which are shown in Appendix 3.2) revealed that non-price pressures, and international and British competition, all tended to *increase* the product-market response, whereas a *reduction* in the latter was associated with price pressure; and product-market responses were unrelated to changes in demand. Both size and industry group were significant influences, with the largest establishments (500+) and 'knowledge-based' marketed services having a higher degree of product-market responsiveness.

Influences of product-market 'pressures' on labour-policy 'responses'

The second stage in the analysis was to explore the influence of product-market pressure on labour-market and work-organization policy.[7] For the purposes of this analysis, labour-market responses were represented by a composite factor derived from a principal component factor analysis of the eight items described above, relating to changes in the work-organization and labour-market policies of firms over the previous two years. Five of these (shiftworking, training to provide cover, group incentives, personal appraisal, and work study) loaded highly on this factor, which we labelled 'qualitative' flexibility. Regression analysis, controlling as before for structural factors, revealed that, of the four product-market pressures (quality, price, delivery dates, and design) which significantly influenced product-market responses, only non-price pressures were a significant influence on this aspect of labour-market policies: qualitative flexibility was increased by non-price pressure. In addition, however, a growing level of demand for products/services was significantly associated with greater qualitative flexibility. An analysis was also carried out for private- and public-sector establishments combined, with the 'non-price pressure' variable being replaced by a single item 'quality pressure'. This produced similar results: influence of demand for products and services was virtually the same as before, although the 'quality' pressure effect on qualitative flexibility, whilst in the same direction, was rather weaker than that of 'non-price' pressure in the private sector. The detailed results of the regression analyses are provided in Appendix 3.3.

The limitation of the above analysis is that the variable 'qualitative flexibility' only reflects five of the eight measures of changes in labour-force policy. Consequently, a series of more detailed analyses was undertaken in which each of the eight labour-policy variables was used in turn as the dependent variable in a logistic regression analysis, with the independent variables being 'demand', 'price pressure', 'quality pressure', and 'British competition', as well as the usual structural dummies. This selection of variables allowed both the private- and public-sector establishments to be used in all eight analyses.

The detailed results of the analysis (with one exception, see below) are not shown here, but the main points can be briefly stated. Quality pressure was a significant influence upon four of the five labour-policy responses which were highly loaded on the qualitative flexibility variable deployed in the previous analysis.[8] However, price pressure was *not* significantly related to four of the five labour-policy responses.[9] Conversely, price pressure significantly and positively influenced use of the policy of reducing surplus labour (numerical rather than qualitative flexibility), whilst quality pressure was unrelated to this response. As is to be expected, a reduction in demand had an extremely strong influence on reducing surplus labour. Increasing pressure from British competition had a significant influence on one variable from each group: on the use of performance assessment, within the group of 'qualitative' labour policies, and on increased use of temporary and other non-permanent workers, among the 'numerical' policies. It is particularly noteworthy that an increase in British competition was the *only* pressure variable to have a significant influence upon the policy of substituting temporary or casual workers in the labour force. It is also notable that *none* of the product-market pressure variables is significantly related to the policy of substituting part-time for full-time workers. This finding is consistent with other indicators from the study that part-time working can largely be interpreted as structurally based, rather than a response to changing economic conditions facing the firm.[10]

The separate analyses of the 'qualitative' labour policy items add relatively little to the overall analysis described in the previous section. Among the 'numerical' labour adjustment policies, relationships to product-market pressures were prominent only in the case of work-force reductions. This last analysis is shown in full in Appendix 3.4. Another notable feature of it is that it reveals significant differences between the local labour markets, with Rochdale having a higher incidence of work-force reductions, and Northampton having a particularly low incidence. It is also worth noting that size of organization was a significant influence on all eight labour policies: the larger organizations tended to make more use both of qualitative and of numerical labour policies. Conversely, smaller establishments are distinguished only by their relative inactivity in use of all these policies (but it must be recalled that the smallest firms, with less than 20 employees, are excluded from all these analyses).

Product-market 'pressures' and 'general' labour policies

The notions of 'pressures' and 'responses' obviously involve changes in the short to medium term. It is also to be expected that pressures, if continuous, will begin to differentiate employers in the longer term, or in a more fundamental way. One would expect the influences to be more slow to emerge and therefore rather more muted in the type of analysis utilized here. To examine these possibilities, four variables reflecting more basic labour-market policies were considered: the rate of internal promotion or transfers, the rate of internal recruitment (which can be expected to be related to both an increase in the labour force and the rate of labour turnover), the proportion of part-time employees, and the proportion of 'marginal' employees (temporary, casual, agency, subcontract, and homeworkers).[11] For recruitment and promotion, predictably, trend in demand over the previous five years was an influential product-market variable. The rate of promotion was also higher on average where there was pressure from domestic competition. For part-time working, the results were rather less expected, with price pressure having a *negative* influence on the part-time employment rate. On the basis of this, part-time working cannot be regarded as a method of 'numerical' flexibility aimed at cost cutting. In addition, part-time working was *positively* influenced by quality pressure. It should be noted that there are rather strong structural influences (area, size, industry group) on the proportion of part-timers employed. This is reflected in a much higher than usual R^2 (proportion of variation accounted for) in the multiple regression equation. Hence the 'product market' effects have to be interpreted as relatively minor influences against a background of strong structural determinants of the incidence of part-time working. On the other hand, part-time working is most usually found in sectors sheltered from foreign competition (and from the price effects of fluctuations in exchange rates)—distribution, hotels and catering, public- and private-sector personal services—where it might be expected that competition would tend to be non-price rather than price. The detailed regression results for promotion, recruitment, and part-time working, are shown in Appendix 3.5.

In the case of the 'marginal worker proportion', neither the product-market pressure nor the structural variables had any significant influence, and the regression equation (with eighteen parameters including the structural dummies) was non-significant—a most unusual occurrence. The two possible interpretations for this are that: (*a*) marginal working represents an area of pure strategic choice (i.e. not influenced by size, area, industrial sector, product market, etc.)—perhaps the only such area in labour-market policy?—*or* (*b*) more probably, and more prosaically, we omitted the crucial product variable(s) in our design of the study (possibly including, for example, variability in demand).

Relationships between 'product-market responses' and 'labour-policy responses'

The conceptualization of the analysis would lead to the presumption that the factors representing 'product-market responses' and the composite factor representing 'qualitative flexibility' within labour policy would be positively and significantly related. This proved to be the case ($r = 0.29$), but it would require further con-

ceptualization and substantial analysis at the item level to establish what this relationship means in detail, a process which we
have not undertaken at this stage. Moreover, it would require
information about whether employers felt they already had
enough 'qualitative flexibility' to respond to product-market pressures without new labour organization initiatives. But this issue
was not addressed by the survey. Both 'product-market
responses' and 'qualitative flexibility' could in theory be parallel
but largely unrelated reactions to product-market pressures.
However, it does seem rather unlikely that increases in the range
of products or services, in the effort put into design and development, in the use of new technology, and in the attention paid to
scheduling work would have no implications for the qualitative
aspects of labour policy.

CONCLUSIONS

This paper reports on a large-scale survey of firms made during a
period of strong recovery following a deep recession in which
there had been a major shake-out of labour, firms, and management. There is very little evidence of a trend towards numerically
flexible labour-market strategies. This study confirms the conclusions derived from other contributions to this volume that the
use of part-time working is confined to particular sectors and
occupations and that such employment forms have not been
widely used in other sectors in response to product-market
changes. There is also little or no evidence of a widespread
increase of other atypical forms of employment contracts. Again
there are important inter-sectoral differences, the reasons for
which are explored elsewhere in this volume (see Gasteen and
Sewell, Ch. 7). The most frequently used form of numerical flexibility was the reduction of the numbers employed surplus to
requirement and this was linked, predictably, to demand and to
price, but not to non-price, product-market pressures. Thus,
when under price pressure, employers have looked for and found
ways of paring down their labour force, but have not generally
sought flexibility by introducing new contractual ways of securing
labour services. But employers do not look for relief in numerical
flexibility when subjected to non-price product-market competi-

tion. Instead, they tend to increase the use of qualitative forms of labour adaptation.

The ways that employers responded are summarized in Figure 3.1. There is no evidence of a significant qualitative response (in the form of product range, new technology, design and development in-put, and improved scheduling of work) to price pressure, but a significant positive response of this nature to non-price pressure and to increased domestic and foreign competition. Moreover, increased non-price pressure and increased demand are positively associated with qualitatively flexible labour-force policies. A particular emphasis on improved product, production, and scheduling is revealed for the market professional service sector and the association between these responses and non-price market pressure is stronger for large firms than small. A

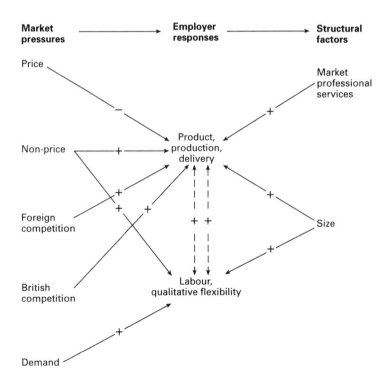

Fig. 3.1 Market pressures and employer responses

significant and positive interrelationship also exists, which we have not explored in detail, between the qualitative product and process response and qualitative flexibility in labour-force strategies.

Is it possible to conclude from this that the era of flexible specialization is upon us? There can be little doubt that this would provide an explanation for the types of product-market pressure to which employers are being subjected and, moreover, the evidence suggests that firms are increasingly qualitatively flexible across a broad range of product, process, and labour-force activities. Whether this is a trend change or a cyclical phenomenon related to the buyers' market conditions of the 1980s cannot be judged from this data although the insistence by customers on improved credit terms indicates buyer power. However, the evidence points away from the possibility that small firms are playing a leading role in this process. For many firms market pressures come mainly through price, and when this is adverse the employers simply lay off workers.

How to interpret the findings on changes in labour-force policies from either a neo-Fordist or a flexible specialization perspective is also problematic. Clearly, training employees to cover jobs other than their own, and the use of group or collective incentives, suggests more co-operation, but the signal is rather in the opposite direction, from the evidence of an increased use of individual performance assessment, work measurement or method study, and shift-working. It may be that the use of telephone-survey methodology, despite its advantage in wide coverage, is unsuitable for exploring fine differences in employer strategies. But it could also be that the polarizing effect of academic debate may have created categories which are too inflexible to capture the full richness of the interaction between economic, technical, organizational, and power relationships active in creating and responding to product-market pressures. The present research, albeit based on simple measures of behaviour of firms, suggests that at the very least there are two distinct dimensions of competitive pressure: price and non-price. This represents at least a doubling of complexity by comparison with theories motivated solely by labour costs.

APPENDIX 3.1. QUESTIONS FROM THE BASELINE SURVEY

1. *Private sector*

The establishments were grouped as (i) manufacturing, wholesale, road haulage extractive, agricultural, and fisheries; (ii) construction; (iii) retail, hotel and catering, personal services, leisure, and other consumer services; and (iv) banks, financial, and business. The form of some of the questions varied between sectors.

A. *Changes in demand conditions*

All establishments were asked:
   Over the past five years, has demand for your products or services
      Increased substantially?
      Increased somewhat?
      Remained more or less the same?
      Decreased somewhat?
      Decreased substantially?
      Don't know

B. *Changes in product-market conditions*

(i) Manufacturing etc.

   Thinking about the past five years, would you say that buyers of your products or services have become more selective in terms of
      Price?
      Quality?
      Design?
      Delivery dates?

(ii) Retailing etc.

   Thinking about the past five years, would you say that customers for your services have become more selective in terms of
      Price?
      Quality?
      Design or appearance?
      Availability?

(iii) Construction

   Thinking about the past five years, would you say that clients have become more selective in terms of

Price?
Quality?
Design?
Completion dates?

(iv) Banking etc.

Thinking about the past five years, would you say that customers for your services have become more selective in terms of
Cost?
Quality?
Presentation?
Speed of service?

C. *Changes in buying policies of customers*

(i) Manufacturing etc.

And has there been a significant increase in
The number of small orders?
Orders with short delivery periods?
The amount of credit you are expected to give?
The time your customers take to pay their accounts?

(ii) Retailing etc.

And has there been a significant increase in
The amount of credit you are expected to give?
The time your customers take to pay their accounts?

(iii) Construction

And has there been a significant increase in
The number of small contracts?
Contracts with short completion periods?
The time clients or main contractors take to pay?

(iv) Banking etc. establishments were not asked this question

D. *Responses to product-market changes*

All establishments were asked (with very slight variation between sectors):
Have changes in competition led to a significant increase in
The range of products or services you supply?
The effort you put into design and development?
Your use of new technology?
The attention you pay to scheduling your work?

E. *Increases in competition*

All establishments were asked:
  Have you been affected by:
    An increase in foreign competition?
    An increase in British competition?

F. *Changes in labour-market and work-organization policies*

All public and private establishments were asked:
  Thinking now of all sections of employees, have any of the following steps been taken over the past two years?
    An increase in shiftworking
    Training of employees to cover jobs other than their own?
    Increased use of group or collective pay incentives?
    Increased use of work measurement or method study?
    Replacement of some full-time employees with part-timers?
    Replacement of some employees with contract or agency staff or casual or temporary workers?
    Reduction of the number employed surplus to requirements?

2. *Public sector*

All public-sector establishments were asked:
  Finally, could I ask you a few questions about changes in economic conditions which could have affected employment?
  Over the past five years, has demand for the services of your establishment
    Increased substantially?
    Increased somewhat?
    Remained more or less the same?
    Decreased somewhat?
    Decreased substantially?
    Don't know
  Over the past five years, has the range of services provided through your establishment become wider, become narrower, or remained the same?
    Wider
    Narrower
    Same
    Not applicable
    Don't know
  Would you say that you are now generally required to provide a higher standard of service than five years ago?
    Yes
    No

Depends on the service
Don't know
Have you been affected by
Increased competition from the private sector?
Changes in the financial practices of government?
Changes in what the public wants?

APPENDIX 3.2. PRODUCT-MARKET 'PRESSURES' AND STRUCTURAL VARIABLES AS INFLUENCES UPON PRODUCT-MARKET 'RESPONSES'

OLS regression: establishments in the market sector with 20 or more employees

	Coefficient	T	p (if <0.05)
Constant term	−0.2561	−1.236	
Aberdeen	−0.0676	−0.489	
Kirkcaldy	−0.0039	−0.028	
Northampton	0.0580	0.413	
Swindon	0.0404	0.293	
Size 50–99 (employees)	−0.1243	−1.109	
Size 100–199	−0.1103	−0.969	
Size 200–499	−0.1522	−1.279	
Size 500+	−0.3956	−2.613	< 0.01
Production industries	0.3755	2.593	< 0.01
'Routine' market services	0.4657	3.134	< 0.001
Price pressure	0.3936	3.568	< 0.001
Non-price pressure	−0.2134	−5.179	< 0.0001
Foreign competition	−0.2330	−2.609	< 0.001
British competition	−0.4352	−5.556	< 0.0001
Reducing demand	0.0378	0.931	

N	611	d.f. of F-ratio	16, 594
Adjusted R^2	0.124	significance	p < 0.0001
F for regression	6.37		

The dependent variable, labelled product-market 'response', is a principal components factor score loading high on: attention paid to scheduling work, effort put into design or development, use of new technology, and increase in range of products or services supplied. Because of the scoring of the dependent variable, the coefficients shown above must be interpreted in the reverse sense: that is, a negative coefficient indicates an influence tending to increase product-market response and vice versa. The reference variables (set to zero) are as follows: for area, Rochdale; for size, 20–49 employees; for industry group, 'knowledge-based' service industries (finance, business services, R. & D.).

APPENDIX 3.3. PRODUCT MARKET 'PRESSURES' AND STRUCTURAL VARIABLES AS INFLUENCES UPON 'QUALITATIVE' LABOUR RESPONSES

(a) Market-sector establishments with 20 or more employees: OLS regression

	Coefficient	T	p (if <0.05)
Constant term	0.3715	1.761	
Aberdeen	0.0248	0.176	
Kirkcaldy	−0.0243	−0.168	
Northampton	−0.1796	−1.192	
Swindon	−0.0925	−0.647	
Size 50–99 (employees)	0.0188	0.166	
Size 100–199	−0.1968	−1.690	
Size 200–499	−0.3261	−2.714	< 0.01
Size 500+	−0.4066	−2.722	< 0.01
Production industries	−0.1498	−1.041	
'Routine' services	−0.2404	−1.620	
Price pressure	−0.0312	−0.281	
Non-price pressure	−0.1997	−4.933	< 0.0001
Foreign competition	−0.1118	−1.224	
British competition	−0.1011	−1.258	
Reducing demand	0.0938	2.276	< 0.05

N	657	d.f. of F-ratio	16, 640
Adjusted R^2	0.088	significance	p < 0.0001
F for regression	4.94		

The dependent variable, labelled 'qualitative' labour responses, is a factor score loading high on: increased use of shiftworking, increased training to provide job cover, increased group incentives, increased personal appraisal, increased use of work study. Because of the scoring of the dependent variable, the coefficient shown above must be interpreted in the reverse sense, that is, a negative coefficient indicates an influence tending to increase labour response and vice versa. The reference variables (set to zero) are as in Appendix 3.2.

(b) All establishments with 20 or more employees: OLS regression

	Coefficient	T	p (if < 0.05)
Constant term	0.6242	3.350	< 0.001
Aberdeen	0.0265	0.237	
Coventry	−0.0489	−0.414	
Kirkcaldy	−0.1215	−0.987	
Northampton	−0.1869	−1.581	
Swindon	−0.1185	−0.033	
Size 50–99 (employees)	0.0312	−0.341	
Size 100–199	−0.1778	−1.919	
Size 200–499	−0.3147	−3.215	< 0.01
Size 500+	−0.3461	−3.016	< 0.01
Production industries	−0.1404	−1.020	
'Routine' market services	−0.2021	−1.423	
'Routine' public services	0.0470	0.289	
'Knowledge-based' public services	0.3026	2.048	< 0.05
Price pressure	−0.1034	−1.109	
Quality pressure	−0.2632	−3.124	< 0.05
British competition	−0.1541	−1.775	
Reducing demand	0.0974	−2.974	< 0.01

N	930	d.f. of F-ratio	18, 911
Adjusted R^2	0.114	significance	$p < 0.0001$
F for regression	6.51		

The dependent variable, and the interpretation of coefficients, are as in analysis (a) of this Appendix. The reference variables are as in Appendix 3.2. The independent variables differ from those in analysis (a) in the following respect: (i) 'routine' public services, and 'knowledge-based' public services (education, health, social services) are added to the industry groups; (ii) a single item, 'quality pressure', replaces the composite item 'non-price pressure', being its leading indicator; (iii) the item 'British competition' has different wording for public-sector establishments, referring to competition from the private sector; (iv) the item concerning 'foreign competition' is omitted, as it was not applicable to most public-sector establishments.

APPENDIX 3.4. PRODUCT-MARKET 'PRESSURES' AND STRUCTURAL VARIABLES AS INFLUENCES UPON WORK-FORCE REDUCTIONS

All establishments with 20 or more employees: logistic regression

	Coefficient	T	p (if < 0.05)
Constant term	−0.5295	−1.155	
Aberdeen	−0.4646	−1.790	
Coventry	−0.8444	−3.047	< 0.01
Kirkcaldy	−0.7947	−3.207	< 0.01
Northampton	−1.0710	−3.984	< 0.01
Swindon	−0.5405	−2.284	< 0.05
Size 50–99 (employees)	0.1710	0.726	
Size 100–199	0.3554	1.494	
Size 200–499	0.5327	2.184	< 0.05
Size 500+	1.199	4.333	< 0.001
Production industries	0.2528	0.741	
'Routine' market services	0.2588	0.720	
'Routine' public services	−0.4480	−1.062	
'Knowledge-based' public services	−0.0133	−0.036	
Price pressure	0.5178	2.082	< 0.05
Quality pressure	0.3523	1.642	
British competition	0.2512	1.536	
Demand same	−0.9701	−4.112	< 0.001
Demand increased	−1.6110	−8.007	< 0.0001

N   949   −2 log likelihood   1151.3

The dependent variable is binary and represents whether or not the establishment had made increased use of reduction in labour which was 'surplus to requirements' in the past two years. The independent variables are the same as in Appendix 3.3, analysis (*b*), except that change in demand is coded with decreasing demand as the reference category (set equal to zero).

APPENDIX 3.5. PRODUCT-MARKET 'PRESSURES' AND STRUCTURAL VARIABLES AS INFLUENCES UPON INDICATORS OF 'GENERAL' LABOUR POLICIES

OLS regression: all establishments with 20 or more employees

(a) Promotions and internal transfers

	Coefficient	T	p (if <0.05)
Constant term	0.2288	1.372	
Aberdeen	−0.0626	−0.632	
Kirkcaldy	−0.1169	−1.057	
Northampton	−0.0580	−0.554	
Swindon	−0.0115	−0.113	
Size 50–99 (employees)	−0.0548	−0.673	
Size 100–199	−0.0609	−0.737	
Size 200–499	−0.0322	−0.371	
Size 500+	0.1517	1.441	
Production industries	−0.3217	−2.616	< 0.01
'Routine' marketed services	−0.1301	−1.012	
'Routine' public services	−0.527	−0.354	
'Knowledge-based' public services	−0.1861	−1.396	
Price pressure	−0.1438	−1.754	
Quality pressure	0.0581	0.773	
British competition	0.1716	2.867	< 0.01
Change in demand	0.6441	2.199	< 0.05

N	906	d.f. for F	17, 888
Adjusted R^2	0.027	p of F	< 0.001
F for regression	2.50		

The dependent variable is the standardized percentage of current employment represented by promotions and internal transfers in the 12-month period before the interview. For explanation of the independent variables, see notes to Appendix 3.2 and Appendix 3.3.

(b) Recruitment

	Coefficient	T	p (if < 0.05)
Constant term	0.1242	1.346	
Aberdeen	−0.0816	−1.476	
Kirkcaldy	−0.0818	−1.332	
Northampton	−0.0472	−0.807	
Swindon	−0.0288	−0.507	
Size 50–99 (employees)	−0.0139	−0.306	
Size 100–199	0.0451	0.983	
Size 200–499	0.0341	0.706	
Size 500+	−0.0177	−0.310	
Production industries	0.0058	0.086	
'Routine' marketed services	0.2535	3.612	< 0.001
'Routine' public services	−0.0463	−0.569	
'Knowledge-based' public services	−0.0524	−0.717	
Price pressure	−0.1235	−2.705	< 0.01
Quality pressure	−0.0612	−1.466	
British competition	−0.0344	−1.039	
Change in demand	0.0688	4.248	< 0.0001

N	901	d.f. for F	17, 883
Adjusted R^2	0.094	p of F	< 0.0001
F for regression	6.49		

The dependent variable was the standardized percentage of current employment represented by recruitment during the 12-months before the survey interview. For further details of the independent variables, see notes to Appendices 3.2 and 3.3.

(c) Proportion of part-time employment

	Coefficient	T	p (if < 0.05)
Constant term	0.0164	0.104	
Aberdeen	−0.2076	−2.214	< 0.05
Kirkcaldy	−0.1628	−1.567	
Northampton	0.0001	0.008	
Swindon	−0.0655	−0.677	
Size 50–99 (employees)	−0.1953	−2.536	< 0.05
Size 100–199	−0.1105	−1.405	
Size 200–499	−0.1198	−1.444	
Size 500+	−0.0276	−0.287	
Production industries	−0.2891	−2.494	< 0.05
'Routine' marketed services	0.7174	5.921	< 0.001
'Routine' public services	−0.0613	−0.443	
'Knowledge-based' public services	1.0800	8.620	< 0.001
Price pressure	−0.2456	−3.139	< 0.01
Quality pressure	0.1680	2.365	< 0.01
British competition	−0.0275	−0.487	
Change in demand	−0.0102	−0.367	

N	944		d.f. for F	17, 926
Adjusted R^2	0.340		p of F	< 0.0001
F for regression	29.56			

The dependent variable was the standardized percentage of current employment represented by part-time employees. For further details of the independent variables, see notes to Appendices 3.2 and 3.3.

NOTES TO CHAPTER 3

1. For an excellent and comprehensive review of this debate see Hyman 1988.
2. A perfectly reasonable supposition given the traumas of the early 1980s recession, the aftermath of which formed a backdrop to the SCELI initiative.
3. The questions asked are given in Appendix 3.1.
4. The percentages in Tables 3.1 to 3.5 relate to numbers of enterprises. The data weighted to employment shares is given in brackets in the tables. It will be seen that the differences in percentages are

usually small. This is because the sample of establishments was constructed approximately 'probability proportional to size', so that in effect it already exhibits a high degree of employment weighting. In the multivariate analyses which follow, the data have not been reweighted, since (*a*) they already incorporate employment weighting, (*b*) size is always controlled in the analyses, and (*c*) reweighting to the population of establishment would give small establishments a weight out of proportion to their importance in the labour market.

5. See Appendix 3.2 for the details of the questions and the pattern of responses.

6. i.e. attention paid to scheduling work; effort put into design and development; use of new technology; and increase in range of products and services supplied.

7. The questions about labour policies covered the two years prior to the survey, compared with the five years for the product pressures and responses. This is a complication which should be kept in mind when interpreting the findings. However, the differences in time-scales should help to strengthen interpretation of the labour policies as responses to (earlier) product-market pressures.

8. It was not significantly related to use of personal appraisals.

9. It was significantly related only to increased use of work study or method study.

10. See Gallie and White in Ch. 2.

11. There are problems of a technical nature arising from the extreme outlying values of these dependent variables. To avoid these, the variables were first standardized, and a few cases where the value was more than five standard deviations from the mean were excluded.

4

Level of Strategy and Regimes of Control

MICHAEL ROSE

INTRODUCTION

Written from the perspective of an industrial sociologist, this chapter is concerned with changes in the social relations of workplaces and their relationship to employer strategy. Not only do firms produce goods and services, they can also be thought of as 'producers' of social structure. The immediate social 'output' of the firm is its own internal organization, which embodies specialist work-roles, authority relations, and ideas explaining and justifying these structures. The social relations of firms, however, have effects on social relations defined more broadly. Occupation remains the main determinant of social status and class. If such boundaries have been blurred, this is a reflection of blurring in work-roles in firms, of changes in reward-structures, in the styles of managing other people, and in the social values and beliefs current in the workplace.

Employees are not simply moulded by workplace social structure and culture (values and beliefs). Workplace organization and management philosophies can be criticized, modified, and sometimes successfully rejected, by individual employees or by trade unions. Management rarely tries to impose new structures without considering their acceptability. But the initiative for designing them lies with management. Management may have social policies which are badly thought out; or it may not realize that technical and commercial decisions may have effects on social relations in the firm and be read by employees as a policy calculated to produce such ends. (Management may often, even typically, lack any such policies.) Yet management, if it wishes to do so, and possesses the necessary resources, has a presumed right to give shape to the social and moral context of the workplace which is supported to some extent by the law. At certain points in history, management concern with reshaping the social relations of the firm increases markedly. Periods of rapid economic and social change, such as the 1980s in Britain, seem to provide the best moment to attempt such programmes. In the 1980s, rapid technical innovation, new products, and market uncertainty provided an opportunity to recast workplace organization and authority in a systematic way, wherever the opportunity was recognized and the wish and will to make the changes existed. In addition, there was strong political endorsement, backed by legislation, for workplace policies that strengthened management authority and expressed a business world-view and scheme of values.

British industrial sociologists thus took as close an interest in employer strategies in the 1980s (Knights *et al.* 1985) as did economists (Wilkinson 1981). The ensuing debate amongst the sociologists was vigorous but suffered from two weaknesses. First, most sociologists and many industrial relations specialists (Hyman 1988) viewed employer strategy as a set of coherent policies concerned with *control over people*; they presumed that employers who had a strategic approach to controlling technical change, product development, or markets, must also have well-defined social and ideological strategies. Secondly, perhaps, researchers were overawed by events at a national level, above all by the decline in the power of trade unions as corporatist bargainers, by the number of new employment laws, and by the action of tough-minded bosses in still-nationalized industries. Some were also influenced by the popularity of 'Human Resources Management' as a theme for articles in the business press and in courses at business schools. Research findings based on extensive case-studies or sample-surveys remained scarce until the end of the 1980s.

It does, of course, seem reasonable to expect that those employers who plan the technical, financial, or marketing aspects of their business further ahead and in more detail than other employers should also be the most likely to have clear policies about employee control. But industrial sociologists may have overstated the importance of social control as a strategic goal for British employers in the 1980s, as well as management's ability to reach it successfully. (Some economists may also have overstated how carefully such activities as product development and marketing were strategically planned.) The view taken in this chapter is that the term 'strategy' needs treating with some care. It is necessary to show that a given firm does behave strategically, or at least more strategically than others, before drawing conclusions about any strategic drive to change social relations or authority structures. This chapter will argue that some claims about trends in workplace social relations in the 1980s prove to be questionable in the light of the SCELI data, though they are valuable as points of reference.

The SCELI data need treating with care. As the appendix on SCELI surveys makes clear, the two main data sets on employers have certain limitations. Neither can be considered a national sample of British employers. Though the employer baseline survey offers a very large sample (almost 1,000 establishments with over 20 staff), its data are very summary and affected by response factors. The detailed case-studies (Employers 30 survey) offers 191 cases, but some were deliberately chosen to detect or follow in detail special circumstances in one or other of the six localities. Thus the thirty or so cases for each SCELI labour market do not necessarily 'sample' local industrial *structure*. Nevertheless, they do provide a degree of detail often missing from large-scale surveys. Conclusions about changing employee relations practice as a whole must be drawn with care—yet on the other hand, there are sufficient cases available to make it unlikely that any of the main trends the data reveals could be regarded as very untypical.

It is important to stress that the question of typicality *per se* is not the concern of this chapter. The sample will be analysed by reference to a variable—levels of strategic planning—which is essentially theoretical. The chapter does not attempt to estimate the proportion of employers who had a strategic approach to employee relations. (The sample is too small and unrepresentative, in sampling terms, to allow exact estimates of this sort.) Rather, it answers the question: did the more strategic firms in this survey also attempt a 'strategic' development of the employment relationship along the lines forecast?

It was possible to proceed in this way because the 191 employers studied in depth were all asked how far ahead they planned

in four main business areas: product-design or service development, marketing, technical change, and staff requirements.
Employers were asked to provide an exact time estimate of the
typical planning period for projects in each business area.
Although some of these business areas did not apply to some
workplaces, the great majority (168, or 88 per cent) of employers
interviewed for the Employers 30 survey provided sufficient information to produce an exact overall or 'strategy score'. These
scores allowed employers to be allocated to one of three almost
equally sized subgroups, each subgroup reflecting at least in an
approximate way the overall level of strategic foresight adopted
in the firms placed in a common band.

In technical terms, the employers have been grouped into
simple ordinal categories. But in order to aid exposition, these
categories have been given labels—Improvisers, Planners, and
Strategists—which are also nominal. These terms reflect the data
to hand. 'Improviser' employers had, overall, significantly shorter
planning horizons than the 'planner' employers, which in turn
planned significantly less far ahead, overall, than the 'strategists'.
But it is important to be clear that these labels *do not* imply
absolute judgements about an employer's readiness to plan or
failure to do so. They merely group the employers in a way that
is convenient for and relevant to the analysis of the chapter, as
well as making exposition easier.

It is also worth pointing out here that this method of grouping
obscures some potentially important detail. There was very close
statistical correspondence in the *relative* readiness to plan one
area of business and to plan any other. Very few employers took
a long-term approach in just one area and a short-term approach
in all others. But the average period of time varied significantly
between activities. The area said to be planned furthest ahead
was, by a very clear margin, technical change. Many firms said
that they planned their technical change twice as far ahead as
any other area. There was none the less very close statistical correspondence between the relative length of planning time in different areas: for example, strategist employers planned technical
change further ahead than marketing, but both areas were on
average planned much further ahead than they were by planner
employers, and very much further ahead indeed than by improviser employers. The level of strategy of an establishment was

closely related to: (i) extent of technical and organizational change experienced during the 1980s; and (ii) the scale of its effort to improve its market position. Data on technical change from the Employers 30 Survey is shown in Table 4.1. More strategist employers had carried out technical change in at least one area, in each of five functional areas, and overall, in the years preceding the survey. Table 4.2 shows data on efforts to improve market position in the same period of time. Although practically all employers did report at least one or two changes, the table shows that strategist employers reported change the most often in all but one area (cutting labour-costs). In all cases, improviser employers reported the least change.

The strategy scores, therefore, do seem to correspond with (and, in a strictly limited sense, to 'predict') readiness to embark upon change in these two key areas. But were the 'strategist' employers the most likely, and the 'improviser' employers the

TABLE 4.1. *Percentage reporting technical/organizational change and level of strategy*

Area in which technical change reported	Sample	Improvisers	Planners	Strategists
Administrative/clerical work	89	77	91	100
Production itself	62	61	54	73
Stock-control/ordering/ despatch	57	54	49	71
Other management systems	61	41	57	86
Product design and development	44	29	40	66
Elsewhere	43	38	44	46
All responses combined*	61	52	58	76

Source: Employers 30 Survey

* The 'responses combined' figures are based upon the overall total 'non-missing' response (67%) for this battery of questions. Missing data (could not say, question not asked, refused to answer) varied from 16% ('administrative/clerical') to 50% ('elsewhere'). It was approximately equal for all subgroups.

Note: The opening question was 'In what areas of your establishment's activities has technical change been introduced?' It was followed by probing questions for each area based on a prompt card. All percentages exclude missing data.

TABLE 4.2. *Percentage reporting effort to improve market position and level of strategy*

Area in which greater effort reported	Sample	Improvisers	Planners	Strategists
Marketing	76	61	79	88
Cutting labour costs	55	46	62	56
Controlling non-labour costs	47	34	47	59
Production response (scheduling)	47	32	46	65
Research and development	42	31	40	55
Stock/raw-material management	40	34	36	50
Design input	38	29	38	50
All responses combined*	49	37	50	62

Source: Employers 30 Survey

* The 'responses combined' figures are based upon the overall total 'non-missing' response (77%) for this battery of questions. Missing data (could not say, question not asked, refused to answer) varied from 19% ('marketing') to 29% ('design input') and for all questions combined was 23%.

Note: The initial question was 'What changes have you made to improve your market position?', the implied context being the 1980s. This was followed by probing questions about specific areas. All percentages exclude missing data.

least likely, also to embark on social innovation in the work-place? To answer this question the chapter will examine three main areas of social control in the workplace: (i) the contract of employment; (ii) work-operations; (iii) forms of employee representation. These areas correspond with common-sense distinctions between management functions. They also make it easier to examine some specific claims, for example that the more strategic-minded employers of the 1980s adopted employee relations policies inspired by human resources management (HRM) theories.

CONTROL BY CONTRACT

The social relations of the enterprise are affected in a fundamental way by the contract of employment. This is not only because this contract specifies status and reward but because it affects treatment in everyday working relationships in the most direct way. Two related developments were often forecast during the 1980s. On the one hand, employment would become more precarious for many staff, through the engagement, at lower levels, of casual, temporary, often part-time staff, many of them supplied by (or under contract to) specialist agencies; at higher staff levels, firms would make much more use of short-term contracts; in addition, more tasks would be undertaken by people employed through, or self-employed as, subcontractors. It was even suggested that a substantial amount of work would be undertaken by people based at home, not merely as traditional low-skilled and heavily exploited outworkers, but as 'networked' professional or managerial level employees. These developments would increase numerical flexibility (Pollert 1988*a*) in the use of personnel. Firms would be able to rid themselves promptly of unwanted staff by allowing their contracts to lapse or simply by dismissing them at short notice. Many non-wage benefits enjoyed by permanent staff would be withheld from temporary and short-term staff. Subcontracting and homeworking would offer additional savings. In addition to its direct financial advantages, numerical flexibility would also promote a more compliant set of work attitudes amongst a growing section of the labour force.

However, the increased insecurity of the 'peripheral' or 'casualized' employees engaged under such brittle contracts of employment would be offset by the second forecast development. Here, highly trained, longer service staff of proven loyalty, with very high market value and (or) scarce firm-specific skills, would be awarded additional security and advantages. In particular, some fortunate manual core employees would be granted a single-status contract of employment, bringing them the same benefits as white-collar or even managerial staff—longer leave entitlements, private health insurance, educational opportunities, or retraining paid for by the firm, etc. The latter changes would favour functional flexibility in the use of staff. Employees would be readier to accept technical change that altered the content of their jobs, or transfers to other departments or sites, once 'class distinctions' had been eradicated from the firm, and with them the 'them-and-us' mentality. The a priori assumption here was that those firms which are more strategic in their planning of technical or financial areas are also the most likely to develop complex policies towards the contract of employment whose outcome would be a split between their core and peripheral labour forces. It was certainly a reasonable hypothesis. However, it escaped proper testing for most of the 1980s.

The SCELI results are valuable in this regard. Table 4.3 is based upon results for the Employers 30 Survey. (Unless otherwise indicated, all data discussed in this chapter are drawn from this source.) It shows that resort to agency workers, subcontractors, and limited contract staff was indeed highest amongst strategist employers and lowest amongst improvisers. There was no difference between employers in their use of homeworkers—which, it is worth noting, was equally rare in all three subgroups. Strategist employers had certainly increased their use of agency workers and subcontractors' staff since 1980. Even so, only one-third had done so. There was no difference between the

TABLE 4.3. *Percentages of different employment contracts and level of strategy*

Current employees	Sample	Improvisers	Planners	Strategists
Workers on short-term contracts	41	37	38	50
Subcontract staff on premises	40	28	37	56
Workers employed by agencies	36	24	28	58
Casual workers	33	32	34	31
Homeworkers or outworkers	3	4	—	4

Source: Employers 30 Survey
Note: The opening question was 'Do you have any of the following working at your establishment?' Probing questions were asked about the total numbers of each type employed, their split between the sexes, the tasks on which they were employed, and the main reasons for employing each grade of labour.

subgroups in their resort to limited contract staff in preceding years. This difference can be further illustrated by examining changes in the use of part-time employees.

Table 4.4 shows that most employers in each subgroup made some use of part-time workers. But strategist employers were the least likely, not as expected the most likely, to have replaced full-timers by part-timers in the previous five years; indeed, they were also the most likely (54 per cent) to find 'particular disadvantages' in employing part-timers at all; and strategist firms lacking part-timers at the time of the survey were significantly more likely to prefer full-time employees than other employers lacking part-timers. On the other hand, it appears that the strategist employers were a little more likely to envisage increasing their use of part-timers over the next five years; but their main reasons for doing so were to ensure their supply of certain grades of labour, not to increase social control.

Similar considerations seem to have underlain the greater use

TABLE 4.4. *Percentages of part-time working and level of strategy*

Part-time employment policy	Sample	Improvisers	Planners	Strategists
Currently has part-timers	66	74	58	69
Mentions particular disadvantage in employing part-timers	44	38	41	54
Establishment likely to increase part-time work-force	26	21	26	31
Has replaced some full-time jobs by part-time jobs in last 5 years	32	39	33	24
Employer has no part-timers but has considered employing part-timers	27	14	28	40

Source: Employers 30 Survey

of agency staff, subcontractors, and limited contract employees acknowledged by the strategist employers. Limited contract employment is attractive to some employers because staff may accept lower money rewards (as well as being easier to dismiss). Only one-third of strategist employers who had such staff at the time of the Employers 30 Survey were more likely to pay lower rates to them than to full-time staff; in this they hardly differed from the two other subgroups. Half of the strategist employers did not have limited contract staff at the time of the survey, and none of these employers said they intended to recruit them in the foreseeable future. Almost one in four of strategist employers had actually abandoned limited contracts during the previous five years—that is, at a time when they were allegedly becoming fashionable as an element of employer control strategy; and their main reason for doing so was the discovery that they led to less efficient working practices. Amongst all employers who did not use limited contracts, by far the most likely to say they intended to avoid using them if they could were the strategist employers. Employers were in fact asked directly whether their use of limited contract workers formed part of a definite strategy of any kind. Slightly more strategist employers claimed that it was, and that it had the aim of increasing numerical flexibility. Yet only two out of every five strategist employers claimed to have this policy. (Planner employers were rather more likely to claim they had this aim.)

Data on strengthening core employment are for the most part indirect. One fairly clear sign of such a policy is a drive to adopt salary-payment for all grades of employees. Others, though they are perhaps less clear-cut, include: (i) establishing a more individualized system of rewards, (ii) introducing a profit-sharing scheme, or (iii) the award of fringe benefits to non-management staff. With regard to payment systems, the data are inconclusive. Strategist employers were no more likely than improvisers or planners to pay their manual workers a salary rather a time-rate wage, but they were more likely to pay their technicians and office-staff a salary (see Table 4.5). Again, one-third of all employers reported a major change in their overall pay-systems in the previous five years. When asked to say in what main way it had changed, strategist employers were much more likely than improviser employers, and somewhat more than planner

TABLE 4.5. *Methods of payment (%) and level of strategy*

	Sample	Improvisers	Planners	Strategists
Monthly salary as main method of payment				
Lower skilled manual	18	14	19	20
Higher skilled manual	19	18	21	18
Technicians (lower graded)	74	72	68	80
Office-workers	87	78	86	96
Managers (lower graded)	92	84	95	96
Overall pay system changes				
Significant change in last 5 years	33	24	36	38
Main change is towards more individualized pay	63	29	63	80

Source: Employers 30 Survey

employers, to cite the individualization of rewards as the main change. Yet a minority (one in five) of those reporting change in payment systems cited a move towards *less* individualization. Not a single strategist employer cited profit-sharing as the main change in their payment system. In addition, by far the most frequent reason for individualizing pay was to increase output through increasing 'employee motivation'. Such motivation does not exclude increased loyalty to an employer. But loyalty itself was never mentioned by strategist employers as their main reason for changing their payment system to a more individualized basis.

With regard to the harmonization of non-money rewards, there were rather clearer differences between the employer subgroups (see Table 4.6). Strategist employers were very much more likely than improvisers, and a little more likely than planners to provide a pension-scheme for their manual, technician, and routine office-workers. (And any part-time workers they had were more likely to share in this benefit.) The strategist employers were also the most likely to provide educational opportunities, membership

TABLE 4.6. *Fringe benefits provided and level of strategy by employee group**

Type of benefit	Private pension	Housing	Health scheme	Training education	Car or travel	Finance
Lower skilled manual	xxxx	—	x	xxxx	—	x
Higher skilled manual	xxxxx	—	x	xxx	—	x
Technician (lower graded)	xxxxx	—	x	x	—	x
Office-workers	xxxxx	—	x	x	—	x
Managers (lower graded)	xxx	—	x	x	x	x

Source: Employers 30 Survey

* Data for full-time employees only

Note: Number of crosses shows the strength of statistical association between level of strategy and provision of a given benefit. Strategist employers were by far the most likely to provide private pension, private health insurance, educational/ training support, and financial help for any group of employees. Manual workers, whether skilled or non-skilled, had exceptional benefits in the area of training and education in these establishments. Very few employers of any kind provided housing benefits for any employee group; car allowances were almost equally rarely provided, except for managers, where once again managers in strategist firms had a moderate (but still statistically significant) advantage over their counterparts employed in other types of firm.

of a private health insurance scheme, financial help, subsidized staff restaurants or meal-expenses, and other fringe-benefits to *all* grades of employee. The only benefits not provided significantly more often by the strategist employers related to housing or running a car.

As Table 4.7 shows, there were great differences between the strategists and other types of employer in their wish to unify non-wage benefits across employee groups. However, the logic of providing these benefits, as reported by the employers themselves in the Employers 30 Survey, was very mixed, with social aims figuring in only a minority of cases in all three subgroups. Strategist employers were a little more likely, and improviser employers a

TABLE 4.7. *Fringe benefits (%) and level of strategy**

Employer policy	Sample	Improvisers	Planners	Strategists
To unify fringe benefits for all grades	29	10	29	47
To 'increase loyalty' or 'woo the workers'	36	30	33	45

Source: Employers 30 Survey
* Full-time employees only

little less likely, to give a reason that could be classified as either 'increasing worker loyalty' or 'wooing the workers' (Table 4.7). But 'wooing the workers' seems to have had an economic rather than social meaning for many of them. Almost as many cited some customary reason ('traditional practice in the industry', 'part of the job', 'a fact of life') far removed from the rationale of human resources management.

To sum up: strategist employers made more use than others of peripheral staff (apart from part-timers), usually with the aim of meeting staff shortages and gaining some numerical flexibility; and they seemed more likely to wish to build a core work-force. Yet still only a minority of them were moving in this direction: it was barely more than in the other subgroups. Nor do the data support any claim that the main logic of such change was an increase in social control. The lasting overall impression is one of considerable stability and continuity in employment practice. Most strategist employers, like most other employers in the survey, had not altered their employment or reward systems in any significant way and did not envisage doing so.

WORK OPERATIONS

In the human resources management scenario of workplace change, the more strategically minded employers are portrayed as careful planners of skills development, and as likely to be the most successful in altering work organization to achieve gains in functional flexibility. Such employers would find it easier to link improvements in work organization and flexibility successfully to the introduction of technical change. Many employees, according to HRM theory, would thus work more efficiently as well as experiencing gains in skill that should enhance their self-esteem, increase their sense of social involvement in the firm, and reinforce their personal commitment to its essential goals. A more flexible response to production pressures, and co-operative versatility in performing their work-tasks, should in turn permit changes in the social roles of employees and in their status in the workplace. Simply put, technical change offers social and psychological opportunities in addition to increasing efficiency. It has already been shown that strategist employers were the most likely, and improviser employers the least likely, to have undertaken major technical change during the 1980s. The strategist employers carried out change in more functional areas too, and the changes were more likely to exploit the electronic technologies. There can hardly be any doubt that the threefold classification scheme of employers does successfully reflect different propensities to innovate, and relative success in the application of new technology, the design of new working methods and systems, and in achieving employee backing for such changes.

Changes in functional flexibility have often been portrayed as requiring the successful combination of technical and social changes in the workplace, reflecting management will to engineer new types of social involvement. The Employers 30 Survey examined growth in two aspects of functional flexibility: (i) *responsiveness*, the ability and readiness of up to eight distinct groups of employee to react promptly and successfully to output or service demands; and (ii) *deployment*, the acceptance of employees in the employee groups present of new functional roles, possibly conflicting with former job demarcations. Table 4.8 shows results for the five of these employee groups that were most often present. Table 4.8 suggests that strategist employers were much more successful in achieving increases in employee responsiveness than were the improviser employers; but overall they were not very much more successful than the planner employers. The same pattern is even clearer in the case of employee deployment: indeed, more planner employers than strategist employers reported significant gains for four of the five employee groups shown.

The gains in efficiency for the work process claimed to have

followed these changes in functional flexibility show a strikingly similar pattern. The improviser employers were less successful innovators—or at least considered themselves less successful—with fewer than 40 per cent claiming gains in efficiency for any one of the five employee groups. The strategist and planner employers, on the other hand, nearly all reported 'some' or 'a great deal' of improvement in efficiency for all job groups. (Proportions vary between 84 and 96 per cent.)

In one respect, however, strategist employers did draw ahead of both other subgroups. This was in the change in the skill level of the employee groups. The Employer 30 data on skill-change is complex. No less than six sorts of overall outcome for skills—once again, for eight employee groups—were allowed for: (i) large net fall; (ii) modest net fall; (iii) no net change (falls and gains cancel out); (iv) no net change (skill of group not affected); (v) modest net gain; (vi) large net gain. Table 4.9 greatly simplifies the data, showing only the proportion of employers in each subgroup that reported either modest or large net gains in skill for the employee group in question. For all employee groups

TABLE 4.9. *Percentages reporting skill changes by employee grade and level of strategy*

Employees showing gains in skill	Sample	Improvisers	Planners	Strategists
Lower skilled manual	26	23	22	31
Higher skilled manual	42	43	57	44
Technicians (lower graded)	50	37	50	58
Office-workers	55	49	54	61
Managers (lower graded)	59	41	65	66

Source: Employers 30 Survey
Note: The probing question on skill-change was placed last in the battery, after detailed questions on flexibility, pace of work, closeness of supervision, etc. in the employee grade concerned. (The battery was repeated for each grade of workers present in the firm.) This may have helped to improve the quality of replies about skill-change. The probe-question itself was: 'To what extent have these technical changes affected the skill-content of the jobs done by [this employee grade]?' Replies were field-coded into the following categories: exclusive increase; mainly increase; about equally increase and decrease; mainly decrease; exclusive decrease; no change; other.

except higher skilled manual workers, strategist employers most often claimed some increase. If results are weighted to allow for proportions claiming 'large' increases, this result is clearer. It may be worth remarking too that the strategist employers also reported most often some change in skill, and in particular changes that were thought to involve no net loss or gain in skill levels for a given employee group, though some overall redistribution had occurred.

Thus the Employers 30 data on work operations shows a similar but less pronounced pattern to that for the employment contract. The improviser employers claimed the least change in two aspects of functional flexibility and in employee skill levels. (Nevertheless, they claimed a substantial amount.) The strategist employers claimed most change in these areas. It is worth noting that these results are in line with the conclusions of the SCELI volume on skill-change. They point to a moderate growth in efficiency based upon successful technical innovation and work redesign in the mid-1980s, rather than upon crude work intensification and the degradation of employee skills. The strategist employers appear to have been the most successful in linking efficiency gains to increases in the challenge of tasks. Significantly, three quarters of strategist employers who were asked the question reported an increase in job-training for all groups of workers over the previous five years, whereas substantial minorities of the other subgroups reported no change or actual falls in their training effort.

These results are, then, consistent with some of the suggestions of HRM for altering the social organization of the workplace by attacking job demarcations and redistributing skills in order to produce an overall growth in the integration and cohesion of a core work-force. Some of the strategist employers, exploiting opportunities for technical change and automation to produce social results, may have been influenced in some way by the HRM scenario. However, it is one thing to show that their behaviour was consistent with HRM doctrine and quite another to show that it was directly inspired and shaped by such ideas. A way of probing for such conscious motivations is to examine the approach of employers to employee representation.

EMPLOYEE REPRESENTATION

The existence of employee representation bodies modifies the social relations of the firm, and in an often radical way when they are trade unions. In the common-sense view, unionized employees are likely to have divided loyalties. (In fact, a large literature in industrial relations documents the pervasiveness and feasibility of 'dual loyalty'.) However, beyond any economic effect of union presence, an active trade union is able to challenge managerial authority and undermine any attempt by managers to develop a control system which has a 'unitarist' philosophy (Fox 1974)—that is to say, one which emphasizes the shared interests of employer and employees.

For these reasons, it might be expected that the more strategically minded employers would seek to minimize union influence, or even to rid themselves of it entirely. In Britain, in the 1980s, additional incentives for them to do so seemed to exist. The 1970s had been marked by a growing, increasingly pervasive trade-union influence within the workplace and at the national level. Union membership rose above 13 million—over 50 per cent of the employed population—by the end of the decade. At a national level, union leaders had participated in corporatist intervention in the economy, above all through prices and incomes policies and industrial planning commissions, where they sat as equals with employers and government representatives. Within many workplaces, shop-floor representatives (shop stewards) or local officials had achieved extensive direct influence over management action. Sometimes, though much more rarely than was generally believed, this union 'voice' amounted to a power of veto on management action.

The first Thatcher government came to office on a wave of reaction against union power as exercised during the strikes of early 1979 (the 'Winter of Discontent'). Ministers promised to abolish the participation of 'union barons' in policy-making. Through tough new employment laws, they would support a drive by management to reassert its authority on the shop-floor. The justification given for this programme was as much social as economic. Reducing union support in workplaces—desirably, removing it entirely—would, it was said, not only speed up technical innovation and work reorganization. It would also restore management prerogatives and authority and enable the reconstruction of the employment relationship and employee attitudes along lines determined by employers.

Coincidentally, the first years of Thatcherism in industrial relations were also those which saw an outpouring of new theories of management, employee motivation, and the reconstruction of the firm. Many of these 'models'—especially those conveyed by the terms HRM or Japanization—seemed to require, or at least to involve, the erosion or suppression of trade unionism in the workplace. In the early 1980s, some commentators were beginning to predict the widespread de-unionization of British workplaces and the adoption of 'unitarist' ideologies of the employer–employee relationship. In doing so, they often pointed to North American experience. In the USA, it is true, employers had been waging an increasingly successful industrial war against unions since the mid-1960s (Goldman and Van Houten 1980). It was all too easy to assume (Hyman and Elger 1981) that this Employers' Offensive would cross the Atlantic to open a second front in Britain. The growing workplace democracy of the previous decade would thus be supplanted by increasingly 'dictatorial' regimes of control (Burawoy 1985) and de-unionization would proceed—literally—with a vengeance.

Other observers took a less drastic view. They pointed out that some versions of HRM were not hostile to at least some employee participation in and representation by trade unions. However, HRM and—*a fortiori*—Japanization of the employment relationship often did advocate the introduction of 'employee involvement' schemes developed by managers themselves and remaining under their firm control. Unions might well be dislodged from their industrial strongholds, in due course, if managers proved capable of building 'superior' forms of employee representation and influence based on the workplace or firm. These observers pointed towards a gradual displacement of unions, rather than to their imminent expulsion from workplaces and consequent rejection by employees.

Some observers were still more cautious. Many British employers, they pointed out, might indeed wish to undertake a de-unionization programme, though even this might be less certain than was often supposed. What remained in some doubt was the capacity of managers to develop such programmes, their skill in devising alternative forms of employee representation, their will to carry out change against perhaps tough opposition, and the extent of backing (financial and psychological) they would have from their own bosses (Batstone 1985; Rose and Jones 1985). Many British employers, they conceded, might exploit selected parts of the new employment legislation to weaken the hold of unions over their work-forces. But their aims would fall short of removing—or even 'marginalizing'—unions. They would merely seek a rationalized, and 'reasonable', form of union involvement in the firm.

This rationalization hypothesis was based on several further considerations. First, existing forms of union-based representation seemingly provided satisfactory technical arrangements, above all in dealing with day-to-day grievances and minor disputes, and for collective pay bargaining. Secondly, though in some 'trouble spots' unions acted as a focus for worker solidarity and industrial militancy, the typical extent of employee commitment to unionism as a social movement or engine of class war was habitually overstated. Thirdly, in the great majority of cases, managers and trade-union representatives developed amicable relationships, and considered their bargaining arrangements effective and legitimate. Significantly, in the more conflict-prone industries or workplaces, shop-floor union militants themselves were much given to condemning what they saw as the collusion of their local officials with plant managers. However, there can be little doubt that most managers—and some local and regional union officials—welcomed the collapse of trade-union power at national level, as the government turned its back squarely on corporatist forms of economic policy-making.

The Employers 30 Survey shows that strategic employers differed in their approach to trade unions and to the establishment of parallel, potentially alternative, forms of employee involvement and representation. Yet they fail to support either the de-unionization or the displacement hypotheses. Table 4.10 shows that the strategic employers had the most highly unionized work-forces, and improviser employers the least, in the straightforward sense that unions were present and had members amongst a given grade of employees. But strategist employers that were unionized also reported significantly more often than unionized

TABLE 4.10. *Percentage reporting union presence and level of strategy, by employee grade*

Employee grade in which at least one union has members	Sample	Improvisers	Planners	Strategists
Lower skilled manual	76	60	80	93
Higher skilled manual	78	68	81	86
Technicians (lower graded)	62	46	61	75
Office-workers	51	26	58	64
Managers (lower graded)	57	35	70	59

Source: Employers 30 Survey

firms in either of the other two subgroups that their manual workers were highly unionized; although, for lower graded technicians, routine office-workers, and lower-level managers, the proportions of planner employers and strategist employers reporting high membership were little different (see Table 4.11). A union may have at least some members, or even many members in a given workplace but fail to gain recognition as a legitimate employee representative and collective bargainer. Once again, the strategist employers were the most likely (73 per cent) to recognize at least one manual-worker trade union—and the most likely (60 per cent) to recognize at least one trade union

TABLE 4.11. *Unionization (%) and level of strategy, by employee grade*

Employee grade with 'high' level of union membership	Sample	Improvisers	Planners	Strategists
Lower skilled manual	62	40	69	74
Higher skilled manual	66	46	72	78
Technicians (lower graded)	51	29	60	60
Office-workers	35	16	49	41
Managers (lower graded)	58	36	68	64

Source: Employers 30 Survey

representing white-collar workers. But were strategist employers also more likely to negotiate with unions once they recognized them? Or were there signs that they, more than any other employer type, were seeking to reduce their contacts with, or recognition of, the unions?

As with the data for skill, the Employers 30 data on negotiation are somewhat complex. It is natural, perhaps, to consider pay issues as the most important subject for negotiation between employers and unions. This overlooks the fact that continuous and intense contacts and negotiation can occur between managers and representatives over a vast range of disciplinary, personal, and domestic questions. Table 4.12 shows that two-thirds of unionized strategist employers reported frequent contacts with

TABLE 4.12. *Percentages reporting particular employer–union relations and level of strategy*

	Sample	Improvisers	Planners	Strategists
Where union for manual workers is recognized				
contacts between local union officials and employer are 'frequent'	48	18	55	63
there are 6+ shop stewards or staff representatives in establishment	45	21	52	56
Pay for manual workers negotiated				
at a 'multi-employer'* level	60	65	59	57
at the 'company' level	45	45	44	47
at the plant/establishment level	52	63	38	60
Where negotiations are at more than one level				
most recent manual-workers settlement was at a 'multi-employer'* level	48	10	50	63

Source: Employers 30 Survey
* 'Multi-employer' designates either national-level or industry-wide negotiation. (Coding did not distinguish between them.)

local union officials, against only one-fifth of unionized improviser employers. (Unionized planner employers had relatively frequent contacts of this sort.) Only one in ten unionized strategist
employers had no shop stewards or staff representatives at all in
the workplace, against one in five for planner employers, and one
in three unionized improviser employers. Again, 56 per cent of
unionized strategist employers had six or more such representatives, against 52 per cent of unionized planner employers, and
only 18 per cent of unionized improviser employers.

An assumption of HRM theory and of government thinking
on industrial relations in the 1980s was that negotiation of pay
and other rewards would—and *should*—take place within companies, and very probably would be decentralized further, to individual establishments, sites, and cost-centres. If it is correct to
say that strategist employers were in the vanguard of change in
general, were they also more likely to pursue this decentralization
of pay bargaining? It is not altogether clear from the SCELI data
that they were. In the Employers 30 Survey, it was recognized
that pay negotiation can occur at many levels. Results confirmed
this. Table 4.12 shows that roughly similar proportions of all
employer types negotiated manual workers' pay at either 'multi-
employer' (national or industry-wide), company, or establishment
level. Many firms—almost half of all types—negotiated pay for
manual workers at two or more levels. To gain some idea of the
relative importance of different levels, these employers were
asked an additional question: where had the most recent settlement for manual workers been negotiated? It was, in the event,
the strategist employers that were the least likely to say the last
manual-worker settlement had taken place at an establishment or
company level, and the most likely to say they had occurred at a
multi-employer level. This is exactly the opposite of what might
have been expected. In a follow-up question, moreover, non-
union employers were asked specifically to say whether manual
workers' pay was negotiated at a company and/or establishment
level. Almost identical, and only rather low, proportions of
employers said that it was.

Nor were there many signs that strategist employers wished to
reduce their contacts with trade unions sharply. This does not
mean, however, that they were less eager than other types of
employer to develop new types of relationship with trade unions.

In point of fact, one in three strategist employers reported a change in their policy towards trade unions in the previous five years (see Table 4.13). The most commonly reported changes were attempts either to reduce the authority of unions or to present a 'tougher' face to them (Table 4.13). Yet only one in six strategist employers had moved in this direction, scarcely more than for the other two employer subgroups. Again, while strategist employers were also the most likely to report an actual change in their relations with trade unions in the previous five years, fewer than half (44 per cent) of them did so—and of these, the great majority (seven-tenths) reported that the change had been towards more understanding or harmonious relations with the trade unions, not a deterioration in them. Regrettably, numbers of cases (40 of all types) are too low to permit many conclusions about exactly what changes the 'changers' were pursuing. But they fail to offer any support to the de-unionization hypothesis. (Only one employer reported an actual attempt to de-unionize: it was an improviser.)

This leaves the possibility of a longer term de-unionization process. All firms with at least one union with members amongst its staff were asked whether they wished to see the level of union influence in the establishment decline over the next five years or so. High and almost identical proportions (four out of five) of each employer subgroup stated that they were happy for union influence to remain at its present level (Table 4.13). When asked why they wished to see union influence maintained, however, strategist employers were more likely to say that having a union made negotiation with the work-force simpler, and that it also made communication with the work-force more effective.

It appears, then, that strategist employers were more likely to have heavily unionized workplaces, to be more willing to negotiate with unions, and to be more confident that they could turn this involvement to their own advantage. Nor is there evidence that any but a tiny minority of the strategist (or any other) employers regarded trade unions as a threat to effective operation of their establishment. Almost two-thirds of the strategist employers said their contacts with local union officials were 'helpful' (64 per cent), and they were by far the most likely (64 per cent again) to claim, in answer to a direct question, that the attitudes of trade unions towards technical change in their own workplace had been favourable (Table 4.13).

The Employers 30 data seem to give no support at all to the de-unionization hypothesis. Hardly any of these employers seem to have been entertaining such aims, even remotely. On the contrary, the majority in all subgroups seem to have felt that their own unions presented them, at the worst, with little trouble and might often be of some help for organizing negotiation, enforcing discipline, and ensuring communication. This still leaves the possibility that many more employers—and especially strategist employers—might have welcomed a slower process of union displacement. There *is* some evidence to support such a conclusion. The strategist employers were the most likely to have introduced some parallel form of employee representation. Some versions of HRM of the early 1980s strongly endorsed the Japanese preference for communication with shop-floor groups through quality circles. Since quality circle meetings are small-scale, discuss human relations problems as well as technical troubles, and are led by supervisors and junior managers, they provide a good opportunity for management to supply information about wider business progress. Trade unions have typically been hostile to quality circles because unions are bypassed, and the meetings can be used, in the union view, to 'brainwash' employees with the firm's viewpoint and scale of values. It might be argued that some strategically minded employers in the Employers 30 Survey were aware of these opportunities, and that union displacement lay at the top of a hidden agenda for change.

Yet it is questionable how much real threat was presented to unions by introduction of these new bodies. Only one in five employers in the Employers 30 Survey who had introduced them considered them 'very effective' means of doing the work they were intended to do (Table 4.13). (Though few improviser employers had introduced them, those who had done so were the most satisfied with their performance: it is possible that, in such firms, they met a real need that was more likely to be fulfilled by unions elsewhere.) It was noted earlier that massive majorities of unionized employers in all subgroups were happy to see union influence remain at its present level. Amongst the few who wanted less union influence, one-third doubted whether it actually would decline, even though they were being asked the question at a moment when public opinion expected a further fall in union influence and probably supported it. Asked about reducing union influence in their own establishments, employers stressed the practical objections to doing so: risks of upset to good local employee relations, the strength of employee loyalty to unions, and the complexity and unpredictability of a de-unionization or displacement process. Above all, they cited reasons which appear to have most to do with lack of interest or will on the part of management itself for embarking on such an uncertain course. In their appraisal of such difficulties, strategist employers differed little from others. On the other hand, they were the most likely to say they encouraged employees to join unions already present in the workplace. These were also the employers who seemed the most likely to have regarded their internal industrial relations as requiring a high-level, professional approach; they were, for example, significantly more likely to report that they had a specialist manager at board level responsible for this function.

Three final aspects of employee relations sharpen this picture. The first concerns non-union negotiation and bargaining in non-union firms. The existence of such arrangements might forestall employee attempts to join a union. Amongst those employers that did not recognize trade unions, were the strategist employers more likely, or less likely, to have developed 'serious' non-union negotiating structures? Non-unionized employers were asked whether they had developed regular procedures for consulting both their manual and non-manual workers, the implication being that some kind of negotiation might thus occur over pay and twelve other possible areas of collective bargaining. Only a minority of the non-union employers actually undertook such consultation. For manual workers the most common area of consultation was pay (24 per cent), followed by staffing levels (22 per cent), transfers between jobs (22 per cent), pace of work (19 per cent), and disciplinary procedures (19 per cent). All remaining areas were reported by far fewer employers, falling to a bare 9 per cent for subcontracting. Consultation by non-union employers with their non-manual employees was reported even less often. Although more of non-union strategist employers did consult their manual workers about pay levels, pay structures, and disciplinary procedures, the difference is marginal and in view of the small numbers involved can be disregarded.

Secondly, strategist employers had no evident preference for single-union representation. Single-unionism has often been pictured since the early 1970s as a stepping-stone to more up-to-date industrial relations, especially by students of Japanese industry (Dore 1973). Multi-unionism, in this perspective, perpetuates artificial skill demarcations, encourages petty status differences, obstructs technical change, and greatly complicates the whole process of collective bargaining. It is regarded as an obstacle to the creation of a sense of common purpose amongst staff. Strategist employers were far more likely to recognize several unions, but they showed no greater wish than employers in the other subgroups to move towards single-union representation. Only one in twenty of those who provided information on the question favoured single-unionism. Over half of them said they were satisfied with multi-unionism or that they lacked any policy towards it. It is clear that the issue was one that was of little interest to the Employers 30 sample as a whole.

Finally, it is worth asking whether the strategist employers made greater resort to the 1980s employment legislation in order to alter their relationship with trade unions. Only one in ten of the strategist employers said that these laws had made a considerable difference to the position of unions in their workplaces, while 53 per cent claimed that they had made no difference at all. Strike ballots were cited as the most important change by those who thought some change had occurred. Planner employers were in fact the most likely to say that the laws had curbed activism and made union members more manageable. What is again somewhat surprising is the very high proportion—over 80 per cent for each subgroup—of all employers who thought the new employment laws had little or no effect on them. In explaining this, the strategist employers were more likely to say that they already had harmonious industrial relations or had already been following procedures now required by the law. A minority of them said they had simply not taken any notice of the legislation.

An equally 'casual' attitude was apparent on the subject of the closed shop. By the time of the Employers 30 Survey, 'post-entry' closed shops, where union membership became compulsory following recruitment, had become illegal, though 'pre-entry' closed shops, which required proof of membership before recruitment, were still legal provided a majority of employees had voted for them in a secret ballot. Employers that still had closed shops (some acknowledged that in effect they maintained illegal pre-entry closed shops) were for the greater part either mildly in favour of them or had no strong opinions on the question. Once again, there were hardly any differences between the employer subgroups. Some field-workers noted that this subject, like that of the new employment laws, aroused far less interest than they had expected.

Overall, the data do point to differences, some of them clear and probably significant ones, between employers in the three subgroups in their attitude to trade unionism. However, most of these differences run counter to the de-unionization and displacement hypotheses, which presume that employers who plan further ahead will seek to marginalize or remove union influence. Only a minority of the strategist employers discouraged union membership or hoped to see a decline in union influence in their workplaces. On the contrary, these employers took an essentially pragmatic view, accepting a greater density of union membership amongst their staff, and routinely negotiating with unions over a wide range of benefits. It is surely important in this regard that the unionized strategist employers were also the most likely to say that they had sought and obtained positive support or involvement from their unions when introducing major technical and organizational changes. True enough, strategist employers had also been the most likely to set up new, non-union bodies to improve communication and build employee involvement. But they had apparently done so without letting these bodies become a challenge to the more traditional role of unions as representatives and bargainers. The weight of evidence, then, is that the main processes of change in establishment-level industrial-relations arrangements and procedures were characterized by rationalization, and that the degree of continuity this implies seems to be clearest amongst the strategist employers.

DISCUSSION

The data show that differences in the planning horizons of key areas of business activity between firms in the Employers 30 sample were related to differences in their handling of three crucial areas of the employment relationship (contract of employment, work organization, and employee representation). Management action in these areas of control can have important effects on the internal social relations of firms. Changes in them which may have a primarily technical or organizational logic can also result in wide changes in social structure. Conversely, change which aims to alter social structure may be 'disguised' as technical and organizational change. The data available provide no direct evidence about how far social aims did shape the technical and organizational change carried out in these organizations. However, some material does throw light indirectly on this question.

Employers were asked about their policies, in the five years leading up to the survey, in six major business areas: marketing, research and development, design of products (or type of service), linkage of production to demand, level of stock-holding, and labour-costs. Employers were asked whether these areas had been paid greater attention or substantially reorganized in the years 1982–7.

Labour-cost issues seem to be those most closely related to some strategic plan for the firm's social structure. But it was marketing which was by far the most often (77 per cent of cases) subject to some important policy-development. New policies for dealing with labour-costs had been introduced by 55 per cent of the employers. Asked to list the actual content of these policies, the great majority listed such changes as staff-cuts, plant closures, use of indirect labour, introduction of new technology, efficiency campaigns, etc. In the light of the literature of HRM or Japanization, it would have been reasonable to expect to find more mention of 'positive' or 'pro-active' staff policies. Only 3 per cent of employers, however, said that their main policy objective was of this nature.

The predominance of a reactive or short-term approach to staffing problems is evident in the data actually used to divide the employers into subgroups. Technical change was most likely to be planned in a medium- to long-term time-frame. Only 20 per cent of employers overall said they planned it less than a year ahead. The planning of staffing requirements involved much shorter average time-scales. Almost three out of five employers (57 per cent) planned for these needs less than one year ahead. True enough, relatively few of these employers were classified as strategist firms, and nearly all the 12 per cent of employers who said they planned their staffing needs over three years ahead were classified as strategists. However, twice as many employers in the sample as a whole planned their marketing, product-design, and technical change over three years ahead. It is startling that as many as one in five employers decided ('planned' is hardly the appropriate term here) their staffing needs 'less than one month' ahead. When the simple supply of labour is regarded as of such low priority beside other business needs, it seems difficult to argue that more than a small minority even of the strategist employers possessed coherent plans for modifying the social structure of the enterprise.

In examining the data on three aspects of control, this chapter has found a distinct pattern. In the first place, technical change (and related changes to the organization of work) had been widespread. The drive towards greater functional flexibility and the overall growth in skills, even if modest, have implications for the way people are managed. They undoubtedly provided opportunities to introduce new supervisory styles or to reshape the ways employees experienced workplace life and the employment relationship. Yet employers had acted with far greater caution in this respect. It seems doubtful that more than a handful of the employers in the sample examined here were taking advantage of the opportunities which had arisen, or perhaps had even considered them. As noted elsewhere, the representativeness of the Employers 30 Survey can be severely questioned. Yet, whatever its limitations, it provides so *little* evidence that the more strategic employers were following up these opportunities, that it seems unlikely that models inspired by human resources management or by Japanese paternalism were being widely followed.

Indeed, in many respects the findings point in a quite different direction. The policy of employers towards trade unionism seems to have changed surprisingly little. Hardly any employers in the sample had contemplated de-unionization. The most strategic employers were also those which had, overall, the most highly unionized work-forces and the most institutionalized relations with trade unions. Where such relations already existed, employers may have rationalized these relations; they did not seek to suspend or abolish them. Likewise, the more strategic employers may have welcomed, and no doubt some had used, the opportunity provided by the insecure market conditions of the early

1980s to reassert control over employees, and especially over enterprise-level industrial relations. They stopped far short of a drive to replace existing systems with HRM models.

APPENDIX 4.1. WHO WERE THE STRATEGISTS?

The chapter does not deal with the question of *which* firms, as defined by such structural variables as size, were the more likely to adopt a strategic approach to their business activities. Rather, it is concerned with the *effects* of a more strategic approach, as far as this is shown by the readiness to plan ahead, on key aspects of the employment relationship. The data does allow some comment on this issue however.

Four types of variable seem especially relevant to the ability to plan ahead: (i) *size of unit* (larger firms have more resources and encounter more complex problems of co-ordination); (ii) *system of production* (industrial sociology has often found that the predictability of production is related to the ability to plan ahead); (iii) *performance* (more successful firms can plan with more security and confidence); and (iv) *ownership* (independent firms are not constrained by centrally determined policies, non-British firms are thought to be more careful planners than British-owned firms). A fifth variable, *age of firm*, is worth considering here too, in view of the claim that more recently founded, 'green-field' units are more likely to plan the development of employee relations in a systematic way.

Approximately 22 per cent of establishments were public-sector units, the remainder private-sector manufacturing units or service providers. Data on the ownership of these private firms are incomplete. Amongst the private-sector firms, about 80 per cent formed part of a larger company or group. Those that were *not* owned by another firm in fact had a very much lower mean strategy-score as a group, though those that were owned by another company had a mean score only just higher than the sample mean. Unfortunately, no data at all are available on any non-British ownership or management control. It was thought that brief enquiries about foreign ownership would not produce valid answers; a visit to Companies House, or other costly verification procedures, might be needed in many cases, and resources did not allow for this work.

For the remaining four variables, there are some (often clear) associations with the strategy-scores. The effect of the other four types of variable is as follows:

1. *System of production.* Units in activities like building and construction had strategy-scores very much lower than average; in vehicles and similar engineering branches it was rather higher than average; units in

metal processing and chemicals had a slightly below average score, those in general services slightly higher. Amongst manufacturing firms (70 out of 168 cases in the sample used here), there was a definite positive association (r = 0.40) between scores and operating at least some continuous production at the site, and an equally clear negative association with carrying out unit production (r = 0.32).

2. *Performance.* The figures for performance which were collected present a severe problem, thanks to missing data. Informants were asked to provide both gross sales and profit figures for the years 1980 and 1985. Some refused to do so, for either year; others provided both figures for 1985, but only one (or neither) for 1980; and interviewers sometimes failed to ask the question or to press for a full reply. An 'exact' comparison is thus available for less than 30 cases; this does not show a strong association with strategy-scores though it does show some link. Where informants did not know or refused to disclose the exact figures, they were asked to give a judgement about the trend in performance over the five years. Around 50 further establishments did in fact provide such estimates for both gross sales and for profits, or judgements about the general trend in them; these figures also show a (rather weak, but statistically significant) positive link with the scores.

3. *Age of establishment.* Overall, there was a relatively strong association with the number of years the establishment had existed on its current site: those with higher strategy-scores were in fact far more likely to be well-established firms. When this link was examined more carefully, it was found that, though the firms founded before 1800 (there were 6) had much higher than average scores, those founded between 1800 and 1949 had scores barely above average, while for those founded since 1950 the link with age reappeared in a particularly clear form. The most important point is that recently established units were by far the least likely to have high strategy-scores, the opposite relationship to that predicted by the 'green-field site' hypothesis.

4. *Size of unit.* The most reliable measure of size of unit available is number of current full-time employees. In the establishments studied, this varied from under 20 in one or two cases to several establishments each employing several thousand persons; the mean number of employees per case is just over 560. The association between strategy-scores and number of employees is positive and very strong. Any other result might perhaps have been surprising: the argument that smaller firms are generally more strategic is a highly questionable one. It is worth bearing in mind, on the other hand, that the number of full-time employees still accounts for only 12 per cent of the variance in strategy scores. There *were* many small or medium-sized firms in the sample with high strategy-scores and several relatively large firms with low ones.

In order to assess the relative importance of the factors discussed, and of some others, such as the degree of independence of the establishment from outside control, a regression analysis was carried out. Only three variables were found to have significant independent effects in this model. In order of importance, they were: size of payroll, forming part of a larger group, and date established at present site. This model did, however, account for 17 per cent of the variance. If the latter two variables were omitted, then operating continuous production and unit manufacture respectively replaced them, with a positive effect in the first case and a negative effect in the second case. However, when this was done, the total variance explained fell somewhat.

II
Localities, Industrial Organization, and Labour-Market Policies

5

Contemporary Relationships between Firms in a Classic Industrial Locality[1]

ROGER PENN

INTRODUCTION

This chapter examines the relations between firms across a wide spectrum of industrial sectors in Rochdale. The analysis is set within three sets of parallel debates in contemporary economic sociology. The first involves the recent renewal of interest amongst economic sociologists and economic geographers in the notion of the industrial district.[2] Rochdale can be examined both as a local industrial district with a distinct network of interrelated firms and also as a part of a wider metropolitan district in and around Manchester. In the latter case, we can compare contemporary Rochdale with the situation in the later nineteenth and early twentieth centuries, when the town formed an element within the wider industrial district of south-east Lancashire. Indeed, this historic industrial district formed the exemplar for Marshall's (1923) original classic economic analysis of industrial districts.

Marshall argued that Lancashire in the period before 1914 could, 'be seen perhaps [as] the best present instance of concentrated organization[3] in the world and that the high levels of specialization amongst the large number of small and medium-sized textile firms in the area represented, 'more than one million [employees] in a composite business'. For Marshall the external economies achieved by this highly differentiated, but spontaneous, network of firms far outweighed any likely advantages accruing from possible co-ordination by a small number of large producers. The present chapter presents a re-examination of the relations between firms within textiles, amongst other industrial sectors, in Rochdale during the 1980s, thereby providing an historical comparison with Marshall's classic analysis.

This chapter also assesses a considerable body of recent international research that has suggested that *co-operation* is a major feature of the normal relations between small and medium-sized firms in a range of spatial contexts (Pyke *et al.* 1991). The International Labour Office (1987) reported that small firms were likely to perform particularly well in localities where they were embedded in social structures that encouraged continuous cooperation. Ravèyre (1986) demonstrated that there had been a significant growth in France of co-operative relations of interdependence between large manufacturing companies and smaller supplier firms, particularly in the area of transferring technological expertise. Ravèyre and Saglio (1984) and Pyke (1987) have shown how networks of firms have developed in association with a mixture of co-operative and competitive practices. Checkland (1981) utilized the metaphor of the Upas tree[4] to explain how the large metal-working firms in Glasgow acted as a barrier to the development of smaller firms in his historical analysis of employment change on the Clyde. Other commentators[5] have focused on the role of Japanese-owned firms, both in Japan and, more recently, in Britain, in combining conventional competitive behaviour within product markets alongside strong co-operative relations in the spheres of research and development.

The most influential analysis along these lines, however, has been Piore and Sable's *The Second Industrial Divide* (1984). Relying considerably on Bagnasco's earlier (1977) exposition of the characteristics of the 'Third Italy', Piore and Sabel argued that the present era was witnessing a conflict between two axial forms of economic activity. The first involved large-scale manufacturing firms utilizing mass production and competitive marketing techniques to supply mass consumption goods. The alternative pattern, revealed in its classic form in the Emilia-Romagna region of Italy in and around Bologna, involved the use of flexible manufacturing systems to provide customized products for a differentiated range of consumer demands. Such firms are portrayed as predominantly small or medium-sized and as operating within a close network of co-operative relations in localized industrial districts. These ideas have enjoyed considerable popularity recently within certain political circles in Britain, particularly those on the left of the political spectrum. Murray (1985) advocated the sponsorship of such networks, a viewpoint incorporated both within the Labour Party's draft programme for the 1990s and the Communist Party's *Manifesto for New Times* (1988). Indeed, part of the thrust of the present chapter is to provide an empirical analysis of *existing relations* between firms in a classic industrial locality with a view to the creation of a clearer picture of how, in fact, firms do interrelate in the present conjuncture in Britain.

FORMS OF RELATIONS BETWEEN LARGE AND SMALL FIRMS

There are at least four forms of relationship between large and small firms that can be identified theoretically. The first involves the classic *satellite* relationship between large firms and a series of independent, smaller firms. Such smaller firms can provide a series of functions for large firms ranging from the supply of components to the production of entire machine modules. These relationships are co-ordinated by market relations between the firms involved.

However, there are two new forms of relations between large and small firms that are thought to have emerged in recent years and that are central to recent debates in economic sociology and economic geography. The first involves a much stronger interaction between the larger and smaller firms whereby the large firm actively engages in the internal functioning of small firms. The classic examples of these types of development are found in Japanese plants, notably those owned by Nissan and Komatsu in north-east England. In these well-publicized instances, the large firm actively penetrates the internal structures of the small components' firms both to ensure adequate quality control and to sponsor technological innovation directly. Of course, such relations can also exist between large firms, as was illustrated by the links between Thames Board and Kelloggs over the development of improved cartonboards for cereal packaging in the mid-1980s (Penn 1988). We can label this mode of relationship as *active engagement*. The second new form of relationship between small and large firms can be illustrated in its purest form in the contemporary clothing industry. Two developments in the retailing of clothes have affected small producers of such clothing.[6] Retailing in Britain is dominated by a small number of large companies, of which Marks & Spencer is the most famous. In addition, there are now five distinct phases to the clothing year in terms of sales. This means that clothing suppliers must react swiftly to the ebbs and flows of customer demand in the shops since retailers do not wish to hold large stocks. Pyke (1987) has shown how small clothing firms in Macclesfield—itself part of a clothing district comprising Macclesfield, Congleton, and Leek—have entered into co-operative relations in order to supply these large orders from the large clothing retailers. Pyke's research revealed that local clothing firms, which for many years had kept their businesses closely guarded, were now openly engaged in discussions as to how they could co-operate together in order to respond to orders which were too large for any individual firm to take on. Pyke has shown in detail the contours of such co-operation. For example, firms may lend each other scarce skilled workers; a firm might have a specialized machine which it allows another firm to utilize from time to time; firms may recommend one another to customers; information on new technology or new market possibilities might be exchanged and assistance with storage might be given. Nevertheless, such co-operation between independent small firms is undertaken under the aegis of the large retailing corporations which intervene to structure these co-operative relations. Crucially, it is they who decide upon the presence of specific small firms within these co-operative relations. Such a pattern of inter-firm relations can be termed *subordinate co-operation*.

The final form of relations between small and large firms is one where small firms acting in concert create an alternative mode of producing to the classic satellite relationship of dependency. Such *independent co-operation* between small firms has been portrayed in detail by Brusco (1986) in Italy and Ravèyre (1986) in France. It is central to the general imagery of post-Fordism and the 'second industrial divide' discussed earlier.[7] However, there has been little rigorous empirical research to determine the salience of this model in Britain. Whilst our data cannot present an exhaustive test of these models, they can provide a partial examination of them within the context of a more general analysis of relations between employers in Rochdale.

This chapter examines the existence of and possible growth of subcontracting relations amongst firms in Rochdale in the late 1980s. Murray (1985), in his much-quoted discussion of Benetton, Atkinson and Meager (1986), in their seminal analysis of flexibility in Britain, and Piore and Sabel (1984), saw the growth of subcontracting as central to their prognoses of contemporary structural transformations. Murray cited the example of the clothing industry in northern Italy where most workers manufacturing Benetton clothes worked not for Benetton itself but for small, independent, subcontracting firms. Murray proclaimed, on the basis of this evidence, that in Britain, 'in industry after industry a parallel restructuring has been taking place'. Atkinson and Meager also saw subcontracting as an essential element of rational corporate action in the contemporary period since, in their view, it reduced labour costs significantly by permitting firms to minimize their direct dependence upon external market fluctuations. Recently, these ideas have become enmeshed in eschatological claims about the transformation of modern capitalist societies from a Fordist to a post-Fordist stage of development (Aglietta 1979; Murray 1988; Harvey 1989). The following systematic assessment of subcontracting relations between and amongst establishments in Rochdale should be seen both as an operationalization of these recent ideas and as an antidote to the rather more speculative mode of analysis now prevalent amongst writers in this area.

THE DEVELOPMENT OF ROCHDALE AS AN INDUSTRIAL LOCALITY

We can identify three historical stages[8] in the development of Rochdale as an industrial locality—see Figure 5.1. Each subsequent stage can be conceptualized as overlaying the former. Indeed, by the mid-1980s, the structure of apparent industrial interconnections within Rochdale manufacturing industry had become highly complex. The first stage in the development of the local industrial district centred upon the rise of textile production in Rochdale. By 1860 Rochdale was a classic urban example of early industrial capitalism, dominated by factory production and containing a large number of mainly manual working-class

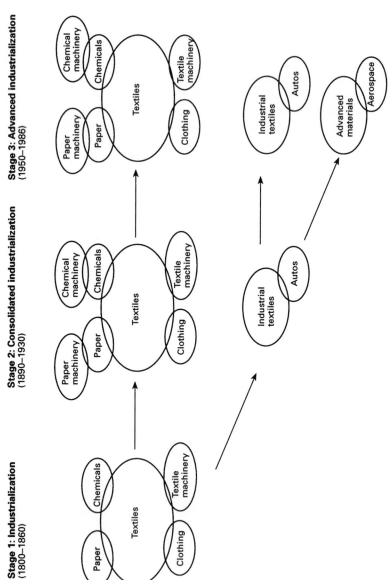

Fig. 5.1 The development of manufacturing industry in Rochdale, 1800–1986

occupations in textiles (Penn 1985). The dynamic behind this social transformation was undoubtedly the general rise of the British textile industry after 1780 (see Penn 1985 for further details). By 1851 there were over 13,000 people employed directly in textiles in Rochdale. Furthermore, within the wider south-east Lancashire belt, of which Rochdale formed a key element, a large number of other industries developed in a symbiotic relationship to textiles. These included clothing production, chemicals for use predominantly in textile finishing activities, and paper manufacture.[9] The latter was located close to textile production since at that time it was manufactured mainly from cotton waste. Furthermore, there were almost one thousand workers employed by 'machine-makers' in Rochdale in 1851, almost all of whom were engaged in the manufacture of textile machinery (Penn 1985).

The second stage in the development of manufacturing industry in Rochdale witnessed the growth of industrial textiles. The classic nineteenth-century textile industry had been based exclusively upon the manufacture of cotton, most of which was designed for direct consumption by households in the form of such items as clothing, curtains, and table-cloths. Industrial textiles, on the other hand, involved the manufacture of specialist fibres that had direct industrial uses. In the case of Rochdale, the initial rise of industrial textiles was centred upon asbestos production. By the early 1920s Turner Brothers Asbestos (TBA) had become the largest local employer, employing well over one thousand people. The output of the Rochdale plant had many uses, including conveyor belts in steel plants, fire-safety curtains, and shed roofing. However, the most significant use was as a core element within the composites used for brake-linings and gaskets in the burgeoning automobile industry.[10]

The newly emergent industrial textile sector overlaid but did not replace the earlier classical structures of industrialized employment. Cotton textile production continued to be of major significance, although its long-term secular decline can be dated from the early 1920s. The local paper industry also flourished in the inter-war period but became more independent of cotton waste as a source of materials. Chemicals likewise became more differentiated, with the development of such specialized activities as the production of paints and industrial inks. Nevertheless, there remained a close symbiosis between chemicals and textile finishing (Penn 1985).

The engineering industry remained heavily focused on the manufacture of textile machinery. Nevertheless, there was a parallel growth of the manufacture of paper and chemical machinery. Since the 1860s, machine-making in Rochdale had developed into an international industry with considerable exports of equipment. Nevertheless, many local textile, paper, and chemical firms purchased locally manufactured machinery (Penn 1985). There were many advantages for both machine-using and machine-making firms in these local links. The users of the machinery could call upon expert advice concerning their equipment close to hand, whilst local machine-makers themselves could learn about new market needs by observation and discussion within these local manufacturing plants.

The third stage in the development of Rochdale manufacturing industry witnessed the emergence of an advanced materials sector. This has grown out of industrial textiles in the period since 1950. Rochdale firms such as TBA and Fothergill & Harvey pioneered the manufacture of carbon and glass fibres, kevlar, and boron filaments.[11] These fibres are often combined with other materials like rubber or plastics to form composites. Rochdale has become a centre for both the manufacture and the engineering of such composites.

The production of advanced materials, industrial textiles, and standard consumer textiles are all present within contemporary Rochdale.[12] Indeed, they are often undertaken by the same firm within the same plant. Each sector of textiles and advanced materials has close links with other industrial sectors. The overall set of industries forms an integrated network of firms within the locality that intersects with a wider network of such firms throughout the south-east Lancashire belt of industrial towns.

Clearly, this picture of the emergence of industrial patterns in Rochdale suggests the strong possibility of a closely interdependent set of local firms in the contemporary period. Indeed, there remained around 100 textile mills and over 350 engineering plants within the Rochdale travel-to-work-area in 1986. A main aim of the empirical research undertaken by the Lancaster Social Change and Economic Life Initiative[13] (SCELI) team in the period between 1986 and 1989 was to develop an empirical analysis of the internal and external relations within and between these firms, particularly between relatively large organizations and smaller putative subcontracting firms. Such an orientation was determined, in part by the wider comparative aims of the initiative (Gallie 1986). The data in this chapter have been derived primarily from two sets of sources: a survey of thirty-two establishments undertaken in 1987 and 1988, and a series of intensive case-studies completed between 1986 and 1989. Both analyses covered organizations in textiles, engineering, paper, chemicals, public services, telecommunications, financial services, retailing, transport, and distribution. The thirty-two-establishment data were collected by two members of the Lancaster research team in face-to-face interviews with managerial representatives at these establishments. Supplementary data were subsequently provided by letter and/or by telephone. Additional information was then obtained from relevant trade-union officers. The case-studies were undertaken by the same two researchers. They utilized either a postal questionnaire or a parallel questionnaire left with respondents, depending upon the sector involved. These questionnaire data were supplemented with semi-structured interviews with other managerial respondents, pertinent trade-union officials, and, wherever possible, work-force representatives.[14]

SUBCONTRACTING IN ROCHDALE

Our data from thirty-two establishments examined details both of the use of subcontractors by firms and whether the firm itself acted as a subcontractor. Respondents were also asked whether subcontracting at the establishment was increasing or decreasing, whether it was a new phenomenon, and the proportion of output or services affected. We also asked respondents about the advantages and disadvantages of subcontracting and, where relevant, their objections to its use. These answers provide a comprehensive picture of current managerial orientations towards economic organization in the town.

The thirty-two establishments were located across a wide range of industrial sectors. They included three consumer and three industrial textile firms, five machine-makers, and three general engineering firms, including one specialist fabricator. The sample

TABLE 5.1. *Use of subcontractors by firms and whether the firm itself acts as a subcontractor (32 establishment data)*

Sector	Subcontractors used	Subcontractor	Size of work-force
MANUFACTURING			
Textiles			
industrial	Yes	No	1,200
	No	No	47
	No	No	100
consumer	No	No	200
	No	No	310
	No	No	90
Engineering			
machine-makers	Yes	Yes	100
	Yes	Yes	220
	Yes	No	120
	Yes	Yes	61
	No	No	245
general	No	No	61
	Yes	Yes	24
	No	Yes	40
Other manufacturing	Yes	No	76
	No	No	200
	No	No	34
SERVICES			
Professional services	No	No	2
	Yes	Yes	18
Government services	No	Yes	154
	No	No	23
	No	No	23
	Yes	Yes	378
	Yes	No	206
	No	No	4
Retail, distribution,	No	No	48
transport	No	No	35
	Yes	No	281
	No	No	66
	Yes	No	960
Financial services	No	No	10
	No	No	4

also included three other manufacturing plants—a paint manufacturer, a chemical firm, and a firm producing components for the textile industry made from paper. We also examined two establishments in professional services, two in financial services, six in government and public services, and five establishments in retail, distribution, and transport.

As is clear from Table 5.1, the use of subcontractors was concentrated overwhelmingly within specific industrial sectors, and in particular within engineering. Four of the five machine-makers used subcontractors, as did the specialist fabricator (itself a subcontractor for larger firms). Three of the five machine-makers acted as subcontractors themselves, as did two of the three general engineering firms. Clearly, therefore, subcontracting was pervasive amongst engineering companies in Rochdale. Elsewhere in manufacturing, however, it was very uncommon. Only two of the nine textile or 'other manufacturing' plants utilized subcontractors. They were only used for specialist engineering activities such as the installation of machinery or machine maintenance at periodic shut-downs. In the latter case, a paper-related plant, this is a common and long-standing practice within the industry (Penn and Scattergood 1985, 1988).

Furthermore, it is evident from Table 5.2 that these subcontracting relations were long-standing features of metal-working in Rochdale. None of the subcontracting relations in this sector was reported as new to the 1980s and in most cases they amounted to less than 10 per cent of overall output. In only one manufacturing plant were these relationships increasing in the 1980s. There was little evidence that subcontracting had increased significantly in the service sector in Rochdale during the decade. Five service-sector establishments reported a use of subcontractors. Within government services these involved specialist (not routine) vehicle maintenance at a local-authority depot and fabric maintenance at a school. Respondents in these establishments reported that it was the policy of the local authority to avoid using subcontracted labour wherever possible. Within retailing, we discovered the use of subcontractors for major (not routine) cleaning at a very large retail store. However, this was new only in so far as the firm had opened its establishment in Rochdale during the 1980s. In addition, a large distribution centre used the British Legion to provide security personnel at their premises.

TABLE 5.2. *Use of subcontractors in Rochdale (32 establishment data)*

Sector	Use	Proportion (%)	Increasing/decreasing	New to 1980s
MANUFACTURING				
Textiles (1/5)	Structural maintenance/ Installation equipment	Small	Decreasing	No
Engineering *machine-makers* (4/5)	Machining (1)	1	Decreasing	No
	Production, small machines (1)	10–30	Constant	No
	Machining (1)	10	Increasing	No
	Fabrication/machining (1)	10	Decreasing	No
general (1/3)	Machine maintenance/ machining (1)	7	Constant	No
Other manufacturing (1/3)	Machine maintenance at shut-downs	1	Constant	No
SERVICES				
Professional services (1/2)	Specialist professional services	5	Constant	No
Financial services (0/2)	None	—	—	No
Government services (2/6)	Specialist vehicle maintenance (1)	1	Increasing	No
	Fabric maintenance (1)	1	Constant	No
Retail, distribution, transport (2/5)	Major cleaning (1)	10	Constant	Yes (firm new)
	Security (1)	Minimal	Increasing	Yes

Overall, then, we found little evidence to support the notion that subcontracting was increasing in the 1980s. It only existed significantly within machine-manufacturing plants. Even here it generally accounted for a small proportion of output. Furthermore, it was a long-standing feature of the industry. The advantages adduced for such subcontracting were traditional examples of economic rationality. The one textile plant employing some subcontractors (itself the largest manufacturing employer in Rochdale) used them for certain specialized ancillary engineering tasks. This had been common practice since at least 1945 and eliminated the need for the firm to train or possess such expert workers. The rationales provided within engineering centred upon the ability of the firm to cope with peaks in demand. The manufacture of machinery, in particular, is both cyclical and intermittent. One firm may have excess skilled labour that can be put to work on subsystems for another local plant. However, this was never the latter management's first choice of action. Only when their domestic skilled work-force could not cope was work contracted out.[15] This was because the firm under pressure could neither directly control the output of the firm to whom work was sent, nor could they be sure about delivery dates. These increased uncertainties meant that firms had to expend greater managerial efforts of control and co-ordination whenever work went outside the plant.

Similar opinions were expressed about the relative advantages and disadvantages of subcontracting within the service sector—see Table 5.3. Indeed, the overwhelming lack of subcontracting and the powerful objections provided against it suggested that Atkinson and Meager's prognosis was highly misleading. Far from improving efficiency or profitability, the extensive use of subcontractors would have created major managerial difficulties in most Rochdale establishments. Indeed, the kind of extensive use advocated by Atkinson and Meager would almost certainly have increased inefficiency and would probably have put most private-sector operations out of business!

TABLE 5.3. *Advantages, disadvantages, and objections to subcontracting in Rochdale (32 establishment data)*

	Advantages	Disadvantages	Objections
MANUFACTURING			
Textiles	Specialized skills in ancillary areas (1)	—	Quality control (3) Cost (1)
Engineering *machine-makers*	Cope with peaks in demand (4)	Quality of work worse (4) Need for tight control (3) More administration (1)	Quality of work (1)
general	Reduce training costs (1) Avoid purchase of machinery (1) No need to hold staff with knowledge that has only limited use (1)	Deliveries often late (1)	—
Other manufacturing		—	—
SERVICES			
Professional services	To provide complete service (1) Cost of employing specialists who would not be fully utilized (1) Useful for intermittent needs (1)	Lack of control (1)	—
Government services		Costs (1)	—
Retailing, distribution, transport	Machinery supplied by contractors (1) Ability to employ people at short notice (1)	Control of quality (1) Cost (1)	— —

RELATIONS BETWEEN FIRMS IN ROCHDALE

If relations between firms (and *pari passu* between large and small firms) were not characterized by any significant degree of subcontracting, how were such firms connected in contemporary Rochdale? Our research identified the following patterns.

Co-operation amongst firms

We discovered a degree of co-operation amongst firms in the locality. This was strongest within the two core areas of manufacturing: textiles and engineering. There were fifty-two engineering firms within the Rochdale District of the Engineering Employers' Federation (EEF). These included almost all the major engineering firms in the town. The Federation provided continuous, local data on wage rates and assisted with wage bargaining with the local engineering union (AEU). This high level of co-operation extended also to apprenticeship training. Local engineering firms funded the Rochdale Training Association which undertook the selection and training of craft and technician apprentices (Bragg 1987). All major local employers except Renold (who had their own training school) participated in this training programme. It was also clear that the local EEF was dominated by its larger local members. Few small firms were members and this applied to almost all the small fabricating firms. We found no evidence that these collective forms of organization extended beyond wage information and training provision into specific market relations between firms. Indeed, it was unlikely that the informal contacts between EEF members could have facilitated significant subcontracting relations.

Most of the largest local textile firms were members of the Oldham and Rochdale Textile Employers' Association. The Association had thirty-eight members, some of whom, like Courtaulds, had a multiplicity of plants in the area. Thirteen member firms were located in Rochdale. They included a preponderance of the larger industrial textile producers. Three member firms manufactured tyre cords and two others were both industrial textile and advanced materials manufacturers. However, the largest textile employer in Rochdale (TBA) was not a member. There was less evidence of significant economic effects resulting from such collective organization amongst local textile producers than had been the case within engineering. Membership of the Association centred upon the supply of general information, particularly concerning local wage patterns.

We concluded that there was considerable generalized co-operation between manufacturing firms in Rochdale but this centred overwhelmingly upon issues of general concern such as wages and training. Employer associations were dominated by larger firms that displayed a strong sense of local identity. This was supported in many cases by the fact that many firms had been in Rochdale for at least eighty years and many had remained with local managements. The intense localism of Rochdale employers was thrown into relief when they successfully rejected attempts by the Training Agency to force them into either Oldham or Bury and Bolton for the purpose of organizing the new employer-led Training and Enterprise Councils within the region.

Market relations between firms

The overwhelming relationship between firms in Rochdale was characterized by classic external market linkages. Indeed, at least three processes currently under way in Rochdale had increased the dominance of these external market relations. First, fewer local plants utilized local machinery in production. There had been a significant expansion of foreign-made equipment within Rochdale plants. In a postal survey of seventy-one textile and engineering plants in 1986, it was revealed that half of the advanced manufacturing equipment used within these plants had not been manufactured in Britain, and the proportion was even higher in the areas of the most sophisticated machinery. Textile production in particular had witnessed a significant utilization of Swiss and West German equipment. One large industrial textile producer reported that they had stopped purchasing locally made equipment because the textile-machinery manufacturers had not kept up sufficiently with their needs for advanced equipment. This view was confirmed when we examined the destination of much of the machinery exported from Rochdale's machinery-making plants. A great deal of it was destined for China, the USSR, and Eastern Europe where the demand was mostly for relatively unsophisticated equipment. Many Rochdale machine-makers had become less and less prominent within the most advanced markets for equipment.

Secondly, subcontractors were used less frequently in manufacturing industry. A subcontractor was used as long as his product proved reliable in terms of quality and delivery. There was little internal monitoring of such contractors' activities and few attempts to promote internal changes within these subcontracting firms by larger firms in the locality. Our research at a specialist fabricator provided further confirmation of this. Only one customer firm had insisted on the fabricating firm obtaining the newest British Standards Institute quality standard. This firm was a relatively new customer and was engaged in the nuclear power industry where high standards of contract work are the norm.

Finally, various large firms in Rochdale had restructured their operations during the 1980s, creating a series of sub-businesses from their previous monolithic structures. Other large firms had instituted decentralized financial regimes of control that had produced parallel results. In both instances, we discovered that traditional internal linkages within such firms had been externalized. For example, at a large metal-working firm, adjacent plants became separate businesses and each had to contract competitively for any work in the other. More often than not in recent years each had been unsuccessful with the other. Likewise, at a large industrial textile producer, three vertically integrated plants were turned into separate businesses and the material inputs down the chain of production were subject to competitive tendering.

The situation of independent small firms in Rochdale

Our research revealed a clear picture amongst small independent firms in Rochdale. They were isolated, highly dependent on larger firms, and financially precarious. There was little evidence of extensive local networks amongst these small firms. There was no evidence of any collective organization by small firms within the locality. Such firms simply did not feature greatly within organized employers' collectivities. Indeed, this pattern proved a serious problem for the Department of Trade and Industry's Inner Cities Task Force in the town when they initially tried to contact small firms. The general lack of collective representation amongst small firms has been a long-standing feature of British societal relations and renders suggestions of any competitive advantage to networks of small firms largely irrelevant in most current situations in Britain. Small independent firms in Rochdale were overwhelmingly dependent upon larger firms. Their relations with these larger dominant firms tended to be co-ordinated through the external market. Such an articulation was financially precarious and there was a large failure rate amongst such businesses in the town during the 1980s.[16]

CONCLUSIONS

Our research revealed a dense set of interrelated industries located in contemporary Rochdale. This pattern had evolved pro-gressively since the advent of industrialization in the early nine-teenth century. There was a close symbiosis historically between textile manufacture and textile machinery-making in the town, which was paralleled by similar relations within chemicals and paper. Such a dense yet differentiated structure of employers in the locality suggested the possibility of extensive inter- and intra-industry linkages. The SCELI research focused particularly on subcontracting between firms in the town. The results revealed that subcontracting was far from pervasive. It was concentrated within the machine-making sector of engineering and was used as a strategy of the last resort by employees when they encountered surges in production that were beyond the capacities of their domestic work-forces. Such subcontracting was a traditional fea-ture of inter-firm relations in this part of engineering and was by no means new to the 1980s. Overall, our research revealed the general absence of subcontracting as a form of inter-firm articu-lation in the present era in Rochdale.

There was superficial evidence of the presence of an industrial district in Rochdale: a series of interlocking industries had emerged progressively over a long period. However, there was strong evidence that the relations between firms within the local-ity were becoming *less* integrated. The machinery-makers were far less connected in either market or non-market terms with local manufacturers in their field of equipment-making. Many machine-makers had become isolated from the most advanced markets for their products as a result of their failure to invest in new equipment or to maintain sufficient innovation within their products. Ironically, some of these advanced markets were located within a few miles of their own manufacturing plants in the 1980s. Local employers in engineering and textiles did co-operate in employers' associations. However, this co-operation was mainly centred upon matters of wages and, less often, training. These organizations were dominated by the larger firms in these two sectors of manufacturing.

We found little or no evidence of extensive networks of small and medium-sized employers in Rochdale. Nor did we find much evidence of the other much vaunted new forms of inter-firm relations that were characterized above as either active engagement or subordinate co-operation. The overwhelming impression of links between small and large firms in Rochdale was one of a classic satellite relationship. Relations between firms were overwhelmingly co-ordinated by external market relations. Paradoxically, the pattern was therefore, in certain respects, similar to that portrayed by Marshall in the 1920s. However, in certain key respects it was different. In the earlier period there was an extensive subdivision of firms which were linked in a complex web of interconnected specialisms. In the modern era, there is the form of such a pattern but its content is quite different. Our evidence suggested that the historic residue of inter-industry linkages remained a significant feature determining the kinds of firms still located in Rochdale. However, there has been a progressive uncoupling of the constituent parts. Today we find a series of large manufacturing firms located in the town which have very limited connections with other such firms in the locality. These large manufacturing plants in engineering do use subcontractors *in extremis* but it is very much a solution of the last resort. The links between these subcontractors and the main contractor are determined overwhelmingly by external market relations and decreasingly by informal or formal networks of inter-firm relations. Given the overall and accelerating dominance of large manufacturing firms within the British economy, it would appear likely that such external market co-ordination of inter-firm relations is far likelier to be the typical pattern for the 1990s than any of the other patterns suggested by commentators.

NOTES TO CHAPTER 5

1. A version of this chapter was first published in *Work, Employment and Society*, 6/2 (June 1992).
2. See e.g. E. Goodman *et al.* (1989).
3. A. Marshall 1923: 600–1.
4. The Upas tree of Java was thought to have the power to destroy other plant growths for a radius of 15 miles.
5. See, e.g., the special issue of the Industrial Relations Journal (Spring 1988), on 'Japanization'.
6. NEDO 1982; 1983.
7. This imagery often goes under the name of flexible manufacturing systems (FMS). For a cogent discussion of this notion, see Pollert 1988.
8. These stages are heuristic.
9. In the mid-nineteenth century, coal was another important local industry, employing almost 1,000 men in Rochdale in 1851. Most of this coal was used to generate power in local textile and metal-working plants. However, most seams were worked out by the last quarter of the nineteenth century.
10. Turner & Newall also owned Ferodo, the major supplier of such products to the British motor industry.
11. See Penn and Scattergood 1987.
12. It is clear that this model of industrial development could not be generated inductively from any available sets of official data. Nevertheless, the model is critical for any adequate understanding of the dynamics of industrial development in the town.
13. Social Change and Economic Life Initiative, ESRC grant no. G13250011.
14. The various research instruments used are available from the Social Change and Economic Life Research Project, Department of Sociology, Lancaster University, Lancaster LA1 4YL.
15. Management preferred to use overtime by existing employees to cope with peaks in demand. Only when this proved insufficient would they contemplate subcontracting work to another plant.
16. Data provided to the author in confidence by the DTI's Inner Cities Taskforce.

from which labour was drawn, the more effectively to retain and control their labour force. Employer paternalism was one distinctive historical form which such strategies took.

In this chapter paternalism is examined first with reference to the historical literature. Our understanding of this employer strategy is based upon two case-studies drawn from the Kirkcaldy area of the SCELI initiative. Our conclusions are based upon extensive oral history interviews carried out in 1987 and 1988, as well as the surviving historical record for this area.

Employer paternalism was a relationship between labour and capital which involved the transfer of non-cash benefits and, in some cases, cash benefits outside the formal wage bargain. It was designed to increase the discretion of the employer and to emphasize and increase the employer's power in the wage relationship. Despite superficial resemblances it was very different from the welfare capitalism developed by firms like the new ICI in the 1930s (Fitzgerald 1988). In the pure form of employer paternalism, the transfer of benefits was firmly identified with the personality or family of the owner-manager capitalist. Although welfare capitalism is sometimes misleadingly called paternalistic, it is in practice quite different. The availability and transfer of benefits and the allocation of jobs and rewards may be sheltered from the market process, but these processes are always guided by rule-based procedures within a bureaucratic structure. As we shall see, the transfer of benefits and allocation of jobs and rewards in a paternalistic structure was often capricious and always identified with the individual owner-employer or employers. These benefits took a wide variety of forms. Employer-provided housing was one of the most important. Many provided some health care. This varied from a recommendation to the local voluntary hospital to the sophisticated medical advice and inspection offered by the Cadbury family for their Bournville employees. (Rowlinson 1988). Many family owned and managed firms provided an unstructured series of bonus or other cash payments outside the normal wage bargain and substantially at the discretion of the owner. These were often given out in person, as if to emphasize the power and independence of the owner. Such individuals made a wide range of contributions to community infrastructure, such as schools, libraries, hospitals, churches, chapels, recreation facilities, and other monumental buildings.

This again varied from the almost total provision of a Sir Titus Salt at Saltaire to the spectacular and visible contributions to more complex urban communities, such as the art gallery and university tower provided for Bristol by the Wills family (Mellor 1976; Jowitt 1986). Finally, there was a variety of carefully structured personal contacts between owner and labour force which spelt out and reinforced the ideological content of the relationship, which we have called the theatre of paternalism.

Recent sociological accounts of paternalism have been dominated by the discussion of contemporary agrarian class relationships. The definition developed by Newby and Bell serves as a useful starting-point because it locates paternalism as an aspect of an unequal and highly stratified society grounded upon the control of producer capital as private property (Newby *et al.* 1978: 29):

> paternalism does not exist in a social vacuum—it is derived from and embedded in a particular system of social stratification, the source of which is basically economic and objectified through property. Paternalism is therefore a method by which class relationships become defined, and grows out of the necessity to stabilize and hence morally justify a fundamentally inegalitarian system. Paternalism—and its obverse, deference—must therefore be regarded as a relationship rather than an attribute of the parties involved . . .

This emphasis on stability, legitimation, and private property was also found in the industrial situation. Our evidence will suggest that the notion of deference needs to be modified, though not rejected. The emphasis in the rural studies upon small and isolated units of production as a suitable environment for paternalism was of little value for understanding industrial paternalism. Indeed, where isolation seemed to be an element in one of our case-studies, the linen settlement of Prinlaws, it was seen to be a socially constructed illusion. By all the rules of geographical contiguity Prinlaws was an industrial suburb of the burgh of Leslie. Its 'owners' ensured that it remained a little 'kingdom', separated in the minds of its inhabitants and in its local government from the local burgh by the pillars which stood on its boundary with Leslie.

The discussion of paternalism has been extended to industrial production by Norris and Bradley (Norris 1978; Lown 1988).

Here the emphasis upon relatively large units of production, selected from amongst firms substantially located in one area and owned by families resident in that area was found in our Fife study, although the notion that 'tradition' is part of the legitimation process was less clear. In one of our examples the 'tradition' of family ownership had to overcome two clear breaks. Traditions can be created relatively rapidly and it is only from the perspective of the 1960s and 1970s, when paternalism was losing its importance, that 'tradition' can seem to have a permanence. Norris suggests that localism is crucial to the success of paternalism by providing physical proximity, a sense of mutual interest, and opportunities for structured personal interaction; its success derived from economic dependence as much as from the welfare element of paternalism (Norris 1978: 485).

The most thorough and coherent examination of paternalism in an historical and industrial context is by Patrick Joyce. His examination of the Lancashire mill towns of Blackburn, Bury, and Bolton revealed the contribution of paternalism to the stabilization of British class relationships in the third quarter of the nineteenth century. He added several elements to our understanding of paternalism. It was bound up with the stabilizing of the technology and workplace relationships after the rapid changes of the previous fifty years. It was identified with the religious and party divisions of the bourgeoisie in the north of England in that period. Employers asserted their identity as Whig, Liberal Nonconformists against Tory Anglicans, as a counter to the potential loyalties and identities of class and status. The family was important as a set of metaphors and authority structures for both community and workplace relationships. Historians have long been aware that the picture of whole families moving from home to factory workplace was demographically impossible, but the gender and age subordinations of the family were very portable (Anderson 1976). Many employers used the celebration of key events in their own family as a means of reinforcing the loyalty and identity of the work-force with the fortunes of the family firm (Joyce 1980). Less widely discussed but equally important has been the work of Melling who showed that employer-provided housing was used in the west of Scotland to attract and keep key members of the labour force (Melling 1980).

The debate which followed Joyce's work suggested that such

paternalism had little real effect and questioned how far such action was limited to rural or urban environments (Rose *et al.* 1989; Huberman 1987 and 1989). The evidence suggests that the employer gains were made in the form of stability, discipline, and, in advanced cases, as with the Cadburys, increased productivity (Rowlinson 1988), rather than in immediate cost savings. In other words, paternalism was a tactic for reducing risk and increasing predictability in the face of market uncertainties. If paternalism was about authority and control, then the relative isolation of a rural labour market may have made the task easier, but urban complexity simply called for more sophisticated tactics.

Closer examination of the historical literature indicates three phases. In the early period between 1780 and 1850, many large industrial establishments were built either in rapidly expanding communities or in isolated rural sites to gain access to water power. In this situation employers were forced to provide housing and other aspects of infrastructure like retail shops to create and keep a labour force. In early mill settlements at New Lanark, Deanston, Catrine, Styal, and Quarry Bank, employers had little choice (Pollard 1964). Some like the Ashworth family at New Eagley were identified in their political life with the *laissez-faire* ideologies of political economy, and not with the romantic urge to create neo-feudal forms of authority. Once involved in the creation of social infrastructure, many employers used the opportunity to extend their economic and ideological dominance over their labour force through the provision of churches, schools, and the manipulation of housing. In the SCELI area, the community of Prinlaws which we selected for detailed study fitted this type.

This led to the next phase in which paternalism was a more consciously developed strategy designed to increase control and authority. Such paternalist ideas and actions developed rapidly between 1820 and 1850 (Roberts 1978: 25). Employers and observers increasingly used the language of paternalism. Sir David Barry, who provided the medical report on Scotland for the 1833 *Factory Commission Report on the Employment of Children in Factories*, pointed out that he had come across no cruelty practised by mill owners but, 'on the contrary, many traits of almost parental kindness on the part of the master, and of corresponding gratitude on the part of the servant, have been brought before me in the course of my enquiries' (Parliamentary Papers, vol. xxi, 1833). For later nineteenth-century and early twentieth-century employers the relative isolation of the factory village was used as the basis for putting a variety of social and philanthropic theories into practice in settlements as diverse as Saltaire, Port Sunlight, and New Earswick. In the urban context, employers did provide many benefits specifically for their own labour force, such as the school which John Marshall attached to his flax mills at Leeds (Rimmer 1960), but because of the size of urban areas and the variety of social influences available to employees (to say nothing of alternative job opportunities), large cities called for a more general and public benevolence (Roberts 1978: 179). Employers in big towns saw paternalism as a useful and suitable strategy but they had to be more explicit about their intentions and about the rights and duties of property. Their actions often merged with the more broadly based efforts of the urban middle class élite to direct and influence cultural production and assert some degree of social control (Morris 1983 and 1990). Our case-study of Michael Nairn of Kirkcaldy fits this pattern.

The origins of such paternalism were varied. Much of the material provision of houses and schools and bonus payments was accompanied by rhetoric and ideology to match. This came from the conjunction of the practical needs of creating a labour force and the political and ideological criticism of manufacturing which developed from the early nineteenth century. The ideological raw material and experience which structured this situation came from two sources.

David Roberts (1978) has provided a historically grounded account of the ideas and values which contributed to nineteenth-century paternalism. The basic elements of paternalism—an assertion of the moral rightness of the authority of property in an unequal and hierarchical society, plus the recognition that the stability of that structure could only be maintained by property which had duties as well as rights—were present in Tudor society. The eighteenth- and nineteenth-century spread of capitalist social and market relationships, the spread of commercialism, of consumer-based status systems, and the economic instability of large-scale production for world markets, were all threats to stable social relationships. The refashioning of paternalist ideology was one response to this instability. It was present in the writing of Tory romantics like Carlyle, Burke, Coleridge, Southey, Wordsworth, Sadler, and Oastler, but the belief in the primacy of private property was the touchstone which enabled it to transfer smoothly from an agricultural and commercial environment to the industrial one. Major landowners did have a central position in the structure of state and political power in eighteenth-century Britain which was sustained well into the twentieth-century (Perkin 1976; Hay *et al.* 1977; Gash 1983; Hanham 1959). The identification of paternalism with the authority structures of the eighteenth-century aristocracy, with land, and with Tory philosophers like Burke, Blackstone, and Archdeacon Paley, leaves a temptation to see paternalism as a reactionary backward-looking strategy. The historical record shows that industrialists did indeed use the raw materials provided by past experience but that paternalism was a dynamic strategy well adapted to the new relationships created by industrial production.

Another source of experience was the employer-dominated household. The seventeenth- and eighteenth-century concepts of household and family were much wider than they became post-1800 in the wake of the evangelical revolution. Households contained not just close kin and domestic servants but apprentices, journeymen, and other servants. This extended household was and remained most important in farming areas, especially in northern Britain, but it was also significant for textiles and many other trades (Laslett 1983). In many sectors of production domination was achieved not by the encapsulation of the worker within the employer's household but by the close proximity of the employer and his employees to each other in small industrial village communities. John Foster identified the breakdown in this relationship as one source of instability in the 1830s and 1840s (Foster 1977). Robin Pearson has shown that the relationship was rebuilt in the weaving villages of the West Riding of Yorkshire around the idea of community (Pearson 1986). Thus the notion of family, enriched and transformed by the domestic and evangelical revolution of the early nineteenth century, was another part of the raw material which provided the role models for industrial paternalism (Davidoff and Hall 1987).

Chandler and his followers have suggested that 'the large

enterprise administered by salaried managers replaced the small traditional family firm as the primary instrument for managing production and distribution' (Chandler 1977: 1) and that, as a result, 'the visible hand of management replaced what Adam Smith referred to as the invisible hand of market forces'. The historical literature and our evidence from Fife indicates that management bureaucracies supplemented and then replaced the visible hand of paternalism as they took on the task of organizing production and distribution in the face of the unpredictabilities of the market. Firms like the Wemyss Coal Company, which operated in our study area, or Alfred Herbert in Coventry, continued into the 1930s with all the essentials of paternalistic style. In the Kirkcaldy area the 'garden village' of Methilhill was built in the 1930s, just as Denbeath had been built in the first decade of the twentieth century (Muir *c.*1947; Geddes 1911). The two systems, family-firm paternalism and managerial capitalism, ran in parallel for fifty years, a feature which has enabled us to examine the working of the system from the employees' point of view through the oral history (Fitzgerald 1988). The French literature suggests the same features of overlap and continuity (Debouzy 1988). The relationship did not lose its importance until the 1950s, by which time it was being undermined by a number of features. Some firms like Cadbury's had transformed themselves quietly and effectively into managerial bureaucracies which happened to contain old family members. In other cases this transformation was less tranquil. At Pilkington's the disappointed expectations raised by paternalistic rhetoric led to a bitter strike (D. Smith 1989; Lane and Roberts 1971). Many paternalistic relationships were like our Prinlaws case-study. They simply died because the families of the owners and managers were no longer able and willing to supply the personnel who would live in the big house and walk through the mill and shopfloor after the old style of men like Sir William Beardmore; 'Beardmore's weel liket—he'll come oot and swear at ye as if he were nae better than yerself' (Hume and Moss 1979: 33). These families often moved into finance, property, and politics (Benwell Community Project 1978). In other cases, the end came when a business was absorbed into the managerial bureaucracies of the multinational or state-owned businesses, as with Nairns and the coal companies of the SCELI area (Massey 1984; Scott and

Hughes 1980; Lawson 1981). This effectively destroyed the conditions of localism which had sustained paternalism. At the same time, the changing nature of the state and the different relationships of employment offered by managerial capitalism further undermined the effectiveness of paternalism as a means of control and as a form of labour organization.

THE INDUSTRIAL CONTEXT OF PATERNALISM IN FIFE

Industrial development was slower and later in the SCELI area than in the west of Scotland, reducing the impact of social and economic dislocations which characterized that area (Campbell 1980). Fife did have long-established indigenous industries, especially linen and coal, but these remained largely small-scale and in many respects more akin to the employer-dominated household pattern than to large-scale production units. The spinning process in linen was mechanized in the early nineteenth century but it was only with the mechanization of weaving in the 1860s that the linen industry entered its golden age, which also saw the eventual displacement of the handloom weaver. Linen remained the largest employer of labour in the County of Fife until 1891 and in Kirkcaldy Burgh until after the First World War. Coal was only developed on a large scale in the final decades of the nineteenth century: from 5,900 miners in 1881 to over 17,000 in 1901—at which point coal surpassed linen as the major employer in Fife. By the outbreak of war in 1914 there were almost 30,000 miners and this massive expansion reversed the trend of out-migration: between 1891 and 1911 Fife's population increased by 80,000 or 43 per cent. Within this general picture there are also smaller, but still significant industries such as paper-making and linoleum (A. Smith 1952; Census of Scotland 1881, 1891, and 1901).

The two case-studies selected allow an examination of the practice of paternalism in terms of old and new industry, as well as in a company-village situation and in an urban environment. The two firms both have long histories, allowing developments to be traced over time. They were John Fergus & Co., flax-spinners and bleachers, and Michael Nairn & Co., linoleum manufacturers. Our methodology involved standard sources, such as company histories, local archives, and Parliamentary Papers, as well as the use of the 1891 census schedules to reconstruct the occupational structure of the local communities, and tape-recorded oral testimonies of former employees and local inhabitants. This latter source is critical in providing the other side of the paternalist story from the myth projected by the employers, though it should be noted that there is no single body of opinion held by the workers but a variety of views and perspectives.

In the County of Fife in 1891 textiles was the largest single source of employment, larger than either mining or agriculture, with 18.1 per cent of the employed population. Within Kirkcaldy Burgh the weight of textiles was even greater, accounting for 26 per cent of the labour force. The county and large burgh level are the only levels at which the printed census reports give details. However, by examining the manuscript census schedules themselves we can extract the occupational structure of our two communities. Not surprisingly, the dominance of linen in Prinlaws was almost total; out of an employed population of 548, 430 or 78.5 per cent were employed in linen, almost certainly all in the Fergus mills. By gender these figures are: 67 per cent of men and 90 per cent of women who were employed worked in the mills. In Kirkcaldy Burgh the proportion employed in the linoleum and floorcloth industry was 9.5 per cent of all workers and 14 per cent of men. In Pathhead—where all Nairn's factories were located—these figures jumped to 20 and 30 per cent respectively. Pathhead had a wider range of occupations and industries than Prinlaws, in the manner typical of urban environments. The 'isolation' of Prinlaws was indicated by the lack of interaction with geographically contiguous labour markets. Paper mills were the major employer of labour in Leslie and the nearby Burgh of Markinch, yet only twelve people in Prinlaws (2.2 per cent of the employed population) worked in that industry.

JOHN FERGUS & CO., PRINLAWS

With the mechanization of spinning, the linen industry in Fife saw the first mills make their appearance in the 1790s. Most were based on the River Leven and by 1800 there were eleven, with almost fifty by the late 1820s. The hand spinning of flax had been done mainly by women working within the household—it was undertaken at home, mainly at night or during the winter. The erection of the mills fundamentally altered the domestic arrangement of the work, though it remained largely an occupation for women and children. The mills of John Fergus & Co. were situated on the Leven beside the old Burgh of Leslie but separate from it. The village which was developed alongside the mills was known as Prinlaws. The site was originally developed around 1800, but Fergus appeared on the scene in 1828 when he sold off his other linen concerns in Kirkcaldy and Kinghorn and bought over the Prinlaws complex. Later on he purchased the East Prinlaws Mill and built a further two, the West Mill in 1836 and the North Mill in 1853. By 1836 there were 320 employees and by 1858 1,500. In 1864 it was commented that, 'the greatest works at present in Fife are those of John Fergus & Co., Prinlaws' (Warden 1967: 516; Bennet n.d.: 66–7). Fergus was undoubtedly a strong representative of the new manufacturing interest in Fife. He was elected as Liberal MP (unopposed) for the Kirkcaldy District of Burghs in 1835, though he did not stand at the subsequent election in 1837. Ten years later he successfully stood for the County seat which he held until his resignation, owing to pressure of business, in 1859 (Bennet n.d.; F. W. S. Craig 1977). Fergus had been elected as MP for Fife in 1847 on an anti-Tory landlord programme, defending the interests of the tenant farmers over the Game Laws (Hutchison 1986: 87). As an industrialist, Fergus had to take on the Earl of Rothes (the largest local landowner) in order to secure successfully the extension of the railway from Markinch to Leslie to service his mills (Hunter 1957: 16, 69).

Fergus died a bachelor in 1865 and the firm was then directed by Andrew Wylie, who had been taken on as a partner. In turn, Wylie took on James Porter, who had originally come to Prinlaws as a clerk, as a partner. Porter subsequently succeeded Wylie. Porter also took on partners but was able to leave the company to the control of his own descendants. In 1925 the firm, still called John Fergus & Co. became a limited liability company. The directors were James Porter, the major shareholder, William Porter, and Edward Jobson. In 1928 James Porter died and his shares were divided equally between his sons William, now the largest shareholder, and James Fergus Porter, who only

became a director in 1953. In 1951, the Porter brothers transferred large amounts of their shares to other members of their
family. In 1954 William Porter died and was succeeded by his
son James. In 1957 the firm went into voluntary liquidation
(Hunter 1957: 69–71; Bennet n.d.: 66–7; Records of Dissolved
Companies).

MICHAEL NAIRN & CO.

Until recently both the smell and the identity of Kirkcaldy was
linked to the linoleum industry and that industry was dominated
by Nairn's. The manufacture of floor covering in the Burgh
began in 1847, but the origins of the firm go back to 1828. It was
at that date that Michael Nairn built a small factory for weaving
heavy canvas from jute. Among his customers was a Bristol firm
which was the only manufacturer of floorcloth in Britain and
which used the canvas for the backing. In 1847 Nairn decided to
produce the finished article by himself and to this end he built a
new manufactory in the industrial suburb of Pathhead, at that
time outwith the Burgh of Kirkcaldy, although more or less continuous with it. This building was dubbed Nairn's folly, due to
local scepticism about its chances of success. Since floorcloth had
to lie in stock for twelve months before it was dry enough for
sale, the risks involved in the business were considerable.

Nairn died in 1858 and the business was carried on by his wife,
his eldest son Robert, and James Shepherd, who had been the
firm's senior commercial buyer. A younger son, Michael Barker
Nairn, entered the partnership in 1861 and soon took over the
effective leadership of the firm. In the early 1860s Nairn's managed to reduce the drying time for floorcloth from twelve to three
months and this innovation allowed other firms to be launched.
Shepherd left Nairn's in 1864 and established a new company
with Michael Beveridge, Shepherd & Beveridge. Other firms were
established around the same time although Nairns continued to
grow into a giant concern. In 1880 a new firm was established,
Barry & Ostlere, and eventually, the two great rival names in
Kirkcaldy were Nairn's and Barry's. The former's growth was
largely generated internally while the latter developed through a
series of take-overs and amalgamations, the most important of

which took place in 1899 when Barry & Ostlere, the Kirkcaldy Linoleum Co., and Shepherd & Beveridge were merged together into the new firm of Barry, Ostlere and Shepherd. John Barry, who was also an Irish Nationalist MP, was appointed chairman and senior managing director.

Linoleum, which was the invention of Frederick Walton of Staines, began to be produced in Kirkcaldy in 1877, when Walton's patent ran out. The new product, being more resilient and warmer, soon displaced floorcloth, though the latter continued to be produced. Nairn's rapidly became an international concern, as did Barry's, with factories and joint ventures in Europe and America. Michael Baker Nairn became a baronet in 1905 and died in 1915, leaving an estate of over one million pounds. In 1909 he had resigned as managing director and was replaced by his son Michael, who also inherited his father's title on Sir Michael's death. Nairn's prospered during the 1920s and 1930s and offered a rare example of productive capacity being moved north during this period. This was in 1933 after the take-over of the Greenwich Linoleum Co. The company successfully moved into the new vinyl floorcoverings after the Second World War and, with the loss of Barry's in 1963, it was the last linoleum firm in Kirkcaldy and Scotland. The Nairn family dynasty finally came to an end in 1975 when the firm was purchased by Unilever. In 1985 Unilever sold Nairn's to the Swiss company Forbo and the Kirkcaldy business now operates under the title of Forbo-Nairn (A. Smith 1952; Muir 1956; Morgan 1986; information from company archive).

THE STRATEGIES OF PATERNALISM

Housing

Employer-provided housing was central to the paternalistic relationship. From the employer's standpoint, the provision of tied housing reduced levels of competition in the labour market. Any gains labour might anticipate from moving from one employer to another had to be balanced against the costs of losing access to housing and community. This must have imposed considerable rigidities and discontinuities in the way in which labour responded to the wage labour market. At Prinlaws the control of housing was used to create and recreate the mainly female labour force. The monopoly of housing in Prinlaws allowed Fergus and Co. to dominate its work-force and community. Even in 1957 after thirty years of council-house building in the area, the company still owned 200 houses.

It was never possible for the Nairns to emulate this level of control, even if they had wanted to. Pathhead, where Michael Nairn situated the first of his factories, already had its own established industries and patterns of property ownership. Pathhead was the area where Adam Smith studied the art of nail-making and by the mid-nineteenth century it was home to a large number of handloom weavers. The ownership of property varied. There were large holdings by individuals, including the Earl of Rothes, several small parcels of land and houses, as well as dozens of individually owned houses. While there is no definite evidence of Nairn's trying to dominate the local housing market, it is clear that the company and family did buy considerable amounts of property and housing in Pathhead. By the early 1900s Nairn's owned around 200 houses in Pathhead and by the 1930s had increased its stock, also purchasing houses from rivals in the linoleum trade (Valuation Rolls, Scottish Record Office). There is evidence, both from the oral testimonies and documentary sources, that Nairn's did seek to reserve houses for its own workers but the actual relationship is not clear. Our oral extracts on this issue all refer to the Prinlaws situation but we are convinced that the experience of some form of tied housing was an extremely common one in many areas of the labour market of lowland Scotland.

At Prinlaws the link between home and work was clear. This relationship was widespread. One respondent described a family life which moved from farm cottage to quarry cottage to mill housing. The extracts shows that the economic dependence was well recognized. It was a dependence which limited the choices of the individuals, mainly women, involved. The deference involved was a simple acknowledgement of power.

[Mr H.] You worked for Fergie Porter, you stayed in Fergie Porter's house and you paid your rent to Fergie Porter. (JSINTER1: 17)

[Mr St.] See what they objected to was Prinlaws—the village, the mills, an' everything—belonged to one man an' if ye fell oot wi' the job—ye were oot o the hoose too. (JSINTER4: 11)

[J.S.] When you were at school did you know that you were going to get a job in the mill?

[[Mrs B.] Well, what happened—we were all born at the East End, 59 High Street. Then, when we were beginnin' to grow up, well ma Dad got to Prinlaws Mill, ye see? Well, ye jist got a house if ye had girls comin' up, so's they would get intae the mill. That's how we happened t'get a house. We had three girls, ye see? So that's why we had t'go t'the mill t'work, because we had got a house down in Prinlaws.

[J.S.] Your father worked in the mill?

[Mrs B.] Yes.

[J.S.] While he was still livin' in Leslie?

[Mrs B.] Uhu.

[J.S.] And then, when you and your sisters were born, he then got a house in Prinlaws?

[Mrs B.] Well, I think I would be about twelve years old when we flitted t' Prinlaws, but these were the conditions—you got the houses if ye had girls that would work in the mill you know? (JSINTER9: 1–2)

[Jim McM.] Was you no in that position where you were asked to leave yer hoose because o' the . . .

[John M.] Yes . . . now, I had a younger brother than me an' an older brother—we had both worked in Prinlaws at that stage—but as I say we were paid off because we demanded a man's wage. Now there wur three of us and when we went down to pay the rent into the office—'Look you've nae work and you'll have to look fur another house'—so of coorse ye couldnae get another house in thae days. Where can ye go? The result is, it came on a wee bit later and thur wur too many people in the same position as us. They couldnae put them a' out, ye see? There were a lot o' folk didnae have work. Thur wur plenty work fur girls but not for men an' the result wis we had to look fur another house but after, maybe, say three or four year I went to be a gardener, which I wisnae skilled in thae days. I've been forty or fifty year as a gardener now, but in thae days I wisnae skilled, but I went tae work in one o' the partner's gardens fur six month an' I wis there fur twenty-five year. [*Laughter*] Now there wis no more this lookin' fur another house.

[J.S.] So you were able to say?

[John M.] I was able to stay and then after it, give time and that, people were able to get houses and things like that, but then they couldnae pit ye oot after a number o' years because ye wur what ye cried [called] sittin' tenants, ye see? But then we didnae have that goin' earlier, what we wur talking aboot that earlier time, but it come after years they couldnae pit ye oot. You wur sittin' tenants. They had tae provide another house if they wanted your house. So it kinda safeguards ye.

[Jim McM.] There was new laws an' that come oot.

[John M.] New laws comin' out, that's right. (JSINTER7: 28–9)

[Mrs D.] They were oot workin' because they were the one that got the hoose. Yer mother was the yin that got the hoose.

[Mrs H.] Of course it came down an' eventually I was the one. My sisters—I had another sister, she had to work hard as well, and they went other place to work when Prinlaws was maybe week about, or three days a week, or something. My older sister, she went away to work in the paper mills along at Markinch for a spell away, and I was the only one left an' I didnae get away because I was the one that was workin' for the house, ye see?

[J.S.] By that time your mother would have stopped?

[Mrs H.] Aye, my mother had stopped by that time.

[J.S.] And what would have happened if you'd left, would the family have lost the house?

[Mrs H.] Well I don't think there was much they could do about it. In fact there was a lot of the girls went away during the war—they were called up for war work and came into good jobs and they simply refused to leave them. They wanted them back—they threatened them but a lot of them just never bothered goin' back an' they couldnae do a thing about it.

[Mrs D.] But I was one o' them that had to go back. I worked in De la Rues during the war. I had a good job and I wanted to keep it.

[Mrs H.] But each householder got a letter that they had to bring their family back into the mill.

[Mrs D.] Either that or they would lose their house, so my mother says, 'Well, you're comin' back an' that's a' there is tae it.' So I had to go back to the dirty, stoory old mill.

[Mrs H.] But by that time I was married and out o' the mill and she was the only one that was left that could possibly go.

[Mrs D.] A place ah detested. (JSINTER2: 6–7)

These extracts also make clear two factors which undermined paternalism. One was the impact of new laws in the late 1940s which increased the rights of sitting tenants. Despite this some of the women felt an almost hegemonistic respect for the power of the mill owner over housing. Hence the importance of the second factor, the presence of managerial capitalism (in these extracts in the form of De la Rue's) which gave some of the women experience of alternative forms of work relationship.

Social Infrastructure

The provision by both firms of social services to their local communities varied both in terms of quality and scale. In Prinlaws it could be said that everything was provided by the firm: not only were the houses built by the firm but so was the school and the church hall; the collection of waste was done by the firm, houses were repaired by the firm, and the water supply and street lighting supplied by the firm. Prinlaws was no model village, with owners committed to public works and improvements. Apart from the school, which later became the chapel, and a small reading-room, there is no evidence that Fergus or any of the subsequent owners built any other public amenities for the village. Nevertheless, Prinlaws was compared to New Lanark in the *Factory Inspectors' Report* (Parliamentary Papers 1833). The company even objected to people improving their own houses by fitting in their own gas or electricity supply, on the grounds that it would encourage everyone to expect the same, and the inhabitants of Fergus houses recall that the company only altered the sanitary arrangements when they were forced to. At the same time there was very little that could be done in or by the village without recourse to the company, so that even the football pitch was given by the firm. There was also the negative side of social provision. Fergus and those who followed him were strongly opposed to drink and so long as the firm remained in operation there was no pub in Prinlaws.

[Mr S.] And they had their own tradesmen. Used to come round and dae a the repairs.

[Mrs S.] Wi had a big gairden. Wi had a big gairden at the back.

[Mr S.] They had their own lightin'. They had a turbine doon at the mill. It used to go off every night—at what? Ten o'clock, was it?

[Mrs S.] At ten o'clock the lights went oot through the week but twelve o'clock was one night—Saturday.

[Mr S.] Saturday night when ye got tae the pictures an' ye had a light to get home wi'.

[Mrs S.] Ye got hame but, eh, eh, ten o'clock through the week.

[J.S.] That's the street lightin'?

[Mr S.] Everything. All the electric power.

[Mrs S.] All the lightin' in Prinlaws—that was jist Prinlaws.

[Mr S.] Street lightin'.

[Mrs S.] Just Prinlaws, Leslie had . . .

[Mr S.] The whole village belonged to the mill, y'see? They had their own power an' a' the rest o' it. They had their own water supply even. (JSINTER4: 12–13)

There were plenty of pubs and licensed grocers in Pathhead but Nairn's provision of amenities tended to be very public and very conspicuous. Even today some of the most prominent landmarks in Kirkcaldy are Nairn constructions, such as the war memorial and the museum and public library. Nairn's was also a prominent contributor to the funds of the Free Kirk and to the YMCA. The family did not, however, confine its activities to writing the cheques. One of the gifts of which Nairn was most proud was the cottage hospital built in 1874. The family interest continued into the twentieth century with the building of a nurses' home in 1926 and even after the creation of the NHS, Nairn still had plans to build a new hospital for Kirkcaldy but was thwarted by the determination of the Health Board to follow its own plan (Morgan 1986).

[Mrs M.] Yes, getting back to the hospital—if anything were needed done floorwise, or any wise really, they just got on to Nairn's.
[Mr M.] Sir Michael.
[Mrs M.] And it was done. . . .
[Mr M.] I can remember one time that he come in and he said, 'I want some layers to go along to . . .'—this was after it had been taken over by the NHS, ye see? 'I want two layers to go along to the hospital, something's wrong with the laying there, it's all bumpy and the rest of it.' So I spoke to the layers and the layers said, 'We cannae do that. That was laid by Thomas Justice and we can't go in and sort their work. We can't sort o' do that.' I says, 'You go and tell that to Sir Michael.' So they went along, but before they went along they phoned Justice and sort of said, 'Look we've had Sir Michael on and there's something wrong—do you mind if we go along and see it?' And they said, 'Oh no.' Of course that was saving them coming down. But that was the thing, he went in there every—once a week sort o' business—he went in. (JSINTER15: 8)

LOCAL LABOUR MARKETS: SECURITY AND SEGREGATION

Both firms were labour intensive, with a large demand for semi-skilled, general workers. The major difference between the two was that Fergus employed mainly women (63 per cent of the work-force), while linoleum was almost exclusively a male industry. Nairn's, however, wove its own canvas backing in one of its factories, which thus had a predominantly female labour force. Both firms faced similar problems in the need to attract a constant and reliable supply of labour and also keep labour costs low. The early theories of dual or segmented labour markets had associated low-paid, relatively unskilled labour working in poor conditions with the creation of 'secondary' employment, involving unstable work habits and high rates of job turnover (Lawson 1981). The historical and contemporary record shows that many employers developed strategies to counter any such tendency which such labour markets may have. Control over housing was one such policy. In Prinlaws this can hardly be exaggerated. There were, however, other strategies available and one of the most important was the regularity of employment offered.

In Prinlaws it was simply understood that young people leaving school would start work in the mill. There was no choice in the matter. Even boys would enter the mill at 14, though they knew there was little chance of them being kept on after they reached 19. For the few men who were kept on—as foremen, tradesmen, or labourers in the batching house—there was every likelihood that they would be there for life. For women it was likely that they would leave on marriage but in Prinlaws women appear to have got married later than elsewhere in our area, meaning they were in paid employment for longer. There was also a higher propensity for married women to continue working in Prinlaws than elsewhere. In Pathhead, Nairn's offered the possibility of secure and regular employment and for a generation entering the labour market in the 1920s and 1930s, this seemed to balance out the small wages. The security offered by Nairn's was even more pronounced for the clerical staff. There was an old saying that, if you got into Nairn's office, they would have to shoot you before you got the sack (JSINTER15: 10).

[Mr H.] I think when you left school in the thirties, like say I left school in '36, you would get a job of some kind. I don't think y'had any doubt that you would get a job, no matter what it wis. (JSINTER1: 25)

[Mr St.] There were nae shortage o' jobs. If you worked in—if yer father or yer folks worked in Prinlaws, there were a job for you tae. Irrespective.

[Mrs St.] Oh aye, that wis one thing, yes, if there wisnae at the time ye werenae long in getting' one, but of course as I said . . .

[Mr St.] There were nae question o' you getting' a job—you got a job. The job was there waitin' on you. (JSINTER4: 23)

[Mrs H.] Straight from the school one day and into the mill the next day.

[J.S.] As quick as that?

[Mrs H.] Yes. Ye never got a spell to think aboot it.

[Mrs D.] Ye didnae get a chance.

[Mrs H.] I was actually—my birthday was in May and I didnae start in July . . . I didn't start work till July because there was no . . . I didnae start workin' then till July because I had missed the leavin' date, y'see, which was in April and my birthday was on the sixth of May, so I got another two or three month's grace before I went into the mill, but I left the school on the Wednesday and was in the mill on the Thursday. I know it is unbelievable to the young ones noo. (JSINTER2: 7)

[Mr K.] I worked in Nairn's from when I left the school in 1920. . . . So that was a long time. It's over—I'm 82 . . . Our father was a worker in Nairn's, he was a printer—making the patterns. My sister worked in the canvas factory which was also Nairn's and then I left the school and went to Nairn's too. We had a regular—we didnae have a big wage but we had a regular wage, where later on, when I was pallin w' a lot o' chaps that were joiners and plumbers and all the engineers— they were three weeks workin' an' four weeks off, maybe four month off. But ma steady wage wis—well, we balanced out pretty well in the hinder end, but the billiard rooms were very full, pretty full. Ye know, boys that didnae have a job, even though they had a good trade. A lot o' them went to America but I stayed here.

[J.S.] You said that your father was a printer?

[Mr K.] He was a hand printer.

[J.S.] Had he been in Nairn's for a long time?

[Mr K.] All his life, aye. He went to the, Nairn's, as a hand printer all his days until, after the Second World War, a hand printer was cut out and they put machines in and they were more or less made redundant. Although they kept them in a job they werenae in the same type o' job and after all the years he had been in the hand printin' he took a wee bit difficult to settle down t'wheelin' barrows of linoleum around and all this sort o' thing and he retired three years early. I think it would be because he was transferred down to a mill where there was dust and everything floatin' about and he wisnae accustomed to that so he jist packed it in and that wis what happened to him. But we had quite a good time in Pathhead.

[J.S.] Did you go to work in Nairn's because, your father being there, was he able to get you . . . a job?

[Mr K.] Well, I was—when I left the school on a Wednesday my mother said, 'Go up and see if ye can get a job at Nairn's.' So I went up and saw the manager on the Thursday mornin' and I got started right away as a message boy. I always remember one of the times Sir Michael Nairn, he called to the factory, and it was pretty wet and he had gum boots on and I was standin' in the Time House and the Time Clerk he was out. Sir Michael walked in, sat down at the fire and I heard somebody say [*adopts English accent*]: 'Pull them off boy, pull them off.' I looked around and it was him huddin up his—and I wis jist gonna say, 'Could ye not pull yer own off?' But a good joab I didn't. [*Laughter*] (JSINTER 14: 1–2)

At the same time both firms imposed a form of loyalty bar through restrictions placed on the mobility of their labour forces. A whole series of arrangements existed amongst local employers—whether in the same industry or not—whereby they agreed not to poach on each other's territory and so enabled each to maintain a separate and geographically located quasi-internal labour market.

[Miss S.] There were a few went fae Prinlaws tae Fettykill but very, very few. Whenever ye gave yer address, that was it.
[J.S.] And that would be because Fettykill would have an agreement wi' Prinlaws?
[Miss S.] I don't know if they had an agreement or no but that was . . .
[J.S.] But they just wouldn't employ them?
[Miss S.] The same at Tullis Russell Paper Mill.
[J.S.] In Markinch?
[Miss S.] If ye stayed in Cadham or Markinch ye got in there no bother, but . . . or if ye had somebody there . . .
[J.S.] Aye, I see—if ye had somebody to speak for ye.
[Miss S.] There was more than unions had closed shops. (JSINTER 3: 3)

[Mr T.] And then—Aw, I forgot to tell ye, when I left Nairn's I went down to Barry's, but before I started in Barry's, Jimmy Grieve— Jimmy Grieve wis the gaffer—and I went down and saw him. He says tae me, 'Bob we're no allowed tae start wan anithers men. Ye see?' But he says, 'Take a joab awa' fur a week or twa [two] some ither place and come back.' I went and started along the base for seven weeks.
[J.S.] Along in the . . . ?
[Mr T.] Naval Base. Rosyth. Fur seven weeks, came back and started in Barry's.
[J.S.] So Barry's widnae employ ye if ye came fi Nairn's and Nairn's widnae employ ye if ye came fi Barry's?

[Mr T.] No. That was a sort of agreement they had. They wouldnae start one another's men. (JSINTER12: 17)

Nairn's also operated a bonus scheme which was formally introduced in 1897. Since it was dependent upon the profits made, there was a clear attempt made to promote the idea that profitability was of mutual benefit. The size of bonus could vary widely, though with office-staff always receiving a higher rate than the workers. This was seen as a reward for doing unpaid overtime. The bonus eventually came to an end around the late 1950s but it had become almost a Pathhead institution. Paid out once a year in January people often planned around the bonus, using it to pay substantial expenses such as their rates for the whole year. Even those who did not work in Nairn's and did not share in the bonus remember it vividly as an event. Fergus did not operate a bonus system or, at least, did not operate anything on such a formal level. We interviewed ex-employees who expressly said there was never a bonus system at the mills, yet others recounted how the master would approach individual men, overseers and long-standing workers, and slip them some cash. This only occurred once a year and would be explained by the master as due to good profits. Nairn's's was a much more formal affair and was a right enjoyed by the work-force, yet it was still a personal contract between the firm and each employee. There was no set of rules by which the bonus was calculated, and the transaction was isolated from anything resembling a market process by the clearly understood instruction that no one was allowed to divulge the amount of bonus received.

[Mr M.] But in addition to that we had a bonus scheme. Let's face it, they were old fashioned in some ways but they weren't so old fashioned in hingmy because they paid their workers and that a bonus at the end of the year. If they had a good year ye got so much and Ciss'll tell you in January we paid our rates.
[Mrs M.] Yes, when we were first married . . . off the bonus. We used to pay something like, no latterly, but in the better days—what we termed the better days—they were paying twenty-five per cent. (JSINTER15: 5–6)

For obvious reasons, the amounts involved are impossible to quantify, but we do have the household account book of a woman whose husband worked in the accounts department of Nairn's in the late 1940s. For some of the years she recorded the amount and uses of the bonus: 1948, £58. 4*s*. 8*d*.; 1949, £61. 6*s*. 8*d*.; 1950, £61. 5*s*. 2*d*. These sums were all net of income tax. The items set against these amounts included, in 1948, repayments to the bank (£12), Jack's suit (£5), and material for wallpapering. Next year another suit was purchased and the debt on the lawn-mower paid off. The impact on local social life can be seen in the number of dance and theatre tickets, and the occasional bottle of gin or whisky, that were purchased. It was clear that these sums of money were in some sense expected but were never predictable and hence were not allowed to be part of normal week-by-week expenditure.

PATERNALISM AS THEATRE

Our study of the Kirkcaldy district has shown that the historic establishment of particular industries within discrete localities often meant that individual firms could and did dominate—economically and politically—specific communities. The identification of the firm with its owner, whether a single individual, family, or partnership, was crucial to the identification of employers as paternalist. What industrial paternalism shares with pre-industrial or the rural paternalism of the great estates is the concentration of power and authority in the person of the owner and employer. This gave paternalism its cutting edge, since the legitimation of the social structure depended not so much on abstraction as the embodiment of social expectations (Joyce 1982: 136; Newby *et al.* 1978: 27).

Paternalism contains within itself an inherent contradiction: it seeks to maintain a degree of hierarchical differentiation between rulers and ruled while, on the other hand, it wishes to cultivate their identification by defining the relationship as an organic partnership in a co-operative enterprise (Newby *et al.* 1978: 29). The theatre of paternalism was the means of making this identification. That firms make efforts to get their employees to identify with the company interest is not a management tactic peculiar to paternalism, but what is distinctive about paternalism is the very personal and physical nature of this identification. The paternalist firm encouraged its work-force to share in the successes of the owner and his family, as well as their tribulations, and to live

through them vicariously. Whether it be commercial success for
the firm at trade exhibitions or family celebrations at the coming
of age of a son or marriage of a daughter, the workers were
expected to join in. As Joyce comments, birth, marriage, and
death comprised the symbolic warp from which the family saga
was woven (Joyce 1982: 183).

This encouragement of identification with the fortunes of the
owner's family could not go so far that it might allow the work-
force too great a sense of familiarity; a proper distance had still
to be maintained. In this respect paternalism was like a public
ritual. It was not only that the firm or family put on a carefully
stage-managed show but also that the work-force and their families were both audience and participants. The one role they could
not be allowed to play, however, was that of a leading character.
The theatre of paternalism may have involved the work-force but
it also reconfirmed their subordination.

In both Prinlaws and Pathhead, celebratory events were consciously organized. The people played their parts more or less
automatically. In the following letter we are given the formal
view of the paternalist employer and it is clear that much preparation must have gone into organizing Sir Michael and Lady
Nairn's garden party after he had received his baronetcy. Here is
the formal view of the paternalist employer, as revealed by the
printed card which was sent to all Nairn employees on the occasion of a trip to the Nairn estate to celebrate Michael Barker
Nairn's baronetcy. It comes from the Nairn Archive.

> Sir Michael Nairn, Bart
> To the Workers of
> Michael Nairn & Co. Ltd.

Rankeillor, Springfield
10 July, 1905

On behalf of Lady Nairn and myself, I wish to give expression to our
gratitude and satisfaction in connection with the Workers Trip to
Rankeillor.

The most important element in the success of an open air gathering is
the weather, and we had the good fortune to be favoured with a perfect
summer day. That, together with the surroundings, and the excellent
arrangements made by the Committee in charge, both for refreshments
and sports, made the event an unqualified success.

We were much surprised by the number and beauty of the banners, and were greatly touched by the flattering terms of some of the mottoes on them. Much labour, and no little skill, has been spent on these banners, and on the other objects that went so far to give the procession dignity and importance. Some of them gave evidence of much artistic taste, and did great credit to the men who produced them.

But what pleased us most of all was the orderly and good behaviour of practically all present. It seemed almost impossible to bring between two and three thousand people together for so many hours without damage being done in some way or other. It is a great pleasure to say that no damage whatever was suffered by anything at Rankeillor. As all seemed to enjoy themselves thoroughly and all got safely home without mishap we shall look back with much pleasure and satisfaction to our Baronetcy Trip of 1905.

Prinlaws provided the perspective of a labour force for whom it was simply the done thing to assemble at the front of the master's house even on such a simple occasion as a children's outing. When the master died the workers already knew their allotted roles in the ceremony.

[Jim] I can mind o' John Aitken tellin' me that they went the school trip, or the Sunday school trip whatever, and the local farmers, they supplied the cairts. Whether it wis the open yarn cairt or whatever, and Jock says they went alang that road there and up West Park Drive to the front o' Porter's hoose and Mrs Porter and Mr Porter they came oot and a' the bairns that wis on the cairts sung a sang or whatever and then they got back ontae the cairts and went up tae Strathenry Field and had their . . .

[Johnny] Had their tea.

[Jim] and dae their games an' that. This was the stop doon the road anyway at the Maister's hoose.

[George] Cried the maister. He a got cried the maister. They a got cried the maister . . .

[Jim] It wis the done thing at that time fur tae go that way up roon the drive an' stop at his hoose . . . Even when Willie Porter died a' the workers went along the drive and he wis brung oot the house—ken? And we walked up the back o the coffin up on tae the High Road an' along the High Road tae the cemetery, which is quite a wee distance, for the aulder men. There wis a full turn oot o' the village. (JSINTER7A: 9–10)

Unknown to those who celebrated the life and death of Willie Porter, they were also celebrating the death of a specific management labour strategy.

CONCLUSION

Paternalism as a strategy was strong in the 1930s but was beginning to disintegrate in the late 1940s and went into rapid decline in the 1950s. Paternalism produced a culture of respect and sometimes awe. There was little affection. Success may be measured in our two examples by the lack of industrial conflict. Nairn's experienced two strikes in their history: one about hours in 1872 and one about union recognition in 1939. Both were about altering the terms of the wage–labour relationship rather than about wages as such. Prinlaws had no recorded strike and no union, although some of our informants had heard of a man who had come up from Kirkcaldy to talk about creating a union. Although some of this success was related to hegemonistic domination in which some of our respondents clearly could not envisage an alternative, this was not the whole story. Fife had a powerful culture of class antagonism which resulted in the election of a Communist MP and a Communist influence in many local authorities (MacDougall 1981; Macintyre 1980). The Prinlaws women remembered the very different attitudes of the lasses from the mining villages who made occasional contributions to the labour force. Some of the success was due to the nature of the bargain: a secure job, access to housing, identity with the success of a family and business, in exchange for low wages, personal subordination, and no industrial conflict. In the conditions of wage labour operating between 1800 and 1950, this was clearly a bargain which many working people, especially women and clerical workers, were prepared to accept.

The forces which broke up this relationship were varied. Local-authority housing and rent legislation modified the tied-house relationship, as well as its attractiveness. An increasing number of new firms like De la Rue, a London-based company which took over one of the old mills on the Leven in 1928 for the manufacture of fountain pens, came into the area. Ownership was no longer that of a local family with its name on churches, schools, and hospitals. Many workers preferred the minimal level of welfare capitalism provided by the new firms to the demanding involvement of the paternalists. The entry of American firms into the west of Scotland in the 1950s had the same sort of effect.

They destroyed the authority of the old family firms and introduced wage scales which challenged the low-wage nature of the Scottish economy (Foster and Woolfson 1986).

Other forces involved the economic and organizational histories of the firms involved. The costs of paternalism are not easy to place in conventional economic categories. The initial cost of the housing, for example, might be perceived as a capital cost for the firm or as an investment for the individual owner. Equally, costs such as a local hospital or library can be seen as capital or as conspicuous consumption designed to purchase local prestige. In any case the initial capital spending was a historic expenditure which by the 1930s and 1940s simply existed as an opportunity cost for firm and owners, with no direct implications for the cash flow of the firm. Paternalism did have direct costs. The housing clearly needed maintenance and the bonus needed to be paid. From this perspective then, paternalism depended upon the prosperity of the firms involved. Nairn's had been an innovating, expanding firm. It had survived the depression of the 1930s because of the booming consumer market in the south of England which furnished its new houses with Kirkcaldy lino. As those profits declined in the 1950s, the bonus ceased to be paid and one link of the personal hold on key staff disappeared. Finally, the demography and ownership structure of paternalism was gone. The local bourgeoisie no longer produced sons and sons-in-law who were able and willing to enter the owner-management of local industry. Families were smaller. Other jobs in finance, in the professions, or in the career structure of large industrial and state bureaucracies, were more attractive. New units of industrial production were generated by the branch-plant economy of the industrial estate which by their nature could not choose the paternalistic style of management (Massey 1984). Willie Porter's heirs were simply unwilling to continue the risks and burdens of management. In 1957 they closed the mill and sold the bits to a property company. Nairn's went more slowly. It was taken over by Unilever, then sold to a Swiss multinational, Forbo, and has just completed the move to a local industrial estate.

Thus, obscured by the ideologies of the welfare state and of market capitalism, a key element in British industrial relationships faded quietly from the scene at a formative point in the social change and economic life which has been the focus of this Initiative. For Scotland, the collapse was associated with the loss of local control of industrial capital and the narrowing of the wages gap between Scotland and England. What has the effect of the collapse of paternalism been? The historical record and the dynamic of paternalism described above gives some basis for suggesting that the growth of state and trade-union power followed in Britain as a whole, as also did an increase in wage inflation and industrial disputes.

Many employees are still offered a variety of benefits outside the direct cash element of the wage bargain. These tend to be delivered by a rule-based bureaucracy, often as a result of formal agreement within a corporate structure. The paternalism of Porter and Nairn, dependent upon personal whim and the ownership of property, was gone. The SCELI survey questionnaire asked questions about employer-provided benefits and together with information on housing this makes an instructive asymmetry. Table 6.1 is based upon the consolidated data set of 1,187 employees drawn from the household survey carried out in the six areas studied by SCELI in 1987. Employers are still anxious to secure the loyalty and stability of their labour force through a variety of benefits that are not negotiated through the normal cash wage. This effort is directed towards upper and middle man-

TABLE 6.1. *Employer-provided benefits and housing by Registrar General's social class as a percentage of each 'class'*

	Employer provides pension	Employer provides health insurance	Lives in local-authority housing
1	90	14	3
2	77	14	10
3.1	56	6	18
3.2	64	9	22
4	46	6	32
5	34	3	47
% of all respondents who were employees	60	9	25

agement, as well as towards the key workers who featured in the paternalist's efforts. Missing from the frame are the semi-skilled and low-wage workers who are now provided for by the state, notably in housing. Both pensions and housing have attracted attention as features which have prevented the labour market working freely and hence have become a target of recent legislation. Employers will continue to attempt to secure and structure their labour market, but structural changes in the control of capital mean that the relationship of paternalism will rarely be available to them. The theatre of paternalism has been replaced by the sponsorship of arts, theatre, and sport. The sons and daughters of those who stood at the roadside to watch Fergie Porter's coffin can watch Raith Rovers playing in the B&Q Scottish Football League, or even go to Edinburgh to see art exhibitions sponsored by BP and IBM, but the hegemonistic effect on their workplace relationships is likely to be very different. They watch a national and international media and their fears and perceptions of what is possible are very different from the women who thought that Fergie Porter could evict them from their houses.

The historical record shows that paternalism was an important management strategy designed to create a stable and reliable labour force amongst the lower paid. Although it had its origins in the practice and ideology of the landed estates, and some affinity with twentieth-century rural labour relationships, industrial paternalism had its own dynamic. Its practice was especially suited to the large or medium-sized firm, identified with one area or community, and with the person or family of the owner-manager capitalist: 'the maister'. The establishment of a paternalistic structure involved considerable capital spending, often in the guise of conspicuous consumption on the part of the owner, and typically involving the creation of housing or of some aspects of community infrastructure. The structure of paternalism needed to be sustained by a variety of current expenditures which varied from property repairs to the annual bonus. Housing, social infrastructure, the bonus (deliberately taken out of the market by denying knowledge to the receivers) were crucial weapons in the strategy. 'Paternalism' of this sort died in the 1950s, much later than the historical literature usually acknowledges. For individual firms with a long history of paternalism, the end of the relationship often coincided with a decline in prosperity, but for some of the firms, and for the strategy as a whole, the decline was related to a loss of motivation and to broader social changes. The welfare capitalism and internal labour markets of the managerial bureaucracies had long existed alongside the paternalists and was increasingly adopted as the preferred strategy. Other social forces made paternalism harder to operate, the growth of legislation, especially regarding housing, the increase in state welfare and housing provision, the growing social and political knowledge of labour, and the lack of a new generation of owner-managers who were willing to live in 'Fergie Porter's house'. For nearly two hundred years industrial paternalism provided an element of stability amongst parts of the low-paid labour force, both for managers and labour, and that paternalism is now gone.

NOTE TO CHAPTER 6

1. We are grateful for the support of the Edinburgh SCELI team and, in particular, to Frank Bechhofer for his comments on an earlier draft. This paper was given originally at the SCELI Employer Labour Force Strategies Conference, Univ. of Cambridge, Sept. 1988, and we would like to thank the members of that working party for comments made in the discussion. Our final acknowledgement is to Jan Adams for her invaluable work in transcribing the taped interviews.

The references JS.INTER refer to interviews carried out by Dr Jim Smyth between Aug. 1987 and Sept. 1988. The original tapes are stored at the Research Centre for Social Sciences, George Square, Edinburgh EH8 9JY. Initial enquiries about the interview material should be made to that address. The references include the number of the tape and the page number of the transcripts which were prepared. In all the interviews, the initials JS refer to the interviewer and all other initials to the respondents.

The following primary sources were consulted:

Census of Scotland, 1891, 1901, and 1911, *Reports*.

Census of Scotland, 1891, MS schedules, Registration Districts 442 and 444.

Forbo-Nairn, Company Records, held by the firm, now partly deposited in Kirkcaldy Museum and Art Gallery.

Household account book of Mary, wife of Jack, an employee in Nairn's accounts dept., opened 26 May 1946. In possession of Linda Ramsey of Edinburgh to whom we are grateful for showing us this book.

Parliamentary Papers, 1833, xxi. *Reports of Factory Inquiry Commission into the Employment of Children in Factories and their Hours of Labour.*

Records of Dissolved Companies, 'John Fergus & Co.', Scottish Record Office, BT2/13825.

Valuation Rolls for the Burgh of Kirkcaldy, various dates, VR27, VR50, VR101, Scottish Record Office.

GLOSSARY OF SCOTS WORDS AND PHRASES USED IN THE INTERVIEWS

a	=	all
ah	=	I
aulder	=	older
awa	=	away
bairns	=	children
cried the maister	=	called the master/boss
dont	=	don't
fi/fae	=	from
fur	=	for
gairden	=	garden
hame	=	home
hingmy	=	that matter or person (for which I don't know the word or name)
hoose	=	house
huddin	=	holding
ither	=	other
jist	=	just
joab	=	job
ken?	=	do you understand?
liket	=	liked
ma	=	my
noo	=	now
oot	=	out
pallin	=	friendly
pit	=	put
sang	=	song
stoory	=	dusty
thur wur	=	there were
wi	=	we
yer	=	your

7

The Aberdeen Offshore Oil Industry: Core and Periphery

ANNE GASTEEN AND JOHN SEWELL

INTRODUCTION

During the last decade several commentators have pointed to profound changes in the nature of product markets, which are taking place on an international scale. There has been a movement away from the supply of mass markets and price competition to the development of market niches and non-price competition (Hayes and Wheelwright 1984; Schonberger 1982) and a complementary shift from mass-production techniques to batch (small-scale) production (Piore and Sabel 1984). The last ten to fifteen years have witnessed the increasing internationalization of Western economies, rapid technological development, faster product obsolescence, falling productivity levels, and service-sector expansion (Safati and Kobrin 1988; OECD 1988; Atkinson 1986). Here, the derived nature of the demand for labour comes into play. Such changes, it is argued (Rimmer and Zappala 1989; Atkinson 1986), have labour-market repercussions. To be able to compete effectively in this volatile, highly competitive environment, firms need a more 'flexible' or adaptable work-force (flexible with respect to numbers and skills employed, intensity of utilization, and labour costs). The gains from increased flexibility would be faster growth of productivity and lower labour unit costs, thereby resulting in improved international competitiveness.

The publication of John Atkinson's NEDO (1986) report acted as a catalyst in generating widespread international interest in the issue of labour-market flexibility and focusing attention upon his concept of the 'flexible firm'. Atkinson identified what he

regarded as a fundamental change in organizations' staffing practices. Firms were said to be moving away from the development
of internal labour markets, increasingly referring to the external
market for labour. In response to more volatile product-market
conditions, they were seeking greater 'flexibility' in the use of
labour which had manifested itself in the spread of peripheral
labour-force strategies (i.e. the use of non-standard forms of
employment, such as short-term contract and/or part-time work).

Whilst others have suggested alternative explanations behind
the desire for flexibility, such as the existence of wage rigidities
(Sloane 1989) and increases in the fixed costs of labour—e.g.
fringe benefits, compulsory social-welfare contributions, and
recruitment and training expenditures—(Hart 1984), product-
market forces have been placed centre stage. Firms' search for
greater flexibility in the organization of labour, and, hence, their
increased use of peripheral workers, has been largely attributed
to the existence of volatility in their product markets. The following is a study of staffing practices in the UK North Sea oil industry which operates in a product market subject to violent price
fluctuations and is renowned for its use of non-standard forms of
employment. The data, extracted from the ESRC's SCELI
Aberdeen Employers Survey, indicate that product-market
volatility alone is too simple an explanation for the use of
peripheral labour by firms. As Michon (1981) suggests, the
nature and organizational characteristics of the production
process must be considered. In the oil industry the technical and
organizational conditions of production would appear to be at
least as significant as product-market volatility in determining the
use of peripheral employment forms.

THE INDUSTRY

The history of the oil industry in Aberdeen effectively begins in
the 1970s with the discovery of very large reservoirs in the
Central and Northern sectors of the North Sea. The inhospitable
production environment of the North Sea imposed exacting
demands on the industry, necessitating the development of technology able to cope with the harsh conditions. North Sea oil production only became a viable commercial proposition as a result

of the quadrupling of oil prices between 1973 and 1980; this enabled profitable development of fields, despite their high costs.

Oil-company activity comprises three main phases: exploration, development, and production. The first stage, exploration (which includes surveying, drilling, and rig hire), is the most sensitive to oil-price changes. Exploration expenditure is determined by expectations of future returns from discoveries and the current cash flows of oil companies, both of which are dependent on present prices. Thus, the 1986 oil-price crash resulted in a substantial downturn in exploration activity.

It is the development phase which involves the largest capital outlay on the part of the companies, on platform, pipeline, storage facilities, and other production-related expenditures. Development activity is sensitive to both changes in the oil price and technology. The effects of the 1986 crash, greater emphasis on cost minimization on the part of the oil companies and increased competition among the oil-related firms, combined with the discovery of smaller fields, mean that expenditure on such activity probably peaked in the 1980s (Kellas 1989). Resulting technological developments, the increasing use of smaller, unmanned structures and sub-sea systems, have significantly reduced the development-phase labour requirements of the companies and, therefore, may subsequently alter work-force organization and staffing policies.

The production or operating stage is the least sensitive to fluctuations in the price of oil. At this stage, development expenditures comprise sunk costs: provided revenue accruing from sales at the current oil price covers operating costs, production will continue. Given technology, employment and other operating costs tend to be constant throughout a field's life. Production employment requirements, however, have been affected by the technological advance, leading to lower present and predicted operating costs.

North Sea oil activity is, then, highly capital intensive and characterized by long-lead times but subject to violent product-market fluctuations. A high proportion of expenditure takes place prior to production on platform construction and other capital outlays. Offshore employment and its sensitivity to product-market fluctuations are directly related to the current phase of company activity, i.e. exploration, development, or production

(Kellas 1989). Offshore and onshore employment encompass a whole spectrum of occupational categories, ranging from unskilled manual workers to specialist engineers, senior management, and executives.

INDUSTRIAL ORGANIZATION

The exploration, development, and production of the offshore fields is managed by the field-operators, subsidiaries of the major oil companies. Despite the claim that Aberdeen is the 'oil capital of Europe', few, if any, strategic decisions are made in the city. Strategic decision-making, including the level of exploration and the commissioning of new fields, is located in the corporate headquarters of the oil majors in London, Paris, Houston, or New York. Nevertheless, the complexity of the field operators' task should not be underestimated. The Aberdeen operators are responsible for the management and co-ordination of a vast range of tasks and specialisms: exploration, drilling, sub-sea engineering and diving, scaffolding, engineering, fabrication, offshore maintenance, catering, navigational positioning, and the supply of labour and materials by land, sea, and air.

Five field operators were interviewed as part of the in-depth Aberdeen Employers 30 Survey. The interviews indicated a sophisticated development of core–periphery concepts of workforce organization. All the operators worked with an explicit core–periphery model; indeed, some of the quotations from management sound as though they might have been extracted from the literature: 'Our philosophy is to have a core number of staff in essential positions and a flexible number of agency contractors' staff in positions that are short-term or not vital.'

The core, then, consists of the operators' own full-time, permanent staff, and the periphery is composed of contractors' or agency workers. The rationale behind the use of such a model, often explicitly recognized by the companies' personnel management, is twofold. First, it is a cost-minimizing strategy designed to accommodate a need for short-term or specialist work and, secondly, it enables the spreading of risk in an industry characterized by volatile product-market conditions. The contracting out of various activities by the operators means that, in the event of any downturn in activity, resulting from, for example, an oil-price fall, they do not bear the entire burden of adjustment. The associated labour and capital costs of reducing activity, e.g. redundancy payments and having expensive capital equipment laying idle, are passed on, in part, to the contractors/agencies.

The operators' activities are supported by the existence of a large network of smaller, oil-related firms, including contractors, subcontractors, and agencies—the providers of the peripheral work-force. Sixteen oil-related companies were interviewed in depth. The range of activities undertaken by the 'oil-related' sector is vast: drilling, construction, maintenance, operation of supply ships, diving, engineering, the manufacture or provision of drilling or other specialized equipment, quay and transport facilities, laboratory and technical services. The oil-related sector, as will be seen below, is comprised of three distinct segments: off-shore services (such as drilling, maintenance, and construction, which are central to the production of oil), oil-related manufacturing, and onshore support services. It is in the offshore service sector that the contracting out and subcontracting of activities, for which the industry is renowned, is most prevalent (contracting out occurs in oil-related manufacturing too, but to a much lesser extent).

The nature of the relationship between the operators and the contractors/agencies in the offshore service sector is one of instant response on the part of the latter to the demands of the former. Immediate increases or reductions in staff numbers are required. Cut-backs are effective at once. Contractors fulfil both the 'numerical' and 'distancing' flexibility requirements of the oil majors. Contracting out allows the operators to adjust the number of labour hours employed to changes in production levels (i.e. numerical flexibility), whilst simultaneously distancing themselves from these activities (through the use of workers not on their payroll) to spread risk. In turn, in order to cope with the required instant response to clients' demands (and, therefore, indirectly the volatile nature of the product market), the contractors themselves, and other oil-related companies, operate numerically flexible staffing regimes. Some engage in distancing strategies, hiring their own contractors, the latter effectively becoming the operators' 'subcontractors'. Thus, oil-related companies, whilst being part of the periphery in terms of industrial organization, also contain core–periphery employment structures. Oil-related core employees, however, are less secure than their oil-company counterparts. One of the interviewed contractors stated that if the firm should lose a contract, 90 per cent of the work-force employed on that job would have to go. Should it be a major contract, the company might need to shed core-staff— e.g. the manager in charge and associated secretarial support.

The pattern of industrial organization in the oil industry is shown in Figure 7.1. At the industry's core are the field

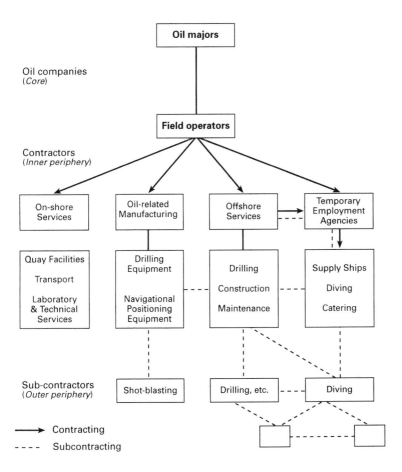

Fig. 7.1 Industrial structure

operators, determining the level of activity within the industry and contracting out short-term or ancillary work. They deal directly with their contractors (and/or employment agencies), located on what may be described as the 'inner periphery', who undertake such work and, in turn, may contract out. If this is the case, the contractors' contractors on the 'outer periphery' become the operators' subcontractors, who may also contract out, and so on. The offshore service sector of the industry is characterized by layer upon layer of contracting out of activity considered to be non-core by the oil majors. The relationship between firms in the industry is one of interdependence, the balance of power depending upon conditions in the market for oil.

RECRUITMENT

All the field operators interviewed described their core work-forces in terms of tightly controlled internal labour markets, with little recruitment of peripheral workers to the permanent labour force. The emphasis was on recruiting young professional and technical staff directly, e.g. graduates in engineering, accounting, and computing, who eventually, having worked their way up the designated hierarchical career structures, would provide the companies with their top management:

We grow our own professional staff and managers. It gives us the opportunity to identify potential early, it represents a return on training, we have knowledge of the individuals, their strengths and weaknesses. We can control the individual's career, it's all part of career development. We are growing the people to run the company. It all underpins safety and operating practices.

The vast majority—80 to 100 per cent—of the operators' top management were recruited through the ranks. Career planning is highly developed, with an individual's potential career planned many years ahead and reviewed regularly. Once future ability has been identified, a training and development programme comes into operation. This involves moving individuals through a number of jobs within the group. The aim is to turn a professional into a 'well-rounded manager' who identifies strongly with the company, so as to ensure 'that we have sufficient people who will be the top management of the company in the future'. The individual operators spoke of the companies as possessing a distinctive corporate style and personality—one manager maintained that, on the graduate 'milk-round', it was actually possible to allocate candidates to different companies on the basis of their personality.

In addition to the core, the operators have worked with significant peripheral work-forces provided by agencies, contractors, and subcontractors, and, therefore, not recruited or employed by the companies themselves. The total peripheral work-force has often exceeded the permanent one. Agency staff and contractors have been used where, 'there is a short-term work requirement, or where the work fluctuates. We use these people in posts where there is a lack of subsequent career development and opportunity, and where the activity is specialised.' Oil-related companies engaged agency and contractors' staff for similar reasons—i.e. work was either short-term and/or of a specialist nature—and in the offshore service sector flexibility (to cope with changes in demand) was introduced into core activities through the use of a variety of 'temporary' employment contracts (documented more, fully in the next section). Oil-related core work-forces tended to be smaller, in both absolute terms and in relation to their periphery, than those of the oil majors, reflecting concentration on a narrower range of tasks. Recruitment of the core, like the operators, is direct. For the periphery, recruitment may be direct or indirect through the use of agencies or (sub)contractors.

Table 7.1 gives examples of the sorts of core and peripheral labour services required by both oil and oil-related companies and indicates that drilling is an ancillary activity for the former. Whilst drilling comprises an integral part of the exploration process, in accordance with the above quotation, demand for it is ultimately short-term and variable (depending on product-market conditions) and there is no opportunity for drillers to develop their careers with the oil majors. Contracting out allowed the non-wage labour costs of such posts (e.g. recruitment, training, national insurance contributions, etc.) to be passed on to the agencies and contractors or subcontractors in the oil-related sector. It will further be seen that in the offshore service sector, drillers may form part of the core work-force, sometimes reaching managerial level, or be located in the periphery, reflecting the

TABLE 7.1. *Examples of labour services required in the oil and oil-related sectors*

Firms	Labour Services			
	Core		Ancillary/ detachable	Specialist services
	Management	Production		
Field operators	Accountants, engineers	Engineers, technicians	Drillers	Systems analysts
Offshore services	Engineers, drillers	Drillers, fitters, welders	Drillers, fitters, welders	Diving, engineering, draughting
Oil-related manuf.	Accountants, design engineers	Turners, machine operators	Painting, shot-blasting	Special finishings
Onshore services		Laboratory technicians, storemen	—	—

duality of employment structures that exists among single-activity firms attempting to cope with the volatility of demand for their services. Moreover, drilling is an occupation where it is still possible for an individual with no formal qualifications or skills to work their way up a rig's occupational hierarchy from Roughneck (i.e. general labourer) to highly paid Driller by learning on-the-job and moving up through the various intermittent grades (Roustabout, Assistant Derrickman, Derrickman, and Assistant Driller).

The continuity of the demand for labour services and, by implication, the degree of security of employment within the various segments of oil and oil-related firms is examined in Table 7.2. The demand for labour services is continuous for the core work-forces of the field operators, hence these employees experience the greatest degree of employment security. Activities which the operators consider to be ancillary, like drilling, will be removed from the remit of the core work-force and whilst they exhibit a continuous demand for labour this is subject to product-market fluctuations; therefore, employment is generally less secure for the employees of the oil-related firms which perform these tasks than

TABLE 7.2. *Continuity of demand for labour services*

Firms	Labour Services			Ancillary/ detachable	Specialist services
	Core				
	Management	Production			
Field operators	Continuous	Continuous		Continuous but detachable from core	Intermittent
Offshore services	Continuous but subject to variation	Continuous but subject to variation		Continuous but subject to variation	Intermittent
Oil-related manuf.	Continuous but subject to variation	Continuous but subject to variation		Continuous but subject to variation	Intermittent
Onshore services	Continuous but subject to variation	Continuous but subject to variation		—	—

it is for oil-company core workers. Operator demand for labour to perform specialist services is intermittent, hence employment with firms providing these specialisms is likely to be more variable.

Among the oil-related firms, the demand for the labour services of core workers is continuous but is more susceptible to the prevailing product-market conditions (given that these companies carry out the operators' ancillary work). While oil-related core workers are less secure than operator core employees, they are more secure than individuals located in the oil-related periphery who work for agencies and subcontractors. There is often no clear distinction between the activities carried out by core and peripheral workers in the offshore services sector (as indicated above by the existence of both core and peripheral drillers) but, to the extent that work is contracted out to other oil-related firms or performed by temporary labour, the associated labour services may be categorized as ancillary or specialist. In this case, the demand for labour services may be continuous, but very much subject to product-market influences, or intermittent where, for instance, a drilling company hires the services of a maintenance firm on a seasonal basis.

The nature of the demand for labour services, i.e. whether it is continuous, continuous but may be 'distanced' (detached), or intermittent, suggests that two distinct forces are at work, serving to shape the form of employment relations in the industry. The first of these might be described as 'technical and organizational', where, *ceteris paribus*, the various productive and bureaucratic processes that a firm is required to undertake may lend themselves to different sorts of cost-minimizing staffing arrangements; for instance, core production and management activities will necessitate continuous employment, whilst other tasks also requiring a continuous flow of labour services (e.g. maintenance, catering, or cleaning) may be detached from the core and some services may be needed only on an intermittent or short-term basis making contracting out cost-effective. The second force at work is product-market volatility; the existence of volatile product-market conditions provides a further explanation as to why firms might wish to deviate from standard, full-time, permanent employment contracts. The existence of these two sets of demand-side forces becomes more evident still in the following discussion of the different types of peripheral employment contracts used in the oil industry.

FORMS OF PERIPHERAL EMPLOYMENT

Oil majors

If the industry is viewed from the perspective of the field operators, three main forms of peripheral worker can be identified. Agency staff are supplied to the operators as and when necessary, usually for a specified and limited period. Their contracts of employment are with the agencies. Contractors' or subcontractors' staff work for firms which provide specific contracted services to the field operators. (These workers may be employed directly as 'permanent' workers by the (sub)contractors, although subject to lay-offs, or they may be employed indirectly through agencies or other (sub)contractors.) Finally, there is the group of peripheral workers employed by hybrid firms of (sub)contractors that also function as agencies.

The oil majors do not directly recruit their peripheral workforces and, as noted earlier, the providers of peripheral labour (the agencies, contractors, or subcontractors) are required to increase or reduce staffing levels instantly. All the non-standard forms of employment contract uncovered in the interviews with oil-related companies were characterized by ease of termination, as the firms sought adjustment to demand fluctuations through the ending of such contracts.

Drilling companies

Most of the drilling companies interviewed used employment agency staff to varying degrees and for different purposes. Offshore, sizeable numbers of such workers were hired for their specialist skills, whilst onshore they were employed to cover for absence or sickness and activities (e.g. draughting) which were not carried out all year round. Agency personnel working for drilling contractors thus tended to be males with specialist skills. This is in contrast to the operators' agency personnel, who tended to comprise female clerical or secretarial staff.

Companies employed (sub)contractors on their own premises to a certain extent. Contractors' staff provided specialist activities not normally undertaken by the company. Among these were the provision of paint crews and the services of various professional and technical staff, including computer analysts. There would thus appear to be considerable overlap between agencies and specialist contractors in providing certain types of personnel to the drilling companies.

Deployment of agency personnel and contractors' staff enhances numerical flexibility and enables the spreading of risk, through the distancing of 'non-core' activities, for drilling companies just as for oil majors. Numerical flexibility was introduced into core activities (e.g. drilling) through the use of 'implicit short-run open-ended' contracts of employment in all the drilling companies. 'Open-ended' contracts comprise conventionally understood employment arrangements. A worker becomes an employee of the company until such time as either party decides to terminate the employment relation by giving a previously agreed period of notice. However, in the North Sea drilling industry, such contracts of employment are implicitly understood by both parties to be of a temporary nature. To paraphrase one interviewee, 'contracts are open-ended, just like any permanent job, but the job is essentially temporary'. The bulk of a drilling company's work-force is then implicitly employed on a short-term basis and subject to being paid off at very little notice in any downturn in activity.

Construction/maintenance companies

The majority of offshore construction/maintenance firms used agency workers to some degree and for various purposes, including specialist on- and offshore work. For some of the firms, agency workers were female administrative, clerical, and secretarial staff, as they are for the oil majors. For all firms agency staff comprised a negligible part of the work-force. Contractors' staff were used by approximately half of the construction/maintenance companies. They tended to be used for highly specialized activities, either not normally undertaken by the company or in response to an increased work-load in such areas. Safety procedures and commissioning work are examples.

The bulk of the direct employees of such firms were skilled manual workers, originally from the construction and shipbuilding industries. For half of the construction/maintenance firms interviewed, the vast majority of the work-force were hired on 'short-term' and 'longer term' rolling contracts, i.e. contracts which are renewable on expiry subject to circumstances; the longer term rolling contracts were more akin to the open-ended contracts of the drilling contractors. Such contracts are used because the work is often short-term and subject to both seasonal and non-seasonal variations in demand; contract termination enabled adjustment to reductions in demand. However, superimposed upon these 'non-permanent' contracts of employment is a traditional 'last-in, first-out' system. Workers were placed on short-run or long-run contracts on the basis of seniority. Length of service thus resulted in increased job security within an unstable employment structure. Pay and conditions are the same for both short- and long-run contract employees; the difference lies in the relatively greater security of employment for the latter. All are ultimately subject to lay-offs.

All these companies had built up a 'nucleus' of long-serving employees who had been working for them for several years. For one company, workers with at least two years' service would be recruited to the core, which was of a predetermined size, when vacancies arose. The remaining maintenance and construction companies had 'permanent' core work-forces, which they augmented by the use of short-term contract workers. The employment structure of these firms was thus of the more traditionally documented 'permanent' versus 'temporary' variety, as opposed to the distinction between short- and long-run contracts outlined above. Compensating differentials operated; for example, contract workers received higher pay than the permanent work-force, their non-pecuniary benefits were worse or non-existent, and the degree of job security, of course, was much less. Very occasionally, recruitment to the permanent work-force occurred, as and when a vacancy arose. As before, the rationale behind the use of such an employment relation lay in the nature of the market in which the companies operated, work being short-term and subject to demand fluctuations.

Other oil-related companies

The remaining firms in the oil-related sector, supplying other support services and products, may be split, very roughly, into three groups: (1) offshore professional, technical, transportation, and supply services; (2) onshore professional, technical, transportation, and supply services; (3) oil-related manufacturing. The use of 'non-permanent' labour, be it agency employees, contractors' staff working on the firms' premises, short-term contract workers, or casuals, was largely restricted to the offshore service sector, which made use of all four to some extent.

Agency workers, for all the firms in this sector, comprised both female administrative, clerical, and secretarial staff and male skilled manual workers and technicians. Contractors' staff working on the firms' premises were specialist computer or engineering personnel. 'Casuals' were either clerical/secretarial staff, brought in to cover for sickness or an abnormally high work-load, or were labourers. However, neither contractors' staff, agency workers, nor casual labour were extensively employed. Greatest use was made of short-term contract workers who tended to be employed in specialist functions offshore, such as radio operators and engineers. Once again, the rationale for using such contracts was that the work is often short-term in nature.

Subcontracting occurred principally among firms supplying offshore services and to a much lesser extent among those in the oil-related manufacturing sector. Offshore service firms subcontracted diving, engineering, and draughting, whilst oil-related manufacturers subcontracted more ancillary activities—painting, shot-blasting, special finishings, and cleaning. In the onshore services and oil-related manufacturing sectors the main adjustment mechanism for coping with changing demand conditions was overtime by full-time workers (also used by one of the offshore service firms). In addition, an oil-related manufacturing firm made use of multi-skilled labour and variations in work effort.

The different forms of peripheral employment contract found in the oil industry are summarized in Table 7.3, which clearly shows that non-standard forms of employment, associated with the contracting out of detachable, ancillary, or specialist activities, are most prevalent among oil companies and offshore service-sector firms. The variety of contractual arrangements that

TABLE 7.3. *Forms of employment contracts*

Firms	Labour Services			
	Core		Ancillary/ detachable	Specialist services
	Management	Production		
Field operators	Full-time permanent	Full-time permanent	Open-ended temporary, fixed/short-term, short-term rolling, long-term rolling	Open-ended temporary, fixed/short-term, short-term rolling, long-term rolling
Offshore services	Full-time permanent	Full-time permanent, open-ended temporary, fixed/short-term, short-term rolling, long-term rolling	Open-ended temporary, fixed/short-term, short-term rolling, long-term rolling	Open-ended temporary, fixed/short-term, short-term rolling, long-term rolling
Oil-related manuf.	Full-time permanent	Full-time permanent	Open-ended temporary, fixed/short-term	—
Onshore services	Full-time permanent	Full-time permanent	—	—

characterize peripheral employment and the range of activities for which they are used provide further support for the distinction between the influence of technical and organizational factors and product-market volatility. In general, contractors' staff appeared to be engaged for technical and organizational reasons, i.e. to carry out specialist work not normally undertaken by the company; only maintenance and construction firms referred to their being used to increase numerical flexibility. The short-term or temporary contractual arrangements covering individuals (whether directly hired or agency workers) reflected a concern with both technical and organizational matters and product-market volatility; individuals were hired to carry out specialist functions or employed on the open-ended temporary, fixed/short-term, short-term rolling, and long-term rolling contracts to enable firms to adjust to product-market changes.

PERIPHERAL LABOUR SUPPLY

The primary focus of attention in this chapter is on the demand-side of the labour market. However, as the implementation of any labour-market strategy is dependent on the availability of labour prepared to accept the implied terms and conditions of employment, a brief discussion of the labour-supply conditions is necessary. Historically, Aberdeen lacked a skilled manual work-force of the sort required by the oil industry; the city is traditionally service-sector-based, fulfilling the role of trading centre for the north-east of Scotland. The scarcity of workers, combined with the need to compensate for the lack of job security and unpleasant working conditions, produces the relatively high wage rates necessary to attract labour from outwith the Aberdeen area.

The political and historical context of staffing strategies are also important in determining their form. A decade of Thatcherism and the progressive deregulation of the labour market popularized the concept of 'flexibility' in employment, thereby legitimizing peripheral jobs. More specifically, the oil industry draws much of its labour from the construction and declining heavy engineering and shipbuilding industries of the central belt of Scotland and the north-east of England. The construction industry has historically operated a contract labour system (its workers being self-employed), whilst employment in shipbuilding has traditionally been temporary. Thus, the oil industry has inherited a work-force endowed with the ideology of self-employment and conditioned to short-term employment contracts.

Finally, the effect of production processes on the demand for labour and how this impacts on the supply of labour has to be considered. The pattern of demand for labour varies between the different sectors within the oil industry and the way this relates to labour availability helps determine the elasticity of supply. For example, the inaccessibility of offshore oil production necessitates the use of shiftwork, the most common form of which is 'two-on and two-off': a worker will spend two weeks on a platform, doing 12-hour shifts, seven days a week, followed by two weeks at home. Such a system widens the hiring catchment area and, therefore, increases the supply of elasticity of labour. Workers from elsewhere in the UK can work offshore in Aberdeen without having to uproot and move house. By contrast, the oil-related manufacturing sector requires a numerically stable, resident work-force to respond to daily demand fluctuations and the local shortage of skilled workers results in a more inelastic supply of labour.

The effect of changes in price and product-market conditions on the elasticity of supply of labour is shown in Table 7.4. Other things being equal, the elasticity of supply of labour will be determined by skill specificity and the size of the pool of available labour. However, if product-market demand is buoyant and prices are high, the available pool of labour would be reduced and supply will be less elastic; in a recession lower product prices would cause the industry to shed labour and supply will become more elastic. Whilst product-market fluctuations impinge upon the oil-industry labour market in the usual manner, firms involved in offshore activities are relatively less constrained by labour-market conditions than onshore firms, as they experience a greater elasticity of supply afforded to them through the use of the two-week shift system. High wages combined with this shift system allow these firms to attract labour with the relevant skills *and* accustomed to 'flexible' employment arrangements.

Table 7.4. Labour-supply conditions

	Product-market conditions	
	Buoyant	Depressed
Labour supply		
elastic (e.g. offshore activity)	less	more
inelastic (e.g. oil-related manufacturing)	more	less
Price	higher	lower

THE COSTS AND BENEFITS OF PERIPHERAL
WORK-FORCES

This section documents the gains and losses associated with peripheral staffing, as identified by both operators and oil-related companies, setting them against the background of the product market demand conditions faced by the different types of firms and notes whether or not such policies are strategic or purely reactive.

Oil majors

For the operators, the main advantage of working to a core–periphery structure is clearly the spreading of risk in a high fixed-cost industry subject to wide price fluctuations. They bear none of the hiring/firing costs of the peripheral work-force and so they can adjust supply to demand without such costs which are passed on to the 'satellite' oil-related companies. Variable costs are thus finely tailored to the pattern of operations.

Disadvantages of a peripheral work-force were focused on those activities where contract workers were involved in tasks also carried out by the operators' core employees. Where an entire activity was subcontracted, e.g. diving, fabrication, catering, or drilling, the specialized nature of the (sub)contractors, together with the discipline imposed by their having to bid for every new contract, was considered sufficient to secure adequate performance. Where agency and individual contract staff were employed, the usual criticisms of a peripheral work-force surfaced.

Lack of quality, poor return on training investment, lack of stability, lack of knowledge of company systems, lack of own management control, lack of management feedstock.

Problem of turn-over, they go if they can pick up more elsewhere. Confidentiality problem. Now try to ensure that sensitive areas not manned with contract people.

Lack of commitment from employee, may affect job development and productivity, turn-over high. Can upset other staff with less pay doing the same work as them.

Agency people work by the clock.

However, these disadvantages were not of an order to deflect the operators away from their chosen strategy of peripheral staffing.

Drilling companies

The drilling companies' rationale for the use of a non-standard employment relation is that the work is temporary in nature and demand can be highly volatile. Managers' perceptions of variation in the overall level of demand for drilling services ranged from slight to substantial yearly fluctuations. Some alluded to a slight seasonal and therefore predictable element, with demand being higher in the summer months. All agreed, however, that non-seasonal variations in demand could not be predicted. Asked about the degree of variation in the overall level of demand, the firms maintained that it had either 'increased' or 'increased substantially' (implying greater uncertainty as a result of the recent slump). All but one company said that the composition of demand had remained constant—it had found that there was no demand for mobile rigs in the winter of 1986 (when the slump in oil activity really began to bite).

All the drilling companies interviewed professed to adjust to variations in the level of demand by terminating the 'open-ended' contracts of employees. Thus, risk was spread across individuals within the companies' work-forces. There were no complaints as such about the loyalty or quality of those employed on an implicitly short-term basis. It should be remembered that such employees are compensated for employment instability and are recruited directly by the company. Alternatively, it could be that implicit, short-run open-ended contracts overcome the adverse psychological effects of being a temporary employee, engendering a degree of loyalty or attachment to the company. Market conditions and not the company are seen to directly dictate employment fortunes. However, the willingness of the firm to discharge their work-forces was also conditioned by their expectations of the future level of demand and not just the current level of activity. One company hoarded labour in the short term in anticipation of winning new contracts. At the time of interview, two rig crews were being maintained on call, at 85 per cent of their normal pay, awaiting decisions on new contracts. The crews were to be paid off (and would then be entitled to redundancy pay) if the contracts did not soon materialize.

Only one drilling contractor exhibited 'distancing'; it subcontracted about a fifth of its work. The advantages of this were seen to be a sharing of the recruitment problem, increased flexibility, and decreased administration costs. The major disadvantage was a failure on the part of workers to identify with the company, resulting in a lack of loyalty which adversely affected performance. The subcontractors' staff were perceived as having jobs less secure than the company's employees; a logical response, as the manager pointed out, since the company used subcontractors because of uncertain demand conditions. The use of agency workers or contractors' staff was deemed to be a reaction to circumstances rather than a conscious personnel strategy by all the drilling companies. However, the use of implicit short-run, open-ended contracts in the face of highly volatile demand is clearly strategic.

Construction/maintenance companies

Construction/maintenance companies too, spread the risk of operating in a volatile market through the use of non-standard employment forms. For all these firms, the overall level of demand was held to vary substantially on a seasonal basis and was therefore predictable. However, during the previous five years, all firms with only one exception had experienced a substantial increase in the degree of variation in the overall level of demand. Half the firms had experienced a substantial change in the composition of demand.

Construction/maintenance companies operating the short-/long-run rolling contract system did not identify any associated disadvantages. This contrasts sharply with firms who resorted to more traditional core–periphery strategies to adjust to uncertainty. These complained of a lack of company loyalty, making the firms vulnerable to poaching and the possible risk that skilled workers, once paid-off, would not be available for re-employment when required to meet an upturn in business.

Two of the maintenance/construction firms used subcontractors for specialized activities comprising only a small proportion of the services offered (less than 10 per cent of work was subcontracted in both cases). Design, electrical, and inspection work were the subcontracted activities. The main advantage was seen to be a reduction in overheads. On the negative side, one of the companies cited lack of loyalty as being a disadvantage.

The use of non-permanent employment contracts, the most important form of flexibility for these companies—covering the vast majority of their employees—was perceived by all as a strategy designed to cope with fluctuations in demand, whether seasonal and predictable, or market-determined and unpredictable. Half the managers perceived the use of contract workers as a reaction to circumstances rather than as a deliberate strategy. Interestingly, although all the construction/maintenance firms face similar market conditions, there is a choice to be made between whether to have all the work-force on contracts of varying lengths or whether to divide it into a permanent core and a temporary periphery.

Other oil-related companies

Other offshore service companies also employed workers on temporary contracts for short-term work. Demand conditions facing firms in this sector varied from substantial annual fluctuations, which were not very predictable (being determined by fluctuations in the price of oil), to the moderate and predictable. Firms facing the more severe fluctuations tended to use (sub)contractors in addition to short-term contract workers. These firms also experienced an increase in the degree of variation in the overall level of demand and a substantial change in its composition.

One of the offshore service firms operated short-term contracts to meet employee preferences for higher pay. Contract workers in all the offshore service firms received higher pay than permanent staff carrying out similar tasks, but their non-pecuniary benefits and job security were less good. They were occasionally recruited to the permanent work-force but only as and when vacancies arose. Disadvantages cited were expense, control, and, for the firm which operated short-term contracts in response to employee preferences, worker commitment. The problem of worker commitment increased with employees' length of service; the longer employees remained with the company, the more integrated they became, and the firm more reliant on workers over which they had no hold.

For oil-related manufacturing firms, which used overtime as their main adjustment mechanism, occasionally supplemented by some limited (sub)contracting, the overall level of demand could vary substantially on a weekly or monthly basis and was not at all predictable. Some had experienced a substantial increase in the degree of variation in demand. Demand for onshore service firms, the other prime users of overtime, varied substantially but was seasonal and predictable.

Cost-saving was the chief gain to be had from the use of (sub)contractors in both the offshore service and oil-related manufacturing sectors, followed by flexibility in the former. Disadvantages, cited by oil-related manufacturers only, were the necessity for supervision and loss of quality control. Among firms exposed to a high degree of volatility in the offshore service sector, the use of contract workers was perceived as a strategy, the objective of which was the minimization of labour costs. Firms facing more stable, predictable demand conditions regarded the use of such labour as a reaction to circumstances.

The costs and benefits of peripheral staffing are summarized in Table 7.5. The benefits of such policies, as identified by the firms, further emphasize the distinction between technical and organizational influences on staffing policies and product-market volatility, with the main users of such labour (the field operators and the offshore service firms) distinguishing between cost minimization (with respect to specialist activities and short-term work or the shedding of recruitment and administration costs for ancillary tasks) and risk-spreading in response to product-market fluctua-

TABLE 7.5. *The costs and benefits of peripheral staffing*

Firms	Costs	Benefits
Field operators	Lack of commitment, unreliable, quality of work	Spreading risk, cost minimization
Offshore services	Lack of commitment, unreliable, quality of work, expense	Short-term work, volatile demand, cost minimization
Oil-related manufacturing	Quality, supervision costs	Cost minimization

tions. A general consensus as to the costs of peripheral staffing appears to exist among the major users, where they identify problems of worker commitment and, therefore, reliability and quality of performance, all of which are likely to stem directly from the nature of such employment relations and the associated lack of job security. However, it should be noted that the drilling companies using open-ended employment contracts and the maintenance/construction firms which operated the rolling contract system reported no such difficulties.

The nature of the product-market conditions encountered by the different segments of the industry and whether or not these are combined with a conscious peripheral staffing strategy can be seen in Table 7.6. The field operators and the offshore service firms are both subject to violent product-market fluctuations and they are the major users of workers hired on non-standard employment contracts; the latter also experience seasonal, and therefore predictable, changes in demand. Oil-related manufacturing firms, on

TABLE 7.6. *Product-market conditions and the operation of a conscious personnel strategy*

Firms	Product-Market Conditions	Staffing Strategy
Field operators	Stable demand, volatile supply which depresses price and profitability necessitating adjustment	Conscious peripheral staffing strategy
Offshore services	Slight to substantial yearly demand fluctuations which are unpredictable; increased demand volatility; slight to substantial seasonal demand fluctuations which are predictable	Conscious peripheral staffing strategy; reaction to circumstances
Oil-related manufacturing	Substantial weekly/ monthly variations; increased demand volatility	Conscious personnel strategy
Onshore services	Substantial seasonal demand fluctuations which are predictable	—

the other hand, also face substantial product-market fluctuations but these are more frequent, i.e. weekly or monthly, than the yearly variations affecting the field operators and the offshore service companies; their use of peripheral manning is limited to the contracting out of ancillary work. Onshore service sector firms, with their seasonal but predictable changes in product-market conditions, make no use of peripheral staffing policies. In general, firms in the three segments which engage in peripheral staffing are operating such strategies consciously.

THE IMPACT OF THE 1986 OIL-PRICE FALL

The interviews took place at a time when the industry was adjusting to the 1986 crash, when the price of oil fell from a high of over $30 per barrel to a low of under $10. The price fall led the oil majors to reassess their activity levels in the North Sea, reducing the level of exploration drilling, reappraising investment programmes, and deferring new projects. The impact of the corporate decisions of the oil majors filtered down through their field operators to the providers of peripheral labour, the agencies, contractors, subcontractors and, ultimately, to individual workers. With the subsequent squeeze in profit margins, the operators not only reviewed their own staffing policies but also passed on the pressure for cost reductions to their (sub)contractors: 'If you are told by headquarters to save 20% of your operation costs you knock hell out of the contractors.'

Major reductions in employment occurred as a result of the 1986 slump, including redundancies among the permanent workforce. The operators had tried to protect their core workers where possible, preferring to pay off agency staff and contractors; however, as the profit squeeze tightened, they came under increasing pressure from their corporate headquarters to reduce operating costs. One of the main ways in which the corporate headquarters sought to control costs was through a reduction in the permanent head-count, believing the operators to be overmanned. The operators were required to undertake extensive staffing reviews which reduced the permanent head-count by redefining the balance between core and periphery employees. Having experienced major job losses affecting the core work-force, the operators were keen to prevent such a situation from recurring, especially as older fields came nearer to the end of their productive life.

> Now there is more emphasis on employing agency staff, we are developing peripheral staff because we are not sure where the industry is going. Also agency staff can now be got cheaper.

> Our philosophy is to have a core, but also depending on circumstances, with the drop in the price of crude, we let people go. Now we take on contractors with possible paying-off in mind. We prefer to pay-off contractors rather than our own people.

> We've increased contract staff to keep labour costs down in a futuristic sense as much as now. We are able to control the number of people we have working in the company. It minimises the administrative costs involved with employment. With contract staff you pay more for the day rate, but save administrative costs, plus there is no long-run commitment.

> Using contractors helps with head office, it keeps the head-count low.

Of the five operators interviewed, four indicated that the proportion of peripheral workers engaged had increased over the past two years. Reductions in both the number of permanent staff and the number of contract staff had followed the oil-price fall, but the effect of this labour shedding and the subsequent re-staffing policies on the relative proportions of core and peripheral workers varied over time. The reaction of the operators had been to increase the number and types of jobs that were peripheral. When new projects came on-stream they were staffed with a higher proportion of contract workers than had been the case with earlier, similar ventures. However, the commitment of the operators to protect those who had been part of the previous core work-force delayed the proportionate increase in contract workers. The initial reaction had been to pay off contract workers in preference to members of the permanent work-force. As permanent staff left and as new project-related opportunities arose, the proportion of contract workers started to rise. The four operators expected the proportion of both agency staff and contractors' staff to increase relative to permanent staff over the next five years. The staffing reviews had identified ancillary or non-core activities which could be wholly contracted out and established lower minimum permanent staff requirements which would maintain the operators' ability to perform core functions. Over-staffing in the permanent work-force was to be eliminated through the increased use of agency staff and contractors. The attraction of peripheral workers also increased with the change in the nature of the work. Large-scale, long-term field commissioning projects were decreasing and there was an anticipation that offshore projects were likely to be of a shorter duration, more varied, more specialist, and less labour-intensive as a result of technological advances.

The benefits of an increase in contract staff are considerable and we expect a considerable increase over the next 5 years, because of our changing organisational requirement, the greater flexibility they give us and also the ability to deal with off-shore manning problems—the abandonment of a field. Increasingly the off-shore industry will be involved in short-term projects and short-term development work.

To ensure a flexible workforce which can meet the changing needs of the company. We are in an industry characterised by change. We have just gone through a big review to enable us to more clearly identify core activities from peripheral activities.

All part of the manpower plan. Identify permanent jobs and non-permanent. We often have short-term projects and for manning these projects they are an integral part of our strategy.

It gives us the use of skills we don't have in-house and the availability of skills we don't wish to have in-house.

It decreases employer responsibility for activities not central to the business of the company. Don't have to invest management time and resources in them.

The degree of flexibility with which the field operators are able to work is constrained by the market conditions facing their suppliers. In the oil-related sector, prior to 1986, when rig day rates appeared to have no ceiling, the larger, more established offshore contractors formed what was effectively a cartel, the Aberdeen Offshore Contractors' Association (AOCA). The idea was to regulate rates to stop 'cowboy' companies with no overheads undercutting AOCA members when tendering for oil-company contracts. Contractors' work-forces were to be certified as being of a certain standard and labour turnover was to be substantially reduced by the payment of almost identical wages, resulting in the development of a more professional image for the industry. When the recession hit in 1986, the infant cartel folded almost immediately. Having failed to consolidate their market power in the heady days of the boom, the contractors, now vulnerable, were squeezed hard by the operators as the oil companies responded to the slump. To quote one contractor's personnel manager, 'The oil companies, having been previously screwed by the contractors, are getting their own back'. The balance of power within the industry had tilted in favour of the operators. The recession and subsequent tightening of oil-company belts meant that only 'necessary maintenance' was carried out. 'Cosmetic maintenance' became a thing of the past. Small companies (usually those without multinational parents) went to the wall. The simultaneous fall in work and competition, as firms went bankrupt, served to increase the supply of available labour to the industry. This in turn enabled surviving contractors to compete for the smaller volume of tenders through wage cutting. As one manager reflected, 'Tenders which used to be won on merit, are now won on wage differentials.' There is evidence to suggest that the operators, having no wish to pay monopoly prices, attempted to spread the smaller volume of work among the surviving contractors to try to preserve the competitive base of the oil-related sector for when the upturn in the industry came.

The fifth of the operators interviewed had embarked on a radically different strategy. The other four field operators were developing staffing policies in a context where new projects were coming on-stream despite the fall in the oil price. Not only was some exploration being carried out but, more importantly, fields where a decision had been taken to commission before the price fall, and where much of the capital expenditure had taken place, were coming on-stream, or existing fields were being further developed.

All the field discoveries of the fifth operator were made in the early years of the North Sea's development. Thus, this company's staffing review took place not against a background of operational change, but in the context of a stable planning environment. Given little likelihood of any new field development, the review revealed predictable, relatively stable labour requirements over the next few years. Equally under pressure from its corporate headquarters to save operating costs, this predictability and stability of future requirements led the company to decide to eliminate the use of contract labour. Savings were to be made by incorporating technical staff and planners who had been contract agency employees in the permanent core. These workers are more expensive when hired on an agency day rate than when employed as staff. As the demand for this type of labour was predictable and stable, the opportunity to make savings arose. Such a strategy is only feasible for a field operator which has reached maturity, and, therefore, attained stability in production.

The very different reaction of this fifth operator to the 1986 crisis again illustrates the importance of technical and organizational factors as well as product-market conditions in determining staffing strategies. All five operators faced a substantial product-market deterioration, but whereas four of the firms, operating against a background of organizational change, increased their post-crisis use of peripheral labour, the fifth, with its stable production environment, enlarged the size of its core work-force to minimize costs. Hence, whilst for four of the operators the use of peripheral labour was a coping strategy for product-market volatility, different technical and organizational factors made it inappropriate for the fifth.

CONCLUSION

Different forms of peripheral staffing practices, with the exception of part-time workers, are endemic in the offshore oil industry. The field operators have traditionally followed a core–periphery model, even when oil prices were high and cost constraints much less rigorous. During this period, shortages of skilled labour and technical staff meant that contract status was desirable for many workers too. The underlying rationale for such a mode of operation is twofold, it minimizes costs whilst accommodating a need for short-term, specialist, or ancillary work, and it allows risk to be spread in a high fixed-cost industry facing volatile product-market conditions. It thus reflects two different influences on a firm's demand for labour: technical and organizational, and product-market volatility. This is exemplified by the operators' strategic decisions which, given common product-market conditions, are dependent upon the stage of the production life-cycle that individual firms have reached.

The fall in the price of crude oil in 1986 resulted in the corporate headquarters of the oil companies exerting pressure on the field operators to reduce costs. The general downward pressure on costs, together with specific head-count limits, led to the operators carrying out extensive staffing reviews. Following the immediate employment reductions, affecting both core and periphery staff, the emergent general strategy within the industry was to place even greater emphasis on the use of peripheral workers when hiring labour. Four of the five operators interviewed, faced with ever-changing patterns of production, minimized labour costs by marginalizing various activities and, in turn, the associated workers. The fifth operator, faced with stable production conditions in the foreseeable future, was able to strengthen the core to make unit labour cost savings over time. Hence, despite the existence of common product-market conditions, technical and organizational variations between firms may lead to the adoption of different labour-market strategies.

The structure of the industry—its (sub)contracting system—not only allows the core companies (the operators) to spread risk and cost burdens across peripheral firms (the oil-related sector), but serves to build a degree of wage flexibility into the periphery. As Gordon (1990) notes, the 1986 crisis tested the effectiveness of the industry's core–periphery structure as a mechanism for adjustment. The operators, under pressure from corporate headquarters to cut costs, squeezed the oil-related companies; the latter responded by cutting the wages of their work-forces.

The oil-related sector may be divided in three: offshore services (at the heart of oil production, encompassing drilling, maintenance, construction, and other support services); oil-related manufacturing; on-shore support services. Demand in the former two sectors varies substantially and is not very predictable. Offshore, variations tend to be on a yearly basis, whilst manufacturing may be subject to monthly or even weekly variations. Hence the frequency and duration of demand fluctuations can be seen to determine their very different numerically flexible staffing regimes. Offshore, immediate swings in demand of a longer duration make an essentially 'hire and fire' adjustment mechanism, based on a variety of contractual arrangements and employment structures, feasible. This is a conscious staffing strategy, evolved in response to market conditions. In manufacturing, turnarounds in demand of a much shorter length, which may well average out to some degree, mean that such an employment policy is not viable because of the greater transactions costs that would be involved (incessant monthly or weekly hiring or firing).

Moreover, the manufacturing sector is further constrained by a relatively inelastic labour supply—the result of a skills shortage in a smaller geographical hiring area—whereas the two-week shift system enables offshore service firms to recruit on a nation-wide basis. Thus, the interaction of product-market volatility (the predictability, frequency, and duration of fluctuations), technical and organizational factors, and labour-supply constraints can be seen to determine the adoption of flexible staffing practices.

In common with manufacturing, the main adjustment mechanism in the onshore service sector is overtime by full-timers. The overall level of demand for onshore services tends to vary substantially, but is seasonal and therefore predictable. Such a pattern allows a wider choice of adjustment mechanisms; however, the historical use of overtime in response to predictable variations in demand has probably not been questioned (Sloane 1989). The onshore service sector, operating as it does under conditions of relative certainty, does not have to consider the use of more drastic labour-force adjustment mechanisms. There is, however, clearly room for manœuvre within the various sectors of the industry with respect to the degree of flexibility of the chosen adjustment mechanism. Witness the split between firms in the maintenance/construction sector. Some chose to have all the work-force on contracts of varying length (the rolling contract system) and others preferred a more traditional permanent–temporary, core–periphery structure.

From an operational point of view, successful adoption of the latter necessitates the isolation of core and peripheral activities. Aside from the well-documented, intrinsic disadvantages of peripheral staffing, such as commitment and quality of performance (which have their roots in the lack of security of employment), further problems occurred, for operators and oil-related companies alike, when permanent employees were detailed to perform the same tasks as temporary workers on higher pay. The drilling companies, using the open-ended contracts of employment, and the maintenance/construction firms, operating the rolling contract system, would seem to have overcome the fundamental disadvantage of peripheral staffing—a lack of company loyalty. In the second case, this has been achieved through the simultaneous development of a seniority-based nucleus of contract workers serving to neutralize the 'temporary psychology'.

In conclusion, core–periphery employment structures in the UK offshore oil industry exist to minimize operating costs, through the pooling of risk, the ensuing wage flexibility, and the smooth adjustment of labour input in response to the changing composition of company activities (e.g. exploration, development, or production). Thus, the main determinants of core–periphery staffing appear to be product-market volatility (qualified by the predictability, frequency, and duration of fluctuations) *and* the firm's technical and organizational conditions of production. The ability of any firm to implement peripheral staffing policies will be constrained by prevailing labour-market conditions (and, therefore, the elasticity of the supply of labour). Successful operation of such employment structures is dependent upon the degree to which core and peripheral activities can be isolated and the fundamental disadvantage of a lack of company loyalty can be neutralized.

III

Employer Policies, Employment Changes, and Individual Perceptions

8

Employer Policies and Individual Life Chances

MICHAEL WHITE AND DUNCAN GALLIE

A central contrast between theories of the labour market is the role that they attribute to employer policies in determining the rewards that employees receive. In neo-classical theory, it is assumed that employers exercise little independent influence on the terms of employment. The market works in an impersonal way to reward employees in terms of their natural abilities or human capital. Employers merely constitute the passive intermediary through which the directives of the market are implemented. In contrast, segmentation theorists assign employers a major role in determining life chances, to the extent that the rewards of employment are sometimes held to be largely independent of the initial skills and experience of individual employees. In particular, such theories point to an important divide between 'primary' and 'secondary' employment practices, which are held to generate quite distinct labour-market segments, offering very different levels of reward to employees.

In Chapter 2, we were critical of the assumptions made by segmentation theorists about the nature of divisions in the labour market. Except in a very small number of 'outlier' cases, employer policies did not cluster in the way that would be theoretically anticipated. Rather, the evidence indicated that employers in practice select from a very wide range of different policy mixes. The pattern that emerged suggested that such policies were less the result of strategic choices designed to optimize the use of labour, than of piecemeal adjustments that reflected limited knowledge and the constraints imposed by the particular path of historical development of the organization. Further, on empirical examination, the various categories of employee that were held to constitute the 'secondary sector' of labour turned out to be very heterogeneous and only a small proportion of such employees met the criterion of cumulative disadvantage. There appeared, then, to be few grounds for conceptualizing either employer policies or employee situations in terms of a small number of types, let alone subsuming the empirical diversity within such overarching concepts as 'primary' or 'secondary'.

However, while the particular conceptualization of the labour market offered by segmentation theorists seems unhelpful, it remains possible that the underlying assumption that employer policies play a significant role in determining the nature and level of employee rewards is still correct. In this chapter, we are concerned to examine empirically the relationship between employer policies and individual outcomes. We will focus upon three types of employer policy. The first are 'internal development' policies, whereby employers seek to develop the skills and commitment of the work-force through providing opportunities for promotion, training, and the recognition of individual performance. The second are part-time employment policies, which are frequently viewed in the literature as directed at the reduction of labour costs and greater numerical flexibility. Finally, we shall look at marginal employment policies, which aim to increase numerical flexibility through the use of employees on relatively short-term contracts. We shall examine the impact of these policies on four types of outcome for employees: occupational level, net pay, satisfaction with pay, and satisfaction with job security.

DATA AND METHODS OF ANALYSIS

The data are again drawn from the six British localities (Aberdeen, Coventry, Kirkcaldy, Northampton, Rochdale, and Swindon) that were studied as part of the Social Change and Economic Life Initiative. In each of the local labour markets, surveys were carried out both of employers and of individuals. Further, the data offer the rare advantage of being able to interlink the two types of survey. The opportunity to achieve a linkage of individual and organizational levels of explanation arose because of the sampling design of the employers' survey. Employers were (except in a minority of cases, added to increase sample size) identified through the individuals in the survey, who were their employees. It was therefore possible to add information, from the employers' data, to the individuals who could be matched with employers. In total, there were 2,005 such individuals, distributed across 981 employing organizations of all types.

The nature of the sample of individuals in this matched data set requires some emphasis. It excluded those employed in establishments outside the study areas (i.e. outward commuters), and those not matched because of missing information or employer non-response. We have no reason to believe that employer's non-response results in a significant bias in the present survey. The exclusion of outward commuters may, however, be of some significance. We would argue that this should lead to an improved analysis in relation to the effects of employers' policies: we are examining only employers in defined local labour markets, and only employees primarily influenced by those same local labour markets.

The individual variables considered in the analyses must first be outlined. The dominant framework in economic analysis is that of human capital, with its emphasis on employee qualifications and work experience as the determinants of individual outcomes. In testing for the impact of employer policies, we decided to control systematically for the types of variables emphasized by human capital explanations, so that it would be clear that any effects that emerged could not be attributed to these. We have adopted this procedure as a methodological device; it does not imply any specific view about the theoretical status of 'human capital' variables. For instance, even if qualifications and work experience eliminated any effects that initially came from employer policies, there could be quite different explanations to those of human capital theory as to why these factors are so important and why individuals differ with respect to them. Such issues could be resolved only through a much more comprehensive research programme.

The survey provided particularly full details of individuals' qualifications, and these were incorporated in the analyses. Individuals' experience was indicated by their time in employment over their working lives, available from work- and life-history data. Aspects of 'human capital' from previous employment, apart from qualifications and experience, we assumed would be captured by the occupational level of the prior employment: we did not habitually include this variable, since to do so considerably reduced the effective size of the data set, but we used it in some control analyses to assess its effect. The survey also contained details of training and length of service in the present employment, but we did not include these as control variables in any analyses, since they should be regarded as outcomes influenced by current employer policies. In addition, we incorporated two variables which sociologists tend to regard as of fundamental importance, both in influencing the acquisition of qualifications and experience, and in continuing to bias chances throughout life: gender and social class of origin (the latter being measured, here, by the Goldthorpe schema of seven classes). We were interested to see how far the outcomes in current employment continued to be affected by these social characteristics, over and above their acting through acquisition of 'human capital'.

The statistical method used was the analysis of covariance within the general linear model (Bock 1975; Winer 1971). In essence, an analysis of covariance can be thought of as an analysis of variance (that is, a cross-classification and comparison of means) where the cell means are first adjusted by a regression procedure. The independent variables used in the regression are referred to, in this context, as the covariates. Within the covariates we always included the variables of qualifications and experience. Gender and social class of origin were usually represented within the cross-classifications for the analysis of variance, but sometimes within the covariates for the technical reason of avoiding an incomplete design (see below).

Within this framework, we were then able to test for the effects of employer policies, as cross-classification variables. From time to time we added further variables either to the covariates or to the cross-classifications. For example, we introduced further individual-level variables to distinguish between policy effects which operate generally across employees, and those which operate selectively by affecting the position of some but not other employees. To give an important example, we included both the variable of being a part-time worker (the individual or contract level) and that of being in an organization with some level of part-time employment (the employer or policy level). The degree of intensity of part-time working in an organization may have additional effects on part-time workers, over and above the effect of their part-time status. In addition, organizations' part-time policies may have effects on full-time workers in those organizations: these can be regarded as 'spillover' effects.

The general approach in these analyses is one of hypothesis testing, not estimation. We wish to know whether the effects upon individuals are different from zero, a task to which the analysis of variance is well suited. Our approach would not be suitable for estimating the dynamic effect of employer policies upon, say, the levels of wages in the labour market. Analysis of variance or covariance provides a framework for hypothesis-testing with a number of practical advantages. The focal independent variables are categorical, so that we avoid problems of outlying values, which are in fact numerous in employer data. Convenient methods exist for testing linearity and non-linearity of effects, and indeed for assessing any other comparisons which we believe to be interesting.

It should be appreciated that the models considered here are all 'unbalanced designs', that is, the numbers of cases per cell are unequal. (We have however taken care to avoid 'incomplete designs' where one or more cells is empty.) The estimates of effects and associated tests of significance for unbalanced designs in the analysis of variance have some of the same limitations as in multiple regression analysis (in particular, the sums of squares are not independent), and the same need for cautious interpretation must be observed.

EMPLOYER POLICY AND OCCUPATIONAL LEVEL

In the first set of analyses to be considered, the individual outcome variable was current occupational level. This outcome is of interest because of its connection with notions of social mobility. Employers' policies could influence mobility in two chief ways: by affecting the opportunities offered to individuals at recruitment and entry-points, and by affecting opportunities within an employment, for example by providing or denying career ladders.

Occupational level was measured by means of the 36-category rank ordering of the Hope–Goldthorpe scale of occupational desirability, derived from the occupational codes of current employment. Despite a number of limitations, the scale (which we will refer to as the HG36) has proved useful as a summary of occupational level which approximates to a continuous distribution for large samples. Research by the originators has shown that the scale is highly correlated with the qualifications deemed necessary for an occupation (Goldthorpe and Hope 1974).

Internal development policies

We formed a simple composite variable to represent policies associated with 'internal labour markets', although we prefer to refer to them by the theoretically neutral term of internal development policies. The composite variable, which had three levels or categories, reflected both the presence or absence of internal promotion, and the use of internal training. These appeared to be the aspects of internal development policy most likely to increase chances of occupational progression. The analysis otherwise contained the standard set of covariates and cross-classifying variables described above. The results of the analysis are shown in Table 8.1, in a condensed analysis of variance table. The importance of the qualification and work-experience variables constituting the regression term should first be noted. The overall regression effect was large and highly significant, a typical result in this set of analyses. Moreover, most of the qualification measures, and the experience measure, contributed significantly to occupational attainment.

Women's average occupational level was shown to be lower than men's, relative to the qualifications and experience they

TABLE 8.1. *Internal development and occupational level*

	Degrees of freedom	F-ratio	p
Regression	17	44.4	0.000
Gender	1	20.7	0.000
Social class of origin	6	3.5	0.002
class 1 contrast	1	15.8	0.000
Internal development	2	3.1	0.046
linear contrast	1	6.1	0.013

Note: The 'within cells' mean-square was 71.41, with 1,757 degrees of freedom.

brought to their current job. The Hope–Goldthorpe scale gives a lower score the higher the occupation. After adjustment by the model, the average male occupational rank was 17.1 while that for women was 19.2. Social class of origin also continued to make a significant difference for those originating from the highest class. Adjusted mean occupational ranks ranged from 16.2, for those from the highest origin class, to 19.4, for those from the lowest.

Individuals in organizations with internal development policies had a higher average occupational level, relative to 'human capital', than in organizations without such policies. The effect was a progressive one (as shown by the significant linear contrast), and this suggests that a more sophisticated measure, reliably reflecting more degrees of internal development policy, could reveal a greater impact upon workers. On available evidence, however, it would seem that the impact of organizational policy in this respect is, on average, less than that of gender or social class of origin. The adjusted mean occupational ranks ranged from 17.5 to 18.8 across the three levels of our simple measure of internal development.

Part-time employment

A somewhat different form of analysis was used to assess part-time employment policy. Social class of origin was removed from the cross-classification variables but incorporated as a dummy variable in the covariate, while gender was cross-classified with whether the individual was a part-time worker, and with the level of part-time employment in the organization. This policy measure was represented as having six levels or degrees of intensity.

The individual part-time employment variable proved to make a very large difference to occupational attainment, controlling for qualifications and experience (F = 48.5, d.f. = 1, 1,694). The gender difference was virtually wholly absorbed within the difference between full-time and part-time individuals. In interpreting this, it must be appreciated that part-time working occurred almost wholly among women: only 20 male part-time workers were found in our sample. The result therefore indicates, very clearly, that women's disadvantage in occupational attainment was chiefly associated with part-time jobs. The effect of different intensities of part-time employment at organizational level (that is, over and above the individual effect of being a part-timer) was not significantly different from zero. The mean occupational rank adjusted for 'human capital' for full-timers was 19.5, while for part-timers it was 23.5.

Marginal employment

We next turn to employers' use of marginal workers (recalling that part-timers were not included within our definition of this group). Here we used our 'standard' form of analysis, with gender and social class of origin as cross-classifying variables. Marginal employment policy was represented as having three levels.

The results for gender and for social class of origin were closely similar to those found in the analysis of internal development policy (see above). Marginal employment policy had an overall effect which was significant, but interestingly this took a non-linear form (overall form $F = 3.9$, d.f. $= 2, 1757$, $p = 0.02$; quadratic contrast $F = 5.0$, $p = 0.025$). The adjusted mean occupational ranks were as follows:

No marginal employment at establishment   18.8
Marginal employment of 1–10 per cent   17.6
Marginal employment of 11 per cent or more   18.3

More establishments using marginal workers fell into the middle category where, it should be noted, there was an increase in the average occupational attainment of individuals, compared with individuals elsewhere. This tallies with previous evidence (see Chapter 2) that marginal employment was positively associated with developmental policies, and further, that individuals on fixed-term contracts were particularly likely to report satisfactory prospects of advancement. In addition, even those establishments with particularly high levels of marginal employment had mean occupational attainment levels higher than those of non-users of marginal workers (though lower than establishments with intermediate levels of marginal employment).

Does the effect of marginal employment policy attach only to workers in marginal employment relations, or are there spillover effects on other workers in organizations using such policies? To examine this a further analysis was performed, in which the individual's contractual position (temporary short contract, fixed-

TABLE 8.2. *Marginal employment and occupational level*

	Degrees of freedom	F-ratio	p
Regression	19	53.3	0.000
Individual contract	2	5.3	0.005
Marginal employment	2	3.7	0.026
linear contrast	1	3.4	0.066
quadratic contrast	1	4.0	0.045

Note: The 'within cells' mean-square was 70.1 with 1,710 degrees of freedom.

term 1–3-year contract, open-ended contract) was cross-classified with the employers' policy. Gender and social class of origin were incorporated in the covariates. The results are summarized in the abridged analysis of covariance table (Table 8.2). For the individual measure, the differences, after adjusting for qualifications and experience, gender, and social class of origin, showed those in short-term employment relatively poorly placed but those on fixed-term contracts situated in above-average occupational ranks. The adjusted mean occupational ranks were as follows:

Temporary (12 months or less)   22.2
Fixed-term (1–3-year) contracts   18.6
Permanent employment   19.4

The results relating to effects of organizational policies (that is, over and above individual differences) were closely similar to those obtained in the previous analysis.

The identification of an organizational alongside an individual effect suggests that marginal employment policy may spill over on to employees with open-ended contracts; alternatively, it may be that organizations with higher than average occupational levels are most able to accommodate marginal workers. The occupational effects of marginal employment appeared to be favourable (an increase in occupational attainment) but unfavourable effects were concentrated upon those with short-term (less than one year) contracts. In addition, the effects were most favourable in organizations which employed a relatively small proportion of marginal workers, and less favourable when more than 10 per cent were employed.

Assessment of 'structural' variables

In Chapter 2, it was noted that employers' policies were quite strongly related to size of establishment and to industry groupings which, in their turn, reflected differences in work-force composition. It is important, therefore, to assess the possibility that the effects of employer policies on individual attainment reflect, at a perhaps deeper level, the influence of these 'structural' variables. To assess this we represented gender and class of origin among the covariates, and then introduced size or industry group of establishment in the cross-classification. This provided a direct comparison of the effects of the structural and employer policy variables.

Industry grouping was particularly associated with part-time employment. Cross-classifying these variables, however, we found that the influence upon occupational attainment of the industry in which an individual worked was non-significant ($F = 1.3$, d.f. 4, 1770), while that of the establishment's part-time employment was significant (overall $F = 2.8$, d.f. 4, 1770, $p = 0.02$; linear trend $F = 10.9$, $p = 0.001$). In a similar analysis with size of establishment, size proved to be significant ($F = 2.5$, d.f. 6, 1751, $p = 0.02$) but the significance of part-time policy was unaffected. When individual status (full-time or part-time) was used instead of establishment part-time policy, the structural variables had no impact on the significance of its effect, while the structural variables themselves were rendered non-significant.

Turning to establishments' internal development policies, we found once more that the influence of industry group was non-significant ($F = 1.67$, d.f. 4, 1780) while that of internal development was slightly reduced but still significant (overall $F = 2.6$, d.f. 2, 1780, $p = 0.08$; but linear trend $F = 5.1$, $p = 0.02$). When size of establishment was introduced as a cross-classification variable, however, neither it nor internal development was significant. A similar result was also obtained for an analysis of size of establishment cross-classified with establishment policy towards employment of marginal workers; neither variable was found to be significant.

It seems, then, that the influence of size and industry upon occupational attainment of individuals is rather small. Employers of different sizes and industry-types may recruit at different occupational levels, but these differences do not in themselves lead to further differentiation of life chances. Nor do these structural differences suppress the adverse occupational effect of part-time working. Size of establishment does suppress the effect of the organizational policies of internal development and employment of marginal workers; but it does so while being, itself, non-significant. The structural variables do not appear to add to an explanation of occupational attainment, and the original set of analyses, excluding them, gives a clearer view. The analyses relating to occupational attainment on balance give support to the notion that employer policies make a difference to workers. Being a part-time worker clearly makes a great deal of difference to occupational level, after making allowance for prior 'human capital'; and the existence of part-timers reflects employer policy. Further, there is evidence that both internal development policies, through training and promotion, and the employment of marginal workers have a positive influence on occupational attainment.

EMPLOYER POLICY AND INDIVIDUAL EARNINGS

Whereas occupational attainment is chiefly of interest to sociologists (although see McNabb and Psacharopoulos 1981) earnings are regarded as of central importance in economic treatments of the labour market. This also applies to many of the contributions in the field of labour-market segmentation theory. 'Secondary' employment policies are regarded as lowering wages by, for example, weakening the bargaining power of workers, while 'primary' employment policies add to the value of workers (by providing internal labour markets) and this leads to higher average wages.

Individual earnings in the current employment were measured in the form of the natural logarithm of net pay per hour. Net pay was used as the closest measure of the actual return to the individual. The notion of 'net pay' is less clean-cut than is sometimes assumed. Ideally, we would like a measure that results from identical items being deducted, whereas in reality partly different things may be netted from case to case. However, it seems unlikely that such variations would be systematic. They are most likely, then, to add to the overall error term, thereby reducing the chances of getting significant results and leading to 'conservative' estimates. Hourly pay was appropriate as the sample included many part-time workers. The log transform is generally used in earnings analyses as it tends to normalize the earnings distribution. Missing data, on earnings or on hours, somewhat reduce the effective sample size for these analyses.

There are advantages and disadvantages to the use of any particular pay measure. The advantages with respect to net pay are that it is likely to be closer to the return to the individual than is gross pay, both objectively and in terms of individual perception. As far as perception is concerned, it will be seen later that there is a marked parallelism between mean net pay measures and mean pay satisfaction measures. We also suspect that, because of its more immediate significance for individual and family budgets, the data for net pay are likely to be more reliable than for gross pay.

The disadvantages are that, for a proportion of employees, it clearly does not represent the overall financial reward that they obtain from their job. In particular, it fails to take account of contributions to company pension schemes. However, such benefits are known to be disproportionately received by higher paid workers. In so far as higher rewards are linked to higher qualifications, such factors will be partly 'carried' by the inclusion of the qualification variables in the analysis. To the extent that such effects are not captured by other variables, we suspect that they lead, in general, to an underestimation in our analysis of the difference between the higher and the lower paid, given that they tend to add to the advantage of those already better off. Our conclusions, then, are likely to represent 'conservative' estimates. Finally, implicit in this type of analysis is the assumption that employers devise policies in the light of some rough conception of the likely implications of the tax structure for employees. This seems a very plausible assumption, although it clearly requires further research.

As is customary in earnings analyses, we have used hourly pay rather than weekly pay. The underlying assumption of an hourly pay measure is that individuals choose their hours of paid work, so that they maximize their returns from both employment and household activity or leisure. If, for example, part-time workers were generally seeking full-time hours, our hourly pay measure would evidently overstate the value of their jobs to themselves. In the British labour market, where there is extensive part-time working and extensive overtime working, the assumption that hours are individually chosen seems broadly reasonable, although there will be a degree of mismatch between preferences and outcomes. In Chapter 2, it was shown that full-timers were on average *less* satisfied with their hours of work.

Internal development policy

To represent internal development of workers, we employed a partially modified composite variable by comparison with the analysis of occupational attainment (described above). One element of the variable remained the presence or absence of internal promotion, but for the other we used the presence or absence of individual assessment schemes (instead of training). These seemed the aspects of internal development policy most likely to influence pay. In the analyses relating to individual earnings, various attempts were made to develop and improve upon the representation of internal development beyond a simple three-point scale. (For example, we distinguished between rates of promotion, and we also added the training variable to the other two, to make a six-point scale.) But the simple three-point scale always outperformed more elaborate versions, and it is therefore this variable to which the reported findings relate.

An initial analysis, using our 'standard' framework of variables, is shown in the abridged analysis of covariance table (Table 8.3). The most striking feature of the results concerns

TABLE 8.3. *Internal development and earnings*

	Degrees of freedom	F-ratio	p
Regression	17	233.6	0.000
Gender	1	113.5	0.000
Social class of origin	6	0.5	n.s.
Internal development	2	8.5	0.000
linear component	1	13.7	0.000

Note: The 'within cells' mean-square was 0.14, with 1,550 degrees of freedom.

gender. The lower pay of women, relative to prior 'human capital', is demonstrated at a very high level of statistical significance. This will involve the effect of women being placed in jobs which are low relative to their qualifications and experience (as shown in the preceding set of results), but also the effect of low within-job-level wages. The adjusted mean net pay for men was £3.03 per hour, while for women it was £2.42, giving men an advantage of 25 per cent. (Note that all earnings are expressed in 1986 values.) It was also notable that social class of origin, which had a significant relation to current occupational level, appeared to have no continuing effect on wages.

The internal development variable, for all its simplicity, yielded quite impressive findings. It was positively related to hourly earnings, and the significance of the relationship was particularly brought out by extracting a linear trend. Although playing a much smaller part than gender differences, the influence of internal development policy seemed more clear cut upon hourly earnings than upon current occupational level. The mean hourly earnings adjusted for the other variables in the model varied as follows:

High internal development   £2.89
Intermediate internal development   £2.65
Low internal development   £2.60

This result concerning the effect of internal development policies was further tested through a number of variants on the basic analysis. First, the non-significant social class of origin was dropped, and the social class of the current occupation was introduced. The thought underlying this analysis was that internal development policy might tend to be more prevalent in organizations where the composition of the work-force was slanted towards higher level (hence higher paid) jobs. But the change did not affect the significance of internal development policy ($F = 8.9$, d.f. 2, 1558, $p = 0.000$): internal development policy raised earnings over and above any effect limited to those in higher job levels.

It could be, however, that employers with internal development policies tend to attract individuals who have already worked in similar organizations and have, accordingly, acquired training which would not necessarily be reflected in our 'human capital' measures. If we assume that such additional training would tend to be reflected in previous occupational attainment, then we can control for this by including prior occupational level (measured again by the HG scale) among the covariates. When this analysis was performed, prior occupational attainment was found to contribute significantly to the regression effect; however, the significance of internal development policy was only slightly reduced as a result and remained highly significant (F = 7.71, d.f. 2, 1250, p = 0.001).

The higher hourly wages apparently earned as a result of being employed where internal development policies are applied, could reflect the size of establishment or type of industry, both of which are known to be associated with differences in earnings. We therefore carried out separate analyses incorporating size of establishment, or industry group, in a cross-classification with internal development policy. In these analyses, gender and social class of origin were included in the covariates. The significance of internal development policy was little affected in these analyses (with size, F = 5.4, d.f. 2, 1554, p = 0.005; with industry group, F = 8.0, d.f. 2, 1571, p = 0.001). The structural variables themselves were significant (size, F = 2.9, d.f. 6, 1554, p = 0.008; industry group, F = 4.4, d.f. 4, 1571 p = 0.002); but one might have expected much larger effects. Presumably much of the differences in earnings between size groups or industries is removed by controlling for gender, qualifications, and experience, at the individual level.

Part-time employment

To analyse the effect of part-time employment policy on pay, we transferred social class of origin to the covariates and added the individual's part-time status (part-timer or not) as a cross-classifying variable alongside gender. The results of this analysis are summarized in the usual abridged form (Table 8.4). It was first of all notable that the addition of the 'part-timer' variable did not take away from the significance of the gender effect on hourly earnings, which remained the salient feature of the results. This was in sharp contrast to the analysis of occupational attainment, where the gender effect operated entirely through part-time status. The part-timer variable was, nevertheless, highly significant. Net

TABLE 8.4. *Part-time employment and earnings*

	Degrees of freedom	F-ratio	p
Regression	18	30.6	0.000
Gender	1	149.8	0.000
Part-timer	1	30.6	0.000
Part-time policy	5	5.0	0.000
linear component	1	22.5	0.000

Note: The 'within cells' mean-square was 0.11 with 1,565 degrees of freedom.

hourly pay was affected both by gender and by part-time status. Furthermore, the establishment's part-time employment policies had a significant effect over and above the individual part-time status effect. The linear trend component of part-time employment policy was, indeed, very highly significant.

If the mean differences in adjusted (ex 'human capital') net hourly pay are examined, it is clear that a part-time employment policy has the general effect of lowering pay for employees. There was a clear differential in favour of employees in establishments with low part-time intensity over those in establishments with high part-time intensity. Since individual part-time status has been controlled for, this indicates the effects of part-time policy for the work-force as a whole rather than for part-timers as a distinct category. Indeed, once other factors have been controlled for, part-timers themselves would appear to receive higher net hourly earnings than full-timers.

One contributory factor in this result was the high average earnings of the very small number of part-time men. To clarify matters, a new composite variable was formed, with categories: 1 = male, 2 = female full-timers, 3 = female part-timers. The analysis was replayed with this variable substituting for both the gender and part-timer variables. Naturally, this composite variable was highly significant (F = 70.9, d.f. 1, 1,571); the significance of the other terms was much as before. The chief interest of the analysis, however, lay in the clarification it provided of the patterns of adjusted mean net hourly pay. These are summarized in Table 8.5.[1] The results confirmed that female part-timers, within

TABLE 8.5. *Hourly earnings adjusted for differences in human capital*

Individual	£
Male (all)	2.76
Female full-time	2.13
Female part-time	2.40
% of part-timers at establishment	
0	2.63
1–9	2.52
10–24	2.43
25–49	2.44
50–74	2.33
75–100	2.20

this sample, had an advantage over female full-timers in terms of net hourly pay, relative to 'human capital'. The overall pattern is that, if no adjustment is made for qualifications and work experience, female part-timers receive lower *gross* hourly pay and equal *net* pay when compared with female full-timers.[2] It is when qualifications and work experience are controlled for that their relative net pay advantage emerges.

Clearly, this should not be taken as indicating any overall advantage in the financial rewards part-timers receive. They are likely to be less well provided for than full-timers in terms of factors such as pensions and holiday pay. Their advantage with respect to net pay in good part reflects the operation of the tax system. However, higher hourly net pay may have significant consequences for people's perceptions of and satisfaction with their jobs. It has been noted elsewhere (Ch. 2) that there is an apparent paradox, with part-time workers showing relatively high levels of satisfaction with relatively low levels of gross hourly pay. Their more favourable position with respect to net hourly pay may be one of the factors that account for this. Finally, the more refined analysis confirmed that establishments with few or no part-timers paid better than those with large proportions of part-timers. This reflects the distinction which was earlier drawn between 'individual', or direct, effects of a policy, and 'spillover' effects. The differential arising from intensity of part-time employment at an establishment is not confined to part-timers.

As with internal development policy, we performed a separate analysis adding prior occupational level (via the HG36 scale) to the covariates. This was intended to provide some control for work-history effects not captured by the 'human capital' measures; for example, current part-time working might reflect a history in which qualifications were disused over a considerable period. Gender and social class of origin were included in the covariates, and part-time policy was cross-classified only with individual part-time status. Adding this variable, however, had little effect upon the significance of the variables relating to part-time status and part-time employment policy, which remained highly significant.

Part-time working was concentrated to a high degree in marketed routine services (retailing, hotels, and catering) and in knowledge-based public services (education, health, and social services). It is important, then, to control for industry to see whether the effect of part-time working can be explained away by industry differences. The establishment-level part-time variable was cross-classified with industry group (with gender and social class of origin among the covariates); part-time working at the individual level was omitted from this analysis, because its inclusion led to an incomplete design. When industry group was present, the effect of part-time policy on hourly earnings was indeed diminished, but not suppressed. The overall test of effect was non-significant ($F = 1.4$, d.f. 4, 1,561), but the linear trend remained just significant ($F = 4.3$, $p = 0.04$). The effect of industry group on hourly earnings was itself chiefly concentrated in marketed routine services (overall effect of industry group, $F = 3.3$, d.f. 4 = 4, 1,561, $p = 0.009$; for routine marketed services, $F = 9.3$, $p = 0.002$). It seems, then, that the effect of part-time employment policy on hourly earnings can be interpreted in part, though not wholly, as a result of the concentration of such policy in the low-wage retail, hotel, and catering industries. Replacing industry group by size of establishment resulted in no substantial change in the effect attributed to part-time employment policy, and indicated that this effect was largely independent of size.

Marginal employment policy

Marginal employment has different characteristics from part-time employment, both from the viewpoint of the employer and from that of the individual (see Ch. 2). We carried out our basic analysis with gender and social class of origin as the cross-classifying variables along with marginal employment policy. The result indicated that marginal employment policy was related to hourly earnings at a just-significant level ($F = 3.1$, d.f. 2, 1,548, $p = 0.045$). This effect arose from a difference between those making any use of marginal workers, and those making no use, with the former group's workers earnings more on average. The adjusted (ex human capital) net hourly earnings were:

No marginal workers used	£2.59
Marginal workers 1–10% of employees	£2.71
Marginal workers 11% plus of employees	£2.70

It should be recalled that the analysis which focused upon current occupational level suggested that use of marginal workers was associated with increased average occupational attainment, relative to 'human capital'. The present finding, that marginal employment policy is also associated with increased hourly pay, suggests that the increased occupational attainment is at least to some extent reflected in earnings.

The small effect of marginal worker employment policy (less than a 5 per cent differential) was shown to be wholly suppressed when size of establishment was introduced into the analysis. The tendency for establishments making use of marginal workers to be linked to higher adjusted net hourly pay, can probably be reduced to the association between use of marginal workers and larger establishments (which also tend to pay more). A further analysis sought to assess the separate effects on net hourly pay of marginal employment policy and of individuals' marginal contractual status. For this analysis, gender and class of origin were shifted to the covariates. The chief findings of this analysis are shown in the usual abridged analysis of variance table (Table 8.6). It can be seen that marginal employment policy continued to have a just-significant effect. Differences between marginal and permanent contracts, however, at the individual level, were associated with substantial differences in net hourly pay (adjusted for human capital, gender, and social class of origin). The estimated means for hourly earnings adjusted for differences in human capital were:

TABLE 8.6. *Marginal employment and earnings*

	Degrees of freedom	F-ratio	p
Regression	19	34.0	0.000
Individual contract	2	21.5	0.000
Marginal employment policy	2	2.6	0.079
linear contrast	1	4.2	0.042

Note: The 'within cells' mean-square was 0.13 with 1,569 degrees of freedom.

Temporary (12 months or less)	£2.34
Fixed-term (1–3-year) contract	£1.97
Permanent contract	£2.60

With 'human capital' and gender controlled, it was the workers on fixed-term contracts who were the least well paid. Those on short-term contracts received a better return, although still substantially below that of the permanent employees.

This analysis demonstrates that marginal workers, in the sense in which we have used the term, are at a considerable disadvantage in terms of pay. There is a strong contrast here, in the case of those on fixed-term contracts, with the findings concerning occupational level. Their relatively favourable occupational attainment was not reflected in pay.

Policies indirectly affecting employment conditions

Employer policies of potential relevance to labour-market differentiation can be separated into inner and outer groups. The inner group consists of the policies directly affecting the employment relationship, while the outer group may influence the use of these inner policies, and so have an indirect effect. The final set of analyses focusing upon hourly earnings related to this group of outer policy variables. In particular, we performed a number of analyses concerning adoption of technological change, and trade-union recognition. If, as we suppose, it is the inner group of policies (internal development, part-time employment, etc.) which chiefly affect outcomes for individuals, with the outer group acting only indirectly, then we would find the latter having relatively weak effects.

Technology

A simple three-level variable represented degree of technological change, based on the presence or absence of new computer systems, and of micro-electronics in new plant and equipment. The standard form of analysis, with gender and social class of origin as cross-classifying variables, resulted in Table 8.7. The overall effect of technology was non-significant, but the linear trend effect was moderately significant, and in the expected direction: increasing technology was associated with higher hourly earnings. Since adoption of technology is strongly associated with size of establishment, we also performed an analysis in which gender and social class of origin were placed in the covariates, and technology was cross-classified with size. This resulted in the complete elimination of a technology effect on hourly earnings ($F = 0.04$), while the size effect was significant to the extent already shown in our previous analyses. These findings suggest that, while the effects of technology upon earnings are not without interest, they are not of a magnitude to force any reinterpretation of the earlier findings concerning employers' policies.

TABLE 8.7. *Technology and earnings*

	Degrees of freedom	F-ratio	p
Regression	17	22.7	0.000
Gender	1	109.9	0.000
Social class and origin	6	0.5	n.s.
Technology	2	2.1	0.119
linear component	1	4.3	0.039

Note: The 'within cells' mean-square was 0.14 with 1,550 degrees of freedom.

Unionization

Trade unionism can be assessed either at the individual level (whether a worker is or is not a member of a union), or at the organizational level (for example, whether or not any trade union has been granted recognition). Both variables were available in the linked data. There is a large literature and a continuing tradition of (largely econometric) research into the 'trade union wage mark-up'. Although our aims were different from this tradition, it appeared desirable that the analysis should incorporate the main variables used there, to provide some degree of comparability. We therefore departed somewhat from our standard practice, and incorporated, as additional variables within the covariates: area (five dummy variables), size (six dummy variables), industry group (four dummy variables), and job level (five dummy variables). Gender and social class of origin were also included in the covariates along with the usual set reflecting qualifications and work experience.

With this formulation, we first used trade-union recognition (the organizational level) as the sole classifying variable. The 'mark-up' was in the expected direction, but it was of small magnitude (about 3 per cent), and non-significant (F = 2.0, d.f. 1, 1,590, p = 0.157). Subsequent analyses, cross-classifying trade-union recognition with (a) part-time intensity, (b) internal development policy, and (c) marginal worker intensity, made little difference to the trade-union effect. In these analyses, the effects of part-time policy and of internal development policy upon net hourly pay remained significant. The effect of marginal worker employment policy was non-significant, but this was as expected since it has already been shown that the inclusion of establishment size suppresses this effect.

It may be that trade-union recognition was too weak an indicator of unionization, which would be better captured by a measure of trade-union density. We therefore turned to the individual-level variable, trade-union membership. Trade-union members are more likely to be found in establishments with high union density, and as this is generally associated with size of establishment, we would expect to find a large proportion of individual members in high-density establishments. Hence, although it is an individual variable, trade-union membership is also associated with and transmits organizational differences. In addition, however, trade-union members in non-union establishments may continue to gain advantages in terms of wages, since employers may feel it is prudent to follow national rates and increases for groups with a union cachet.

Using trade-union membership as the sole classifying variable, we found that it was, indeed, highly significant (F = 8.5, d.f.1, 1,600, p = 0.005). The adjusted average net hourly pay for trade-union members was £2.64, while for a non-member it was £2.49, a mark-up of 6 per cent. Trade-union membership was then cross-classified with part-time employment policy, with the result given in Table 8.8. The effect of trade-union membership upon earnings was unaffected by the inclusion of part-time employment policy. The overall effect of part-time policy was reduced in this analysis, but the linear trend remained highly significant. Moreover, the reduction in the effect could be attributed to the presence in the covariates of the structural variables, especially industry group.

TABLE 8.8. *Union membership, part-time employment, and earnings*

	Degrees of freedom	F-ratio	p
Regression	38	23.1	0.000
Part-time policy	5	1.8	0.105
linear component	1	8.1	0.005
Union membership	1	8.7	0.003

Note: The 'within cells' mean-square was 0.11 with 1,590 degrees of freedom.

Broadly similar results were obtained when union membership was cross-classified with internal development policy. The significance of union membership was unaffected (F = 9.0, d.f. 1, 1,596, p = 0.003), while that of internal development policy was somewhat reduced, but remained highly significant (overall effect F = 4.9, d.f. 2, 1,596, p = 0.008). When cross-classified with marginal worker employment policy, the effect of union membership on pay was again unchanged, while the effect of the other was non-significant, probably once more because of the presence of size of establishment among the covariates.

These results, taken as a whole, suggest that our original conceptualization of trade unionism as a contextual influence upon employers' work-force policies needs to be modified. Union membership and work-force policies appear to act upon earnings rather independently of one another. For example, it is clearly not the case that the effect of unionism requires internal development policies, or a curtailment of part-time employment, to be transmitted. Equally, it is evident that these work-force policies are more than a mere expression of wider differences between highly unionized and less unionized establishments.

SATISFACTION WITH ASPECTS OF EMPLOYMENT

Finally, we have examined the impact of employer policy on people's satisfaction with their pay and with their job security. There were several reasons for interest in these measures. First and foremost, the feelings aroused in working life (both positive and negative) extend beyond what can be measured in terms of economic rewards. Hence it is inherently important to attend to the effects upon individual satisfactions which may result from employer policies. Furthermore, the findings which we have outlined above suggest that employers are able to alter individuals' returns to their 'human capital' through the policies which they apply. Why do workers accept such differentiation, in cases where it works to their apparent detriment? Part of the answer may lie within the plane of personal satisfactions and perceptions.

It appeared sensible to retain, for analyses of satisfaction, the framework already used in the analysis of current occupational level and of hourly earnings. Hence our covariates include qualifications, work experience, gender, and social class of origin. The interpretation of these variables, however, is different when connected to satisfaction. We regard them as influences upon expectations, which are here not directly measured, and it is relative to expectations that satisfaction is formed and expressed. Qualifications and work experience will tend to raise expectations and hence, other things being equal, to have negative effects on satisfaction: the expectations of the more highly qualified or the more experienced will be greater than those of the less qualified or less experienced. Expectations, similarly, may vary because of the social conditioning attaching to gender and to class of origin. (This form of model of satisfaction has been extensively developed and applied by psychologists: see Adams 1963, 1965; Goodman 1974; Lawler 1971; Locke 1976.) The main focus remains the influence of employers' work-force policies, and these continue to be represented as cross-classifying variables. The analysis of satisfaction does, however, introduce some new questions, which require extra variables to be included, and these will be discussed as they arise.

Satisfaction with pay

In analysing satisfaction with pay, there were two additional influences to be taken into account. One was, naturally, the actual level of pay. By controlling for actual pay, one makes the adjusted satisfaction variable as far as possible a subjective response. If one did not do so, the analyses of pay satisfaction could very well simply cover the same ground already covered in our analyses of actual pay. Accordingly, we placed the log of net hourly pay among the covariates. However, to minimize reductions in the effective sample size, we imputed missing pay values through the average pay calculated for each broad occupational group in the survey.

Another possibility was that satisfaction with pay was conditioned by the individual's satisfaction with hours. This appeared to be particularly important, because of our interest in the influence of part-time working upon pay satisfaction. If a part-time worker seeks short working hours as a priority, and if low wages are seen as inseparable from part-time employment, then a lowering of wage expectations will result, and this will lead, other things being equal, to a raising of pay satisfaction. A difficulty in using satisfaction with hours of work to 'predict' satisfaction with pay is that each is certain to be related to general or overall satisfaction with employment, so that a spurious correlation will result. To counter this, we separately regressed both pay satisfaction and hours satisfaction upon a measure of overall satisfaction with employment, and used the standardized residuals from these analyses as the new 'net' satisfaction variables.

To recapitulate, the analysis on which we shall report contained the following variables: in the covariates, the usual measures of qualifications and experience, gender, social class of origin, actual log hourly net pay, and 'net' hours satisfaction. The first analysis to be reported contained, in the cross-classification, individual part-time status, employer part-time policy, and internal development policy. In this way, we brought together in one analysis two of the main employer policies known to have an influence upon actual pay.

Considering the covariates first, the analysis revealed the expected effects upon satisfaction of the qualification variables. Five qualification dummies were significant (on a univariate test), and of these four had negative influences upon satisfaction; the one positive influence was attached to the lowest level of qualification coded. Actual pay was, also as expected, very strongly and positively related to pay satisfaction. Satisfaction with working hours was, likewise, strongly and positively related to pay satisfaction. There was some tendency for women to be more satisfied than men with their pay, suggesting lowered expectations, but this fell just short of significance on a univariate test.

It can be claimed, then, that the covariates provide a reasonably coherent background view of pay satisfaction, although (as is usually the case in studies of satisfaction) the degree of explanation achieved by these 'objective' variables was much smaller than in the case of the analysis of occupational level or actual pay. From this we can proceed to look at the effects of the employer policies. These are summarized in Table 8.9. The first point to be noted is that internal development policy had no discernible effect on pay satisfaction. This was not wholly surprising, since the earlier analyses suggested that internal development raised current occupational level as well as current earnings; it was likely, therefore, to raise pay expectations, if these develop relative to occupational level. It might be thought that the nonsignificant result here was brought about by a dominating effect

TABLE 8.9. *Part-time employment, internal development, and satisfaction with pay*

	Degrees of freedom	F-ratio	p
Regression	26	6.2	0.000
Part-timer	1	7.0	0.008
Part-time policy	4	3.1	0.016
'none' v. 'any'	1	11.1	0.001
Internal development	2	0.6	n.s.

Note: The 'within cells' mean-square was 0.9 with 1,688 degrees of freedom.

of the part-time variables, but this was not the case. A separate analysis, in which both the part-time variables were omitted, showed internal development policy to have no effect on pay satisfaction even when considered on its own.

The most interesting part of the table concerns the part-time variables themselves. To recapitulate the earlier analyses, assessing influences on actual pay, the part-time influences on pay were partitioned between an individual level and an organizational level. When this was done, and when the measure of pay was net hourly earnings adjusted for prior 'human capital', it was found that (a) all kinds of workers in establishments with high intensities of part-time working were paid less than workers in establishments with low intensities of part-time working, but (b) part-time women workers earned higher net hourly pay than full-time women workers. Table 8.9 shows that both these aspects of part-time working continued to have highly significant effects upon pay satisfaction. It should be recalled that this was after controlling both for actual differences in pay and for differences in satisfaction with hours. The adjusted mean pay satisfaction scores showed that attitudes conformed very closely to the real differences in net pay which were established by the previous analyses. Part-timers were more satisfied with their pay than were full-timers; those in establishments with higher proportions of part-timers were less satisfied than those in establishments with lower proportions. There was a particularly marked difference in satisfaction in favour of those in establishments without any part-timers, compared with the rest.

Within the bounds of these labour markets, it appears that part-time employment was associated for women with some advantage in terms of net hourly pay as well as with a high level of satisfaction with work hours. Not unreasonably, this was reflected in their positive satisfaction with pay. However, it would clearly be mistaken to infer, from this, that workers were oblivious to the organizational, as opposed to individual, implications for pay of different policies. On the contrary, they appear to perceive that part-time working, *qua* organizational policy, is linked to reduced pay levels, and react accordingly. This negative reaction to part-time employment policy is not, of course, confined to part-time workers, but applies also to full-time workers.

The final analysis of satisfaction with pay was concerned with the effects of marginal employment policy and of the associated differences in individual contracts. It was found that both the establishment-level and the individual-level aspects of marginal employment were non-significant in overall terms (for establishment level, $F = 2.7$, on 2, 1,798 degrees of freedom, $p = 0.07$; for individual level, $F = 2.4$, $p = 0.09$); but they were significant in terms of particular contrasts. The effects are most simply presented in terms of the estimated mean satisfaction scores, adjusted for covariates (Table 8.10). The highest average levels of satisfaction were displayed by those on short-term contracts, and by employees in establishments which employed considerable proportions of marginal workers. The previous analyses of actual pay showed that marginal workers, and especially those on fixed-term contracts, were poorly paid (ex 'human capital' and gender) by comparison with permanent workers. That this was not reflected in satisfaction, presumably reflects differences in expectations. Temporary workers (on contracts lasting less than twelve months) had in many cases experienced unemployment (see Ch. 2), and, as shown earlier in the present chapter, they tended to be employed at a low occupational level relative to qualifications and experience.

TABLE 8.10. *Marginal employment, contract type, and satisfaction with pay*

	Adjusted mean satisfaction*
No marginal workers at establishment	−0.03
1–10% marginal workers	−0.06
11+% marginal workers	0.10
Temporary (less than 12 months)	0.15
Fixed-term (1–3 year) contract	−0.06
Permanent employment	−0.07

* Standardized satisfaction scores.

Satisfaction with job security

Writers on labour-market differentiation have generally stressed the importance of job security, and the emphasis on this has become particularly salient with the development of theories of labour-market segmentation. These have generally associated precariousness with non-standard contracts of employment, and so our analysis revolves around policies of part-time and marginal employment. However, it is far from obvious that precariousness resides wholly or even mainly in these contracts. In the first place, part-timers generally have, at face value, high levels of satisfaction with security (see Ch. 2). In the second place, previous research has shown that large proportions of workers succumbing to prolonged unemployment during the 1980s did so after substantial periods of service under standard contractual forms (White 1983; White and McRae 1989). So other aspects of employers' policies, such as their propensity to make work-force reductions, may be important for feelings of job security or insecurity among workers of all kinds. In all the analyses, therefore, we included a variable, from the employers' survey, which reported whether or not there had been a reduction of workers deemed 'surplus to requirements' during the preceding two years.

An initial analysis was designed to clarify the relative roles of part-time working at the individual and organizational levels. The work-force reduction variable was placed in the covariates, along with gender, social class of origin, qualifications, and experience. The cross-classified variables were the individual's part-time status, and the employer's part-time policy. The dependent variable was standardized satisfaction with job security. The chief results are displayed in the usual abridged analysis of variance table (Table 8.11). Although the regression term was significant, only one variable was significant on a univariate test. This was the work-force reduction variable: absence of work-force

TABLE 8.11. *Part-time employment and satisfaction with job security*

	Degrees of freedom	F-ratio	p
Regression	25	2.6	0.000
Part-timer	1	1.2	n.s.
Part-time policy	4	3.7	0.005
'none' v. mean	1	10.8	0.001

Note: The 'within cells' mean-square was 0.98 with 1,708 degrees of freedom.

reductions was very strongly related to satisfaction with job security. Gender was near-significant, with women tending to be, to a small extent, more satisfied.

The striking and somewhat unexpected finding was that, when satisfaction with job security was partitioned between the individual and organizational levels of part-time working, it was the organizational variable which proved significant. With part-time intensity represented at five levels, the adjusted mean satisfaction scores were as follows:

No part timers	−0.16
1–9% part-timers	0.07
10–19% part-timers	−0.06
20–49% part-timers	0.03
50–100% part-timers	0.10

Establishments with low but non-zero levels of part-time working departed from an otherwise orderly pattern, the establishments with no part-timers being the least satisfied with job security and those with a predominance of part-timers being the most satisfied.

A similar analysis was carried out to examine how marginal working affected feelings of job security, except that work-force reduction was shifted to the cross-classifying variables so as to assess its effect on a par with those of marginal working. The findings are summarized in Table 8.12. The covariates weakly affected satisfaction with job security. Turning to the main effect variables, the analysis chiefly confirmed that there were great dif-

TABLE 8.12. *Marginal employment, work-force reductions, and satisfaction with job security*

	Degrees of freedom	F-ratio	p
Regression	24	1.9	0.005
Contract	2	177.8	0.000
short-term v. mean	1	347.8	0.000
1–3 years v. mean	1	8.6	0.003
Marginal working	2	0.1	n.s.
Work-force reductions	1	48.0	0.000

Note: The 'within cells' mean-square was 0.81 with 1,790 degrees of freedom.

ferences in feelings of security or insecurity depending upon contractual status, and upon the presence or absence of work-force reductions in the establishment. The differences in satisfaction between individuals with different types of contract show permanent workers, here, with a marked advantage:

Temporary (less than 12 months)   −1.47
Fixed-term contract   −1.03
Permanent employment   0.09

The extent to which marginal working had been utilized by the establishment however, made no difference to feelings of security; this indicates that there was no spillover effect from marginal workers to others in the establishments which used them.

Part-time and marginal employment policies have been often regarded as rather similar in generating higher levels of job insecurity. The analysis above, however, suggests that their implications are altogether different and that part-time employment is actually associated with increased security. Why should this be the case? Explanation needs to be at the organizational rather than the individual level, since individuals in organizations with part-time employees tend to feel more secure, whether they themselves are full-timers or part-timers. The effect of recent workforce reductions upon employees' sense of insecurity points to part of the explanation. Part-time workers, it is generally agreed, provide organizations with flexibility, and we suggest that one of the consequences of this flexibility is the ability to make adjustments to the work-force without resorting to overt work-force reductions.

This proposition was tested by cross-tabulating individuals by combinations of their establishments' part-time policies and work-force reduction policies. Figure 8.1 summarizes the results by plotting proportions of individuals in establishments with work-force reductions, by intensities of part-time employment in the establishments. It can be seen that the proportions being confronted with work-force reductions tended to fall in the establishments with high proportions of part-timers, although the relationship was not linear. Work-force reductions were highly unusual in establishments with a predominantly part-time workforce. The higher satisfaction with job security of individuals in such establishments in this sense reflects reality.

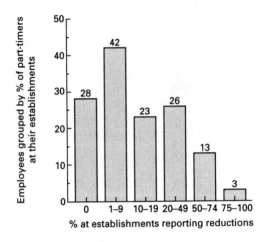

Fig. 8.1 Part-time proportions and work-force reductions

Does the employment of marginal workers, similarly, provide organizations with a means of avoiding recourse to work-force reductions? The answer turns out to be a clear 'No'. Of those individuals in establishments with no marginal workers, 20 per cent had been in a situation of work-force reductions; of those in establishments with 1–10 per cent of marginal workers, 32 per cent, and of those in establishments with more than 10 per cent of marginal workers, 33 per cent. Moreover, satisfaction with job security was lower for permanent workers in organizations with work-force reductions, than where there were no reductions, as in the case of temporary workers and of those on fixed-term contracts. A separate analysis (not shown here) indicated that the interaction between contractual status and presence or absence of work-force reductions, in terms of influence upon satisfaction with security, was non-significant. In short, permanent and marginal workers alike are present where reductions take place and are adversely affected by them.

The findings taken as a whole, therefore, indicate that part-time working and marginal employment policies have quite different consequences both for those workers with the contractual status in question, and for permanent or 'standard contract' workers in the same establishments. Substantial levels of part-time working reduce the probability of work-force reductions, and increase the feeling of job security in equal measure for part-time and full-time workers. The use of marginal workers, however, is associated with increased recourse to work-force reductions, and while the brunt is borne by the marginal workers themselves (especially those employed on a short-term basis), even permanent workers in such establishments are not insulated from this main source of insecurity.

The most important point to emerge is that, despite a tightening of the labour market in 1986–7, when these surveys were being conducted, and despite falls in unemployment at that time, by far the dominant influence upon individuals' sense of security or insecurity was whether or not their employer had cut the work-force. A serious limitation of the notion that 'precariousness' is essentially a matter of contract, lies in diverting attention from the sense of insecurity which can be felt by workers on standard contracts.

INTERPRETATION OF THE EFFECTS OF EMPLOYER POLICIES ON INDIVIDUALS

The findings have confirmed that qualifications and experience did indeed contribute in a very important way to individual outcomes: most of all in regard to occupational attainment, but also in regard to earnings. They also entered, although less strongly, into explanations of satisfaction with pay and with pay security. The theoretical implications of this depend partly on views about the precise functions of qualifications and experience within employment. It should also be remembered that there is now a very substantial literature showing that educational achievement is not simply a matter of individual choice but reflects social milieux and differential opportunity (see *inter alia* Halsey *et al.* 1980).

At the same time, the results demonstrated that employer policies brought about differentiation (or distortion) of individuals' returns to their qualifications and experience. Moreover, the effects of these policies were, in important instances, not confined to the individuals directly affected by them, but also spilled over on to other employees in the same establishments. These spillover effects will be particularly difficult to explain for unaugmented human capital theory, or for any theory based wholly on individual contributions and returns.

The effects of particular policies on individuals were not uniformly advantageous or disadvantageous. The picture was one of rather complex sets of exchanges and trade-offs, with each policy having its up side as well as its down side. To emphasize this point, Table 8.13 draws together the findings for the three main policies investigated in the linked analyses, showing whether the effect of each was favourable to the individual (+), unfavourable (−), or neutral (0). The patterns revealed suggest that employers were not able to impose conditions unilaterally upon individuals through their choice of policies. Some attention was seemingly being paid by employers to offering inducements, or to making the bargain a palatable one, whatever policy they were using.

TABLE 8.13. *Relations of policies to individuals' returns to human capital*

	Occupational attainment	Net hourly earnings	Satisfaction	
			Pay	Security
Internal development	+	+	0	0
Part-time				
individual	−	+	+	0
establishment	0	−	−	+
Marginal employment				
individual	+/−	−	−/+	−
establishment	+/−	(+)	(+)	0

+	favourable effect
−	unfavourable effect
0	no effect
+/− or −/+	mixed effect

An attraction of this type of interpretation, by comparison with those of segmentation theories, is that it allows both employers and workers to behave, on the whole, in a reasonable way. Although employers sometimes underutilize qualifications and experience—as in the case of part-time workers—they do not disregard them. And employers' apparent efforts to offer something attractive to workers, whatever the policy, suggest that workers are careful of their own well-being, a point sometimes in doubt within some versions of segmentation theory.

This is not to deny that some individuals, or groups, may be employed under wholly disadvantageous conditions. The point is that such conditions are not likely to flow from any single employer policy or contract-type, nor indeed from any combination of the broad policies or contract-types which we have investigated. In general, one would expect that wholly disadvantageous conditions would arise for workers where they were unable to make use of market mobility and had become tied to or dependent upon their employers. Explanation of such cases of disadvantage will presumably involve analysis in the individual side of the labour market of influences, such as immigrant status, race, handicap, or unemployment; as well as analysis of the labour market and social contexts which affect mobility. Employers' policies and contract-types offer no short cut to a painstaking analysis of disadvantage.

Contract-types, it has been stressed, do not align with either favourable or disadvantageous effects upon individuals. In addition, there are the spillover effects: the tendency for the whole establishment to be affected by the policy of employing some workers on non-standard contracts. These spillover effects, it should be recalled, sometimes work in a contrary direction to the effects at the individual contract level. Taken in combination, these observations suggest that, in paying much attention to non-standard contracts in recent years, too little has been devoted to 'standard' contracts, that is, to workers in full-time permanent employment. Standard contracts seem to emerge from the present analysis as problematical as non-standard ones. They appear problematical, both in the sense that there are evidently important policy differences to consider within the scope of the standard contract-type, and in the sense that individuals on standard contracts may face substantial problems.

The existence of these policy differences within standard employment leads to forms of 'distortion' of the labour market which are peculiarly difficult to explain in terms of conventional human capital theory. We will simply note one of these, by way of illustration. Internal development policies, according to our (admittedly exploratory) estimates, were associated with a 7 per cent advantage in occupational attainment and an 11 per cent advantage in terms of net hourly pay. It seems most unlikely that differences of this magnitude could be accounted for by the cumulative in-job additions to 'human capital' arising from training and promotion. (Promotion rates were very low, with the majority of establishments having no promotion in the previous year, and the typical non-zero value being 1 per cent. In addition, the cumulative effects of promotion will tend to be dampened by bringing in new recruits to fill posts vacated by promotion.) A more sensible interpretation is that internal development policies form part of a wider pattern of efficient 'human capital' utilization, which permits jobs of a given level to be filled by individuals with lower qualifications and less experience than is the case elsewhere. But such an interpretation requires that other establishments (lacking internal development policies) make a less than efficient utilization of qualifications and experience; and many of these inefficient users will be operating wholly or mainly with full-time permanent workers. We are left, therefore, with a problem of explaining differences in 'human capital' utilization of considerably wider scope than attempted even within segmentation theories.

In terms of individual disadvantage, again, our findings lead to a renewed interest in the problems of full-time 'permanent' workers. The most obvious example concerns the particularly low returns to qualifications and experience, for female full-time workers, and the negative spillover effects upon full-time workers (both male and female) of high proportions of part-time workers within the establishment. But perhaps the most important change of perspective coming from our findings concerns precarious employment. If attention is confined to insecurity arising from non-standard employment conditions, then precariousness would appear to attach to no more than the 7 per cent on temporary and fixed-term contracts. However, a more endemic form of insecurity arose from the policy of work-force reductions in many establishments, and this effect applied to workers on standard as well as non-standard contracts. These work-force reductions cannot be regarded as random events or transitory disturbances. In Chapter 3 by Wilkinson and White, it is shown that they are strongly related to product-market circumstances of, at least, the medium term, and have a good claim to be regarded as a policy response.

The findings, then, have to a large extent disengaged issues of individual disadvantage, or advantage, from issues of contractual status. The issues of individual disadvantage, or advantage, not only remain but increase their scope. The 'distortions' of returns to 'human capital' are present across the whole range of employers and contract-types. The life chances of individuals, even within the category of standard employment, may be differentiated by employers' policies. In conclusion, employers' policies not only differentiate individuals' life chances to an appreciable degree, but do so in a complex, patterned way which appears to rule out an interpretation based on conventional human capital theory. We have also ruled out any interpretation based upon labour-market segmentation, in the sense of a relatively simple partitioning of employers, employers' policies, or types of employment contract. Instead, our findings suggest that employers' policies create a very complex pattern of labour-market differentiation, through generating multi-directional processes of change across the labour market.

NOTES TO CHAPTER 8

1. The figure estimated for men (£2.76) differs from that estimated above when assessing the effects of internal development policy on earnings (£3.03). These are the means predicted by each model, rather than the observed means, and the application of different models results in different figures being estimated. However, the relative earnings of men and women remain stable across the two models.

2. The equality of net pay (unadjusted) between full-timers and part-timers in these data accords with the findings of the national 'Women in Employment' Survey (Martin and Roberts 1984). This source, while quoting earnings gross for full-time workers and part-time workers, also provides information on the proportions of earnings deducted through tax and national insurance contributions, from which net earnings may also be estimated.

9

Perceptions of the Labour Market: An Investigation of Differences by Gender And by Working-Time[1]

BRENDAN BURCHELL, JANE ELLIOTT,
AND JILL RUBERY

INTRODUCTION

Studies of labour-market structures or divisions have primarily been concerned with describing the practices and processes by which divisions in the labour force are created or reinforced. These studies tend to fall into two types: those concerned with charting employer policies and practices (Osterman 1982; Baron and Bielby 1980; Atkinson 1985a; Rubery 1988), or with the demand side of the labour market, and those concerned with work- and life-history data which reveal the interaction of the supply and the demand side of the labour market on individuals' and groups' life chances without being able to differentiate adequately between these different influences (Hunt 1988). An aspect of the labour market that has been less systematically explored is how individuals who participate in the labour market actually perceive labour-market opportunities and labour-market barriers. Studies of employer policies or of life histories may reveal a significant effect of, for example, internal labour markets on labour-market position (see Ch. 8 by White and Gallie) but there is little research which identifies whether individuals perceive themselves to be in an internal labour market.

The work-attitudes/work-histories survey enables us to explore the perceptions of how the labour market functions from the perspective of individual agents in the labour market. Much of recent research has revealed the creation of divisions in the labour market, related on the one hand to employer policies and practices, and on the other to differences between labour-market groups, for example differences by gender. These two sources of divisions are interrelated: employer policy has been argued to lead to the creation of internal labour markets for more advantaged male labour and to the confinement of women workers to peripheral jobs often organized on a part-time basis. The segmentation and the gender debates in the literature (see the introduction to this volume) also provide the focus for our study of perceptions of the labour market: what are the perceptions of individual agents in the labour market of the form and role of employer policy and practice and to what extent do these perceptions differ by gender? Evidence from studies using SCELI data (Horrell *et al.* 1990; Gallie 1991) and from other analyses of the female labour market (Humphries and Rubery 1992) however suggest that the experience of women in the labour market may be strongly affected by whether women are in full- or part-time employment, although less agreement is found on whether this difference relates to the objective characteristics of their jobs or to differences in the type of employees and their commitment to wage labour (see Chs. 2 and 8, and Hakim 1991).

In practice this means that, in order to explore differences in labour-market experience, it is useful to divide the respondents into three groups: male full-timers, female full-timers, and female part-timers. Male part-timers constitute too small a category of respondents for useful analysis. Where appropriate, divisions found between these groups will be compared to those found for more conventional labour-market groups. In particular we will use Registrar General's 1980 social class categories as a basis for comparing between occupational categories.

The Social Change and Economic Life Initiative provides an important source of new data which can be used to explore some of these issues. The work-attitudes and work-history questionnaire was administered to a random sample of 1,022 adults in Northampton, including 616 who were currently employed, aged between 20 and 60, in the summer of 1986. Information was collected on various aspects of the respondents' experience of and perceptions of structured labour markets. The inclusion of both men and women in the survey allows for the direct comparison of men's and women's experiences in the labour market, thus overcoming problems of interpreting results on some similar issues from the 'Women and Employment' survey (Martin and Roberts 1984), where comparisons were made primarily between full- and part-time women workers and previous studies which included only men (e.g. Blackburn and Mann 1979).

The evidence concerning respondents' experience of and perceptions of labour-market structure will be presented in two main sections, the first concerned with the present situation of respondents and the second with their expectations of future labour-market opportunities. The data allow us to explore how individuals perceive the influence of organizational and structural factors on labour-market chances and how well these perceptions of the labour-market structures and opportunities differ by gender and by full-time and part-time status.

STRUCTURED EMPLOYMENT OPPORTUNITIES AND CURRENT JOB

The first area of individuals' experience of structured labour markets that we explore relates to their current job. The survey included questions concerned with both the respondents' access to their current job and their access to promotion opportunities. The questions investigated these issues in several different ways, from questions about their own experience to their perceptions of the types of recruitment and promotion criteria adopted by their employer.

Access to current job

Individuals' experience of and perceptions of recruitment methods and criteria are of direct interest to the study of structured labour markets. Differences in recruitment both create a structured labour supply by limiting access, and reflect differences in the labour-supply structure. For example, methods of recruitment will vary according to expectations of the job-search activity patterns of the targeted group. The use of screening processes have been justified in neo-classical literature on the grounds that hiring involves costs and that cheaply identifiable characteristics such as qualifications or gender can provide employers with a way of reducing the probability of making a mistake, even if these screens will result in discrimination either for or against individuals who deviate from the 'norms' ascribed to their labour-force group (Stiglitz 1975). It has been argued from this by neo-classical theorists that one would therefore expect the use of screens to be prevalent primarily in more skilled jobs, where the costs of recruiting the wrong person are high, while in lower grade jobs the assumption that workers and jobs are interchangeable still prevails. Thus women could be expected in general to be in jobs with more open recruitment than men. Labour-market segmentation theorists would also expect more structuring of access to better jobs (Doeringer and Piore 1971). However, this approach has been developed to look not only at technical but also social attributes of the work-force; motivation and control may be an issue for all job groups and firms may use recruitment criteria to increase the chances of acquiring a worker with the right motivation, social background, or tacit skills (Manwaring 1984). One of these social criteria could in fact be gender, where the requirement is not related to technical productivity but to fitting into the work group (Curran 1988).

Two questions included in the SCELI work-attitudes questionnaire related to recruitment into the respondent's current job. One question asked the respondent how they first came to hear about their present job; this question thus identifies which recruitment method by the firm was the one to attract their future employee's first attention (even though other methods may also have been used by the firms and may have involved expenditure of more resources). The second question was not directly related to the individual's perceptions of the types of recruitment criteria used by the firm in selecting people for their type of job.

First, analyses of how men and women found their current job revealed interesting differences by gender and between full- and part-time workers. Subsequent more detailed analysis showed these differences to be in part related to the type of job, and thus related to gender and working-time primarily through the pattern of job segregation. Nevertheless, some interesting differences in gender and working-time remain even after controlling for job-type.

The results for all occupations for male full-time workers, female full-time workers, and female part-time workers are shown in the first column of Table 9.1. Of the six routes by which respondents might have come to hear about their current job the two most common for all three groups were through family or friends or through local adverts or employment agencies.[2] However, female part-timers were most likely to have heard through family or friends and female full-timers through local adverts, with male full-timers occupying a mid-way position. The other main difference between these groups was that full-timers, both male and female, were more likely to have heard about their jobs through national adverts than female part-timers.

The rest of Table 9.1 disaggregates the data by social class. This disaggregation at first sight appears to reduce gender and working-time differences but in fact reveals some systematic patterns, as well as helping to clarify the reasons for the aggregate differences. For example, the higher share of full-timers using national adverts is mainly the result of the higher share of full-timers with jobs in the professional classes. However, even those part-timers who have jobs in these categories are much less likely to have heard about their jobs through national adverts; part-time jobs are thus local jobs, whatever their employment category. The tendency of women part-timers to make more use of family and friends in finding out about jobs than either women full-timers or men is found to be present systematically in all job categories except for skilled manual work, where men were the most likely to have used this method. Here the numbers of women are so small as to make comparisons by gender difficult. It is, however, this job category which accounts for full-time men being more likely than full-time women to have heard about their job through family or friends. Nearly half of the total number of men who found out about their job through this method were in this job category, and 48 per cent of skilled manual men found their job this way compared to shares between 26 and 31 per cent in other job categories.

Women full-timers were generally more likely to make use of local adverts irrespective of job category (semi- and unskilled manual work being the only exception) but a contributory reason for the high share of this method in the total was the high concentration of women full-timers in clerical work (over 50 per cent) and the importance of local adverts and employment agencies for this job category (58 per cent of all women in full-time clerical jobs found their job this way).

Recruitment method appears strongly related to both the social class of the job and the working-time, but not directly or system-

TABLE 9.1. *How respondents first came to hear about their current job, by gender, working-time, and social class*

			Social class			
		All	1 and 2	3.1	3.2	4 and 5
Family and	MFT	35	26	30	48	31
friends	FFT	25	21	20	53	36
	FPT	37	31	40	0	44
National	MFT	10	22	2	4	0
advert	FFT	11	29	0	0	3
	FPT	2	8	0	7	0
Contacted	MFT	10	8	18	8	15
employer	FFT	13	15	13	21	3
	FPT	16	29	13	0	14
Employer	MFT	10	15	6	5	9
approach	FFT	8	10	10	0	0
	FPT	12	17	11	14	10
Local advert	MFT	36	29	45	35	45
or agency	FFT	44	26	58	26	58
	FPT	33	15	36	79	32
Sample	MFT	283	101	27	99	55
numbers	FFT	161	61	62	14	21
	FPT	132	27	49	8	49

Chi-squared significant at 1% signifying statistically reliable differences in job search between the three types of employees. Sample numbers refer to the total sample; percentages exclude those who chose the 'other' category in response to the question. Note that the percentages total to 100% across the five information channel categories within each of the three employee-type categories.

MFT = male full-timers, FFT = female full-times, FPT = female part timers.

Social class: 1 and 2, managerial and professional; 3.1, clerical; 3.2, skilled manual; 4 and 5, semi and unskilled.

atically related to gender. Women in full-time work may be more likely to participate in an open, competitive recruitment system, than male full-timers, where networks for entry into skilled manual work are widespread. The predominance of informal recruitment methods for part-timers requires further exploration. It is not clear if these systems prevail because of employers' concern to minimize fixed costs such as adverts, or to ensure that local labour is employed to minimize the probability of turnover; or alternatively if employers are striving for more general objectives of, for instance, recruiting workers who fit into the company by having appropriate social attitudes and motivations. These data are at least compatible with the hypothesis that tacit skills are as important for part-time jobs as they have been argued to be for full-time manual labour. Part-timers do not participate in a fully open employment network where the relative advantages of different jobs on offer can be compared. Instead they rely on access to information about jobs through networks.

In the second question relating to recruitment, respondents were asked to select from a list of factors, any which they considered would make it difficult for someone to get a job like theirs in their organization, thereby exploring indirectly the respondents' perceptions of recruitment criteria adopted by their employer. Respondents were free to select as many or as few items as they wanted. The two most frequently mentioned factors (see Table 9.2) by men and women, and by full- and part-timers, were 'no experience of similar work' and 'lack of good references', although a markedly lower percentage of part-timers mentioned experience compared to full-timers (42 per cent, compared to 69 per cent of male and 62 per cent of female full-timers). The next most commonly mentioned factor by full-timers was 'lack of appropriate qualifications' (46 per cent of women, 35 per cent of men) but this factor ranked only sixth in the part-timers list, being mentioned by only 22 per cent of the sample. Experience in the organization was also stressed more by full-timers than part-timers, being mentioned by only 7 per cent of part-timers compared to nearly a quarter of full-timers. From these responses we can see that part-timers are less likely to see their job as related to a structured career path requiring specific qualifications, work experience, or previous employment within the organization. Moreover, entry is perceived as being less restricted by age than for full-time jobs, reinforcing the idea of the casual, unstructured job sector. However, there is evidence to suggest that entry is not entirely open. In the first place, being female is a relatively frequently mentioned requirement; 29 per cent of part-timers thought men would find it difficult to get their job compared to only 19 per cent of female full-timers. Gender was in fact only

TABLE 9.2. *Perceptions of factors which would make it difficult for someone to get a similar job to that of the respondent*

	Male full-timers		Female full-timers		Female part-timers	
	% who mentioned	Rank	% who mentioned	Rank	% who mentioned	Rank
Having no personal contacts	12	10	6	9	15	8
Being under 20	33	4	41	4	24	5
Being over 40	28	6	14	8	17	7
Being a man	0	11	20	7	30	4
Being a woman	30	5	3	11	2	10
Being white	12	9	6	10	0	11
Lack of experience of similar work	69	1	62	1	42	2
Not having the right educational qualifications	35	3	46	3	22	6
Having heavy domestic commitments	26	7	38	5	38	3
Lack of good references	48	2	56	2	47	1
Lack of experience in the organization	25	8	23	6	7	9

marginally less important in restricting access to part-time jobs than for male full-time jobs, where 31 per cent thought women would have difficulties getting their type of job. Gender segregation thus appears to take on greater importance at the top and the bottom of the hierarchy. Female part-timers are also more likely to say that not having personal contacts within the firm might make it difficult to get their type of job, thereby reinforcing our earlier findings that access to part-time jobs is not necessarily open but bounded by informal social contacts and networks. Structuring of access to employment may thus take many forms and is by no means limited to the use of formal qualifications and experience criteria.

Access to promotion

Employers not only structure access into entry-level jobs but also access to higher level jobs through their systems of internal and external recruitment. Respondents were probed about the system of access to promotion in a number of different ways. In the work-history part of the schedule they were asked for each job to say if they considered, when they took the job, that it had promotion prospects. Ambiguities clearly arise in interpreting the implications of the results of this question for internal labour markets as some may have responded with respect to the advantages the job would confer on the external labour market. However, the question related to the promotion opportunities that came with the job, and are thus part of the picture of how access to employment positions has a long-term impact on career advancement.

Table 9.3 reveals major disparities in promotion opportunities in current job by gender and by working-time. Of men, 63 per cent said that their job offered promotion prospects, compared to only 44 per cent of women. Only 29 per cent of women in part-time jobs had promotion prospects, compared to 52 per cent of women in full-time jobs, but this latter percentage was still well below the share of men with promotion prospects. Promotion prospects were also related to social class but differences in distribution by social class did not explain the gender and working-time differences. For example, of those in professional or managerial jobs, only 40 per cent of women in part-time employ-

TABLE 9.3. *Percentage who believed when taking their current job that it offered promotion prospects*

	Sample	Social class				
		All	1 and 2	3.1	3.2	4 and 5
Male full-timers	293	63	75	82	50	53
Female full-timers	161	52	57	57	29	35
Female part-timers	137	29	40	30	39	21

Chi-squared significant at 1% for MFT/FFT/FPT and for MFT by social class.

ment felt they had promotion prospects, compared to 57 per cent of women in full-time employment and 75 per cent of men in full-time employment.

Respondents were also asked about their perceptions of the system of promotion associated with their current job. Asked if currently working for the organization was an advantage or a disadvantage, if there was a vacancy for a better job in their organization, over 70 per cent of males and females considered it be either an advantage or a major advantage and less than 30 per cent considered it to be neither an advantage or disadvantage, or to be a disadvantage (see Table 9.4). Part-timers were even more adamant about the advantages given to internal candidates, with 80 per cent seeing it to be an advantage to be already working for the organization. These results suggest that firms' preferences for their own employees over outsiders is perceived as more general than hypothesized in dual-labour-market theory. However,

TABLE 9.4. *Percentage who believed it to be an advantage to be already working in the organization when a better job becomes available in it*

	Sample	All	Jobs with promotion prospects	Jobs without promotion prospects
Male full-timers	291	72	77	66
Female full-timers	160	72	82	59
Female part-timers	124	80	95	74

Chi-squared significant at 1% for FFT and FPT.

this question did not tap frequency with which vacancies occurred, so that internal promotion opportunities could still be quite limited. This question was not specifically linked to internal promotion opportunities for the individual respondent, as the purpose of the question was to separate personal barriers to upward mobility from perceptions of the use of internal advancement. However, there is some evidence of a relation between perceptions of advantages to being already employed in an organization and personal opportunities for promotion in the case of women, and in particular women currently in part-time jobs. Thus only 5 per cent of women in part-time jobs who considered that they had promotion opportunities in their current job did not consider it to be an advantage to be already employed, compared to 26 per cent in jobs without promotion prospects. Similar patterns were found for women in full-time jobs, with only 18 per cent of those with promotion prospects considering it not to be an advantage to be employed, compared to 41 per cent for those without promotion prospects. A much smaller difference, 23 per cent with promotion prospects compared to 34 per cent without, was found for men in full-time jobs. These results suggest a possible greater correlation between having promotion prospects and being in an advantaged internal labour market, in the case of women, and particularly part-time women. These groups could reasonably be expected to be extremely pessimistic about their opportunities for promotion if they considered there were no internal avenues open to them where their competence and other attributes might help them overcome the disadvantage of being a part-time employee.

The investigation of these various aspects of promotion thus support the view that females in general, but those in part-time jobs in particular, are the least likely to see themselves as being in jobs with promotion prospects. However, these differences do not emerge because of perceived differences in the advantages of being employed within the organization; in short, it is not that women are employed in firms where external recruits are preferred and men in firms where internal recruits are preferred.

STRUCTURED LABOUR MARKETS AND EMPLOYMENT PROSPECTS

So far we have seen that women's current experience of the labour market does differ significantly from that of men's in terms of their access to promotion within organizations. However, the survey also explored individuals' perceptions of their potential or future employment prospects within the labour market as a whole and, where appropriate, the influence of structural as well as personal variables on these expectations.

Prospects in external and internal labour markets

The cost of being employed in an internal labour market may be that one acquires such firm-specific skills that transfer to other employers becomes difficult, particularly within the local area. To see to what extent respondents were 'trapped' in their current employment we asked how easy or difficult it would be for them to find a job as good as their current one, and how easy or difficult it would be to get a job where they could use the same skills in the local area.

Women were much more likely than men to feel that they could easily get an equivalent job to their current one and one in which they could use similar skills (see Table 9.5). These findings fit with the predictions of segmentation theory that women are more likely to be in casually organized labour markets, in jobs requiring either general or low-level skills. However, there is some evidence to suggest that this finding is more specific to the female labour market, and that for female part-time labour, than to 'low-grade' or 'secondary' employment in general. No relationship was found between ease of finding an equivalent job and social class, thus suggesting that not all lower skilled jobs operate within a casual employment system. Over 63 per cent of women in both full- and part-time jobs consider their skills to be transferable, compared to only 44 per cent of men (see Table 9.6), but it was only female part-timers who were significantly more likely to think they could easily find as good a job elsewhere (39 per cent, compared to 29 per cent of female full-timers and 23 per cent of male full-timers). These findings for part-timers may reflect the poor quality of their current job. They may also, and

TABLE 9.5. *Percentage who would find it very or quite easy to find a job as good as their current one*

	Sample	% very or quite easy			Social class			
		All	Aged under 40	Aged over 40	1 and 2	3.1	3.2	4 and 5
Male full-timers	294	23	28	13	23	18	20	30
Female full-timers	167	20	33	19	27	34	23	21
Female part-timers	137	39	47	26	34	40	59	37

Chi-squared significant at 1% level for all by MFT/FFT/FPT; at 1% for MFT by age; at 5% for FPT by age. Social class: see Table 9.1.

TABLE 9.6. *Likelihood of respondents finding another job in the Northampton area in which they could use the same skills as in their current job*

	Sample	% likely or very likely			Social class				
		All	Aged under 40	Aged over 40	1 and 2	3.1	3.2	4 and 5
Male full-timers	293	44	50	34	37	45	44	55
Female full-timers	162	63	68	54	61	57	83	68
Female part-timers	136	65	65	64	60	66	50	68

Chi-squared significant at 1% level for all by MFT/FFT/FPT; at 5% for MFT by age.

perhaps even more significantly, reflect the buoyancy of demand for part-time labour in similar low-level jobs. Between September 1984 and September 1987 female part-time employment grew by 26 per cent in Northampton, compared to growth rates of female full-time and male full-time employment of 15 and 8 per cent respectively.

Older employees were also relatively pessimistic about getting an equivalent job but in this case it is not clear whether these responses are influenced by perceptions of age restrictions on recruitment, or because they had progressed so far up the internal market hierarchy that they would lose considerable status and skill if they were to move.

These findings on expectations in the external labour market are supportive of the view that women in particular are less likely to be in an internal promotion system, so that external mobility does not involve so high a cost. However, there is very little difference between men and women when we look at where their best chances of obtaining a better job might be: 55 per cent of men in full-time jobs and 53 per cent of women in full-time jobs thought their best chance of a better job was with their current employer. The share for part-timers fell to 44 per cent, but this ratio was perhaps higher than expected for jobs so strongly associated with a casual labour market. Thus, while women were more confident than men about their ability to find an equivalent job on the external labour market, this external-labour-market power did not extend to providing more opportunities to find a better job. Moreover, women's preference for their current employer was not as strongly related to personal factors such as age as in the case of men. Again these results could suggest that older men have more to lose because they have achieved more in the internal labour market, or that men are more likely to perceive age discrimination in recruitment. Older part-time women showed no tendency to favour the internal over the external labour market, either because of the poor opportunities internally or because of the lack of age restrictions on recruitment in the part-time labour market.

Women's chances of promotion appear to be relatively low in both the internal and the external labour market, so that exclusion from an internal promotion system does not necessarily lead to women choosing the external market as a better option.

However, if women are in jobs with promotion prospects they are more likely to see their best chances to lie with their current employer (62 per cent, compared to 45 per cent for those without promotion prospects for female full-timers; 60 to 39 per cent for female part-timers: see Table 19.7). Men were also more inclined to favour their current employer if they felt they had promotion prospects but the differences were smaller (58 compared to 48 per cent). These results may suggest that the most effective internal labour market policy, if measured by the likelihood of retaining employees, would be one designed for female employees, particularly part-timers, as male employees may still have more opportunities for seeking external promotion.

Labour-market pessimists and labour-market optimists

So far we have been concerned with *where* the respondents felt their chances of a better job might lie. We also need to look at how optimistic or pessimistic they were about obtaining a better job in the near future. Women were not as pessimistic about their opportunities of obtaining a better job over the next two years as their current concentration in jobs without promotion prospects might suggest. No significant differences were found in the shares of male full-timers, female full-timers, and female part-timers who thought they had a good chance of a better job over the next two years (see Table 9.8).

However, disaggregation by age revealed similar shares in all three groups (over 60 per cent) for those under 40, but in the over-40 age group the female part-timers were the most optimistic, with 38 per cent thinking they had a very or quite good chance of a better job, compared to 29 per cent of female full-timers and 24 per cent of male full-timers. The optimism of the young is likely to be at least in part related to objectively better chances of advancement; the optimism of the older female part-timers may not only reflect the less structured nature of the part-time labour market, with fewer restrictions on entry by age or specific experience, but also the fact that their current jobs are low-status and low-paid relative to the employees' potential and qualifications. If one is already at the bottom of the hierarchy, then the chances of upward mobility may in fact increase. Alternatively, it may be a reflection of their attributing their

TABLE 9.7. *Percentage who consider their best chance of a better job would be to stay with their current employer*

	Sample	All	Aged under 40	Aged over 40	Jobs with promotion prospects	Jobs without promotion prospects
Male full-timers	285	55	49	64	58	48
Female full-timers	160	53	48	62	62	45
Female part-timers	133	44	44	44	60	37

Chi-squared significant at 5% level for MFT by age; for FFT by promotion prospects; for FPT by promotion prospects.

TABLE 9.8. *Percentage who consider they have a very or quite good chance of getting a better job over the next two years*

| | Sample | All | Aged under 40 | Aged over 40 | Social class | | | |
					1 and 2	3.1	3.2	4 and 5
Male full-timers	289	48	62	24	58	78	34	41
Female full-timers	166	52	63	29	55	63	29	26
Female part-timers	127	52	61	38	56	53	59	47

Chi-squared significant at 1% level for MFT and FFT by age; at 5% for FPT by age; and at 1% for MFT and FFT by social class. Social class: see Table 9.1.

current low status in the labour market to a relatively temporary domestic situation (for example, having pre-school children). Once the domestic commitment is lifted, they might realistically expect a boost in their labour-market standing. This interpretation of the results is supported indirectly by the analyses of responses by social class. Part-timers were the only group where optimism was not positively related to social class. Those employed in manual occupations were just as optimistic about opportunities for a better job as those in non-manual, in contrast to the results for full-timers where the non-manual groups were much more optimistic than the manual. The responses by full-timers may be more related to the existence of structured career opportunities, and those by part-timers to the low status and pay of their current jobs.

Two further pieces of evidence can be introduced to suggest that part-timers' optimism was not related to perceptions of significant chances for advancement; only 22 per cent of female part-timers considered that they 'had a career', with all the implications of upward mobility that such a term confers, compared to 56 per cent of female full-timers and 62 per cent of male full-timers (see Table 9.9). Moreover, while considering they had a career was positively related to optimism about a better job in the case of full-timers, the relationship for part-timers was weaker and non-significant.

Major problems thus emerge in interpreting individual responses about optimism of obtaining a better job, as the results are confounded by the characteristics of the respondents' current position as well as their objective chances for upward mobility. In the extreme, someone who has reached the top of his or her internal labour market can be rightly pessimistic about chances for advancement, without this being an indication of low labour-market status. Under these circumstances it was not surprising that we in practice found little relationship between optimism about getting a better job and variables which might be expected to be related to being in an internal labour market.

Similar problems emerge in interpreting responses to a question about which factors would be most likely to stop respondents getting a better job over the next two years. These data should provide some indication of how individuals perceive barriers to promotion and advancement as they affect their own

TABLE 9.9. *Percentage who considered they were 'having a career'*

	Sample	All	Aged under 40	Aged over 40	Social class				Chances of a better job	
					1 and 2	3.1	3.2	4 and 5	Good	Poor
Male full-timers	292	62	67	53	83	89	49	32	75	48
Female full-timers	165	56	64	38	86	43	29	19	64	45
Female part-timers	138	22	30	9	62	16	31	4	28	14

Chi-squared significant at 1% by MFT/FFT/FPT; at 5% MFT by age; at 1% for MFT, FFT and FPT by social class; at 1% for MFT and at 5% for FFT by chances of a better job. Social class: see Table 9.1.

individual prospects. However, included in the sample are those who may not really perceive any *major* barriers (but nevertheless have selected some items from the list just to accommodate the interviewer) and those who see the barriers as primarily related to their own stage in the life-cycle. We have thus selected out the responses of those who could be considered labour-market pessimists; that is, they said they had quite or very poor chances of obtaining a better job within the next two years, but they did not consider that being too old was likely to be a factor hindering them in the labour market. This age factor was the most frequently mentioned barrier amongst those with poor chances of a better job, and was mentioned less frequently by labour-market optimists, thus supporting the hypothesis that pessimism and life-cycle are closely related. To see what factors may lead people to be pessimistic about the labour market for reasons other than their own life-cycle position, it is useful to concentrate instead on the 'younger' labour-market pessimists (see Table 9.10).

For this group, the most frequently mentioned barrier was 'lack of jobs to apply for'; approximately 50 per cent of this group mentioned this factor (55 per cent of women and 45 per cent of men), compared to 36 per cent of the total sample including all labour-market pessimists and optimists. The ordering of the other factors was relatively similar for labour-market pessimists and optimists, with personal factors such as qualifications and lack of experience being stressed above more structural forms of discrimination such as sexism (with ageism being the main exception to this pattern). Little can be concluded about another form of structural discrimination, racism, with this data set; there were too few members of ethnic minorities in the sample to perform any meaningful analysis on them. The major difference between full and part-timers was in the frequency with which they cited heavy domestic commitments as a barrier, but this factor was important to both labour-market optimists and pessimists among the part-timers.

Structural factors, in the shape of lack of job opportunities, are thus frequently perceived as a constraint on labour-market advancement by those who are pessimistic about their own chances. At least a significant minority of labour-force participants see their 'choice' over employment as being limited by structural factors.

TABLE 9.10. *Perceptions of barriers to getting a better job over the next two years*

	Labour-market pessimists			Whole sample		
	MFT	FFT	FPT	MFT	FFT	FPT
Not having the right contacts	21	23	12	19	16	10
I'd be too young	11	5	2	9	7	0
I'd be too old	NA	NA	NA	38	35	32
Not having the right skills	33	22	25	27	27	24
Being a man	0	NA	NA	1	NA	NA
Being a woman	NA	2	6	NA	6	3
Not being the right colour	3	0	0	1	1	0
My qualifications	44	39	34	30	34	34
My references	0	3	0	3	2	1
My domestic commitments	1	14	40	1	9	38
My experience	22	10	11	20	15	12
Not being in good enough health	5	0	0	5	4	9
Lack of jobs to apply for	45	55	54	32	42	36
Sample	72	80	80	289	166	127

Pessimists were defined as respondents who considered they had a poor chance of a better job over the next two years, excluding those who said they were too old. 52% of the MFT category were classed as pessimists, as were 52% of FFT and 37% of FPT respondents.

Preferences for changing jobs

We have already seen that a significant minority do identify structural factors as constraining their labour-market opportunities and choices. We can gain some further information on the extent to which individuals feel constrained by labour demand factors from a question which asked respondents whether they would wish to change their jobs if there were plenty of jobs available, thereby trying to distinguish labour demand from other factors leading individuals to prefer to stick to their current job. Around 40 per cent of both male and female full-timers would wish to change their job, but only 32 per cent of part-timers expressed a desire to do so (see Table 9.11). This represents a

TABLE 9.11. *Percentage who would wish to change their jobs if there were plenty available*

| | Sample | % who wish to change jobs | Of these, % who would like to change | | |
			Their employer	Their occupation	Both employer and occupation
Male full-timers	298	40	34	17	49
Female full-timers	160	39	36	18	46
Female part-timers	139	32	9	35	56

Chi-squared significant at 5% by type of change desired.

very significant slice of all labour-force groups that would wish to change their jobs if they felt there was a significant degree of choice in the labour market, and provides an interesting alternative measure of job satisfaction. Although the straightforward question on job satisfaction confirmed the results of other surveys by showing individuals to be likely to indicate high levels of satisfaction, other indirect questions in the survey such as this one indicated a much higher underlying level of discontent or dissatisfaction (Agassi, 1982).

The greater commitment of part-timers to their current job may reflect their awareness of the few opportunities, as a part-timer, to improve their job position. Alternatively, it may reflect the importance of domestic commitments in determining part-timers' labour-market behaviour. Part-timers are not particularly likely to wish to change jobs to obtain full-time work (see Table 9.12). Only 23 per cent would be willing to consider a full-time job if they were looking for a new job, while 54 per cent of female full-timers would consider a part-time job (indeed 21 per cent would *only* consider a part-time job). Involuntary full-time working among women is thus apparently more common than involuntary part-time working.

Those respondents who replied that they would want to change their jobs if plenty were available were asked a second question to determine whether it was their employer, their occupation, or both their employer and occupation that they would want to change. Those part-timers who would wish to change their job were much more likely to wish to change their occupation than were full-timers; 91 per cent of part-timers wanted to change their occupation compared to under two-thirds of full-timers, while over four-fifths of full-timers wished to change employers, compared to under two-thirds of part-timers. There is thus a significant number of part-timers who are dissatisfied with the type of work that they do, while full-timers are more likely to be committed to their particular occupation, so that their dissatisfaction with work hinges on the quality of their employer. The high percentage who would wish to change their employer also provides indirect evidence for the structural hypothesis that employers have a significant and relatively independent effect on the terms and conditions of employment, even after controlling for occupation. This 'employer' effect may indeed be less marked for

TABLE 9.12. *Percentage who would consider a full-time, a part-time, or both types of job if they were looking for another job*

	Sample	Part-time only	Full-time only	Part-time or full-time	Total % willing to consider	
					Part-time	Full-time
Male full-timers	298	3	81	17	20	97
Female full-timers	166	21	46	33	54	79
Female part-timers	140	77	6	17	94	23

Chi-squared significant at 1%.

part-timers if there is a greater tendency for all employers to provide poor pay and employment prospects for part-time employees.

CONCLUSIONS: GENDER AND THE STRUCTURING OF LABOUR MARKETS

The structuring of the employment system by gender, which has
been frequently observed and documented through studies of
firms, has also been found in the perceptions of a random sample
of individuals in a local labour market of their current employment position and prospects. The respondents' perceptions of
labour-market processes fitted well with previous models, derived
primarily from the demand side, of how labour markets are
structured (C. Craig *et al.* 1985*a*). However, divisions by gender
and by full-time and part-time jobs were often more illuminating
than divisions between low- and high-skilled jobs, suggesting that
gender is a stronger structuring variable than, for example, occupational level. Those in part-time jobs saw their labour markets
as less restricted by such factors as age or direct experience than
those in full-time jobs, but other types of barriers to entry, such
as lack of personal contacts, were perceived. Women, and in particular those in part-time jobs, were more likely to believe they
could get an *equivalent* job in the external labour market. This
apparent optimism with respect to their chances on the external
market did not lead to them seeing the external market as offering any better chances for promotion than the internal labour
market. Yet it was those in part-time jobs who were least likely
to be in jobs with internal promotion prospects. These perceptions are compatible with a view of the female labour market,
particularly for women returners, where pay levels are all relatively similar and compressed, so that it is much more possible to
obtain an equivalent job than a markedly better job.

Perhaps one of the most interesting issues to arise from the
analysis is the fact that it is not necessarily advantaged workers
that are the most attached to their employers. Attachment
depends on external opportunities as well as internal advantages.
Older workers or others who have limited opportunities outside
may feel that their current employer is more important in their

lifetime opportunities than a more advantaged worker who has greater internal and external promotion opportunities. Thus female part-timers in jobs with promotion prospects are much more likely to believe their best chance lies with their current employer than is the case for male full-timers. This issue makes it difficult to interpret responses to questions about labour-market prospects, as they will be influenced both by structural and personal factors. Nevertheless it provides a useful antidote to neoclassical and many labour-market-segmentation theories which have concentrated on differences between firms in their pay or promotion prospects as the main factor leading to job attachment on the part of workers. This demand-side approach has failed to take into account the structuring of the labour market into advantaged and disadvantaged groups which results in job attachment, not because of the advantages of the job but because of the limited external opportunities. It should be noted that these divisions of the labour supply are in some cases structural and long-term (for example those between men and women); in some cases associated with life-cycle patterns (women looking after children, older workers), and in some cases are erected by unforeseen events (redundancy and unemployment, ill-health). In some cases disadvantage may be reinforced (through unstable patterns of employment) but in other cases individuals may move between advantaged and disadvantaged positions through their life-cycle.

This perspective may be particularly important in understanding the relationships between labour-market structuring and gender. Women may be relatively stable workers in jobs which offer little chance of promotion, largely because of their limited opportunities for advancement on the external market, particularly if they are returning to work after having children. Firms might find that it is in female employment areas that strategies to retain labour at little extra cost could be the most effective. Women who find themselves in jobs with promotion prospects appear to be much more likely to believe that staying with their current employer offers them the best chance of a better job than is the case for men. There is evidence that management had begun to receive similar messages to counteract an impending skills shortage in the late 1980s; firms such as the banks introduced career-break systems and other strategies to keep their skilled labour forces within their internal-labour-market system. It would not be surprising, on the basis of this evidence, if even marginal improvements to women's employment prospects within the organization would be sufficient to induce a high degree of attachment from the female labour force, even in times of labour shortage. The problem for women is that the skills shortage was too rapidly replaced by recession, so that the stimulus to firms to experiment with new employment systems for women tended to recede before most firms had had the time to review their employment policies. In the mean time, gender divisions persist, with men enjoying better promotion opportunities in both internal and external labour markets. Women in part-time jobs remain confined to a labour market with so few opportunities for real promotion that employers can extract loyalty and commitment from their work-force without offering any of the advantages of a formal internal-labour-market system.

NOTES TO CHAPTER 9

1. This paper is based on analysis of the Northampton part of the work-attitudes/work-histories survey. The authors would like to acknowledge the contributions of other members of the SCELI initiative to the construction and collection of the data. A particular debt is owed to other members of the Cambridge team who participated in the construction of the questionnaire from which these data are drawn.
2. Note this six-way classification has been constructed from a more detailed breakdown in the questionnaire.

10

Internal Labour Markets from Managers' and Employees' Perspectives

BRENDAN BURCHELL AND JILL RUBERY

INTRODUCTION

Interest in internal labour markets has recently been fuelled by a variety of different considerations. These range from the theoretical concerns of the new institutionalist economics to the more practical issues of the role of Japanese-type employment systems on labour productivity. All perspectives have, however, taken as their starting-point the employment policy system as described and understood by management. Within the neo-classical framework, one assumption has been that workers' responses to the employment policy are expected to be based on 'rational' assessments of the relative advantages of staying with their current employer compared to changing employer. A second implicit assumption has been that the data or information on which employees are expected to act are directly congruent with those held by management; it is this second assumption that this chapter sets out to explore empirically. If it turns out to be the case that employees and their employing managers have divergent perceptions of the firm's employment practices, the predicted results of those theoretical practices on the structuring of the labour market will have to be reconsidered.

For example, in the 'efficiency wage' literature, it is hypothesized that it may, in the longer term, be less costly for employers to pay above the 'going rate' of wages in the external labour market. It is argued that by doing so one is increasing the cost to the employee of leaving the establishment, either voluntarily or through dismissal. Thus, not only will the costs of recruiting labour be reduced (for instance, the costs of advertising vacan-

cies, interviewing applicants, and training them) but, it is hypothesized, there will also be an incentive for employees to work
more conscientiously in order to minimize their risk of dismissal.
If employees think that they could easily obtain another job with
the same pay and conditions as their current job, then there is
little to be lost through dismissal. However, if they feel that they
are currently being paid above the rate being offered by other
employers, then a dismissal for 'shirking' or other forms of pro-
ductivity-reducing behaviour would be actively avoided by the
employee. There may be other benefits to the employer of achieving low rates of employee turnover too, such as the acquisition of
enterprise-specific skills which accumulate 'incidentally' in the
course of employment. Other forms of on-the-job training, such
as learning to use other machines within the firm and the development of loyalty, can also be considered to be 'costless assets'
that develop in establishments with stable internal labour markets.[1] If, however, employees are not aware that they are being
paid above the 'going rate' then that employment policy could
not achieve its objective, or if the employees' information about
their pay relative to similar jobs in other organizations was frag-
mentary and incomplete, then the premium that would have to
be paid to have the desired effect on reducing turnover on shirking might have to be so great as to be prohibitively expensive.
For the efficiency-wage theory to be understood at its most basic,
one needs to examine the effects of the *employer's* policy on the
employees' perceptions of their position in the labour market.
Studies to date have simply examined the employer's policy and
employer's perceptions. Yet it is the employee who has the
option of mobility, not the employer.

Similarly, if employers decide to adopt an internal promotion
policy to encourage stability of the labour force, employees are
expected to perceive an improvement in their chances of advancement. With this assumption of straightforward communication
between employees and employers, it thus becomes sufficient to
collect information on employment policies from management,
with possibly some check on the 'outcome' of the policy by looking at actual promotion statistics, turnover rates, etc. While this
latter type of data can help monitor the validity of management's
description of their employment policies, there is no direct examination of the motivation and perceptions which underlie

employee behaviour. For example, most vacancies might be filled by internal recruits, but if the number of vacancies is limited employees could still be unaware of the employer's preference for internal promotion. Similarly, low turnover rates may reflect a period of economic contraction in the company or be a response to the lack of vacancies in the external market. In short, it is not possible to infer employee motivations and perceptions from aggregate observed behaviour as there are too many possible factors which could give rise to similar, undifferentiable outcomes.

Perceptions of internal labour market systems

The concept of an internal labour market has often not been very clearly defined (see Rubery in Ch. 1, for an elaboration of this argument). For some it refers primarily to the use of internal recruitment and promotion systems, but for others the main emphasis is on pay, such that the distinguishing characteristic is that of an employer which sets pay levels independently of and usually above external opportunity wages for the employees. One approach thus stresses the independence of the establishment in terms of labour allocation and one in terms of pay; moreover, many analyses assume that these two factors are necessarily related. In fact, within a basic neo-classical competitive labour market model, the existence of enduring pay differentials for similar types of jobs (other aspects of the jobs, such as job security, being equal) can only be justified at the theoretical level if there are barriers to the free mobility of labour associated with internal promotion systems. However, if an underlying tendency towards a neo-classical competitive labour market is not assumed, divergences in employment systems can persist which may not be explained by specific barriers to labour mobility but by such factors as divergences in industrial structure, variations in employers' competitive policies and their implications for the organization and costs of labour, differences in the ways employers deal with 'the incompleteness of the labour contract', the segmentation of labour supply into advantaged and disadvantaged groups, the existence of collective ideologies within organizations, and so on. Indeed, within this approach, high pay and promotion opportunities may not necessarily be complements but may be considered to be alternative labour-market policies. Promotion from within may be used to avoid paying high wages to external recruits, and high pay may be sufficient to retain workers with few external promotion opportunities without the construction of an internal promotion ladder. Thus, in order not to assume here that there is a necessary link between high pay and frequent promotion opportunities, these two distinct features of an internal labour market system will be investigated separately. The adopted definition of an internal labour market system is that there should be evidence of relative independence from the external market, either in pay or in labour allocation. These two issues provide the focus for the first two sections of empirical analysis.

One reason for employers adopting an internal labour market system may be that the types of people recruited into that occupation or the establishment overall are likely to have long-term career aspirations, either within the organization or by seeing the job in the organization as a stepping-stone to better jobs with other employers. They are concerned not only with the terms and conditions in their current job but also with whether or not it offers them longer term chances of advancement or a career. However, management may make these decisions based on their own perceptions of the likelihood that employees in a particular occupation have a career orientation.

In order for employers to be able to exert control over their employees' mobility, these theories of employer strategies also require management to understand and act upon the employees' perceptions of their positions *vis-à-vis* the local labour market. Rational employers' policies ought to take account of *employee's perceptions of* the availability of other jobs that they might consider moving to. There may be no advantage in paying above-average wage rates to reduce job turnover, if, in fact, there were no other jobs that a particular set of employees might consider moving to. Similarly, the employers' decisions to provide training to their current employees as a mechanism to reduce turnover or increase motivation would only be effective if employers knew which groups of employees would be keen to undertake training.

THE SURVEY OF MANAGERS AND EMPLOYEES

If we are to understand how labour markets actually work it seems reasonable to investigate directly how employees perceive the employment structures in which they are located, rather than assume that their perceptions directly match the description of the structure provided by management. As a special study within the Social Change and Economic Life Initiative, the Cambridge team undertook a study of twenty-three Northampton employers which involved detailed interview surveys of a selection of employees employed in a representative range of occupations within the establishment. In addition, management was asked a set of directly comparable questions about each of the occupations selected for the survey. These two data sets thus provide us with a basis for comparing management's views of their employment system (as it relates to a specific occupation) with the perceptions of some of those employed in that occupation. As a more exact test of some of the theories discussed above, we could have asked managers how the employees perceived these attributes, rather than asking them for their own estimates of the attributes. It might thus have been possible for a manager to effect a policy whereby employees were misinformed and erroneously believed that they were being paid at above average rates. However, in our discussions with managers, there was no evidence that they differentiated between 'facts' (or their perceptions of those facts) and the perceptions of their employees of those facts. Furthermore, if it had been found that managers stated that they were paying relatively lower than employees thought that they were being paid, then this would have been consistent with a system whereby employers had knowingly fostered falsely optimistic perceptions on the parts of their employees. As will be demonstrated later in this chapter, employers were actually more optimistic about their employees' pay and promotion opportunities than the employees themselves. It is difficult to reconcile this state of affairs with employers differentiating between their own and their employees' perceptions of relative pay when formulating labour-market policies.

The occupations sampled were chosen to be representative of the range of occupations in the labour market, but the numbers interviewed in each occupation reflected the relative weight of the occupation within the establishment's employment structure. Thus an attempt was made to select at least one occupation from each of the seven occupational classifications adopted by SCELI for the employer survey[2] provided that there was one such occupation within the establishment. However, we also chose to interview up to four employees in occupations which were relatively numerous and only one employee in occupations which were of more minor importance in the employment structure. This procedure should result in the sample being relatively representative both of the occupational bands in the labour market as a whole, and of the occupational structure of the individual establishment. In comparing management's and employees' responses, the management questionnaire for an occupation has been compared to each of the individuals within the occupation taken separately. We have not assumed that we can construct an 'average employee' perspective, but the management's questionnaire could be expected to bear some relationship to the responses of individuals within the occupation. Where managers felt it necessary to give different responses for different employees within the groups, they were invited to do so.

Once the occupations were selected, the employees to be interviewed were chosen, as far as possible, on a random basis. Nevertheless, the sample cannot be taken to be a strictly representative sample of the Northampton labour market; the selection of employers aimed to achieve a reasonable proportion of the main types of industries (manufacturing, public and private services, distribution, etc.) and of large and small employers, but, given these parameters, one of the main criteria by which they came to be included was the willingness of management to participate in the survey. There are some reasons for believing that this procedure has biased our sample towards the range of 'good employers' in Northampton, to those most concerned with their public image in the community. Not all the participating employers fitted this category, but it was certainly the case that some of the employers providing the worst employment conditions refused to participate in this part of the initiative. In addition, our sample of employees was clearly biased in favour of established employees, if only because selections were made from employee lists that were often several weeks out of date, and the process of selection and interview was often spread over two or three months so that completely new recruits would not be likely to appear in the sample. Thus we avoided the problem that some of a completely random sample of employees could be expected to give divergent answers to management simply because they had not yet acquired sufficient knowledge of the organization. Because of this problem, and the non-independence of cases (i.e. the responses of one personnel manager could contribute scores to several employees), the data analysis techniques will be descriptive rather than inferential, with significance levels only being given where no other visual or descriptive measure of size of effect is readily available.

The interview schedule for employees came in two parts, one administered by an interviewer, and a separate self-completion section usually given to the respondent ahead of the interview. The interviews were carried out at the employee's place of work and lasted 45 minutes on average; the self-completion section took approximately 20 minutes to complete. The purpose of the self-completion was simply to extend the range of questions that could be asked within the constraints of the budget and the time which managers considered reasonable for the employee interviews.

The survey comprised 270 employees of whom 246 completed both the self-completion and the main questionnaire, and had a questionnaire relating to their job completed by a manager. These 246 individuals (approximately half of them men) were doing one of 148 different jobs, in one of the 23 establishments where these interviews took place in the Northampton 'travel-to-work area'. The Northampton travel-to-work area was typical of many British local labour markets in 1987, when the survey data was collected. It had been going through a restructuring phase for a considerable period while its traditional footwear industry was in decline. Service industries were on the increase during this time; according to the 1984 and 1987 Censuses of Employment there had been an increase of 17 per cent overall in service-sector employment, but with increases of 39 per cent in 'financial services', and 17 and 21 per cent in 'other services' and 'transport and communication' respectively. Much of this increase was in part-time female employment, where there was a 26 per cent increase across all SIC divisions, compared to an overall rate of increase in total employment of under 14 per cent.

Five attributes relevant to internal labour market policies

Perceptions of managers and employees were compared in terms of five attributes of jobs and employees: pay, promotion opportunities, job opportunities outside of the establishment, career aspirations, and training aspirations. It is not being claimed that this list is exhaustive, merely that it will be revealing. Other attributes that might be investigated, such as job satisfaction, may be of similar interest. The exact wording of the questions in the managers' questionnaires is recorded in Table 10.1; the wording in the employees' questionnaire was in all cases as similar as possible.

Errors, bias, and heterogeneity

In making these comparisons between managers' and employees' perceptions, there are three questions that might be of interest. First, how closely are the perceptions of managers and employees correlated? Put another way, how much *error* is there in managers' and employees' perceptions of the same attributes? Secondly, we ask whether there are any consistent *biases* between the two sets of perceptions. For instance, are managers likely to be systematically more or less optimistic concerning promotion opportunities than the employees? Thirdly, the perceived *spread* of some of the job attributes will be of interest. If, in the vast majority of cases, managers claim to be, for instance, paying 'about average', then theories that assume that employer's explicit policies are a significant factor in the structuring of labour markets might be questioned. Conversely, if there is a considerable amount of spread in pay above or below the 'going rate', this would be supportive of the notion that employers are active players in the labour market rather than passive ciphers of market forces. Similar arguments can be made for the spread in employees' perceptions; if employees are widely dispersed in their perception of their pay this would be supportive of labour-market theories which emphasize the importance of the variation between employers. These three issues can be summarized as error, bias, and spread respectively.

To answer the first of these questions, correlation coefficients[3] will be used to measure the level of agreement between managers and employees. The level of agreement can also be gauged graphically from Figures 10.1 to 10.7, where the sizes of the circles represent the number of joint manager and employee responses to each possible combination of responses (they can be thought of as similar to scattergrams, but modified to cope with the large number of 'ties'). If agreement is good, one would observe most of the cases to fall on or near to a straight line drawn diagonally up the middle of the graph.

The questions of bias and heterogeneity can also be gauged from Figures 10.1 to 10.7. Bias would be apparent if cases were not evenly spread above and below the diagonal; that is, if the managers were consistently more or less optimistic in their responses than employees. This can be tested for statistically by a Wilcoxon matched-pairs signed-ranks test for paired data, which contrasts the number of cases where the managers are more optimistic with the number of cases where the employees are more optimistic. Finally, the heterogeneity issue can be determined by inspecting the amount of spread away from the central categories on the graph. One final aspect of the data is also of interest, the frequency with which managers and employees use the 'Don't know' response category. If employees reply that they do not know how pay compares with other jobs requiring similar skills in the local labour market, then this implies that, for those individuals, the processes which determine mobility between employers are unlikely to be affected by the competitive processes assumed to be central in neo-classical theories. And if employers claim ignorance of the pay relativities of their employees compared to the 'going rate' in the local labour market, then that also suggests that they are not operating any active employment policies of the sort described by the efficiency-wage theories. They may, for instance, have been setting the pay levels according to nationally agreed union rates or the minimum wage rates set by wages councils. However, it is difficult to ascertain the level of uncertainty which makes individuals answer 'Don't know' when responding to questionnaires, rather than hazarding a guess.

Perceptions of pay levels relative to similar jobs in the Northampton area

Both managers and employees were asked how well they thought the job in the establishment was paid compared to other similar jobs in the Northampton labour market. This question has relevance for internal labour markets in two respects; establishments are unlikely to be pursuing an independent pay policy within the establishment if they respond that pay for each occupation is about average for similar jobs in the area. A very high clustering on the 'about average' response could be taken as indirect evidence of pay being determined by external forces, even allowing for the fact that some establishments which pursue relatively independent pay policies will nevertheless from time to time happen to coincide with the local average. If pay is above average the employer may be using high pay to attract and keep workers; however, paying below average may also indicate relative independence from the market, possibly through the use of relatively disadvantaged labour, by compensating for low pay with aspects of the employment contract such as job security for risk-averse groups of workers, or by relying on employee 'loyalty'. However, the need to find some explanation of how employers succeed in paying rates which are below the average may be less imperative if the employees are not fully aware of where their pay rates are in fact pitched, in relation to similar jobs in the Northampton labour market.

The extent of congruence in our sample is shown by the correlation coefficients in the first row in Table 10.1; the correlation between manager's and employee's perceptions of relative pay is 0.27,[4] or 0.33 for men but only 0.17 for women. To emphasize the size of these correlations, the corresponding R^2s indicate that the shared variances are 7, 11, and 3 per cent respectively. These meagre correlations cast doubt on the similarity of relative pay perceptions of managers and employees, or in the efficiency of their mutual communications about relative pay levels. However, before proceeding, it is important to consider whether there are other factors, such as measurement error or methods artefacts that might be suppressing the magnitude of these correlations.

For instance, the response categories that are being used here—'well above average', 'above average', etc.—are rather subjective and may well be interpreted in different ways by different individuals. Furthermore, whenever a continuous variable is measured in a small number of categories, correlations will be reduced. However, inspection of Figures 10.1, 10.2, and 10.3 shows that differences are clearly not limited to simple

TABLE 10.1. *Correlations between managers' and employees' perceptions of internal-labour-market advantages*

Item from manager's questionnaire	All employees	Men	Women
Thinking about other similar jobs in the Northampton area, how well would you say this job is paid?	0.27	0.33	0.17
How frequently are people in this type of job offered a better job within the organization?	0.27	0.21	0.20
How keen do you think the employees in this job would be to undertake training or further training that might help them get a better job in the future, not necessarily in this organization?	0.16	0.19	0.11 (not significant)
How likely do you think that it is that employees in this type of job could find another job in the Northampton area in which they could use the same skills as those in their current job?	0.22	0.20	0.21
How often do people in this type of job see themselves as having a career?	0.38	0.26	0.42
Approximate valid sample sizes	220	110	110

Note: Figures are Spearman's Rho, but are very similar in all cases to Pearson's R, and can thus be squared to estimate the component of shared variance.

definitional difficulties; the level of disagreement is two or more categories in 19 per cent of cases. While it is not possible, using these data, to determine exactly the proportion of the variance caused by these artefactual problems (and thus adjust the values of R^2 up accordingly), the data do strongly suggest a large scope for divergences in the judgements of managers and employees. One pragmatic way of looking at this issue is to compare the correlations found here with those found using other 'matched' variables in the data set. For instance, in our investigations into

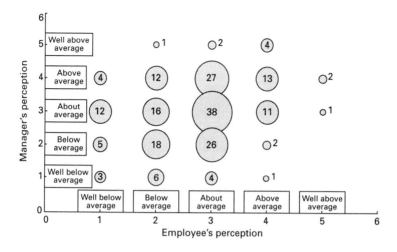

Fig. 10.1 Relative pay, all employees

managers' and employees' perceptions of skill and responsibility, correlations in the range of 0.4 to 0.7 and above were found in some cases (although here, too, low correlations were more common). Thus it is unlikely that methodological issues alone can account for these low correlations. One further morsel of relevant evidence can be gleaned from the correlations between employees and other employees. Where there was more than one employee in a particular occupational category for an establishment, a correlation could be calculated between those employees. Although this led to small sample sizes,[5] the correlation within employees ($r = 0.34$) was marginally higher than the correlation between employers and employees. This counters the argument that it is a high level of 'random error' in the employees' responses that is bringing down the correlations between employers and employees.

One further possibility that was investigated was that employees who obtained their jobs through informal channels were less likely to share management's view of the pay level than employees who had gone through formal job-search procedures. There was no evidence of this whatsoever; if anything, there was more consensus between managers and employees where informal job-search techniques had been used.

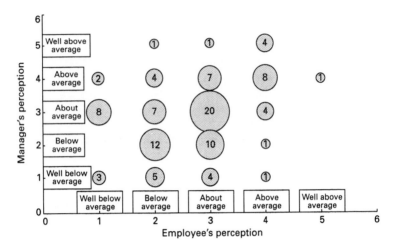

Fig. 10.2 Relative pay, men

A second problem regarding different choices of comparison groups by employers and employees is more difficult to deal with. For instance, it is possible that managers are comparing their employees with other workers with similar skills *and similar employment contracts*, whereas employees are comparing their

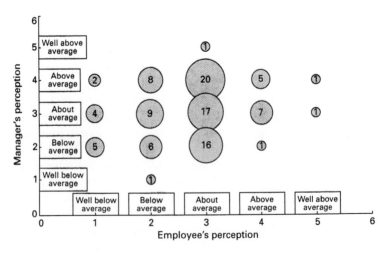

Fig. 10.3 Relative pay, women

pay with, say, freelance workers who have higher hourly rates but may have many other costs to cover (such as advertising) and higher risks associated with their contracts. Whilst this issue cannot be dealt with here without more detailed questioning of managers and employees about their comparison groups, it is implausible that this effect, in itself, could account for more than a small amount of the large incongruences apparent in the observed correlation coefficients.

The second issue of interest concerning relative pay is that of bias; are managers systematically more or less optimistic than employees about their pay relative to other employers in the local labour market? For both men and women the median case falls in the 'About average' category, but overall there are more cases where the employees are less optimistic about pay (i.e. above the diagonal in Figure 10.1) than more optimistic; in 40 per cent of cases the employees are less optimistic than the employers, in 25 per cent of cases employees are more optimistic than employers, and in the remaining 35 per cent of cases they agree. This effect, whilst not striking in its magnitude, is statistically significant (Wilcoxon matched-pairs signed-rank test, $z = 3.3$, $p = 0.001$). This mismatch was larger for women than it was for men.

By inspection of Figures 10.1, 10.2, and 10.3 it is clear that there is a considerable amount of spread on either side of the 'about average' category, in the perceptions of both managers and employees. In only about one-third of cases did managers state that they were paying the going rate, and just under half of the employees thought that their relative pay was 'About average'. Ten per cent of managers claimed to be paying either 'Well above average' or 'Well below average' rates, and 13 per cent of employees claimed to be receiving 'Well below' or 'Well above' average rates. There was an unexpected gender effect here, with managers much more likely to use both of the extremes on the scale for men; 18 per cent of men were rated by managers as getting well above or well below the going rate, compared to only 2 per cent of women. Whilst this may simply be an artefact of the higher levels and great variation in male pay, it is nevertheless a potentially interesting finding worthy of further investigation.

One explanation of the large spread above and below the paying of the 'going rate' might be that there are factors distancing some employers from local labour-market conditions. For

TABLE 10.2. *Percentage of 'Don't know/Cannot really say' responses to each question*

Item from manager's questionnaire	Manager's response	Male employee's response	Female employee's response
Thinking about other similar jobs in the Northampton area, how well would you say this job is paid?	0.4	13	9
How frequently are people in this type of job offered a better job within the organization?	1.2	15	17
How keen do you think the employees in this job would be to undertake training or further training that might help them get a better job in the future, not necessarily in this organization?	0.8	0.7	0.8
How likely do you think that it is that employees in this type of job could find another job in the Northampton area in which they could use the same skills as those in their current job?	1.2	8	6
How often do people in this type of job see themselves as having a career?	0.4	0.7	1.6

instance, they may have pay structures that are no longer in line with local labour-market conditions; in other words, some employers may not even have enough of a strategy to make any attempt at keeping in line with local rates. However, from the case-study interviews with all of the companies represented in this data set, this seemed unlikely to be true. In almost all instances managers reported some sort of attempt to acquire information about pay levels in other establishments in Northampton, through channels such as informal contacts in the chamber of commerce or job advertisements in local newspapers. A second, related objection to this explanation is the very low level of managers' responses in the 'Don't know' category (0.4 per cent, from Table 10.2), suggesting that managers do take an active interest in acquainting themselves with levels of pay in the local labour market. These data are, therefore, very strongly suggestive of the fact that many managers are using relative pay as part of an active strategy in an attempt to exert control over either the labour market or labour costs.

The infrequency with which managers used the 'Don't know/Cannot really say' response category was striking;[6] only 0.4 per cent of responses were thus coded. While it might be rather arbitrary, in a situation like this, as to when one's knowledge is so limited that one uses the 'Don't know' category, nevertheless this is a remarkably low proportion of managers who claim to be ignorant of pay relativities with the local labour market, particularly when it must be remembered that for many of the establishments in the public sector, or which are parts of larger organizations, the managers have no part in the setting of pay levels. By contrast, 13 per cent of male and 9 per cent of female employees reported that they did not know how their pay compared with similar jobs locally but outside the organization. While it is plausible that the managers are better informed about the local labour market than employees, this very relevant possibility has not been considered in a critical analysis of efficiency-wage theories. An interesting possibility would be that employers could make use of this ignorance of going rates in the local labour market by paying those employees below the 'going rate'. However, inspection of the data for those employees responding 'Don't know' shows that the employers' policies seem to be independent of the levels of employees replying 'Don't know'; even when managers thought that they were paying above average, 13 per cent of the employees claimed to be ignorant of their pay relative to the local rates.

All this seems to point to the conclusion that if the managers are attempting to enact strategies, and the spread above and below the 'going rate' suggests that some of them are, their strategies might be unsuccessful in a large number of cases simply because employees were not perceiving the strategies in the way that was intended. Alternatively, because employers might be using other strategies to employ workers at less than competitive rates, such as the formation of a culture of loyalty or paternalism, relative pay rates might be a secondary consideration for large segments of the work-force. In support of this hypothesis, analyses of other data sets collected in the same local labour market (Burchell and Rubery 1990) have shown that there are large, stable segments of the work-force characterized by high levels of job satisfaction and low levels of job-search behaviour or the desire to change jobs. For these workers, actively seeking information about the external labour market would have been at odds with their beliefs that their best chances of advancement lay with their current employer.

Frequency of internal promotion opportunities

Even more closely associated with the concept of internal labour markets than high relative pay is the existence of opportunities for internal promotion. These internal promotion systems have been argued to be used not simply as a means of recruiting labour with suitable skills to higher grade jobs, but also as a means of retaining workers in lower grades through the carrot of promotion. The desire for low labour turnover is associated with the costs incurred by the establishment in recruiting and training their employees. However, if promotion opportunities are to act as a carrot to retain existing staff, it is essential that the employees concerned actually perceive that these opportunities exist. The evidence casts considerable doubt on this hypothesis. Both managers and employees were asked to say how frequently they thought people in that particular occupation were offered a better job within the organization, using a six-point scale from 'Almost always' to 'Very rarely or never'. Figure 10.4 compares their responses; again, if there was perfect congruence, all the observations should lie on the diagonal. The important features of the (mis)match will be discussed from the perspectives of error, bias, and spread (or heterogeneity).

The correlations between the responses of employees and managers were low. For men and women together the correlation was 0.27, falling even further to 0.21 and 0.20 for men and women separately (see Figures 10.5 and 10.6). This means that there was even less agreement between the two parties than there was with

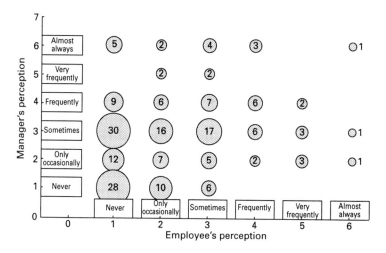

Fig. 10.4 Promotion opportunities, all employees

pay. (Again it was the case, however, that the correlations between employees in the same occupational group with the same employer were higher, $r = 0.32$, $N = 45$.) However, when the correlations were recalculated separately for each of the seven job categories, there were subsamples of the employees where the

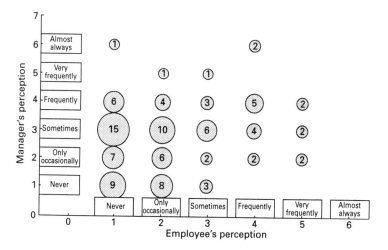

Fig. 10.5 Promotion opportunities, men

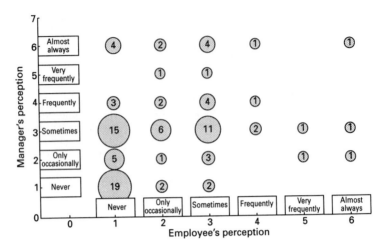

Fig. 10.6 Promotion opportunities, women

correlations between managers and employees were high; this was true of both the "Higher professionals and scientists' (rho = –0.63) and 'Middle management' (rho = 0.66). While this may be revealing about the greater communication or shared understanding between management and other higher skilled white-collar workers, the low sample sizes within those two groups might mean that generalizing from these data is a little risky.

It would have been fascinating to go on to see which other types of employees or employer showed greater levels of agreement over relative pay or promotion prospects. For instance, did employees who have been with the same employer longer come to have views of promotion opportunities which are more congruent with those employers? Did employees who have only just been selected into their jobs through the external labour market have more congruent perceptions of their relative pay? Did employers who claimed to put a lot of effort into communication have higher levels of agreement between employer and employees than others? Unfortunately, because of the small numbers of employees, and even smaller number of employers, this data set is not capable of providing satisfactory answers to these questions. However, exploratory analyses failed to find much evidence at all of any such systematic differences, except those in skill type referred to above and the gender differences referred to throughout the chapter.

The bias in responses between the two sides was even more striking, with managers having far greater levels of expectation about promotion frequencies than employees. In exactly half of the cases, managers were more optimistic than employees, whereas employees were only more optimistic than managers in 20 per cent of cases ($p < 0.001$). This mismatch was even greater amongst the female employees, with the ratio of 'manager optimist' cases to 'employee optimist' cases in excess of three to one. Put another way, the model response category was 'Sometimes' for managers, but 'Very rarely or never' for employees. The reason for these two very different portraits being painted of the very same establishments probably reflects the two different perspectives on internal recruitment, seemingly confused by managers and theorists alike (see Ch. 1). Even though the question was explicitly worded so as to refer to the proportion of each category that are promoted, rather than the proportion of places that are filled from these employees, managers were probably confounding the two. Because of the pyramid nature of organizations, with fewer places at each successive level in the hierarchy, combined with higher rates of turnover lower down the hierarchy, it is quite possible to fill all places internally whilst simultaneously only a small number of each stratum are ever offered promotion.

Again, there is a considerable level of dispersion amongst both employees and managers in their responses, although the interpretation of this is somewhat different from the case of pay; presumably differences in promotion opportunities reflect different organization structures, which may be market- or technology-led rather than explicit attempts to control labour turnover. Differences in promotion opportunities between industrial sectors supports this hypothesis, although, with only twenty-three establishments in the data set, further subdivisions by establishments are prone to unreliability. Nevertheless, the findings of greater optimism about promotion among private service firms in the sample is suggestive of the need for further investigation. The greater formalization of promotion procedures (such as the mandatory advertising of vacant positions) might be a factor in keeping the levels of internal promotions low in the public sector. Differences in frequency of promotion opportunities were also found by job category. A hierarchy by occupation emerges, with frequency of promotion being seen as greatest by both managers and workers for 'Higher professionals and scientists' and 'Middle management', followed by the lower non-manual categories, the operatives, and the category 'Lower professionals' with the least frequent opportunities. However, the bias between employees and managers was still very evident within all of these categories.

The final point to be made about the data on frequency of promotion is the low levels of 'Don't know' responses. Only 1.2 per cent of managers' responses purported not to know about frequencies of internal promotions, contrasted to 15 per cent of men and 17 per cent of women (see Table 10.2). As with pay, promotion opportunities seem to be an important issue for managers. However, evidence from employees would suggest that, if this internal promotion is taking place, they are by and large either unaware of it or apply a different notion of frequency than is used by management, such that the speed of internal promotion is so slow that it may not act as an important means of retaining labour within the establishment.

The competition for labour: Employee opportunities outside the organization

As discussed above successful employer labour-market strategies might be expected to take account of the ease with which employees could find employment using similar skills outside the organization. However, it should come as no surprise by now that there was plenty of latitude for error and bias in the comparison of managers' and employees' responses. Correlations were again very low (rho = 0.22, 0.20, and 0.21 for all employees, men, and women respectively, see Figure 10.7). Furthermore, there were systematic differences between the levels of 'optimism' from the two sides of the employment contract. As can be seen from Figure 10.7, managers were generally much more optimistic than employees concerning the employees' chances of finding other jobs in the local labour market; the divergence of opinion was particularly acute for the male employees. This finding is consistent with the conclusions of another set of analyses on this

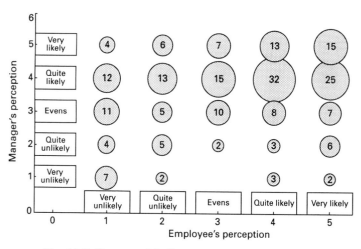

Fig. 10.7 Chances of finding another job, all employees

data set (Burchell *et al.* 1994) that employees see their own jobs as being more skilled than their managers do, particularly in the levels of organizational skill and discretion required. If employees see themselves as being more specialized in their skills, then they may think that it would be difficult to find other jobs requiring those same high levels of skill. The overall pattern was similar for men and women, except that women declared that they would find it easier to find other jobs in Northampton than men, reflecting perhaps the lower level of specialization found in women's jobs.

Career orientations of the employees

It could be expected that employers would do more to offer promotion opportunities and other benefits associated with 'internal labour markets' in occupations where they believed the workforce to have strong career orientations. In other words, internal promotion structures may not be constructed in situations where the employees concerned have weak career orientations, even if the technical characteristics of their jobs, such as high levels of establishment-specific skills, would favour such employment forms. Where workers do not expect or anticipate career advancement over their lifetime it may not be either necessary or effective to try to provide such advancement within the confines of the organization. Again, however, if such a fine tuning of employment policy is to be pursued by management, it would be essential for managers to perceive 'correctly' whether or not the employees concerned had career expectations. Our data can again be used to explore the matching of managers' perceptions of whether or not their employees were likely to consider that they were 'having a career' with the employees' own responses to the question. The managers' response was related to *how often* they felt employees in the particular job 'saw themselves as having a career', while the employees were only allowed the choice between 'Yes' and 'No'. The format of the question is not necessarily ideal, as whether or not an individual sees him or herself as having a career will not necessarily be independent of the current work situation. We are not therefore really investigating whether or not the employees when first recruited, or when they first entered the labour market, expected to have a career; we are looking instead at an orientation which will reflect both past and present experience in the labour market. However, from the perspective of management, the only question which can be asked must concern the present career orientation of employees, as they would not have the knowledge to describe career orientations prior to employment within the establishment. Nevertheless, the degree of congruence found here did seem to be only a little better than in the other cases considered so far.

Table 10.3 shows the percentage of men and women who responded affirmatively to the question concerning careers, broken down by the manager's perceptions of whether they saw themselves as having careers, in four categories from 'Almost always' to 'Rarely/Never'. As can be seen, there is a fair congruence in managers' and employees' perceptions of career orientation, corresponding to the highest correlations in Table 10.1 (rho = 0.38 for all employees, 0.26 for men and 0.42 for women), better than in the cases of perceptions of promotion opportunities or relative pay. This (marginally) higher level of agreement is particularly striking as, being an attribute of individual employees (unlike pay and promotion opportunities which are attributes of the situation), there was considerable scope for variation between employees within each of our job categories, which the

TABLE 10.3. *Percentage of employees who 'see themselves as having a career', by gender and manager's judgement of frequency having career in job category*

	Manager's judgement			
	Almost always	Frequently	Sometimes	Rarely or never
Men	77 (31)	79 (42)	75 (20)	39 (28)
Women	95 (19)	55 (20)	40 (40)	29 (34)

Note: The percentages are followed by the total number in each cell.

employers would have to aggregate over, causing additional error variation.

At the extremes, 84 per cent of employees said they were having a career in jobs where managers thought that employees almost always had careers, compared to 25 per cent of employees in jobs where managers felt that employees never saw themselves as having a career.[7] In between these two extreme values the percentages of those seeing themselves as having a career declined in accordance with managers' perceptions of frequency of career orientation. Managers were much less likely to see women as having a career (only 35 per cent of managers' responses in relation to women's jobs put the score as high as 'Almost always' or 'Frequently', compared to 51 per cent in the case of men); but in some respects the managers' and employees' perceptions in the case of women were better matched, with the percentages of women saying they had a career ranging from 95 per cent in the 'Almost always' category to only 11 per cent in the 'Never' category. There was also a good matching between managers' perceptions of career orientations by job grade and employee responses, with the ranking of managers' responses by share in the 'Almost always' or 'Frequently' category following exactly the rank order of job groups by share of employees who said they were having a career. There were no surprises in the rank ordering of job groups, running from 'Middle management' through 'Higher professional', 'Lower professional', 'Administrative and lower management', 'Higher skilled operatives', 'Routine clerical', to 'Lower skilled operatives', with the lowest levels of career aspirations.

Further analysis of the relationship between managers' perceptions of career aspirations amongst their employees is confounded by a number of features. For instance, careerists might be attracted to jobs with internal promotion opportunities, but individuals might also be more likely to report that they had a career if they were in jobs with a good chance of advancement. This is explained, somewhat, by findings from the main SCELI data (Burchell, Elliott, and Rubery, in Ch. 9) that, for many individuals, advancement is more dependent on moves between establishments than on vertical moves within an establishment. Furthermore, an upward trajectory is only one meaning of the word career—for many professions (such as dental or general practitioners) their 'career' often involves attaining a prestigious position soon after their training is finished, and remaining at that level for the rest of their working lives. Still, managers and employees alike were both willing to answer the question about careers; the 'Don't know' response was used by only one management rating of an employee and by three employees in the whole sample (Table 10.2). What is clear, none the less, is that the structural limitations on internal promotions means that there is a much larger proportion of the work-force who have career aspirations than who are in jobs with good opportunities for internal advancement.

Opportunities for training

One other way in which managers might use long-term goals as a stabilizing influence on the work-force is by providing training opportunities for their employees that would allow them to get better jobs (either internally or externally) at some point in the future. For a strategy based upon the provision of training opportunities to be effective, it would have to be targeted at those employees who were keen to undertake training. However, it was in the comparison between managers' perceptions of employees' keenness for training and employees' own reported keenness for training that gave rise to the very lowest of correlations, being only 0.16 overall (see Figure 10.8). While the correlation was slightly higher for men (rho = 0.19) it was very low for women (rho = 0.11). There was also an apparent tendency of managers to underestimate systematically the readiness of

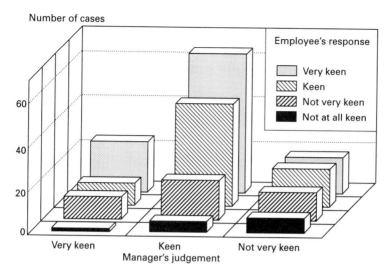

Fig. 10.8 Keenness to undertake training, by manager's judgements

employees to undertake training; if anything, this effect was stronger for male employees, where the modal response was 'Very keen' in all cases, even where managers declare them to be 'Not very keen'.

DISCUSSION AND CONCLUSIONS

This chapter has sought to explore the question of the existence and function of internal labour markets from a different and somewhat novel perspective, that is, whether there is any agreement between managers and employees as to what type of employment practices or policies exist within an establishment. The results do in fact suggest that this is a perspective on the operation of the labour market that requires further investigation, as employees' perceptions of labour-market processes seem to be quite different from those of managers. These differences in perceptions must be expected, *ceteris paribus*, to result in different labour-market behaviour from that predicted by models based on a managerial view of the labour-market system. Not only has this exploration of the data supported the need to carry out this type of research, but it has also pointed up some interesting specific findings which may have implications for labour-market analysis if they were to be substantiated in other data sets.

The first point of this type is that the incongruence between perceptions of relative pay between managers and employees is so great as to make any efficiency-wage policy very *inefficient* in its implementation. The premium would probably have to be so large for it to be widely recognized that it would be very costly to implement. However, as managers seem to be unaware of this rift in perceptions, efficiency wages may have a life of their own; it seems unlikely that managers, confident of their judgements of pay relativities, would suspect the lack of consensus as being an Achilles' heel in their attempt to control their labour mobility.

The second specific point of interest to emerge from the results is the pessimism among employees about the frequency of promotion opportunities within the establishment. Not only are they pessimistic relative to management but also in absolute terms, with two-thirds saying that better jobs are offered 'Only occasionally' or 'Never' and only 6 per cent saying they are offered 'Almost always' or 'Very frequently'. It would be instructive to compare perceptions of frequency of promotion to actual past practice within an establishment, so that it could be seen whether there are straightforward differences of perception between managers and employees or whether employees have a different understanding of what is meant by 'frequently'. It has, in fact, been argued elsewhere (see Ch. 1) that it is necessary to distinguish between an internal labour market from an employer's perspective, where most of the jobs are filled internally, and an internal labour market from an employee's perspective, where most employees are offered better jobs. These different perspectives on internal labour markets could lie behind some of the differences between managers' and employees' response in these data.

The third main conclusion is that there is even less consensus about the competitive conditions in the external labour market than in the internal labour market. Implicit in the use of pay and promotion to affect labour turnover or 'shirking' is the assumption that managers know how strong the competition for labour is, or perhaps more importantly, how easy the employees *think* that they could get another job in another organization. Again, not only is this assumption highly questionable, but there is also evidence that managers are systematically overestimating the transferability of their employees' skills to other organizations relative to the employees' own views of the transferability of their skills. This is further evidence for the inefficacy of an efficiency-wage strategy; managers may be making costly efforts to retain their employees when, in fact, there is nowhere for those employees to go!

Finally, managers may be out of tune with the personal dispositions of their employees that would make them differentially amenable to different strategies. In particular, managers may seriously underestimate their employee's keenness to undertake training which may benefit them in the future. However, and rather surprisingly, the highest correlations found in the whole study were those between managers' subjective estimations of the career-mindedness of their employees and the individual's self-assessment of whether they had a career. The consequence of a low consensus at this level (albeit higher than in the other cases examined) is that managers may be trying to use pay as a carrot for employees when the provision of training or internal advancement might be more appropriate, and vice versa.

Put into a more general context, these findings might be symptomatic of a more general problem with neo-classical theories, such as the efficiency-wage theory, which fail to take adequate account of the nature of lay knowledge and lay understanding of the labour market. Lawson (1987) for instance points out the paradox that individuals often claim a high level of certainty in their beliefs, even when there are, in fact, high levels of uncertainty. This may well be exactly what is happening in this instance; managers were willing to express their beliefs apparently without reservation, yet those beliefs might be very imprecise and erroneous. From the more detailed interviews conducted with the managers of the enterprises involved in this study, and from the literature on internal labour markets, the researchers were not given any hint that the managers' beliefs about the state of the labour market would bear little relationship to the beliefs of the employees. Yet overconfidence concerning one's beliefs is a well-documented psychological phenomenon (see, for instance,

Kahnemann *et al.* 1982) and the case in point would seem to be an ideal arena for such a bias to operate, with little possibility of adequate feedback for managers to correct their erroneous judgements. However, whilst employees were equally averse to using the 'Don't know' response when describing their personal attributes, they used it with frequencies ranging between 7 and 17 per cent when asked about relative pay, promotion opportunities, and the availability of jobs for them in the local labour market. It would be of great interest to explore the decision-making processes of those 'unknowing' individuals further, but it is unlikely that the mobility of those individuals would be readily amenable to influence in the manner theorized by efficiency-wage considerations.

Lawson (1989) points to another flaw in the way in which economists use assumptions to build theories, which he likens to scaffolding in the erection of a building. Whereas the building eventually stands when the scaffolding is removed, economic theories, particularly theories involving the assumption of perfect competition, may well fall completely if the assumptions are discredited. Efficiency-wage theory and other 'New Institutionalist' theories might well be a case in point.

However, this does not mean that employers are powerless to act out any policies to structure the labour market to their own ends. All that this investigation has shown is that it is unlikely and implausible that the phenomena of segmentation associated with internal labour markets occur through simple wage or promotion incentives as is hypothesized in the neo-classical treatment of the efficiency-wage theory. Rather, there are a number of other mechanisms which might act to segment the labour market into non-competing groups due to the nature of internal labour markets. For instance, employers may do so by enhancing the loyalty and cohesiveness of their employees, by using existing kinship networks, or by ensuring that the internal labour market is seen to operate according to legitimate as opposed to unjust principles, to give but a few examples. However, these mechanisms may differ from those posited in neo-classical models at a fundamental level. Whilst the individual is seen as the primary agent in the efficiency-wage theory, it is highly likely that the processes at work can only be understood at a collective level. These processes can best be explored through the detailed case-studies of existing practice, and through an analysis that treats labour markets as social as well as economic phenomena. Theories which limit themselves to considerations of efficiency, human capital investment processes, and price incentives will, at best, fail to understand the dynamic processes involved in the labour market and, at worst, fail even to identify the principal structuring agents in the labour market.

NOTES TO CHAPTER 10

1. It should also be noted that there can be costs to an employer of having a stable internal work-force, such as their greater collective power to seek 'productivity rents' in wage negotiations and their ability to engage in 'collective shirking'.
2. Namely: lower skilled operatives, higher skilled operatives, lower professionals, higher professionals, routine clerical, administrative and lower management, middle and upper management.
3. Spearman's Rho was used due to the sometimes irregular distributions of the variables. However, as they were in all cases very similar to Pearson's product-moment correlations, an indication of R2 can be obtained by squaring the coefficients.
4. All correlation coefficients and other test results are statistically significant unless explicitly stated otherwise. However, as the responses of one manager may be incorporated into several employee's questionnaires, the test statistics are probably less reliable than in situations where the independence assumption is more strictly adhered to.
5. Of the 156 different occupational groups, only 65 had more than one employee, and of these only 57 provided two valid responses to the question.
6. These responses were treated as 'missing' for all of the other analyses and graphs presented here.
7. The 'Rarely' and 'Never' categories have been combined together in Table 10.3 to alleviate the small numbers in the 'Never' category, especially among men.

METHODOLOGICAL APPENDIX

The Social Change and Economic Life Initiative

DUNCAN GALLIE

1. INTRODUCTION

The Social Change and Economic Life Initiative (SCELI) focused on six local labour markets—Aberdeen, Coventry, Kirkcaldy, Northampton, Rochdale, and Swindon. These were selected to provide contrasting patterns of recent and past economic change. In particular, three of the localities—Coventry, Kirkcaldy, and Rochdale—had relatively high levels of unemployment in the early and mid-1980s, while the other three had experienced relatively low levels of unemployment.

In each locality, four surveys were carried out designed to provide a high level of comparability between localities: the Work Attitudes/ Histories Survey, the Household and Community Survey, the Baseline Employers Survey, and the 30 Establishment Survey. The interview schedules for these surveys were constructed collectively by representatives of the different teams involved in the research programme. In addition a range of studies was carried out that were specific to particular localities. These were concerned to explore in greater depth a number of themes covered in the comparative surveys.

A distinctive feature of the research programme was that it was designed to provide for the possibility of linkage between the different surveys. The pivotal survey (and the first to be conducted) was the Work Attitudes/Histories Survey. This provided the sampling frame for the Household and Community Survey and for the Employers Baseline Survey. The Baseline Survey in turn provided the listings from which organizations were selected for the 30 Establishment Survey.

The field-work for the Work Attitudes/Histories Survey and for the Household and Community Survey was carried out by Public Attitudes Surveys Research Ltd. The Baseline Employers Survey was a telephone survey conducted by Survey and Fieldwork International (SFI). The interviews for the 30 Establishment Survey were carried out by members of the research teams.

TABLE A.1. *The Work Attitudes/Histories Survey 1986: achieved sample*

	Aberdeen	Coventry	Kirkcaldy	Northampton	Rochdale	Swindon	TOTAL
Eligible addresses	1,345	1,312	1,279	1,400	1,350	1,321	8,007
Achieved sample							
Main sample	997	990	1,011	957	987	955	5,897
Booster sample	48	23	—	65	18	60	214
Total interviewed	1,045	1,013	1,011	1,022	1,005	1,015	6,111
Response rate (%)	78	77	79	73	74	77	76

2. THE WORK ATTITUDES/HISTORIES SURVEY

This survey was concerned primarily with people's past work careers, their current experience of employment or unemployment, attitudes to trade unionism, work motivation, broader socio-political values, and the financial position of the household.

Two pilot studies were carried out in the preparation of the Work Attitudes/Histories Survey, testing questionnaire items, the placing of the work history schedule, interview length, and the contact procedure. The main field-work was conducted between June and November 1986. The objective was to secure an achieved sample of 1,000 in each of the six localities. As can be seen in Table A.1, the target was marginally exceeded, providing an overall sample of 6,111.

The sampling areas were defined in terms of the Department of Employment's 1984 Travel to Work areas (TTWA), with the exception of Aberdeen. In Aberdeen, where the TTWA was particularly extensive and included some very sparsely populated areas, the Daily Urban System area was used to provide greater comparability with the other locations.

A random sample was drawn of the non-institutionalized population aged 20–60. The electoral register was used to provide the initial selection of addresses, with probabilities proportional to the number of registered electors at each address. A half open-interval technique was also employed, leading to the identification of a small number of non-registered addresses in each locality. Doorstep enumeration of 20- to 60-year-olds was undertaken at each address followed by a random selection using the Kish procedure of one 20- to 60-year-old at each eligible address.

To provide sufficient numbers for analysis, it was stipulated that there should be a minimum of 150 unemployed respondents in each locality. A booster sample of the unemployed was drawn in the localities where this figure was not achieved through the initial sample. The booster sample was based on a separate random sample of addresses, with a higher sampling fraction in the wards with the highest levels of unemployment. As with the main sample, addresses were selected from the electoral register. But, for the selection of individuals, only the unemployed were eligible for inclusion. This booster sample was implemented in five of the six localities, producing a total of 214 respondents. Response rates for the combined main and booster sample were approximately 75 per cent in each of the localities, ranging from 73 per cent in Northampton to 79 per cent in Kirkcaldy (see Table A.1).

Where appropriate, weights have been used to take account of the booster sample, using the estimates of the proportion of unemployed available from the initial sample. There are also weights to provide a Kish adjustment for household size and to correct for an over-representation of women in the achieved sample (3,415 women compared with 2,696 men). The sex weight assumes equal numbers of men and women in the relevant population, as is shown to be almost exactly the case by examination of census data.

The interview consisted of two major sections. The first was a life and work history schedule in which information was collected about various aspects of the individuals' labour market, family, and residential history over the entire period since they had first left full-time education. Information about family and residential history was collected on a year grid basis. Information about labour market history—including spells of unemployment and economic inactivity—was collected on a sequential start-to-finish date-of-event basis. In the case of 'employment events' further information was collected about *inter alia* the nature of the job, the employer, hours of work, number of employees, gender segregation, and trade union membership. The second part of the interview schedule was a conventional attitudinal schedule, with a core of common questions combined with separate subschedules designed specifically for employees, for the self-employed, and for the unemployed and economically inactive.

While the greater part of the questions in the schedules provides direct comparability between localities, some scope was given for teams to introduce questions that would be asked only in their own locality (or in a subset of localities). This usually involved teams introducing a broader range of questions for investigating one or more of the themes covered in the common questions.

3. THE HOUSEHOLD AND COMMUNITY SURVEY

In 1987 a follow-up survey was carried out involving approximately one-third of the respondents to the 1986 Work Attitudes/Histories Survey. This focused primarily on household strategies, the domestic division of labour, leisure activities, sociability, the use of welfare provision, and attitudes to the welfare state. The survey was conducted in each of the localities, with the field-work lasting between March and July. The survey produced an achieved sample of 1,816 respondents, of whom 1,218 were living in partnerships and 588 were living on their own. Where applicable a range of questions was asked of partners as well as of the original respondents.

The sampling lists for the survey were generated from computer listings of respondents to the Work Attitudes/Histories Survey who had agreed to being reinterviewed. To ensure that a sufficiently large number of the unemployed respondents from the Work Attitudes/Histories Survey were reinterviewed, it was decided to specify that, in each locality, approximately 75 of the households in the follow-up survey would be from households where the respondent was unemployed at the time of the Work Attitudes/Histories Survey. For sampling, the lists were stratified into four groups, separating the unemployed from others and people who were single from those with partners. The sampling interval was the same for those of different partnership status, but different sampling intervals were used for the unemployed and for others to obtain the target numbers of people who had been unemployed at the time of the first survey.

In the event, 87 per cent of respondents (ranging from 84.8 per cent in Coventry to 89.7 per cent in Aberdeen) had indicated that they were willing to co-operate in a further phase of the research. Since the sampling areas were once more defined in terms of local labour markets, there was a further attrition of the original eligible sample due to people leaving the area (between 7 per cent and 9 per cent, depending on the locality). Response rates (for those that had agreed to be reinterviewed and were still in the area) were 75 per cent or better in each locality, ranging from 75 per cent in Rochdale and Northampton to 77 per cent in Kirkcaldy. The structure of the achieved sample is given in Table A.2. It should be noted that the table describes respondents with respect to their characteristics at the time of the Work Attitudes/Histories Survey, 1986, since this was the relevant factor for the sampling strategy. The economic and partnership status of a number of respondents had changed by the time of the second interview. For instance, while 1,223 of these respondents were classified as having had partners in 1986, the number with partners at the time of interview in 1987 was 1,218.

The questionnaire for this survey consisted of three sections: an interview schedule including questions of both respondents and partners, a respondent's self-completion, and a partner's self-completion. There was a shorter separate schedule for single people. The questionnaires included an update of the life and work histories of the original respondent and a full work history was collected for partners interviewed. The self-completion for respondents and partners was used at different points in the interview to collect independent responses from partners where it was thought that issues might be sensitive or that there was a danger of contamination of responses. The respondents and their partners filled in the relevant sections of the self-completion in the presence of the interviewer, but without reference to each other. The great majority of questions were common to all localities, but, again, a limited number of locality specific questions were allowed.

The *Time Budget Survey*. The data available through the Household and Community Survey interview was extended through a linked time

TABLE A.2. *The Household and Community Survey 1987: achieved sample by characteristics at time of Work Attitudes/Histories Survey*

	Aberdeen	Coventry	Kirkcaldy	Northampton	Rochdale	Swindon	TOTAL
Total issued	390	400	399	404	402	394	2,389
Achieved sample							
Employed/non-active with partner in 1986	153	162	167	163	155	175	975
Employed/non-active, single in 1986	68	54	62	60	68	48	360
Unemployed with partner in 1986	42	42	40	40	45	39	248
Unemployed, single in 1986	41	44	40	38	32	38	233
Total interviewed	304	302	309	301	300	300	1,816
Response rate (%)	78	76	77	75	75	76	76

budget survey. This project was directed by Jonathan Gershuny of the University of Oxford. The final five minutes of the Household and Community Survey were devoted to introducing the time budget diaries to the individual or couple present. The diaries were designed to cover a full week starting from the day following the household interview. They required natural-language descriptions of the diarist's sequences of activities to be kept on a fifteen-minute grid, for the whole week, together with any secondary (i.e. simultaneous) activities and a record of geographical location and whether or not others were present during the activities carried out. Interviewers left behind addressed, reply-paid envelopes for return of the diaries at the end of the diary week.

Forty-four per cent of those eligible (802 of the original 1,816 respondents and 533 of their 1,218 partners) completed usable diaries for the whole week. This low rate of response, though not unexpected from a postal survey, raises the issue of the extent of non-response biases. In anticipation of this problem, a number of questionnaire items were included in the original Household and Community Survey interviews which were intended to 'shadow' or parallel evidence from the diaries (i.e. questions about the frequency of participation in leisure activities and about the distribution of responsibilities for domestic work). An analysis of the two sources of data showed that the distribution of frequencies of the questionnaire responses of those who failed to complete diaries was very similar to the distribution of questionnaire responses for those who did keep diaries. From this we may infer an absence of bias at least with respect to estimates of these leisure and unpaid work activities (for a fuller account, see Gershuny 1990).

4. THE EMPLOYER SURVEYS

The implementation of the Baseline Employers Survey, which was a telephone survey, was the responsibility of Michael White of the Policy Studies Institute. The schedule was drawn up in collaboration with a working party of representatives from the different teams involved in the SCELI programme.

The survey involved a sample of establishments. The major part of the sample was drawn from information provided from the Work Attitudes/Histories Survey about people's employers. Each of the 1,000 individuals interviewed in each locality was asked, if currently employed, to provide the name and address of the employer and the address of the place of work. The sample was confined to establishments located within the travel-to-work areas that formed the basis of the research programme. Approximately 12 per cent of establishments initially listed

TABLE A.3. *The Baseline Employer Survey*

	Aberdeen	Coventry	Kirkcaldy	Northampton	Rochdale	Swindon	TOTAL
Sample from survey	345	280	229	287	233	273	1,647
Booster sample	52	54	32	51	55	39	283
Out of area	1	30	16	27	11	4	89
Eligible	396	304	245	311	277	308	1,841
Interviews	308	203	174	209	177	240	1,311
Response rate (%)	77.7	66.7	71.0	67.2	63.9	77.9	71.2

could not be included in the sample because of insufficient information or closures. The sample covers all types of employer and both the public and the private sectors.

This method of generating a sample differs from a straight random sample drawn from a frame of all establishments. The latter would have resulted in a very large number of small establishments being included, while there was considerable theoretical interest in medium-sized and large establishments as key actors in the local labour market. The method used in SCELI weights the probability of an establishment's being included by its size: the greater the number of employees at an establishment, the greater its chance of having one or more of its employees included in the sample of individuals (and hence itself being selected).

The above method is closely related to sampling with probability proportional to size (p.p.s.); however, there are generally too few medium-sized and large establishments to generate a true p.p.s. sample. To increase the numbers of these medium-sized and large establishments, an additional sample of private sector employers with fifty or more employees was drawn from market research agency lists, supplemented by information from the research teams. The booster consisted of all identifiable establishments in this size range not accounted for by the basic sampling method. The sampling method, then, was designed to be as comprehensive as possible for medium-sized and larger employers. In practice, 70 per cent to 85 per cent of the sample by different localities were provided through the listings from the Work Attitudes/Histories data, while only 15 per cent to 30 per cent were from the booster sample. The structure of the achieved sample is presented in Table A.3. The sample so generated under-represents smaller, and over-represents larger, establishments, but provides adequate numbers in all size groups. It is also approximately representative of employment in each area, but it is possible to use weighting to achieve an even more precise representation of local employment. This was carried out using tables of employment by size group of establishment within industry group within each local labour market, from the 1984 Census of Employment (by courtesy of the Statistics Division, Department of Employment).

There were five stages of piloting over the summer of 1986, particularly concerned to develop the most effective contact procedure. The main field-work period was from October 1986 to February 1987. The overall response rate was 71 per cent, ranging from 64 per cent in Rochdale to 78 per cent in Aberdeen and Swindon.

The interview schedules focused particularly upon occupational structure, the distribution of jobs by gender, the introduction of new technologies, the use of workers with non-standard employment contracts, relations with trade unions, and product market position. Different questionnaires were used for large and small organizations, with fewer questions being asked of small organizations. There were also minor variations in the schedules for public and private organizations, and for different industries. The four industry subschedules were: (1) manufacturing, wholesale, haulage, extractive, agriculture; (2) retail/hotel, catering/personal, and other consumer services; (3) banks, financial and business services, and (4) construction. These were designed to provide functionally equivalent questions with respect to product market position for different types of organization.

In each locality, there were follow-up interviews in at least thirty establishments—the 30 Establishment Survey—designed in particular to explore the motivation behind particular types of employer policy. While steps were taken to ensure that cases were included across a range of different industries, the composition of the follow-up sample was not a random one, but reflected team research interests. In contrast to the other surveys, the data from this survey should not be assumed to be generalizable to the localities.

5. THE RELATED STUDIES

Finally, most teams also undertook at least one smaller-scale further enquiry in their localities, each being designed exclusively by the team itself and funded separately from the three main surveys. These Related Studies sometimes built upon previous fieldwork a team had undertaken in its locality, and upon the resulting network of research contacts. Adopting for the most part documentary, case-study, or open-ended interviewing techniques of enquiry, the Related Studies dealt with special issues ranging from local socio-economic history to present-day industrial relations trends.

In one sense, then, the Related Studies can be thought of as freestanding research projects. At the same time, however, in interpreting the findings from a related study, a team could take advantage of the extensive contextual data provided by the main surveys. What is more, thanks to their use of methodologies permitting enquiry in depth and over time, the Related Studies could throw more light on many of the quantitative (and at times somewhat summary) findings of the main surveys. Several Related Studies were of particular value in validating and extending core-survey findings.

BIBLIOGRAPHY

Abraham, K. 1988. 'Flexible Staffing Arrangements and Employers' Short-Term Adjustment Strategies', in R. Hart (ed.), *Employment, Unemployment and Labor Utilization* (Boston, Mass.: Unwin Hyman).

Adams, J. S. 1963. 'Towards an Understanding of Inequity', *Journal of Abnormal and Social Psychology*, 67: 422–36.

—— 1965. 'Inequality in Social Exchange', in L. Berkowitz (ed.), *Advances in Experimental Social Psychology*, ii (New York: Academic Press).

Agassi, J. B. 1982. *Comparing the Work Attitudes of Men and Women* (Lexington, Mass: Lexington).

Aglietta, M. 1979. *A Theory of Capitalist Regulation* (London: New Left Books).

Anderson, M. 1976. 'Sociological History and the Working Class Family: Smelser Revisited', *Social History*, 1/3: 317–34.

Armstrong, P. 1982. 'If it's Only Women it Doesn't Matter So Much', in J. West (ed.), *Work, Women and the Labour Market* (London: Routledge & Kegan Paul).

Atkinson, J. 1985a. 'Flexibility: Planning for an Uncertain Future', *Manpower Policy and Practice*, 1 (Summer): 26–9.

—— 1985b. *Flexibility, Uncertainty and Manpower Management* (Report 89; Brighton: Institute of Manpower Studies).

—— 1986. *Changing Work Patterns: How Companies Achieve Flexibility to Meet New Needs* (London: NEDO).

—— and Meager, N. 1986. *Changing Work Patterns* (London: NEDO).

Bagnasco, A. 1977. *Tre Italie: La problematica territorale dello sviluppo italiano* (Bologna: Il Mulino).

Baron, J., and Bielby, W. 1980. 'Bringing the Firms Back in: Stratification, Segmentation and the Organization of Work', *American Sociological Review*, 45/5 (Oct.): 737–65.

—— Davis-Blake, A., and Bielby, W. T. 1986. 'The Structure of Opportunity: How Promotion Ladders Vary within and among Organisations', *Administrative Science Quarterly*, 31 (June): 248–73.

Barron, R. D., and Norris, G. M. 1976. 'Sexual Divisions and the Dual Labour Market', in D. L. Barker and S. Allen (eds.), *Dependence and Exploitation in Work and Marriage* (London: Longman).

Batstone, E. 1985. *Working Order: Workplace Industrial Relations over Two Decades* (Oxford: B. Blackwell).

Becker, G. 1964. *Human Capital: A Theoretical and Empirical Analysis with Special Reference to Education* (New York: National Bureau of Economic Research).

Bennet, G. P. n.d. *The Past at Work* (Markinch: [publisher unknown]).

Benwell Community Project 1978. *The Making of a Ruling Class: Two Centuries of Capital Development on Tyneside* (Benwell Community Project, Newcastle upon Tyne).

Berger, S., and Piore, M. 1980. *Dualism and Discontinuity in Industrialised Societies* (Cambridge, Cambridge UP).

Best, M. H. 1990. *The New Competition* (Cambridge: Polity Press).

Bills, D. 1987. 'Costs, Commitment and Rewards: Factors Influencing the Design and Implementation of Internal Labour Markets', *Administrative Science Quarterly*, 32 (June): 201–11.

Blackburn, R., and Mann, M. 1979. *The Working Class in the Labour Market* (London: Macmillan).

Blanchflower, D., and Oswald, A. 1988. 'Internal and External Influences upon Pay Settlements', *British Journal of Industrial Relations*, 26 (Nov.): 363–70.

Blauner, R. 1964. *Alienation and Freedom: The Factory Worker and his Industry* (Chicago: Univ. of Chicago Press).

Bock, R. D. 1975. *Multivariate Statistical Methods in Behavioural Research* (New York: McGraw Hill).

Bowles, S. 1985. 'The Production Process in a Competitive Economy: Walrasian, Neo-Hobbesian and Marxist Models', *American Economic Review*, 75/1 (Mar.): 16–36.

Boyer, R. 1979. 'Wage Formation in Historical Perspective: The French Experience', *Cambridge Journal of Economics*, 3/2 (June): 99–118.

Boyson, R. 1970. *The Ashworth Cotton Enterprise: The Rise and Fall of a Family Firm* (Clarendon Press: Oxford).

Bradley, H. 1988. 'Change and Continuity in History and Sociology: The Case of Industrial Paternalism', unpubl. paper given to BSA Edinburgh Conference.

Bragg, C. 1987. 'Apprenticeship Training in the Contemporary Rochdale Engineering Industry', MA thesis, Lancaster Univ.

Braverman, H. 1974. *Labour and Monopoly Capital: The Degradation of Work in the Twentieth Century* (New York: Monthly Review Press).

Brown, C., and Reich, M. 1989. 'When does Union-Management Co-operation Work? A Look at NUMMI and GM-Van Nuys', *California Management Review*, 31/4: 26–44.

Brown, C. V. 1983. *Taxation and the Incentive to Work* (Oxford: Oxford UP).

Brusco, S. 1982. 'The Emilian Model: Productive Decentralisation and Social Integration', *Cambridge Journal of Economics*, 6/2 (June), 167–84.

—— 1986. 'Small Firms and Industrial Districts: The Experience of Italy', in D. Keeble and E. Weever (eds.), *Regional Development in Europe* (London: Croom Helm).

Burawoy, M. 1979*a*. *Manufacturing Consent: Changes in the Labour Process under Monopoly Capitalism* (Univ. of Chicago Press: Chicago).

—— 1979*b*. *Manufacturing Consent: The Transformation of Work in the Twentieth Century* (New York: Basic Books).

—— 1985. *The Politics of Production* (London: Verso).

Burchell, B., and Rubery, J. 1987. 'Segmented Jobs and Segmented Workers', DAE mimeo, SCELI project, presented to the International Working Party on Labour Market Segmentation Conference, Turin.

——, —— 1990. 'An Empirical Investigation into the Segmentation of the Labour Supply', *Work, Employment and Society*, 4/4 (Dec.): 551–75.

—— Elliott, B. J., Rubery, J. C., and Wilkinson, S. F. 1994. 'Job Content and Skill: Manager's and Employees' Perspectives', in R. Penn, M. Rose, and J. Rubery (eds.), *Occupations and Skill* (SCELI series, Oxford UP, forthcoming).

Burns, T., and Stalker, G. M. 1961. *The Management of Innovation* (London: Tavistock).

Campbell, R. H. 1980. *The Rise and Fall of Scottish Industry, 1707–1939* (Edinburgh: John Donald).

Carter, I. 1979. *Farm Life in Northeast Scotland, 1840–1914* (Edinburgh, John Donald).

Chandler, A. D., jun. 1977. *The Visible Hand: The Managerial Revolution in American Business* (Cambridge, Mass.: Belknap Press).

Checkland, S. G. 1981. *The Upas Tree: Glasgow 1875–1975* (Glasgow: Univ. of Glasgow Press).

Craig, C., Rubery, J., Tarling, R., and Wilkinson, F. 1982. *Labour Market Structure Industrial Organisation and Low Pay* (Cambridge: Cambridge UP).

—— Garnsey, E., and Rubery, J. 1985*a*. *Payment Structures in Smaller Firms: Women's Employment in Segmented Labour Markets* (Dept. of Employment Research Paper no. 48; London: Dept. of Employment).

——, ——, and —— 1985*b*. 'Labour Market Segmentation and Women's Employment: A Case-Study from the United Kingdom', *International Labour Review*, 124/3 (May–June): 267–80.

Craig, F. W. S. 1977. *British Parliamentary Election Results 1832–1885* (London: Macmillan).

Curran, M. 1988. 'Gender and Recruitment: People and Places in the Labour Market', *Work, Employment and Society*, 2/3 (Sept.): 335–51.

Daniel, W. W. 1990. *The Unemployed Flow* (London: Policy Studies Institute).

Davidoff, L., and Hall, C. 1987. *Family Fortunes: Men and Women of the English Middle Class, 1780–1850* (London: Hutchinson).

Davies, J. 1986. 'A Twentieth Century Paternalist: Alfred Herbert and the Skilled Coventry Workman', in W. Lancaster and A. Mason (eds.), *Life and Labour in a Twentieth Century City: The Experience of Coventry* (Coventry: Cryfield).

Debouzy, M. 1988. 'Permanence du paternalisme?' *Le Mouvement sociale*, 144: 3–15.

Doeringer, P., and Piore, M. 1971. *Internal Labour Markets and Manpower Analysis* (Lexington, Mass.: D. C. Heath).

Dore, R. 1973. *British Factory, Japanese Factory* (London: Allen & Unwin).

Dunlop, J. 1957. 'The Task of Contemporary Wage Theory', in G. Taylor and F. Pierson (eds.), *New Concepts in Wage Determination* (New York: McGraw-Hill).

Dutton, H. I., and King, E. 1982. 'The Limits of Paternalism: The Cotton Tyrants of Northern Lancashire, 1836–54', *Social History*, 7/1: 59–73.

Edwards, R. 1979. *Contested Terrain: The Transformation of the Workplace in the Twentieth Century* (London: Heinemann).

Elias, P., and White, M. 1991. *Recruitment in Local Labour Markets: Employer and Employee Perspectives* (Dept. of Employment Research Paper No. 86; London: Dept. of Employment).

Everitt, B. S. 1977. *The Analysis of Contingency Tables* (London: Chapman & Hall).

Fitzgerald, R. 1988. *British Labour Management and Industrial Welfare, 1846–1939* (London: Croom Helm).

Foster, J. 1977. *Class Struggle and the Industrial Revolution* (London: Methuen).

—— and Woolfson, C. 1986. *The Politics of the UCS Work-In Class Alliances and the Right to Work* (London: Lawrence & Wishart).

Fox, A. 1974. *Beyond Contract: Work, Power and Trust Relations* (London: Faber & Faber).

Friedman, A. 1978. *Industry and Labour* (London: Macmillan).

Gallie, D. 1986. 'The Social Change and Economic Life Initiative: An Overview' (ESRC Social Change and Economic Life Initiative Working Paper 1, Oxford: Nuffield College).

Gallie, D. 1991. 'Patterns of Skill Change: Upskilling, Deskilling or the Polarisation of Skills?' *Work, Employment and Society*, 5/3: 319–51.

Gash, N. 1983. *Aristocracy and People: Britain 1815–1865* (London: Edward Arnold).

Geddes, P. 1911. *The Civic Survey of Edinburgh* (Edinburgh: The Civic Department).

Gershuny, J. I. 1990. 'International Comparisons of Time Use Surveys: Methods and Opportunities', in R. von Schweitzer, M. Ehling, and D. Schafer (eds.), *Zeitbudget erhebungen* (Stuttgart: Metzer- Poeschel).

Gilbert, G. N. 1981. *Modelling Society: An Introduction to Loglinear Modelling for Social Researchers* (London: George Allen & Unwin).

Gilbert, N. (ed.) 1992. *Fordism and Flexibility: Divisions and Change* (London: Macmillan).

Goldman, P., and Van Houten, D. R. 1980. 'Uncertainty, Conflict and Labour Relations in the Modern Firm: Parts 1 and 2', *Economic and Industrial Democracy*, 1, 63–98 and 236–87.

Goldthorpe, J. H., and Hope, K. 1974. *The Social Grading of Occupations* (Oxford: Clarendon Press).

Goodman, P. S. 1974. 'An Examination of Referents Used in the Evaluation of Pay', *Organizational Behaviour and Human Performance*, 12/2 (Oct.): 170–95.

Goodman, E., Barnford, J., and Saynor, P. 1989. *Small Firms and Industrial Districts in Italy* (London: Routledge).

Gordon, A. J. 1990. 'The North Sea Oil Industry: A Case Study of Flexibility', unpublished dissertation, Dundee Institute of Technology.

Gordon, D. M., Edwards, R., and Reich, M. 1982. *Segmented Work, Divided Workers* (Cambridge: Cambridge UP).

Guest, D. 1987, 'Human Resource Management and Industrial Relations', *Journal of Management Studies*, 24/5: 503–22.

Hakim, C. 1987. 'Trends in the Flexible Workforce', *Employment Gazette* (Nov.): 549–560.

—— 1990. 'Core and Periphery in Employers' Workforce Strategies: Evidence from the 1987 ELUS Survey', *Work, Employment and Society*, 4/2 (June): 157–88.

—— 1991. 'Grateful Slaves and Self-Made Women: Fact and Fantasy in Women's Work Orientations', *European Sociological Review*, 7/2: 101–21.

Halsey, A. H., Heath, A. F., and Ridge, J. M. 1980. *Origins and Destinations: Family, Class and Education in Modern Britain* (Oxford: Oxford UP).

Hanham, H. J. 1959. *Elections and Party Management: Politics in the Time of Disraeli and Gladstone* (London: Longmans).

Haraszti, M. 1977. *A Worker in a Worker's State* (Harmondsworth: Penguin).

Hart, R. A. 1984. *The Economics of Non-Wage Labour Costs* (London: Allen & Unwin).

Harvey, D. 1989. *The Condition of Postmodernity* (Oxford: B. Blackwell).

Hassan, J. A. 1980. 'The Landed Estate, Paternalism and the Coal Industry in Midlothian 1800–1880', *Scottish Historical Review*, 59/1: 73–91.

Haughton, G. 1985. 'The Dynamics of the Rochdale Labour Market', Lancaster University Social Change and Economic Life Initiative, Working Paper 3.

Hay, D., Linbaugh, P., Rule, J. G., Thompson, E. P., and Winslow, C. 1977. *Albion's Fatal Tree: Crime and Society in Eighteenth Century England* (Harmondsworth: Penguin).

Hayes, R., and Wheelwright, S. 1984. *Restoring our Competitive Edge: Competing Through Manufacturing* (New York: John Wiley & Sons).

Hicks, J. 1963. *The Theory of Wages* (2nd edn. London: Macmillan).

Hirst, P., and Zeitlin, J. 1989. *Reversing Industrial Decline? Industrial Structure and Policy in Britain and her Competitors* (Oxford: Berg).

Horrell, S., and Rubery, J. 1991. *Employers' Working-Time Policies and Women's Employment* (Equal Opportunities Commission Research Series; London: HMSO).

—— Rubery, J., and Burchell, B. 1990. 'Gender and Skills', *Work, Employment and Society*, 4/2 (June): 189–206.

Huberman, M. 1987. 'The Economic Origins of Paternalism: Lancashire Cotton Spinning in the First Half of the Nineteenth Century', *Social History*, 12/2: 177–92.

—— 1989. 'The Economic Origins of Paternalism: Reply to Rose, Taylor and Winstanley', *Social History*, 14/1: 99–103.

Hume, J. R., and Moss, M. S. 1979. *Beardmore: The History of a Scottish Industrial Giant* (London: Heinemann).

Humphries, J., and Rubery, J. 1992. 'The Legacy for Women's Employment: Integration, Differentiation and Polarisation', in J. Michie (ed.), *The Economic Legacy 1979–1992* (London: Academic).

Hunt, A. (ed.) 1988. *Women and Paid Work* (London: Macmillan).

Hunter, A. J. 1957. *The Auld Toon O' Leslie* (Leslie: [publisher unknown]).

Hutchison, I. G. C. 1986. *A Political History of Scotland 1832–1924: Parties, Elections and Issues* (Edinburgh: John Donald).

Hyman, R. 1988. 'Flexible Specialisation: Miracle or Myth', in R. Hyman, and W. Streek (eds.), *New Technology and Industrial Relations* (Oxford: B. Blackwell).

Hyman, R. and Elger, T. 1981. 'Job Controls, the Employers' Offensive, and Alternative Strategies', *Capital and Class*, 15: 115–49.

Incomes Data Services 1989. *Retail Pay and Conditions* (Study 446; London: Incomes Data Services).

International Labour Office 1987. 'Smaller Units of Employment: A Synthesis', report on industrial reorganization in industrialized countries (Geneva: ILO).

Jacquemin, A. 1987. *The New Industrial Organization: Market Forces and Strategic Behaviour* (Oxford: Clarendon Press).

Jowitt, J. A. (ed.) 1986. *Model Industrial Communities in Mid-Nineteenth Century Yorkshire* (Bradford: University of Bradford).

Joyce, P. 1982. *Work, Society and Politics: The Culture of the Factory in Later Victorian England* (London: Methuen).

—— 1984*a*. 'Labour, Capital and Compromise: A Response to Richard Price', *Social History*, 9/1: 67–76.

—— 1984*b*. 'Languages of Reciprocity and Conflict: A Further Response to Richard Price', *Social History*, 9/2: 225–31.

Kahn, L. 1975. 'Unions and Labour Market Segmentation', Ph.D. thesis, Univ. of California, Berkeley, Calif.).

Kahnemann, D., Slovic, P., and Tversky, A. 1982. *Judgement under Certainty: Heuristics and Biases* (Cambridge, Cambridge UP).

Kellas, G. K. 1989. 'Oil and the Local Economy', in R. F. Elliott and A. E. H. Speight (eds.), *Unemployment and Labour Market Efficiency: A Study of the Aberdeen and Grampian Experience* (Aberdeen: Aberdeen UP).

Kerr, C. 1954. 'The Balkanisation of Labour Markets', in E. W. Bakke and P. M. Hauser (eds.), *Labour Mobility and Economic Opportunity* (New York: MIT Press).

Knights, D., Willmott, H., and Collinson, D. (eds.) 1985. *Job Redesign* (Aldershot: Saxon House).

Kochen, T. A., Katz, H. C., and McKersie, R. B. 1986. *The Transformation of American Industrial Relations* (New York: Basic Books).

Konzelmann Smith, S. 1991. 'Technological Integration and Fragmented Labour Market Structures: The Decline and Restructuring of the US Steel Integrated Sector', *International Contributions to Labour Studies*, 1: 25–57.

Lane, A., and Roberts, K. 1971. *Strike at Pilkingtons* (London: Fontana).

Laslett, P. 1983. *The World We Have Lost—Further Explored* (London: Methuen).

Lawler, E. E. III. 1971. *Pay and Organizational Effectiveness: A Psychological View* (New York: McGraw Hill).

Lawson, T. 1981. 'Paternalism and Labour Market Segmentation Theory', in F. Wilkinson (ed.), *The Dynamics of Labour Market Segmentation* (London: Academic Press).

—— 1987. 'The Relative/Absolute Nature of Knowledge and Economic Analysis', *Economic Journal*, 97: 951–70.

—— 1989. 'Abstraction, Tendencies and Stylised Facts: A Realist Approach to Economic Analysis', *Cambridge Journal of Economics*, 13/1: 59–78.

Lester, R. A. 1952. 'A Range Theory of Wage Differentials', *Industrial and Labour Relations Review*, 5 (July): 483–501.

Lindbeck, A., and Snower, D. 1985. 'Explanations of Unemployment', *Oxford Review of Economic Policy*, 1/2: 34–59.

Locke, E. A. 1976. 'The Nature and Causes of Job Satisfaction', in M. D. Dunette (ed.), *The Handbook of Industrial and Organizational Psychology* (Chicago: Rand McNally).

Lown, J. 1988. ' "Père plutôt que maître . . .", le paternalisme à l'usine dans l'industrie de la soie à Halstead au xixe siècle', *Le Mouvement sociale*, 144: 51–70.

MacDougall, I. (ed.) 1981. *Militant Miners: Recollections of John McArthur, Buckhaven, and Letters, 1924–26, of David Proudfoot, Methil, to G. Allen Hunter* (Edinburgh: Polygon Books).

MacInnes, J. (1987). 'The Question of Flexibility', Research Paper No. 5, Centre for Research into Industrial Democracy and Participation, Univ. of Glasgow, Aug.

Macintyre, S. 1980. *Little Moscows: Communism and Working Class Militancy in Inter War Britain* (London: Croom Helm).

Mackay, D., Boddy, D., Brack, J., and Jones, N. 1971. *Labour Markets under Different Employment Conditions* (London: George Allen & Unwin).

Main, B. G. M. 1988. 'Women's Hourly Earnings: The Influence of Work Histories on Rates of Pay', in A. Hunt (ed.), *Women and Paid Work* (Basingstoke: Macmillan).

Manwaring, T. 1984. 'The Extended Internal Labour Market', *Cambridge Journal of Economics*, 8/2: 161–87.

March, J. G., and Simon, H. A. 1958. *Organizations* (New York: Wiley).

Marchington, M., and Parker, P. 1990. *Changing Patterns of Employee Relations* (Hemel Hempstead: Harvester Wheatsheaf).

Marris, R. 1964. *The Economic Theory of Managerial Capitalism* (London: Macmillan).

Marsden, D. 1986. *The End of Economic Man?* (Brighton: Wheatsheaf).

Marshall, A. 1923. *Industry and Trade: A Study of Industrial Technique and Business Organisation* (London: Macmillan).

Martin, J., and Roberts, C. 1984. *Women and Employment: A Lifetime Perspective* (London: HMSO).

Massey, D. 1984. *Spatial Divisions of Labour: Social Structures and the Geography of Production* (London: Macmillan).

Maurice, M., Sellier, F., and Silvestre, J.-J. 1984. 'The Search for a Societal Effect in the Production of Company Hierarchy: A Comparison of France and Germany' in Osterman 1984.

——, ——, and —— 1986. *The Social Foundations of Industrial Power* (Cambridge, Mass.: MIT Press).

McKenna, F. 1976. 'Victorian Railways Workers', *History Workshop*, 1: 26–73.

McNabb, R., and Psacharopoulos, G. 1981. 'Further Evidence of the Relevance of the Dual Labour Market Hypothesis for the United Kingdom', *Journal of Human Resources*, 16: 442–8.

McNabb, R. and Ryan, P. 1990. 'Segmented Labour Markets', in D. Sapsford and Z. Tzannatos (eds.), *Current Issues in Labour Economics* (London: Macmillan).

Meacham, S. 1977. *A Life Apart* (London: Thames & Hudson).

Meegan, R. 1988. 'A Crisis in Mass Production?' in J. Allen and D. Massey (eds.), *The Economy in Question* (London: Sage).

Mehaut, P. 1988. 'New Firms' Training Strategies and Changes in the Wage-Earning Relationship', *Labour and Society*, 13/4: 443–56.

Melling, J. 1980. 'Non-Commissioned Officers: British Employers and their Supervisory Workers 1880–1920', *Social History*, 5/2: 183–222.

Mellor, H. E. 1976. *Leisure and the Changing City, 1870–1914* (London: Routledge & Kegan Paul).

Michon, F. 1981. 'Dualism and the French Labour Market: Business Strategy, Non-Standard Job Forms and Secondary Jobs', in F. Wilkinson (ed.), *The Dynamics of Labour Market Segmentation* (London: Academic Press).

Middlemas, K. 1979. *Politics in Industrial Society: The Experience of the British System since 1911* (London: Andre Deutsch).

Morgan, N. 1986. 'Sir Michael Nairn', 'Sir Michael B. Nairn', and 'John Barry' in A. Slaven *et al.*, *Dictionary of Scottish Business Biography, 1860–1960*, i. *The Staple Industries* (Aberdeen: Aberdeen UP).

Morris, R. J. 1983. 'Voluntary Societies and British Urban Elites 1780–1850: An Analysis', *Historical Journal*, 26: 95–118.

—— 1990. *Class Sect and Party: The Making of the British Middle Class, Leeds, 1820–50* (Manchester: Manchester UP).

Muir, A. *c.*1947. *The Fife Coal Company Limited: A Short History* (Cambridge: W. Heffer).

—— 1956. *Nairn's of Kirkcaldy: A Short History of the Company, 1947–1956* (Cambridge: W. Heffer).

Murray, R. 1985. 'Benetton Britain: The New Economic Order', *Marxism Today*, 29/11 (Nov.): 28–32.

—— 1988. 'Life after Henry (Ford)', *Marxism Today*, 32/10 (Oct.): 8–13.

NEDO 1982. *Changing Needs and Relationships in the UK Apparel Fabric Market* (London: NEDO).

—— 1983. *The Cotton and Allied Textiles Industry: A Report on the Work of the Cotton and Allied Textiles Economic Development Committee* (London: NEDO).

Newby, H., Bell, C., Rose, D., and Saunders, P. 1978. *Property, Paternalism and Power: Class and Control in Rural England* (London: Hutchinson).

Norris, G. M. 1978. 'Industrial Paternalist Capitalism and Local Labour Markets', *Sociology*, 12: 469–89.

OECD 1986a. *Labour Market Flexibility* (May; Paris: OECD).

—— 1986b. *Flexibility in the Labour Market* (Nov.; Paris: OECD).

—— 1988. 'Labour Flexibility in Europe: A Comparative Analysis of Four Countries', unpubl. MS.

Oi, W. 1962. 'Labour as a Quasi-Fixed Factor', *Journal of Political Economy*, 52 (Dec.): 53–5.

Osterman, P. 1982. 'Employment Structures within Firms', *British Journal of Industrial Relations*, 3: 349–61.

—— (ed.) 1984. *Internal Labour Markets* (Cambridge, Mass: MIT Press).

—— 1987. 'Choice of Employment Systems in Internal Labour Markets', Industrial Relations, 26/1 (Winter): 46–67.

—— 1988. *Employment Futures* (New York: OUP).

Pankhurst, K. 1990. 'The Quality of Labour', Ph.D. thesis; Univ. of Cambridge.

Pearson, R. 1986. 'The Industrial Suburbs of Leeds in the Nineteenth Century: Community Consciousness amongst the Social Classes', Ph.D. diss.; Univ. of Leeds.

Penn, R. D. 1985. *Skilled Workers in the Class Structure* (Cambridge: Cambridge UP).

—— 1988. 'The Internationalization of the Contemporary Paper Industry', Industry Research Working Paper 1 (Lancaster University Press).

—— and Scattergood, H. 1985. 'Deskilling or Enskilling? An Empirical Investigation of Recent Theories of the Labour Process', *British Journal of Sociology*, 36/4: 611–30.

—— —— 1987. 'Corporate Strategy and Textile Employment', Lancaster University, Social Change and Economic Life Initiative, Working Paper 12.

—— —— 1988. 'Continuities and Change in Skilled Work: A Comparison of Five Paper Manufacturing Plants in the UK, Australia and the USA', *British Journal of Sociology*, 39/1: 69–85.

Perkin, H. J. 1976. *The Origins of Modern English Society, 1780–1880* (London: Routledge & Kegan Paul).

Pfeffer, J., and Cohen, Y. 1984. 'Determinants of Internal Labour Markets in Organisations', *Administrative Science Quarterly*, 29 (Dec.): 550–72.

Phillips, A., and Taylor, B. 1980. 'Sex and Skill: Notes towards a Feminist Economics', *Feminist Review*, 6: 79–88.

Piore, M. J., and Sabel, C. F. 1984. *The Second Industrial Divide* (New York: Basic Books).

Pollard, S. 1964. 'The Factory Village in the Industrial Revolution', *English Historical Review*, 79/3: 513–31.

Pollert, A. 1987. 'The Flexible Firm: A Model in Search of Reality', *Warwick Papers in Industrial Relations*, 19 (Dec.).

—— 1988*a*. 'The Flexible Firm: Fixation or Fact', *Work, Employment and Society*, 2/3: 281–306.

Pollert, A. 1988*b*. 'Dismantling Flexibility', *Capital and Class*, 34: 42–75.

Price, R. 1983. 'The Labour Process and Labour History', *Social History*, 8/1: 57–76.

—— 1984. 'Conflict and Co-operation: A Reply to Patrick Joyce', *Social History*, 9/2: 217–24.

Purcell, J. 1987. 'Mapping Management Styles in Employee Relations', *Journal of Management Studies*, 24/5: 533–48.

—— and Sisson, K. 1983. 'Strategies and Practice in the Management of Industrial Relations', in A. Bain (ed.), *Industrial Relations in Britain* (Oxford: B. Blackwell).

Pyke, F. 1987. 'Industrial Networks and Modes of Cooperation in a British Context', North West Industry Research Unit, Manchester Univ.

—— 1988. 'Cooperative Practices among Small and Medium-Sized Establishments', *Work, Employment and Society*, 2/3 (Sept.): 352–65.

—— Becattini, G., and Sengenberger, W. (eds.) 1991. *Industrial Districts and Inter-Firm Co-operation in Italy* (Geneva: International Institute for Labour Studies).

Ravèyre, M.-F. 1986. 'Small and Medium-Sized Firms in Saint-Cobain', intermediate report, CLYSI: Univ. of Lyons.

—— and Saglio, J. 1984. 'Les Systèmes industriels localisés', *Sociologie du Travail*, 1984 (2): 157–76.

Rimmer, M., and Zappala, J. 1989. 'Labour Market Flexibility and the Second Tier', *Australian Bulletin of Labour*, 14: 564–91.

Rimmer, W. G. 1960. *Marshalls of Leeds, Flax Spinners, 1788–1886* (Cambridge: Cambridge UP).

Roberts, D. 1978. *Paternalism in Early Victorian England* (London: Croom Helm).

Robinson, E. (ed.) 1970. *Local Labour Markets and Wage Structures* (London: Gower).

Rose, M., and Jones, B. 1985. 'Managerial Strategy and Trade Union Response', in Knights et al. 1985.

Rose, M. B. 1986. *The Gregs of Quarry Bank Mill: The Rise and Decline of a Family Firm* (Cambridge: Cambridge UP).

—— Taylor, P., and Winstanley, M. J. 1989. 'The Economic Origins of Paternalism: Some Objections', *Social History*, 14/1: 89–98.

Rowlinson, M. 1988. 'The Early Application of Scientific Management by Cadbury', *Business History*, 30: 377–95.

Rubery, J. 1978. 'Structured Labour Markets, Worker Organisation and Low Pay', *Cambridge Journal of Economics*, 2/1 (Mar.): 17–36.

—— 1987. 'Flexibility of Labour Costs in Non-union Firms', in R. Tarling (ed.), Flexibility in the Labour Market (London: Academic).

—— 1988. 'Employers and the Labour Market', in D. Gallie (ed.), *Employment in Britain* (Oxford: B. Blackwell).

—— (ed.) 1988. *Women and Recession* (London: Routledge & Kegan Paul).

—— and Wilkinson, F. 1981. 'Outwork and Segmented Labour Markets', in Wilkinson 1981.

—— Tarling, R., and Wilkinson, F. 1987. 'Flexibility, Marketing and the Organisation of Production', *Labour and Society*, 12/1 (Jan.): 131–51.

Sabel, C. 1989. 'Flexible Specialisation and the Re-emergence of Regional Economies', in Hirst and Zeitlin 1989.

Safati, H., and Kobrin, C. (eds.) 1988. *Labour Market Flexibility: A Comparative Anthology* (Aldershot: Gower).

Schonberger, R. J. 1982. *Japanese Manufacturing Techniques* (New York: Free Press).

Scott, A. (ed.) forthcoming. *Gender Segregation in British Labour Markets* (SCELI ser.; Oxford: Oxford UP).

Scott, J., and Hughes, M. 1980. *The Anatomy of Scottish Capital: Scottish Companies and Scottish Capital* (London: Croom Helm).

Sengenberger, W. 1981. 'Labour Market Segmentation and the Business Cycle', in Wilkinson 1981.

Sewel, J. 1993. 'Trade Unionism and Employer Policies in the Aberdeen Oil Industry', in D. Gallie, R. Penn, and M. Rose, *Trade Unionism in Recession* (Oxford: Oxford UP).

Skinner, W. 1986. 'The Production Paradox', *Harvard Business Review* (July/Aug.): 55–9.

Sloane, P. J. 1989. 'Flexible Manpower Resourcing: A Local Labour Market Survey', *Journal of Management Studies*, 26: 129–50.

Smith, A. 1952. *The Third Statistical Account of Scotland: The County of Fife* (Edinburgh: Oliver & Boyd).

Smith, D. 1989. 'Perils of Paternalism: Transatlantic Comparisons', Strategic Innovation Research Group, Aston University, Working Paper 7.

Smout, T. C. 1986. *A Century of the Scottish People, 1830–1950* (London: Collins).

Stiglitz, J. 1975. 'The Theory of Screening, Education and the Distribution of Income', *American Economic Review* (June): 283–300.

Storey, J. 1985. 'The Means of Management Control', *Sociology*, 19/2: 192–211.

—— 1989. *New Perspectives on Human Resource Management* (London: Routledge).

Streeck, W. 1989. 'Skills and the Limits of Neo-liberalism: The Enterprise of the Future as a Place of Learning', *Work, Employment and Society*, 3/1 (Mar.): 89–104.

Tarling, R. 1981. 'The Relationship between Employment and Output: Where does Segmentation Theory Lead us?' in Wilkinson 1981.

Thurow, L. 1975. *Generating Inequality: Mechanisms of Distribution in the US Economy* (London: Macmillan).

Warden, A. J. 1967. *The Linen Trade, Ancient and Modern* (London: Frank Cass; originally publ. in 1864).

Weber, M. 1947. *The Theory of Social and Economic Organisation* (New York: Free Press).

White, M. 1983. *Long-Term Unemployment and Labour Markets* (London: Policy Studies Institute).

—— and McRae, S. 1989. *Young Adults and Long-Term Unemployment* (London: Policy Studies Institute).

Wholey, D. 1985. 'Determinants of Firm Internal Labour Markets in Large Law Firms', *Administrative Science Quarterly*, 30 (Sept.): 318–75.

Wilkinson, F. (ed.) 1981. *The Dynamics of Labour Market Segmentation* (London: Academic).

Williamson, O. 1975. *Markets and Hierarchies* (New York: Free Press).

—— 1986. *The Economic Institutions of Capitalism* (New York: Free Press).

—— Wachter, M., and Harris, J. 1975. 'Understanding the Employment Relation: Analysis of Idiosyncratic Exchange', *Bell Journal of Economics*, 6: 256–80.

Winer, B. J. 1971. *Statistical Principles in Experimental Design* (2nd edn. New York: McGraw Hill).

INDEX